T0220857

Lecture Notes in Computer Science   9024

Commenced Publication in 1973
Founding and Former Series Editors:
Gerhard Goos, Juris Hartmanis, and Jan van Leeuwen

More information about this series at http://www.springer.com/series/7410

Berna Ors · Bart Preneel (Eds.)

Cryptography and Information Security in the Balkans

First International Conference, BalkanCryptSec 2014
Istanbul, Turkey, October 16–17, 2014
Revised Selected Papers

 Springer

Editors
Berna Ors
Istanbul Technical University
Istanbul
Turkey

Bart Preneel
Katholieke Universiteit Leuven
Leuven
Belgium

ISSN 0302-9743   ISSN 1611-3349 (electronic)
Lecture Notes in Computer Science
ISBN 978-3-319-21355-2   ISBN 978-3-319-21356-9 (eBook)
DOI 10.1007/978-3-319-21356-9

Library of Congress Control Number: 2015943046

LNCS Sublibrary: SL4 – Security and Cryptology

Springer Cham Heidelberg New York Dordrecht London

Printed on acid-free paper

Springer International Publishing AG Switzerland is part of Springer Science+Business Media
(www.springer.com)

Preface

This volume contains the papers presented at BalkanCryptSec 2014, the first international conference on cryptography and information security in the Balkans, held October 15–16, 2015, in Istanbul, Turkey.

As a result of the Call for Papers, 36 submissions were received from 21 countries. Each submission was reviewed by at least three, and on average 3.8, Program Committee members. After the conference a second round of reviews was held for the revised papers. The committee decided to select 15 papers for the proceedings. The proceedings also include an overview paper authored by one of the invited speakers.

The Program Committee consisted of 51 members representing 22 countries. These members were carefully selected to represent academia and industry, as well as to include world-class experts in various research fields of interest to BalkanCryptSec. The Program Committee was supported by 20 external reviewers.

Additionally, the workshop included four excellent invited talks. Katerina Mitrokotsa from Chalmers University of Technology discussed her vision of authentication, in a talk entitled "Authentication in Constrained Settings." Aggelos Kiayias from University of Connecticut, described his research in a talk entitled "Cryptocurrencies: Bitcoin and Beyond." Benedikt Gierlichs from KU Leuven and iMinds discussed his vision of secure embedded systems in a talk entitled "Embedded Security." Mariye Umay Akkaya from the Turkish Standards Institution discussed her vision of common criteria in a talk entitled "Crypto Module Standardization (ISO/IEC 1970 and 24759) and Common Criteria."

We wish to thank everyone who made the conference possible. First and foremost the authors who submitted their papers, the presenters of the accepted papers, and the invited speakers. The hard task of reading, commenting, debating, and finally selecting the papers for the conference fell on the Program Committee members. The Program Committee also used external reviewers, whose names are listed on the following pages, to extend the expertise and ease the burden. We want to express our deepest gratitude to them as well.

We would like to thank the Turkish Standards Institution (TSE) for sponsoring our workshop and specially Mariye Umay Akkaya for her assistance in acquiring this sponsorship.

We would also like to thank the very hard working local Organizing Committee, consisting of nine wonderful research and teaching assistants of the Department of Electronics and Communication Engineering at the Istanbul Technical University: Mehmet Akif Ozkan, Ramazan Yeniceri, Emre Goncu, Ahmet Cagri Bagbaba, Buse Ustaoglu, Busra Tas, Emrah Abtioglu, and Latif Akcay.

Special thanks to the EasyChair team that provided a friendly environment for handling the submissions and creating these proceedings.

The dream of having a cryptography and security conference in the Balkans belongs to Svetla Nikova and Tsonka Baicheva. We deeply thank them for their dream and for their hard work to make it come true. We hope this newborn conference will have a long life.

April 2015   Berna Ors
                                                                                              Bart Preneel

Organization

Program Committee

Sedat Akleylek	Ondokuz Mayis University, Turkey
Elena Andreeva	KU Leuven, Belgium
Elli Androulaki	IBM Research, Zurich, Switzerland
Tsonka Baicheva	Institute of Mathematics and Informatics, Bulgaria
Lejla Batina	Radboud University Nijmegen, The Netherlands
Ioana Boureanu	Akamai Technologies Limited, UK
Claude Carlet	University of Paris 8 and LAGA, France
Jean-Sebastien Coron	Université du Luxembourg, Luxembourg
Reza Curtmola	New Jersey Institute of Technology, USA
Paolo D'Arco	University of Salerno, Italy
Ricardo Dahab	University of Campinas, Brazil
Vesna Dimitrova	Ss. Cyril and Methodius University, Republic of Macedonia
Zoran Djuric	University of Banja Luka, Bosnia and Herzegovina
Christophe Doche	Macquarie University, Australia
Stefan Dziembowski	University of Warsaw, Poland
Gerhard Frey	University of Duisburg-Essen, Germany
Dieter Gollmann	Hamburg University of Technology, Germany
Bogdan Groza	Politehnica University of Timisoara, Romania
Tim Güneysu	Ruhr University of Bochum, Germany
Sokratis Katsikas	University of Piraeus, Greece
Aggelos Kiayias	University of Connecticut, USA
Lars Knudsen	Technical University of Denmark, Denmark
David Lubicz	Université Rennes I, France
Stephen Mclaughlin	Pennsylvania State University, USA
Nasir Memon	Polytechnic Institute of NYU, USA
Miodrag Mihaljevic	RCIS-AIST, Japan, and Mathematical Institute of SANU, Serbia
Svetla Nikova	K.U. Leuven, Belgium
Claudio Orlandi	Aarhus University, Denmark
Berna Ors	Istanbul Technical University, Turkey
Elisabeth Oswald	University of Bristol, UK
Charalampos Papamanthou	Polytechnic Institute of NYU, USA
Bart Preneel	K.U. Leuven, Belgium
Christian Rechberger	Technical University of Denmark, Denmark
Kui Ren	State University of New York at Buffalo, USA

Panagiotis Rizomiliotis	University of the Aegean, Greece
Erkay Savas	Sabanci University, Turkey
Zulfukar Saygi	TOBB ETU, Turkey
Michael Scott	Dublin City University, Ireland
Ali Selcuk	TOBB ETU, Turkey
Dimitris. E. Simos	SBA Research, Austria
Johannes Skaar	Norwegian University of Science and Technology, Norway
Ercan Solak	Isik University, Turkey
Francois-Xavier Standaert	UC Louvain-la-Neuve, Belgium
Berk Sunar	WPI, USA
Ferucio Laurentiu Tiplea	Alexandru Ioan Cuza University of Iasi, Romania
Nikos Triandopoulos	Boston University, USA
Serge Vaudenay	Ecole Polytechnique Fédérale de Lausanne, Switzerland
Vesselin Velichkov	University of Luxembourg, Luxembourg
Frederik Vercauteren	K.U. Leuven, Belgium
Lawrence Washington	University of Maryland, USA
Tolga Yalcin	UIST St. Paul the Apostle, Macedonia

Additional Reviewers

Bilgin, Begul
Chabanne, Hervé
Ege, Baris
Hinterwalder, Gesine
Kaskaloglu, Kerem
Kirlar, Baris
Merino Del Pozo, Santos
Millerioux, Gilles
Mischke, Oliver
Papadopoulos, Dimitrios
Papagiannopoulos, Kostas

Peeters, Roel
Pieprzyk, Josef
Pöppelmann, Thomas
Renauld, Mathieu
Susil, Petr
Yalcin, Tolga
Yang, Yang
Yilmaz, Ramazan
Zhang, Bingsheng
Zhu, Bo

Contents

Invited Talk

Authentication in Constrained Settings

Aikaterini Mitrokotsa[✉]

Chalmers University of Technology, Gothenburg, Sweden
aikmitr@chalmers.se

Abstract. Communication technologies have revolutionized modern society. They have changed the way we do business, travel, manage our personal lives and communicate with our friends. In many cases, this crucially depends on accurate and reliable authentication. We need to get authenticated in order to get access to restricted services and/or places (i.e. transport systems, e-banking, border control). This authentication is performed in constrained settings due to: (i) privacy issues, (ii) noisy conditions, (iii) resource constraints. Privacy-preservation is essential for the protection of sensitive information (i.e. diseases, location, nationality). Noisy conditions refer to physical noise in the communication channel that may lead to modification of the transmitted information, or natural variability due to the authentication medium (e.g. fingerprint scans). Resource constraints refer to limited device power/abilities (i.e. sensors, RFID tags). It is a very challenging problem to develop privacy-preserving authentication for noisy and constrained environments that optimally balance authentication accuracy, privacy-preservation and resource consumption. In this paper, we describe the main challenges of the problem of authentication in constrained settings, the current state-of-the-art of the field and possible directions of research.

1 Introduction

Authentication used to rely on visual evidence and physical tokens (mechanical keys, signatures, official seals). As time progressed the use of communication technologies has had a tremendous expansion and a transformative impact in our life. Wireless and resource constrained technologies have already become widespread and are bound to become even more in the near future. Tiny and weak microprocessors, smart cards, RFID tags and sensors are now pervasive in machinery, supply chain management, environmental monitoring, smart home appliances, healthcare applications, keyless entry in automobiles, highway toll-collection and NFC (Near Field Communication)/WiFi payments. Often, these devices are required to perform critical authentication processes under noisy conditions, while respecting the privacy of the involved parties. Smart grids, energy efficiency, transport systems, vehicular networks, healthcare, inventory control and mobile communication are just a few of the domains that benefit from reliable authentication.

Naturally, these new technologies suffer from serious limitations and security and privacy risks. Attackers might attempt to impersonate a legitimate user

© Springer International Publishing Switzerland 2015
B. Ors and B. Preneel (Eds.): BalkanCryptSec 2014, LNCS 9024, pp. 3–12, 2015.
DOI: 10.1007/978-3-319-21356-9_1

and get access to restricted services/locations while dishonest legitimate users may try to abuse their access rights. Numerous recent studies have shown that existing authentication systems can be easily broken.

Authentication is especially challenging when it appears under *constrained settings* due to: (i) *privacy* issues, (ii) *noisy* conditions, and (iii) *resource* limits. This is a significant research challenge that needs to be addressed in order to guarantee reliable and secure communication and prepare us for the future Internet of Things (IoT) rather than the partial solutions of the "Intranet of Things".

By *privacy issues*, we refer to the risks raised by leaving our digital fingerprint whenever we get authenticated for a service/place. Especially for wireless communications the danger that private information shall be collected silently and cheaply is great.

By *noisy* conditions, we refer to the physical noise in the communication channel that may lead to transmission errors and subsequently to modification of the transmitted information. Additionally, noise might be due to the natural variability of the authentication information. For instance, two different scans of the same fingerprint would result to different captured data (i.e. due to the difference in finger pressure during the fingerprint scanning).

By *resource* limits, we refer to communication technologies with limited resources or high cost. These include wireless technologies such as wireless ad hoc networks, WSN (wireless sensor networks) and RFID (Radio Frequency Identification Systems) that are increasingly being deployed in a broad range of applications. There is a pertinent need for reliable but lightweight authentication mechanisms that can be deployed in such inherently resource-deprived technologies. Things become more challenging if we consider that authentication often involves the communication between heterogeneous devices with diverse computational and communication capabilities as well as storage power.

Due to these limitations, service providers and users become more reluctant on using resource-deprived devices that may jeopardise the reliability of a service and the user's privacy.

2   Current State of Research in the Field

We divide the research field into two main areas: (i) authentication in *noisy conditions*, and (ii) *privacy-preserving* authentication. Both of these areas include *resource constrained* devices.

2.1   Authentication in Noisy Conditions

Noisy authentication & decision making: Authentication is a *decision making* problem where we need to decide whether or not to accept the credentials of an identity-carrying entity; a decision that becomes very challenging under noisy conditions. The different regions of the authentication process depending on the certainty of the verifier (due to noise about the identity of the prover – legitimate user or adversary) could be discriminated into the following categories [6]: (i) the *honest region* represents the cases for which the verifier has high confidence that the prover is a legitimate user. This could be when the prover is close enough to the verifier and thus erroneous responses are very few, (ii) the *uncertainty region* represents the area where noise makes the verifier's decision difficult leading to errors, (iii) the *adversarial region* represents the area where the verifier has high confidence that the entity that attempts to get authenticated is an adversary. This *decision making* process can be modeled using *game theory* [10]. The authentication problem is formulated as a two-player game between the authentication system (verifier) and the prover. Nevertheless, existing approaches [10] are based on unrealistic assumptions such as knowing the adversary's utility (payoff). It is an open question how to apply decision making techniques when the utility of the adversary and the model parameters are unknown.

Below we describe some representative cases of authentication in noisy conditions that are directly connected to the research problem of authentication in constrained settings.

Distance-bounding authentication: In many cases, we can only have access to a service by proving we are sufficiently close to a particular location. For instance, in applications such as automobile and building access control the key (prover) has to be close enough to the lock (verifier). In these cases, proximity can be guaranteed through signal attenuation. However, using additional transmitters an attacker can *relay* signals from a key that is located arbitrarily far [30]. This type of attack can also be mounted against bankcards [27], mobile phones, proximity cards [32] and wireless ad hoc networks. Thus, the problem is: *How can the verifier check the distance of a prover?*

Distance-bounding (DB) protocols [17], are challenge-response authentication protocols, that allow the verifier, by measuring the time-of-flight of the messages exchanged, to calculate an upper bound on the prover's distance. The time-critical part of this authentication process is performed under noisy conditions, which implies that we should allow the responses to be partially incorrect. It is not easy to balance correctness with accuracy, while the resource constraints make this problem even more challenging. For this reason, many attacks [8,11,13,41,42,44,45] onto DB protocols [19,36,54,60] continue to be published. Recently, the first family of provably secure DB protocols – called SKI [14–16] – has been proposed, that is secure even under the real-life setting of noisy communications, against the main types of relay attacks. Another provably secure protocol that attains quite strong relay attack resistance requirements has been proposed recently by Fischlin and Onete [29]. A detailed comparison between the SKI family of protocols and the Fischlin and Onete protocol [29] is given by Vaudenay [65].

Additionally, for this class of protocols an analysis of the expected loss when authenticating an attacker and when legitimate users are not authenticated [23,24] has been performed. However, the security of DB protocols is dependent on the underlying communication channel. It is an open question whether the proposed DB protocols can be applied in practice in conventional channels similar to those in NFC.

Biometric authentication: Biometric techniques [39] are a potential simple and efficient method for authentication. However, this is not straightforward. The data collecting process has a high degree of variability. For instance, two different scans of the same fingerprint would result to different captured data (i.e. difference in finger pressure during the fingerprint scan, orientation and dirty finger). The biometric comparison and the approximate equality between a fresh biometric trait and a stored biometric template is a challenge for any biometric scheme. Different approaches have been proposed to efficiently perform this comparison based on error-correcting codes [57], fuzzy commitments, fuzzy vaults [33], fuzzy extractors [26]. Many of these approaches have been shown to be vulnerable to multiple attacks. More robust approaches are those based on secure multi-party computation [62] algorithms. Among the most challenging problems in biometric authentication are: (i) the resistance to impersonation attacks [63], (ii) the irrevocability of biometric templates, and (iii) guarantee that personal information will remain private. Furthermore, biometrics can be used for authentication in mobile devices [22,59] but in this case the authentication problem becomes more challenging considering the limited available resources.

Other cases: Captchas and Physically Unclonable Functions (PUFs) are also strongly connected to the authentication problem under noisy conditions. Captchas are employed in online transactions to make sure that the entity that attempts to get authenticated is a human being and not a machine [7]. The challenge consists of a set of puzzles, which the prover must solve. Erroneous response may be given by humans due to simple mistakes or comprehension difficulties. While the security of captcha-like puzzles has been analyzed for the case where the error rates are known [58], it is an open question whether captchas with a certain performance profile can be automatically designed. PUFs are used mainly for device identification and authentication [51,55] as well as for binding software to hardware platforms [31,37] and anti-counterfeiting [61]. PUFs authentication involves generating a response that depends both on the received challenge as well as on physical properties (i.e. ambient temperature, supply voltage) of the object in which the PUF is embedded. Thus, a PUF will always return a slightly different response for the same challenge.

2.2   Privacy-Preserving Authentication

Often, we need to get authenticated without revealing sensitive information. We consider two types of privacy preservation: privacy-preservation of *context information* such as the location of a sensor or an RFID tag as well as privacy-preservation of *content information* such as biometric templates or information related to our medical history, our nationality etc.

Location & identity privacy: Location and identity can be easily leaked when using wireless communications by eavesdropping transmitted messages, checking signal strengths and messages' arrival times. A survey of privacy preservation in wireless sensor networks is presented in [38], while [64] investigates the identity privacy problem in the context of RFID communication. More general privacy problems have been studied in the fields of data mining [4] and databases [5] both of which are intrinsically linked to the authentication problem. Rasmussen and Čapkun have proposed a location privacy-preserving distance bounding protocol (RČ) [49]. Nevertheless, this protocol has several problems [8, 42]. A new DB protocol [42] that improves the basic construction of the RČ protocol has been proposed. However, location privacy considering the information leakage at the physical layer is quite challenging. It has been shown recently [43], that for protocols with a beginning or a termination, it is theoretically impossible to achieve location privacy for very powerful adversaries (omniscient). However for limited adversaries, carefully chosen parameters enable computational, provable location privacy.

Privacy & biometrics: Biometric authentication involves the comparison between a fresh and a stored biometric template. This comparison is usually performed using some distance or divergence between the fresh and stored template. Later on the distance is compared to a pre-defined threshold and an authentication decision is taken (acceptance/rejection). Numerous approaches have been proposed in order to guarantee privacy-preserving biometric authentication: quantization schemes [40], fuzzy extractors [26], fuzzy commitment [34], cancelable biometrics [50], and fuzzy vault [33], while the most secure are based on secure-multi party computation techniques including oblivious transfer [48], homomorphic encryption [47] as well as private information retrieval [21]. Multiple privacy-preserving biometrics authentication protocols have been proposed based on secure multi-party computation [9, 18, 56]. Nevertheless, it has been proven that many of these schemes are vulnerable to threats [52], such as cross-matching [53] and hill-climbing [1–3, 52]. More precisely, it has been recently proven that all biometric authentication protocols (including privacy-preserving ones) that rely on leaking distances (e.g. Hamming distance, Euclidean distance) are susceptible to leakage of information that may lead to the disclosure of stored biometric templates (even if the latter are encrypted). Pagnin et al. [46] provide a formal mathematical framework to analyse this leakage.

Privacy & machine learning: The authentication problem especially using biometrics relies extensively on machine learning techniques. Privacy-learning has been studied by research communities in security, databases, theory, machine learning and statistics. Recently, the strands of this work have begun to merge, with the formalism of *differential privacy* [28]. Differential privacy offers a formal framework that can be used to bound the amount of info that an adversary can discover. Much work has been done to understand how algorithms and methods can guarantee differential privacy and performance [12, 35]. Recently Dimitrakakis et al. [25] have generalized the concept of differential privacy to arbitrary dataset distances and proved that Bayesian learning is inherently private. Recently a number of differentially-private versions of machine learning algorithms have been proposed (e.g. [20]).

3   Open Questions and Challenges

In order to solve the problem of authentication in constrained settings we need to address the following questions:

- How robust is an authentication system performing under noisy conditions and resource constraints?
- How can we minimise the resource cost?
- How can we maximize (/*minimise*) the probability to authenticate a legitimate user (/*an attacker*)?
- How can we preserve the privacy rights of the parties involved in the authentication process in a collective way?

Many of existing authentication protocols use informal models and are poorly grounded theory. Additionally, in many cases the information leakage is addressed locally without considering that an adversary may have access to multiple services or devices. The following dimensions of the problem need to be taken into account when we design reliable and privacy-preserving authentication protocols for constrained settings.

(*i*) The privacy implications of wireless communication may lead to oppressive electronic data surveillance. The wireless medium renders the privacy preservation a big challenge. To combat eavesdropping and the involvement of untrusted parties (e.g. databases) secure multi-party computation and differential privacy are valuable tools that could be employed. However, there is a need for development of lightweight techniques for resource-constrained devices where the trade-off between privacy and computation is tuned according to the target application.

(*ii*) Designing provably secure protocols resistant to relay attacks is a very challenging task. Accurate authentication could be strengthened by relying on cross-layer authentication protocols that employ properties of the physical layer (e.g. noise of the communication channel, response time) in order to provide high security guarantees and efficiency in realistic conditions.

References

1. Abidin, A., Matsuura, K., Mitrokotsa, A.: Security of a privacy-preserving biometric authentication protocol revisited. In: Gritzalis, D., Kiayias, A., Askoxylakis, I. (eds.) CANS 2014. LNCS, vol. 8813, pp. 290–304. Springer, Heidelberg (2014)
2. Abidin, A., Mitrokotsa, A.: Security aspects of privacy-preserving biometric authentication based on ideal lattices and ring-lwe. In: Proceedings of the IEEE Workshop on Information Forensics and Security 2014 (WIFS 2014). Atlanta, USA. December 2014
3. Abidin, A., Pagnin, E., Mitrokotsa, A.: Attacks on privacy-preserving biometric authentication. In: Proceedings of the 19th Nordic Conference on Secure IT Systems (NordSec 2014), pp. 293–294. Tromso, Norway. October 2014
4. Agrawal, R., Evfimievski, A., Srikant, R.: Information sharing across private databases. In: Proceedings of ACM SIGMOD 2003, pp. 86–97. ACM, NY (2003)

5. Agrawal, R., Srikant, R.: Privacy-preserving data mining. In: Proceedings of ACM SIGMOD 2000, pp. 439–450. ACM, NY (2000)
6. Ahmadi, H., Safavi-Naini, R.: Secure distance bounding verification using physical-channel properties (2013). arXiv:1303.0346
7. Ahn, L.V., Blum, M., Hopper, N.J., Langford, J.: Captcha: using hard ai problems for security. In: Proceedings of the 22nd International Conference on Theory and Applications of Cryptographic Techniques, EUROCRYPT 2003, pp. 294–311. Springer, Heidelberg (2003)
8. Aumasson, J.-P., Mitrokotsa, A., Peris-Lopez, P.: A note on a privacy-preserving distance-bounding protocol. In: Qing, S., Susilo, W., Wang, G., Liu, D. (eds.) ICICS 2011. LNCS, vol. 7043, pp. 78–92. Springer, Heidelberg (2011)
9. Barbosa, M., Brouard, T., Cauchie, S., de Sousa, S.M.: Secure biometric authentication with improved accuracy. In: Mu, Y., Susilo, W., Seberry, J. (eds.) ACISP 2008. LNCS, vol. 5107, pp. 21–36. Springer, Heidelberg (2008)
10. Barni, M.: A game theoretic approach to source identification with known statistics. In: Proceedings of ICASSP 2012. pp. 1745–1748. Kyoto, Japan. March 2012
11. Bay, A., Boureanu, I., Mitrokotsa, A., Spulber, I., Vaudenay, S.: The bussard-bagga and other distance-bounding protocols under attacks. In: Kutyłowski, M., Yung, M. (eds.) Inscrypt 2012. LNCS, vol. 7763, pp. 371–391. Springer, Heidelberg (2013)
12. Blum, A., Ligett, K., Roth, A.: A learning theory approach to non-interactive database privacy. In: STOC 2008, pp. 609–618 (2008)
13. Boureanu, I., Mitrokotsa, A., Vaudenay, S.: On the pseudorandom function assumption in (secure) distance-bounding protocols. In: Hevia, A., Neven, G. (eds.) LatinCrypt 2012. LNCS, vol. 7533, pp. 100–120. Springer, Heidelberg (2012)
14. Boureanu, I., Mitrokotsa, A., Vaudenay, S.: Practical and provably secure distance-bounding. In: Proceedings of the 16th Information Security Conference (ISC). Dallas, Texas, USA. November 2013
15. Boureanu, I., Mitrokotsa, A., Vaudenay, S.: Secure and lightweight distance-bounding. In: Proceedings of LightSec 2013. Gebze, Turkey. May 6–7 2013
16. Boureanu, I., Mitrokotsa, A., Vaudenay, S.: Practical and provably secure distance-bounding. Journal of Computer Security (2014)
17. Brands, S., Chaum, D.: Distance bounding protocols. In: Helleseth, T. (ed.) EURO-CRYPT 1993. LNCS, vol. 765, pp. 344–359. Springer, Heidelberg (1994)
18. Bringer, J., Chabanne, H., Izabachène, M., Pointcheval, D., Tang, Q., Zimmer, S.: An application of the goldwasser-micali cryptosystem to biometric authentication. In: Pieprzyk, J., Ghodosi, H., Dawson, E. (eds.) ACISP 2007. LNCS, vol. 4586, pp. 96–106. Springer, Heidelberg (2007)
19. Bussard, L.: Trust Establishment Protocols for Communicating Devices. Ph.D. thesis, Ecole Nationale Supérieure des Télécommunications, Institut Eurécom, Télécom Paris (2004)
20. Chaudhuri, K., Monteleoni, C., Sarwate, A.D.: Differentially private empirical risk minimization. JMLR **12**, 1069–1109 (2011)
21. Chor, B., Kushilevitz, E., Goldreich, O., Sudan, M.: Private information retrieval. J. ACM **45**(6), 965–981 (1998)
22. Clarke, N., Furnell, S.: Authentication of users on mobile telephones - a survey of attitudes and practices. Comput. Secur. **24**(7), 519–527 (2005)
23. Dimitrakakis, C., Mitrokotsa, A., Vaudenay, S.: Expected loss bounds for authentication in constrained channels. In: Proceedings of INFOCOM 2012, pp. 478–85. Orlando, FL, USA. March 2012
24. Dimitrakakis, C., Mitrokotsa, A., Vaudenay, S.: Expected loss analysis for authentication in constrained channels. Journal of Computer Security (2014)

25. Dimitrakakis, C., Nelson, B., Mitrokotsa, A., Rubinstein, B.I.P.: Robust and private bayesian inference. In: Auer, P., Clark, A., Zeugmann, T., Zilles, S. (eds.) ALT 2014. LNCS, vol. 8776, pp. 291–305. Springer, Heidelberg (2014)
26. Dodis, Y., Ostrovsky, R., Reyzin, L., Smith, A.: Fuzzy extractors: how to generate strong keys from biometrics and other noisy data. SIAM J. Comput. **38**(1), 97–139 (2008)
27. Drimer, S., Murdoch, S.J.: Keep your enemies close: distance bounding against smartcard relay attacks. In: Proceedings of USENIX 2007, pp. 7:1–7:16. Berkeley, CA, USA (2007)
28. Dwork, C., McSherry, F., Nissim, K., Smith, A.: Calibrating noise to sensitivity in private data analysis. In: Halevi, S., Rabin, T. (eds.) TCC 2006. LNCS, vol. 3876, pp. 265–284. Springer, Heidelberg (2006)
29. Fischlin, M., Onete, C.: Terrorism in distance bounding: modeling terrorist-fraud resistance. In: Jacobson, M., Locasto, M., Mohassel, P., Safavi-Naini, R. (eds.) ACNS 2013. LNCS, vol. 7954, pp. 414–431. Springer, Heidelberg (2013)
30. Francillon, A., Danev, B., Čapkun, S.: Relay attacks on passive keyless entry and start systems in modern cars. In: Proceedings of NDSS 2011. San Diego, CL, USA (2011)
31. Guajardo, J., Kumar, S.S., Schrijen, G.-J., Tuyls, P.: FPGA intrinsic PUFs and their use for IP protection. In: Paillier, P., Verbauwhede, I. (eds.) CHES 2007. LNCS, vol. 4727, pp. 63–80. Springer, Heidelberg (2007)
32. Hancke, G.P., Mayes, K.E., Markantonakis, K.: Confidence in smart token proximity: relay attacks revisited. Comput. Secur. **28**(7), 404–408 (2009)
33. Juels, A., Sudan, M.: A fuzzy vault scheme. J. Des. Codes Crypt. **38**(2), 237–257 (2006)
34. Juels, A., Wattenberg, M.: A fuzzy commitment scheme. In: Proceedings of CCS 1999, pp. 28–36. NY, USA (1999)
35. Kasiviswanathan, S.P., Lee, H.K., Nissim, K., Raskhodnikova, S., Smith, A.: What can we learn privately? In: Proceedings of FOCS 2008, pp. 531–540 (2008)
36. Kim, C.H., Avoine, G., Koeune, F., Standaert, F.-X., Pereira, O.: The swiss-knife rfid distance bounding protocol. In: Lee, P.J., Cheon, J.H. (eds.) ICISC 2008. LNCS, vol. 5461, pp. 98–115. Springer, Heidelberg (2009)
37. Kumar, S.S., Guajardo, J., Maes, R., Schrijen, G.J., Tuyls, P.: Extended abstract: the butterfly PUF protecting IP on every FPGA. In: Proceedings of the 2008 IEEE International Workshop on Hardware-Oriented Security and Trust, HST 2008, pp. 67–70. IEEE Computer Society, Washington, DC (2008)
38. Li, N., Zhang, N., Das, S.K., Thuraisingham, B.: Privacy preservation in wireless sensor networks: a state-of-the-art survey. Ad Hoc Netw. **7**(8), 1501–1514 (2009)
39. Li, S.Z., Jain, A.K. (eds.): Encyclopedia of Biometrics. Springer, New York (2009)
40. Linnartz, J.P., Tuyls, P.: New shielding functions to enhance privacy and prevent misuse of biometric templates. In: Proceedings of AVBPA 2003, pp. 393–402. Springer-Verlag, Heidelberg (2003)
41. Mitrokotsa, A., Dimitrakakis, C., Peris-Lopez, P., Castro, J.C.H.: Reid et al'.s distance bounding protocol and mafia fraud attacks over noisy channels. IEEE Commun. Lett. **14**(2), 121–123 (2010)
42. Mitrokotsa, A., Onete, C., Vaudenay, S.: Mafia Fraud Attack against the RČ Distance-Bounding Protocol. In: Proceedings of IEEE RFID-TA 2012, pp. 74–79. Nice, France. November 2012
43. Mitrokotsa, A., Onete, C., Vaudenay, S.: Location leakage in distance bounding: why location privacy does not work. Comput. Secur. **45**, 199–209 (2014)

44. Mitrokotsa, A., Peris-Lopez, P., Dimitrakakis, C., Vaudenay, S.: On selecting the nonce length in distance-bounding protocols. Comput. J. **56**(10), 1216–1227 (2013)
45. Munilla, J., Peinado, A.: Attacks on a distance bounding protocol. Comput. Commun. **33**, 884–889 (2010)
46. Pagnin, E., Dimitrakakis, C., Abidin, A., Mitrokotsa, A.: On the leakage of information in biometric authentication. In: Proceedings of the 15th International Conference on Cryptology in India INDOCRYPT 2014. pp. 265–280. New Delhi, India. December 2014
47. Paillier, P.: Public-key cryptosystems based on composite degree residuosity classes. In: Stern, J. (ed.) EUROCRYPT 1999. LNCS, vol. 1592, pp. 223–238. Springer, Heidelberg (1999)
48. Rabin, M.O.: How to exchange secrets with oblivious transfer. IACR Cryptology ePrint Arch. **2005**, 187 (2005)
49. Rasmussen, K., Čapkun, S.: Location privacy of distance bounding. In: Proceedings of CCS 2008, pp. 149–160. ACM (2008)
50. Ratha, N.K., Chikkerur, S., Connell, J.H., Bolle, R.M.: Generating cancelable fingerprint templates. IEEE Trans. Pattern Anal. Mach. Intell. **29**(4), 561–572 (2007)
51. Sadeghi, A.R., Visconti, I., Wachsmann, C.: Enhancing RFID security and privacy by physically unclonable functions. In: Sadeghi, A.R., Naccache, D. (eds.) Towards Hardware-Intrinsic Security, Information Security and Cryptography - THIS 2010, pp. 281–305. Springer, Heidelberg. (2010)
52. Simoens, K., Bringer, J., Chabanne, H., Seys, S.: A framework for analyzing template security and privacy in biometric authentication systems. IEEE Trans. Inf. Forensics Secur. **7**(2), 833–841 (2012)
53. Simoens, K., Tuyls, P., Preneel, B.: Privacy weaknesses in biometric sketches. In: IEEE Symposium on Security and Privacy, pp. 188–203. May 2009
54. Singelée, D., Preneel, B.: Distance bounding in noisy environments. In: Stajano, F., Meadows, C., Capkun, S., Moore, T. (eds.) ESAS 2007. LNCS, vol. 4572, pp. 101–115. Springer, Heidelberg (2007)
55. Mauw, S., Piramuthu, S.: A PUF-based authentication protocol to address ticket-switching of rfid-tagged items. In: Jøsang, A., Samarati, P., Petrocchi, M. (eds.) STM 2012. LNCS, vol. 7783, pp. 209–224. Springer, Heidelberg (2013)
56. Stoianov, A.: Cryptographically secure biometrics. In: Proceedings of SPIE 7667, Biometric Technology for Human Identification VII, vol. 76670C, pp. 76670C–76670C-12. April 2010
57. Sukarno, P., Phu, M., Bhattacharjee, N., Srinivasan, B.: Increasing error tolerance in biometric systems. In: Proceedings of MoMM 2010, pp. 50–55. ACM, New York (2010)
58. Baignères, T., Sepehrdad, P., Vaudenay, S.: Distinguishing distributions using chernoff information. In: Heng, S.-H., Kurosawa, K. (eds.) ProvSec 2010. LNCS, vol. 6402, pp. 144–165. Springer, Heidelberg (2010)
59. Tresadern, P., Cootes, T.F., Poh, N., Matejka, P., Hadid, A., Levy, C., McCool, C., Marcel, S.: Mobile biometrics: combined face and voice verification for a mobile platform. IEEE Pervasive Comput. **12**(1), 79–87 (2013)
60. Tu, Y.J., Piramuthu, S.: RFID Distance Bounding Protocols. In: Proceedings of EURASIP Workshop on RFID Technology, pp. 67–68. Vienna, Austria. September 2007
61. Tuyls, P., Batina, L.: RFID-tags for anti-counterfeiting. In: Pointcheval, D. (ed.) CT-RSA 2006. LNCS, vol. 3860, pp. 115–131. Springer, Heidelberg (2006)

62. Tuyls, P., Skoric, B., Kevenaar, T. (eds.): Security with Noisy Data: On Private Biometrics, Secure Key Storage and Anti-Counterfeiting. Springer, Heidelberg (2007)
63. Une, M., Otsuka, A., Imai, H.: Wolf attack probability: a new security measure in biometric authentication systems. In: Lee, S.-W., Li, S.Z. (eds.) ICB 2007. LNCS, vol. 4642, pp. 396–406. Springer, Heidelberg (2007)
64. Vaudenay, S.: On privacy models for RFID. In: Kurosawa, K. (ed.) ASIACRYPT 2007. LNCS, vol. 4833, pp. 68–87. Springer, Heidelberg (2007)
65. Vaudenay, S.: On modeling terrorist frauds. In: Susilo, W., Reyhanitabar, R. (eds.) ProvSec 2013. LNCS, vol. 8209, pp. 1–20. Springer, Heidelberg (2013)

Symmetric Cryptography

Optimizing the Placement of Tap Positions

Enes Pasalic[1], Samir Hodžić[1 (✉)], Samed Bajrić[1], and Yongzhuang Wei[2]

[1] University of Primorska, FAMNIT and IAM, Koper, Slovenia
enes.pasalic6@gmail.com, samir.hodzic@famnit.upr.si, samed.bajric@upr.si
[2] Guilin University of Electronic Technology, Guilin, P.R. China,
and Also with the State Key Laboratory of Integrated Services Networks,
Xidian University, Xi'an 710071, People's Republic of China
walker_wei@msn.com

Abstract. Although there are many different approaches used in crypt-analysis of nonlinear filter generators, the selection of tap positions in connection to guess and determine cryptanalysis has not received enough attention yet. In a recent article [18], it was shown that the so-called filter state guessing attack (FSGA) introduced in [15], which applies to LFSR based schemes that use (vectorial) Boolean filtering functions, performs much better if the placement of tap positions is taken into account. In this article, for a given LFSR of length L, we analyze the problem of selecting n (where $n \ll L$) tap positions of the driving LFSR (used as binary inputs to a filtering function) optimally so that the complexity of FSGA like attacks is maximized. An algorithm which provides a subop-timal solution to this problem is developed and it can be used for real-life applications when the choice of tap positions is to be made.

Keywords: Stream ciphers · Filtering generator · Guess and determine cryptanalysis · Filter state guessing attack · Tap positions

1 Introduction

Nonlinear filter generator is a typical representative of a hardware oriented design in stream ciphers. It consists of a single linear feedback shift register (LFSR) and a nonlinear function $F : GF(2)^n \longrightarrow GF(2)^m$ that processes a fixed subset of n stages of the LFSR. This fixed subset of the LFSR's cells is usually called the *taps*.

There are many cryptanalytic approaches that have been applied to non-linear filter generators during the last two decades. These methods mainly use the cryptographic weaknesses of the filtering function giving rise to Berlekamp-Massey linear complexity attacks [10], linear distinguishing and inversion attacks of Golić [5–7], algebraic attacks [4], probabilistic algebraic attacks [2,17], and so on. To protect a nonlinear filter generator against these attacks, the filtering function should satisfy multiple cryptographic criteria that include high nonlin-earity, high algebraic degree [14], high algebraic immunity (AI) [11], and many others.

© Springer International Publishing Switzerland 2015
B. Ors and B. Preneel (Eds.): BalkanCryptSec 2014, LNCS 9024, pp. 15–30, 2015.
DOI: 10.1007/978-3-319-21356-9_2

Apart from resisting the attacks using the properties of the filtering function, a nonlinear filter generator should also have sufficient security margins against other generic cryptanalytic methods, e.g. time-memory-data tradeoff attacks [1,8,9], and guess and determine attacks. A classical guess and determine attack is a method based on guessing some portion of the secret key (state bits) in order to decrease the complexity of obtaining the remaining unknown key (state) bits. Recently, a new guess and determine attack, named Filter State Guessing Attack (FSGA), was introduced in [15]. The basic idea behind the FSGA is to perform a guess and determine attack on the preimage space of the filtering function $F : GF(2)^n \longrightarrow GF(2)^m$. Since for uniformly distributed F there are 2^{n-m} such preimages , for any observed m-bit output block the attacker may for each choice of 2^{n-m} many possible inputs (over the whole set of sampling instances) set up an overdefined system of linear equations in secret state bits. This attack turns out to be successful only for relatively large m, more precisely for approximately $m > n/2$.

In certain cases, the running time of the FSGA may be lower than the running time of a classical algebraic attack (cf. [15]). In particular, a superior performance of the FSGA over classical algebraic attacks was demonstrated in the case the filtering function belongs to a class of vectorial Maiorana-McFarland functions (see e.g. [3]). Notice that the tap positions of a nonlinear filter generator are of no importance for the FSGA in [15]. More precisely, only one bit of the information was considered to be known from the previous sampling points. The complexity of the attack was significantly improved in [18], where the information from the neighbouring taps, in the attack named GFSGA (Generalized FSGA), was used for a further reduction of the preimage space. In particular, the attack complexity of GFSGA is very sensitive to the tap placements, though no algorithm for their choice was provided in [18]. The reader should however notice that there exist other kind of attacks on nonlinear filtering generators such as e.g. decimation attacks [12] and attacks that take the advantage of the normality of Boolean functions [13] whose complexity does not depend on the choice of tap positions.

The main motivation for this work relies on the fact that even after more than two decades of extensive research on the security and design of filtering generators the selection of tap positions has not been rigorously treated yet. The designers, well aware of the fact that a proper tap selection plays an important role in the design, mainly use some standard (heuristic) design rationales such as taking the differences between the positions to be prime numbers (if possible), the taps are distributed over the whole LFSR etc. Intuitively, selecting the taps at some consecutive positions of the LFSR should be avoided, and similarly placing these taps at the positions used for the realization of the feedback connection polynomial is not a good idea either. Another common criterion is to ensure that a multiset of differences of the tap positions is mutually coprime. This means, that for a given set of tap positions $\mathcal{I} = \{i_1, i_2, \ldots, i_n\}$ of an LFSR of length L (thus $1 \leq i_1 < i_2 < \ldots < i_n \leq L$) all the elements in the difference set formed as $\mathcal{D} = \{i_j - i_l : i_j, i_l \in \mathcal{I}, i_j > i_l\}$ are mutually coprime. In many situations, in real-life applications, this condition turns out to be hard to satisfy. To the best of our knowledge, no algorithm for determining an optimal tap placement, for given n and L, has been provided so far.

In this article, we firstly demonstrate some potentially misleading design rationales from the security point of view and discuss the complexity issues related to optimality. Indeed, for a standard size of an LFSR used in these schemes, say $L = 256$, and a recommended number of inputs $n \geq 16$, any exhaustive search over the set of $\binom{L}{n}$ elements is clearly infeasible. Therefore, we propose a suboptimal algorithm for this purpose, which at least when applied to LFSRs of relatively short length performs optimally (giving the best choice over all possibilities) . It is also shown that certain choices of tap positions in real-life stream ciphers such as SOBER-t32 and SFINX could have been (slightly) further optimized with respect to guess and determine cryptanalysis, in particular their resistance to GFSGA would have been better.

The rest of the article is organized as follows. In Sect. 2, basic definitions regarding Boolean functions and the mathematical formalism behind their use with LFSRs is given. A brief overview of FSGA and GFSGA is given in Sect. 3. Section 4 discusses the relation between the complexity of the GFSGA attack and the number of repeated equations used in the reduction of the preimage space. Two versions of the algorithm for determining (sub)optimal tap positions for a given n and L are presented in Sect. 5, and their application for the choice of tap positions in SOBER-t32 and SFINX is discussed.

2   Preliminaries

A Boolean function is a mapping from $GF(2)^n$ to $GF(2)$, where $GF(2)$ denotes the binary Galois field and $GF(2)^n$ is an n-dimendional vector space spanned over $GF(2)$. A function $f : GF(2)^n \rightarrow GF(2)$ is commonly represented using its associated algebraic normal form (ANF) as follows:

$$f(x_1, ..., x_n) = \sum_{u \in GF(2)^n} \lambda_u (\Pi_{i=1}^{n} x_i{}^{u_i}),$$

where $x_i \in GF(2)$, $(i = 1, ..., n)$, $\lambda_u \in GF(2)$, $u = (u_1, ..., u_n) \in GF(2)^n$. A vectorial (multiple output) Boolean function $F(x)$ is a mapping from $GF(2)^n$ to $GF(2)^m$, with $(m \geq 1)$, which can also be regarded as a collection of m Boolean functions, i.e., $F(x) = (f_1(x), ..., f_m(x))$. Commonly, $F(x)$ is chosen to be uniformly distributed, that is, $\#\{x \in GF(2)^n | F(x) = z\} = 2^{n-m}$, for all $z \in GF(2)^m$. Moreover, for any $z = (z_1, ..., z_m) \in GF(2)^m$, we denote the set of preimage values by $S_z = \{x \in GF(2)^n \mid F(x) = z\}$.

2.1   Nonlinear Filtering Generator

A filtering generator consists of a single LFSR of length L whose n fixed positions (taps) are used as the inputs to a filtering function $F : GF(2)^n \rightarrow GF(2)^m$ (also represented as $F(x) = (f_1(x), ..., f_m(x))$), thus outputting $m \geq 1$ keystream bits at the time. A general description of a filter generator is as follows:

$$(z_1^t, ..., z_m^t) = (f_1(\ell_n(\mathbf{s}^t)), ..., f_m(\ell_n(\mathbf{s}^t))),$$

where $\mathbf{s}^t = (s_0^t, \ldots, s_{L-1}^t)$ is the secret state of the LFSR at time t, the notation $\ell_n(\mathbf{s}^t)$ means that a subset of n bits of $\mathbf{s}^t = (s_0^t, \ldots, s_{L-1}^t)$ (at fixed positions) is passed as the input to Boolean functions $f_1, \ldots, f_m$, and $z_1^t, \ldots, z_m^t$ are the corresponding output keystream bits.

Due to linearity of its feedback connection polynomial, at any $t > 0$ we have $\ell_n(s_0^t, \ldots, s_{L-1}^t) = (\psi_1^t(\mathbf{s}), \ldots, \psi_n^t(\mathbf{s}))$, where the linear functions $\psi_i^t(\mathbf{s}) = \sum_{j=0}^{L-1} a_{i,j}^t s_j$, $(i = 1, \ldots, n)$, are unique linear combinations of the initial secret state bits $\mathbf{s}^0 = (s_0, \ldots, s_{L-1})$, at time $t = 0$. The LFSR is updated by computing the update bit s_L (as a linear combination of $s_0, \ldots, s_{L-1}$ determined by the connection polynomial) and shifting its content to the left (while at the same time outputting the bit s_0), so that $\mathbf{s}^1 = (s_1, \ldots, s_L)$. The binary coefficients $a_{i,j}^t$ above can therefore be efficiently computed from the connection polynomial of LFSR for all $t \geq 0$.

3 Overview of FSGA and GFSGA

For self-completeness and due to the close relation with subsequent sections, we briefly describe the main ideas behind FSGA and its extension GFSGA. For both attacks there is no restriction on $F : GF(2)^n \to GF(2)^m$, thus F satisfies all the relevant criteria including a uniform distribution of its preimages.

3.1 FSGA Description

For every observation of the cipher output $z^t = (z_1^t, \ldots, z_m^t)$ at time t, there are 2^{n-m} possible inputs $x^t \in S_{z^t}$. Moreover, for every guessed preimage $x^t = (x_1^t, \ldots, x_n^t) \in S_{z^t}$, one obtains n linear equations in the secret state bits $s_0, \ldots,$ s_{L-1} through $x_i^t = \sum_{j=0}^{L-1} a_{i,j}^t s_j$, for $1 \leq i \leq n$. The goal of the attacker is to recover the initial state bits $(s_0, \ldots, s_{L-1})$ after obtaining sufficiently many keystream blocks $z^t = (z_1^t, \ldots, z_m^t)$. If the attacker observes the outputs at the time instances $t_1, \ldots, t_c$, so that $nc > L$, then with high probability each system of nc linear equations is independent but only one system will provide a consistent (correct) solution.

As there are $2^{(n-m)c}$ possibilities of choosing c input tuples $(x_1^{t_1}, \ldots, x_n^{t_1}), \ldots,$ $(x_1^{t_c}, \ldots, x_n^{t_c})$, and for each such c-tuple a system of nc linear equations in L variables is obtained. The complexity of solving a single overdefined system of linear equations with L variables is about L^3 operations. Thus, the complexity of the FSGA is about $2^{(n-m)c}L^3$ operations, where $c \approx \lceil \frac{L}{n} \rceil$.

3.2 GFSGA Description

The major difference to FSGA is that the GFSGA method efficiently utilizes the tap positions of the underlying LFSR. Let the tap positions of the LFSR be specified by the set $\mathcal{I}_0 = \{i_1, i_2, \ldots, i_n\}$, $1 \leq i_1 \leq i_2 \leq \ldots \leq i_n \leq L$. If at the time instance t_1, we assume that the content of the LFSR at these tap positions is given by $(s_{i_1}^{t_1}, \ldots, s_{i_n}^{t_1}) = (a_1, \ldots, a_n)$, then at $t = t_1 + \sigma$ we have $(s_{i_1+\sigma}^{t_1+\sigma}, \ldots, s_{i_n+\sigma}^{t_1+\sigma}) = (a_1, \ldots, a_n)$, where cutting modulo L can be performed if necessary. Notice that the state bits at positions $i_1 + \sigma, \ldots, i_n + \sigma$ does not necessarily intersect with $\mathcal{I}_0$, thus if the intersection is an empty set no information from the previous sampling can be used at the sampling instance $t_1 + \sigma$. However, we can always select σ so that at least one bit of information is conveyed. More formally, the observed outputs at $t_1, \ldots, t_c$, where $t_i = t_1 + (i-1)\sigma$ and $1 \leq \sigma \leq (i_n - i_1)$, may give rise to identical linear equations since the equations $x_i^{t_u} = \sum_{j=0}^{L-1} a_{i,j}^{t_u} s_j$ (where $1 \leq i \leq n$) may be shifted to $x_l^{t_v} = \sum_{j=0}^{L-1} a_{i,j}^{t_v} s_j$, for some $1 \leq i < l \leq n, 1 \leq u < v \leq c$.

It is of importance to determine how many identical linear equations will be obtained for all the sampling instances $t_1, \ldots, t_c$. By introducing $k = \lfloor \frac{i_n - i_1}{\sigma} \rfloor$, and for $\mathcal{I}_0 = \{i_1, i_2, \ldots, i_n\}$ defining recursively:

$$
\begin{aligned}
\mathcal{I}_1 &= \mathcal{I}_0 \cap \{i_1 + \sigma, i_2 + \sigma, \ldots, i_n + \sigma\}, \\
\mathcal{I}_2 &= \mathcal{I}_1 \cup \{\mathcal{I}_0 \cap \{i_1 + 2\sigma, i_2 + 2\sigma, \ldots, i_n + 2\sigma\}\}, \\
&\vdots \\
\mathcal{I}_k &= \mathcal{I}_{k-1} \cup \{\mathcal{I}_0 \cap \{i_1 + k\sigma, i_2 + k\sigma, \ldots, i_n + k\sigma\}\}.
\end{aligned}
\tag{1}
$$

the analysis in [18] showed that the complexity of the GFSGA is closely related to the parameter $r_i = \#\mathcal{I}_i$, where $i = 1, \ldots, k$.

Remark 1. For instance, the above notation means that for some $i \in \mathcal{I}_1$ (and therefore $i \in \mathcal{I}_0$) the state bit $s_i^{t_2}$ was used in the previous sampling since it was at the position $i - \sigma \in \mathcal{I}_0$ at time t_1, where $t_2 = t_1 + \sigma$. The idea is easily generalized for $\#\mathcal{I}_i = r_i$, where $i = 2, \ldots, k$.

The number of identical equations obtained in [18] is given as follows. If $c \leq k$, then in total $\sum_{i=1}^{c-1} r_i$ identical linear equations are obtained, whereas for $c > k$ this number is $\sum_{i=1}^{k} r_i + (c - k - 1)r_k$. Note that in this case $r_k = r_{k+1} = \cdots = r_{c-1}$ due to the definition of k, which simply guarantees that after k sampling instances the maximum (and constant) number of repeated equations is attained. Consequently, the time complexity of the attack for $c \leq k$ was estimated as,

$$
\begin{aligned}
T_{Comp.}^{c \leq k} &= 2^{(n-m)} \times 2^{(n-m-r_1)} \times \ldots \times 2^{(n-m-r_{(c-1)})} \times L^3 \\
&= 2^{(n-m)c - \sum_{i=1}^{c-1} r_i} \times L^3,
\end{aligned}
\tag{2}
$$

and similarly, if $c > k$, the time complexity for $c > k$ was given by

$$
\begin{aligned}
T_{Comp.}^{c > k} &= 2^{(n-m)} \times 2^{(n-m-r_1)} \times \ldots \times \\
&\quad \times 2^{(n-m-r_k)} \times 2^{(n-m-r_k) \times (c-k-1)} \times L^3 \\
&= 2^{(n-m)c - (\sum_{i=1}^{k} r_i + (c-k-1)r_k)} \times L^3.
\end{aligned}
\tag{3}
$$

Remark 2. If $n - m - r_i \leq 0$, for some $i \in \{1, \ldots, k\}$, then the knowledge of these r_i bits allows the attacker to uniquely identify the exact preimage value form the set of 2^{n-m} possible preimages, i.e., we assume $2^{(n-m-r_i)} = 1$ when $n - m - r_i \leq 0$.

Table 1 (cf. [18]) gives a complexity comparison of FSGA, GFSGA and CAA (Classical algebraic Attack). The tap positions and the sampling difference σ are given below:

(1) $\{3, 8, 13, 16, 21, 29, 32, 37, 44, 52, 67, 79, 92, 106, 111, 125, 155\}$, $\sigma = 5, c = 23$.
(2) $\{2, 7, 17, 25, 27, 31, 48, 58, 61, 73, 82, 91, 103, 115, 123, 134, 146, 156\}$, $\sigma = 3$, $c = 20$.

Table 1. Complexity comparison for different (n, m) and $(K = 80, L = 160)$.

(n, m)	$(17, 6)$	$(18, 7)$
$FSGA$	2^{123}	2^{121}
CAA	2^{75}	2^{75}
$GFSGA$	$2^{53.97}$	$2^{64.97}$

4   Complexity Versus the Number of Repeated Equations

The complexity of GFSGA, which is a generic attack for this particular encryption scheme, strongly depends on the choice of tap positions, see also [18]. Therefore, our goal is to maximize this complexity which is certainly related to the minimization of the parameters $r_i = \#\mathcal{I}_i$, but not completely equivalent. Notice that by optimizing the resistance of these schemes to GFSGA does not necessarily imply the optimality of tap selections, though for the targeted filtering generator we cannot see other reasonable approaches in the context of the guess and determine cryptanalysis.

Let R denotes the number of repeated equations regardless of this number being $\sum_{i=1}^{c-1} r_i$ for $c \leq k$, or $\sum_{i=1}^{k} r_i + (c - k - 1)r_k$ for $c > k$. From [18], it somehow appears that an (sub)optimal choice of tap positions is the one that minimizes the number of repeated equations R, which is a bit misleading as illustrated by the following example.

Example 1. Let the tap positions be given by $\mathcal{I}_0 = \{1, 5, 13, 25, 41, 65, 77\}$, for $L = 80$, $n = 7$, and $m = 3$. Computing the complexity $T_{Comp.}$ for all sampling differences $\sigma = 1, 2, 3, \ldots, 76$, one can verify that the best choice of σ for the attacker is $\sigma = 12$, with the minimal complexity $T_{Comp.} \approx 2^{23.97}$ and having $R = 177$ as the number of repeated equations. However, the computation below shows that for $\sigma = 4$, $R = 353$ is maximum possible, but in that case $T_{Comp.} \approx 2^{27.97}$.

To see why $\sigma = 4$ is not optimal for the attacker, we first compute $r_i = \#\mathcal{I}_i$,

$$\mathcal{I}_1 = \{5\}, \ \mathcal{I}_2 = \{5, 13\}, \ \mathcal{I}_3 = \{5, 13, 25, 77\}, \ \mathcal{I}_4 = \{5, 13, 25, 41, 77\},$$
$$\mathcal{I}_5 = \{5, 13, 25, 41, 77\}, \ \mathcal{I}_6 = \{5, 13, 25, 41, 65, 77\},$$
$$\mathcal{I}_j = \{5, 13, 25, 41, 65, 77\}, \ for \ j = 7, 8, \ldots, 61.$$

The number of sampling points c, for $k = \lfloor \frac{77-1}{4} \rfloor = 19$, is determined from the condition $nc - (\sum_{i=1}^{k} r_i + (c - k - 1)r_k) > L$, i.e., $c = 62$ is the smallest positive integer satisfying the condition. The terms $2^{(n-m-r_i)} \neq 1$ in (3), for which $r_i < n - m$ so that the number of preimages is greater than one, only appear for $r_1 = 1$ and $r_2 = 2$, i.e.,

$$T_{Comp.} = 2^{(n-m)} \times 2^{(n-m-r_1)} \times 2^{(n-m-r_2)} \times L^3 \approx 2^{27.97}.$$

For $j = 3, \ldots, 61$, we have $2^{(n-m-r_j)} = 1$, in accordance to Remark 2.

Similarly, for $\sigma = 12$, which implies that $k = 6$, we obtain $c = 37$ (where c is derived from $nc - (\sum_{i=1}^{k} r_i + (c - k - 1)r_k) > L$) and "only" $R = 177$ repeated equations. The intersection sets in this case are given as,

$$\mathcal{I}_1 = \{13, 25, 77\}, \ \mathcal{I}_2 = \{13, 25, 65, 77\}, \ \mathcal{I}_3 = \{13, 25, 41, 65, 77\},$$
$$\mathcal{I}_j = \{13, 25, 41, 65, 77\}, \ \ for \ j = 4, 5, \ldots, 36.$$

The complexity computation in this case involves only $r_1 = 3$, i.e.,

$$T_{Comp.} = 2^{(n-m)} \times 2^{(n-m-r_1)} \times L^3 \approx 2^{23.97}.$$

Notice that for $j = 2, \ldots, 36$, we have $2^{(n-m-r_j)} = 1$.

Remark 3. A lower complexity in the above example (for a larger number of repeated equations) is entirely due to a low difference between n and m so that many of the repeated equations could not be efficiently used since the preimages could be identified uniquely even without using these equations.

More formally, if σ' gives the maximal possible value of R though the attack complexity is not minimal, and σ'' gives the minimal attack complexity without maximizing R, then it holds

$$\sum_{r_j \in H_{\sigma''}} (n - m - r_j) < \sum_{r_i \in H_{\sigma'}} (n - m - r_i) \qquad (4)$$

where $H_{\sigma'} = \{r_i < n - m : r_i \text{ obtained by } \sigma', i = 1, 2, \ldots, c - 1\}$ and $H_{\sigma''} = \{r_j < n - m : r_j \text{ obtained by } \sigma'', j = 1, 2, \ldots, c - 1\}$. In the above example, we have $H_{\sigma'} = \{r_1, r_2\} = \{1, 2\}$ with $\sigma' = 4$, and $H_{\sigma''} = \{r_1\} = \{3\}$ with $\sigma'' = 12$, for which (4) holds.

Another problem related to the approach of finding the intersection sets given by (1) is that the information contained in R and the cardinalities r_i alone does not fully specifies the properties of the repeated equations. The equations corresponding to the numbers in the sets $\mathcal{I}_i$ may be repeated and found in other sets $\mathcal{I}_j$, where $i \neq j$, and even though they efficiently reduce the preimage space they do not contribute to the rank of the systems of linear equations that need to be solved. An alternative method of tracking the repeated equations, illustrated in the example bellow, turns out to give a deeper insight to the problem of selecting the tap positions optimally.

Example 2. Let the tap positions be given by $\mathcal{I}_0 = \{l_1, l_2, l_3, l_4, l_5\} = \{1, 4, 8,$ $9, 11\}$, $L = 15$, and the sampling distance $\sigma = 2$. Let $\mathbf{s}^{t_i} = (s_{0+(i-1)\sigma},$ $s_{1+(i-1)\sigma}, \ldots, s_{14+(i-1)\sigma})$, denote the LFSR state over $c = 10$ sampling instances $t_i = (i-1)\sigma$, for $i = 1, 2, \ldots, 10$. Moreover, at these different sampling instances, we represent the output bits of LFSR $s_0, s_1, \ldots$ via their indices in $\mathbb{N}$, i.e., $s_k \to (k+1) \in \mathbb{N}$. For instance, in Table 2 the number 27 corresponds to the bit s_{26} which becomes a part of the LFSR state $\mathbf{s}^{t_9}$ at position l_5. The LFSR state bits at tap positions $\mathcal{I}_0 = \{l_1, l_2, l_3, l_4, l_5\}$ are illustrated in Table 2.

Table 2. The LFSR state bits at given tap positions for $\sigma = 2$.

States	l_1	l_2	l_3	l_4	l_5
$\mathbf{s}^{t_1}$	$s_0 \to 1$	$s_3 \to 4$	$s_7 \to 8$	$s_8 \to 9$	$s_{10} \to 11$
$\mathbf{s}^{t_2}$	$s_2 \to 3$	$s_5 \to 6$	$s_9 \to 10$	$s_{10} \to 11$	$s_{12} \to 13$
$\mathbf{s}^{t_3}$	$s_4 \to 5$	$s_7 \to 8$	$s_{11} \to 12$	$s_{12} \to 13$	$s_{14} \to 15$
$\mathbf{s}^{t_4}$	$s_6 \to 7$	$s_9 \to 10$	$s_{13} \to 14$	$s_{14} \to 15$	$s_{16} \to 17$
$\mathbf{s}^{t_5}$	$s_8 \to 9$	$s_{11} \to 12$	$s_{15} \to 16$	$s_{16} \to 17$	$s_{18} \to 19$
$\mathbf{s}^{t_6}$	$s_{10} \to 11$	$s_{13} \to 14$	$s_{17} \to 18$	$s_{18} \to 19$	$s_{20} \to 21$
$\mathbf{s}^{t_7}$	$s_{12} \to 13$	$s_{15} \to 16$	$s_{19} \to 20$	$s_{20} \to 21$	$s_{22} \to 23$
$\mathbf{s}^{t_8}$	$s_{14} \to 15$	$s_{17} \to 18$	$s_{21} \to 22$	$s_{22} \to 23$	$s_{24} \to 25$
$\mathbf{s}^{t_9}$	$s_{16} \to 17$	$s_{19} \to 20$	$s_{23} \to 24$	$s_{24} \to 25$	$s_{26} \to 27$
$\mathbf{s}^{t_{10}}$	$s_{18} \to 19$	$s_{21} \to 22$	$s_{25} \to 26$	$s_{26} \to 27$	$s_{28} \to 29$

Our goal is to determine when some equation (state bit) is repeated on the tap positions $l_1, \ldots, l_4$ at the sampling instances t_i. Hence, we observe the repetition of all consecutive tap positions $l_{j+1} - l_j$, then the differences $l_{j+2} - l_j$, etc. Let D be a set of all differences between consecutive tap positions, i.e.,

$$D = \{d_j | d_j = l_{j+1} - l_j, j = 1, 2, 3, 4\} = \{3, 4, 1, 2\}.$$

To consider all possible repetitions of the equations on all tap positions, we design a scheme of all possible differences:

Table 3. The scheme of all possible differences for the set D.

Row\Columns	Col. 1	Col. 2	Col. 3	Col. 4
Row 1	d_1	d_2	d_3	d_4
Row 2	$d_1 + d_2$	$d_2 + d_3$	$d_3 + d_4$	
Row 3	$d_1 + d_2 + d_3$	$d_2 + d_3 + d_4$		
Row 4	$d_1 + d_2 + d_3 + d_4$			

Table 4. The scheme of all differences for $D = \{3, 4, 1, 2\}$.

Row\Columns	Col. 1	Col. 2	Col. 3	Col. 4
Row 1	3	4	1	2
Row 2	7	5	3	
Row 3	8	7		
Row 4	10			

In Table 3, Column 1 specifies the repetition of some equations at the tap position l_1, Column 2 gives the repetition of equations on l_2, etc. Similarly, Row 1 takes into account the consecutive repetitions from l_{i+1} to l_i, Row 2 regards the repetition from l_{i+2} to l_i, etc. In our example, by Table 3, we have Assuming the attacker starts the sampling with some step σ, the total number of repeated equations R is the sum of all equations which repeat on each of the tap positions l_j, where $j = 1, 2, 3, 4$.

Since Table 3 can be designed for an arbitrary set D, $\#D = n - 1$, the repetition of the same equations can be tracked as follows. We are looking for the first number in each column such that it is divisible by σ, which implies that we have the repetition of equations, otherwise there are no repetitions. Notice that in Table 4, in Column 1, $\sigma \nmid 3$, which implies that there is no repetition of equations from l_2 at l_1. Also, since $2 \nmid 7$, there is no repetition from l_3 at l_1. However, $2 \mid 8$, which implies that the equation(s) from l_4 will appear on l_1 after $\frac{8}{2} = 4$ sampling instances (cf. Table 2 where 9 appears at l_1 when the content of the LFSR is $\mathbf{s}^{t_5}$). Thereafter, one equation from l_4 appears at l_1 for every state $\mathbf{s}^{t_i}$, for $i \geq 5$. Further, the fact that $2 \mid 8$ and $2 \mid 10$ implies that $2 \mid d_4 = 2$, which means that we have a repetition from l_5 to l_1 at every LFSR state $\mathbf{s}_i^t$, $i \geq 2$. Since Column 1 already contains this number 8 which is divisible by 2, all the repeated equations from l_5 to l_1 are already taken into account, and we do not use number 10 (Table 4, Row 4) when calculating the number of repeated equations. So, $\frac{d_4}{2}$ is related to the repetitions of equations from l_5 to l_4. Hence, the number of repeated equations R, for $c = 10$, is calculated as follows.

1. On l_1, there are $(c - \frac{d_1+d_2+d_3}{\sigma}) = 10 - \frac{8}{2} = 6$ repeated equations.
2. On l_2, there are $(c - \frac{d_2}{\sigma}) = 10 - 2 = 8$ repeated equations.
3. On l_3, there are NO repeated equations, since we do not have the differences divisible by $\sigma = 2$.
4. On l_4, there are $(c - \frac{d_4}{\sigma}) = 9$ repeated equations.

In total, we have $R = 6 + 8 + 0 + 9 = 23$ repeated equations.

The analysis performed in the above example leads to the following result concerning the number of repeated equations.

Proposition 1. *Let* $\mathcal{I}_0 = \{l_1, l_2, \dots, l_n\}$ *be a set of tap positions, and let*

$$D = \{l_{i+1} - l_i \mid i = 1, 2, \dots, n-1\} = \{d_1, d_2, \dots, d_{n-1}\}.$$

The number of repeated equations is calculated as

$$R = \sum_{i=1}^{n-1} \left(c - \frac{1}{\sigma} \sum_{k=i}^{m} d_k\right), \tag{5}$$

where $\sigma \mid \sum_{k=i}^{m} d_k$ for some $m \in \mathbb{N}$, $i \leq m \leq n - 1$ and $\frac{1}{\sigma} \sum_{k=i}^{m} d_k \leq c - 1$. Moreover, if $\frac{1}{\sigma} \sum_{k=i}^{m} d_k \geq c$, for some $1 \leq i \leq n - 1$, then $(c - \frac{1}{\sigma} \sum_{k=i}^{m} d_k) = 0$. This means that the repetition of the same equations (bits) starts to appear after the LFSR state s^{t_c}.

Remark 4. The importance of the above proposition lies in a fact that the counting method of repeated equations does not depend on the relation between the number of sampling points c and k (where $k = \lfloor \frac{i_n - i_1}{\sigma} \rfloor$), i.e., it holds for both $c \leq k$ and $c > k$.

Notice that, in order to minimize the number of repeated equations, the terms $(c - \frac{1}{\sigma} \sum_{k=i}^{m} d_k)$, $i \leq m \leq n - 1$, should be minimized. Hence, we want to avoid the divisibility by σ in the scheme of differences as much as possible. Moreover, for a given length L of LFSR, the differences between $d_i \in D$ should be maximized under the constraint $\sum_{i=1}^{n-1} d_i \leq L - 1$, which is also conditioned by $1 \leq l_1 < l_2 < \ldots < l_n \leq L$. In other words, the goal is to distribute the tap positions over entire LFSR while at the same time keeping the divisibility by σ as low as possible. Clearly, if $\sum_{i=1}^{n-1} d_i = L - 1$, then $l_1 = 1$ and $l_n = L$.

5   Two Algorithms Towards an Optimal Selection of Taps

It turns out that the problem of optimizing the choice of $\mathcal{I}_0$ is closely related to the divisibility of the elements in the corresponding (multi)set of differences D by an arbitrary σ. Thus, instead of searching the set $\mathcal{I}_0$ directly, we focus on the set of differences D. The construction of the set D is however out of reach to be done exhaustively for moderately large L and n, and consequently we use some heuristic techniques to specify D (sub)optimally.

In what follows, we present a method of constructing the set D which gives a low number of repeated equations (confirmed by computer simulations) for every σ. The set D is specified using some heuristic design rationales (see below) and at the same time the differences d_i are maximized.

Step A: Find the elements of the set D. To do this and avoid the divisibility by σ, the following pattern is applied.

1. Prime numbers are the most favourable to join the set D. Since higher values of n dictate the repetitions of some elements in D, the repetition should be kept on minimum with a general tendency to choose co-prime differences. If some even numbers are taken, then the set D should contain just few of them, because they can result in many common (high) factors in the rows of Table 3.

2. Maximize the differences d_i under the constraint $\sum_{d_i \in D} d_i \leq L - 1$.

Step B: Find the best ordering of the chosen differences, which basically means that ordering of D is also important. This can be done using the following algorithm with the complexity $O(n! \cdot K)$, where K corresponds to the complexity of calculation $T_{Comp.}$ for all possible σ.

INPUT: The set D and the numbers L, $n = \#D + 1$ and m.

OUTPUT: The best ordering of the chosen differences, that is, an ordered set D that maximizes the complexity of the attack.

STEP 1: Generate a list of all permutations of the elements in D;
STEP 2: For every permutation, find the minimal complexity for all steps σ
         from 1 to L;
STEP 3: Generate a list of all minimal complexities from Step 2;
STEP 4: Find the maximal value in the list of all minimal complexities;
STEP 5: Return the corresponding permutation of the maximal value.

Open Problem 1. *Find an efficient algorithm, which returns the best ordering of the set D without searching all permutations.*

Remark 5. To measure the quality of a chosen set of differences D with respect to the maximization of $T_{Comp.}$ over all σ, the computer simulations indicate that an optimal ordering of the set D implies a small value of an optimal sampling distance σ. This is also a criterion that a set D is most likely chosen well (a sub-optimal choice). The term "most likely" concerns the difficulties of capturing the whole process of choosing the tap positions explicitly, due to a very complicated relation between σ, R, D and $T_{Comp.}$ through the scheme of differences. When choosing an output permutation (cf. Step 5 below), we always consider both σ and $T_{Comp.}$ though σ turns out to be a more stable indicator of the quality of a chosen set D.

Note that, the above algorithm performs an exhaustive search over all permutations of the input set. For practical values of L, usually taken to be $L = 256$, the time complexity of the above algorithm becomes practically infeasible already for $n > 10$. To reduce its factorial time complexity, we modify the above algorithm to process the subsets of the multiset D separately within the feasibility constraints imposed on the cardinalities of these subsets.

STEP 1: Choose a set X by **Step A**, where $\#X < \#D$ for which **Step B** is
         feasible;
STEP 2: Find the best ordering of X using the algorithm in **Step B** for
         $L_X = 1 + \sum_{x_i \in X} x_i < L$ and $m_X = \lfloor \#X \cdot \frac{m}{n-1} \rfloor$;
STEP 3: Choose a set Y by **Step A**, where $\#Y < \#D$ for which **Step B** is
         feasible;
STEP 4: "Generate" a list of all permutations of the elements in Y;

STEP 5: Find a permutation (Y_p) from the above list such that for a fixed set X, the new set Y_pX obtained by joining X to Y_p, denoted by Y_pX (with the parameters $L_{Y_pX} = 1 + \sum_{x_i \in X} x_i + \sum_{y_i \in Y_p} y_i \leq L$ and $m_{Y_pX} = \lfloor \#Y_pX \cdot \frac{m}{n-1} \rfloor$), allows a small optimal step σ, in the sense of Remark 5;

STEP 6: If such a permutation, resulting in a small value of σ, does not exist in Step 5, then back to Step 3 and choose another set Y;

STEP 7: Update the set $X \leftarrow Y_pX$, and repeat the steps 3 - 5 by adjoining new sets Y_p until $\#Y_pX = n - 1$;

STEP 8: Return the set $D = Y_pX$.

Remark 6. The parameters L_X and m_X are derived by computer simulations, where L_X essentially constrains the set X and m_X keeps the proportionality between the numbers $m, \#X$ and $\#D = n - 1$.

An illustration of our modified version of the above algorithm is given in the following example. Namely, for a rather practical choice of the parameters L, n and m, the whole procedure of defining the set of differences that eventually yields the tap positions is discussed. Some suboptimal choices of tap positions for varying input parameters L, n, m along with the time complexity of the GFSGA and the time complexity of applying our algorithms are given in Appendix (cf. Tables 5 and 6).

Example 3. Let $n = 17$, $m = 6$, and $F(x) : GF(2)^{17} \longrightarrow GF(2)^6$. Let $L = 160$ bits, the length of the secret key is $K = 80$ bits.

Let $X = \{5, 13, 7, 26, 11, 17\}$ be obtained using the algorithm in **Step B** for $L_X = 80$, $m_X = 2$. Let $Y = \{1, 2, 9, 15, 23\}$. Then, a permutation $Y_p = \{9, 1, 2, 23, 15\}$, i.e., the set

$$Y_pX = \{9, 1, 2, 23, 15, 5, 13, 7, 26, 11, 17\},$$

where $L_{Y_pX} = 130$ and $m_{Y_pX} = 4$, gives that $\sigma = 1$ is an optimal sampling distance for the attacker. Since $L_{Y_pX} \leq 160$, then we choose the set $Z = \{3, 4, 5, 7, 11\}$. Then, a permutation $Z_p = \{5, 11, 4, 3, 7\}$, i.e., the set $Z_pY_pX = \{5, 11, 4, 3, 7, 9, 1, 2, 23, 15, 5, 13, 7, 26, 11, 17\}$, where $L_{Z_pY_pX} = L = 160$ and $m_{L_{Z_pY_pX}} = m = 6$ gives the optimal step $\sigma = 1$ for the attacker. Then we have

$$D = \{5, 11, 4, 3, 7, 9, 1, 2, 23, 15, 5, 13, 7, 26, 11, 17\},$$

and thus

$$\mathcal{I}_0 = \{1, 6, 17, 21, 24, 31, 40, 41, 43, 66, 81, 86, 99, 106, 132, 143, 160\}.$$

Hence, $\sigma = 1$ is optimal, with the minimal complexity $T_{Comp.} = 2^{86.97}$, which is essentially an extremely good choice of tap positions (non-exhaustively confirmed to be an optimal choice).

In what follows, we apply the above algorithms to two well-known stream cipher SOBER-t32 [16], [18] and SFINX [19].

SOBER-t32: An application of the GFSGA attack on unstuttered SOBER-t32 was considered in [18]. The tap positions of SOBER-t32 are given by $\mathcal{I}_0 = \{1, 4, 11, 16, 17\}$ (corresponding to the reverse order of the taps $1 \leftarrow s_{16}$, $4 \leftarrow s_{13}$, etc.) and the sampling distance used in [18] was $\sigma = 3$. Due to the reverse order of the bits s_i, we consider the set D in reverse order, i.e. $D = \{1, 5, 7, 3\}$ instead of $\{3, 7, 5, 1\}$, since this ordering corresponds to our consideration of the LFSR states presented in Table 2. Regarding the set D, the set of all $r_i = \#\mathcal{I}_0$ is $\{1, 1, 2, 2, 3, 3, 4, 4, 4, 4, \ldots\}$, i.e. $r_1 = r_2 = 1$, $r_2 = r_3 = 2$, $r_4 = r_5 = 3$ and $r_k = 4$, $k \geq 7$. At each sampling point we derive $40 - 8 \times r_i$ linear equations (cf. [18]). Therefore, the number of repeated equations is given by

$$40 + 32 + 32 + 24 + 24 + 16 + 16 + 8 \times (c - 7) + c, \tag{6}$$

which for $c = 47$ gives $R = 550$ linear equations (6). Thus the complexity of the attack can be estimated as

$$T_D = (17 \times 32)^3 \times 2^{35} \times 2^{2 \times 27} \times 2^{2 \times 19} \times 2^{2 \times 11} \times 2^{39 \times 3} = (17 \times 32)^3 \times 2^{266}.$$

Since $\#D = 4$, we can easily apply **Step A** and **Step B**, to come up with the new set $D^* = \{5, 2, 7, 2\}$, and get the set $\{0, 2, 2, 2, 3, 3, 4, 4, 4, 4, \ldots\}$ of all $r_i = \#\mathcal{I}_0$. The inequality

$$40 + 40 + 32 + 32 + 32 + 24 + 24 + 8 \times (c - 7) + c \geq 544$$

implies $c = 42$, and $R = 546$ equations. The complexity is estimated as

$$T_{D^*} = (17 \times 32)^3 \times 2^{2 \times 35} \times 2^{3 \times 27} \times 2^{2 \times 19} \times 2^{34 \times 3} = (17 \times 32)^3 \times 2^{291}.$$

This means that our algorithm gives the tap selection with much better resistance against GFSGA.

SFINX: The design details of SFINX can be found in [19]. The set of the tap positions of SFINX is given as

$$\mathcal{I}_0 = \{1, 2, 7, 10, 20, 22, 45, 59, 75, 99, 106, 135, 162, 194, 228, 245, 256\},$$

and $D = \{1, 5, 3, 10, 2, 23, 14, 16, 24, 7, 29, 27, 32, 34, 17, 11\}$. An optimal step of the GFSGA attack on this set of tap positions, is $\sigma = 2$ which requires $c = 27$ sampling points, resulting in $R = 200$ sampled equations for obtaining an overdefined system. The corresponding complexity in this case is $T_{Comp.} = 2^{256}$. Note that $\sum_{i=1}^{16} d_i = 255$ with optimal step $\sigma = 2$, which indicates that the set of tap positions $\mathcal{I}_0$ of SFINX is chosen well. However, we can use the elements of the given set D and our algorithm to create the set of differences "by parts", in order to decrease the number of repeated equations R and increase the complexity (slightly). Starting with the set $X = \{29, 32, 17, 34, 27, 11\}$, and permuting the set $Y_p = \{2, 23, 14, 16, 24, 7\}$ for $L_{Y_p X} = 237$, we get the set

$Y_pX = \{2, 23, 14, 7, 16, 24, 29, 32, 17, 34, 27, 11\}$ with an optimal step $\sigma = 8$ for the attack. Then, taking the set $Z_p = \{1, 5, 3, 10\}$, we get the set $D^* = Z_pY_pX$ given as

$$D^* = \{1, 5, 3, 10, 2, 23, 14, 7, 16, 24, 29, 32, 17, 34, 27, 11\},$$

with the optimal steps $\sigma \in \{1, 2\}$ for the attack. The estimated complexity for both optimal steps is $T_{Comp.} = 2^{257}$ with $R = 167$ repeated equations, thus only a minor improvement has been achieved.

It would be of interest to consider the problem of optimizing the placement of tap positions in case the GFSGA attack with a variable sampling step (σ is not fixed) is used, which is left for the extended version of this article.

Acknowledgments. Enes Pasalic was supported in part by the Slovenian Research Agency research program (P3-0384) and research project (J1-6720). Samir Hodžić was supported in part by the Slovenian Research Agency (research program P3-0384 and Young Researchers Grant). Yongzhuang Wei was supported in part by the Natural Science Foundation of China (61100185,61201250), in part by the National Basic Research Program of China (2013CB338002), in part by the project of Outstanding Young Teachers' Training in Higher Education Institutions of Guangxi.

Appendix

In Table 5 we give several instances for determining suboptimal tap positions of LFSRs of different length. The following parameters are used:

- L is the length of LFSR;
- n and m are parameters related to vectorial Boolean function $F : GF(2)^n \to GF(2)^m$;
- D is a set of differences between tap positions;
- c is the minimal number of observed outputs needed for an overdefined system
- R is the number of repeated equations for given c outputs;
- σ is an optimal step of the GFSGA attack;
- $T_{Comp.}$ is the time complexity of GFSGA.

Table 5. Specifications of difference sets for LFSRs of different lengths.

L	(n, m)	D	R	c	σ	$T_{Comp.}$
80	(7,2)	$\{5, 13, 7, 26, 11, 17\}$	24	15	1	$2^{69.97}$
120	(13,3)	$\{5, 7, 3, 13, 6, 11, 5, 11, 7, 13, 21, 17\}$	61	14	3	$2^{99.7}$
160	(17,6)	$\{5,11,4,3,7,9,1,2,23,15,5, 13, 7, 26, 11, 17\}$	128	17	1	$2^{86.97}$
200	(21,7)	$\{3, 7, 9, 13, 18, 7, 9, 1, 2, 9, 1, 2, 23, 15, 5, 13, 7, 26, 11, 17\}$	175	18	1	$2^{108.9}$
256	(27,9)	$\{5, 9, 13, 4, 7, 19, 3, 7, 9, 13, 18, 7, 9, 1, 2, 9, 1, 2, 23, 15, 5, 13, 7, 26, 11, 17\}$	227	18	1	2^{135}

Remark 7. From the difference sets D in Table 5 we easily obtain the tap positions.

Table 6. Time complexities for finding tap positions in Table 5.

L	(n,m)	Cardinality of parts	Complexity	Times in sec
80	(7,2)	no parts	$O(K \cdot 6!)$	135
120	(13,3)	(6,6)	$2 \cdot O(K \cdot 6!)$	125+162=287
160	(17,6)	(6,6,4)	$2 \cdot O(K \cdot 6!) + O(K \cdot 4!)$	137+198+8.5=343.5
200	(21,7)	(6,6,4,4)	$2 \cdot O(K \cdot 6!) + 2 \cdot O(K \cdot 4!)$	137+96+7.7+9.5=250
256	(27,9)	(6,6,4,4,6)	$3 \cdot O(K \cdot 6!) + 2 \cdot O(K \cdot 4!)$	250+369.3=619.3

Remark 8. Note that the time required to create some particular set of differences depends on the cardinality of parts. It means that the smaller cardinalities implies the lower time complexity, though such an approach may provide the solutions that are "far" from optimal. Table 6 presents the following:

- Cardinality of parts refers to the modified algorithm on Page 10, bottom. For instance, $(6, 6, 4)$ means that we take $\#X = 6$ elements and finding its optimal permutation requires 137 sec with our permutation algorithm. Then, we take another $\#Y_p = 6$ elements and determine its best order which fits to the set X, which requires 198 seconds (modified algorithm). Finally, the same procedure is applied to the set $Y_p X$ by adding $Z_p = 4$ elements using again our modified algorithm (requiring 8.5 sec). The resulting set of differences is given as $D = Z_p Y_p X$.
- Complexity refers to the complexity of the permutation algorithms **Step B** and its modification used to construct the set D.
- The constant K regards the procedure described in the permutation algorithm (**Step B**): creating the list, searching, etc.

References

1. Biryukov, A., Shamir, A.: Cryptanalytic time/memory/data tradeoffs for stream ciphers. In: Okamoto, T. (ed.) ASIACRYPT 2000. LNCS, vol. 1976, pp. 1–13. Springer, Heidelberg (2000)
2. Braeken, A., Preneel, B.: Probabilistic algebraic attacks. In: Smart, N.P. (ed.) Cryptography and Coding 2005. LNCS, vol. 3796, pp. 290–303. Springer, Heidelberg (2005)
3. Carlet, C.: A larger class of cryptographic boolean functions via a study of the Maiorana-McFarland construction. In: Yung, M. (ed.) CRYPTO 2002. LNCS, vol. 2442, pp. 549–564. Springer, Heidelberg (2002)
4. Courtois, N., Meier, W.: Algebraic attacks on stream ciphers with linear feedback. In: Boneh, D. (ed.) Advances in Cryptology-EUROCRYPT 2003. LNCS, vol. 2656, pp. 346–359. Springer, Heidelberg (2003)

5. Golić, J.D.: Intrinsic statistical weakness of keystream generators. In: Pieprzyk, J., Safavi-Naini, R. (eds.) Advances in Cryptology-ASIACRYPT 1994. LNCS, vol. 917, pp. 91–103. Springer, Heidelberg (1995)

6. Golić, J.D.: On the security of nonlinear filter generators. In: Gollmann, D. (ed.) Fast Software Encryption 1996. LNCS, vol. 1039, pp. 173–188. Springer, Heidelberg (1996)

7. Golic, J.D., Clark, A., Dawson, E.: Generalized inversion attack on nonlinear filter generators. IEEE Trans. Comput. **49**(10), 1100–1109 (2000)

8. Hellman, M.: A cryptanalytic time-memory tradeoff. IEEE Trans. on Inform. Theor. **26**(4), 401–406 (1980)

9. Hong, J., Sarkar, P.: New applications of time memory data tradeoffs. In: Roy, B. (ed.) ASIACRYPT 2005. LNCS, vol. 3788, pp. 353–372. Springer, Heidelberg (2005)

10. Massey, J.L.: Shift-register synthesis and BCH decoding. IEEE Trans. Inform. Theor. **15**(1), 122–127 (1969)

11. Meier, W., Pasalic, E., Carlet, C.: Algebraic attacks and decomposition of Boolean functions. In: Cachin, C., Camenisch, J.L. (eds.) EUROCRYPT 2004. LNCS, vol. 3027, pp. 474–491. Springer, Heidelberg (2004)

12. Mihaljević, M.J., Fossorier, M.P.C., Imai, H.: A general formulation of algebraic and fast correlation attacks based on dedicated sample decimation. In: Fossorier, M.P.C., Imai, H., Lin, S., Poli, A. (eds.) AAECC 2006. LNCS, vol. 3857, pp. 203–214. Springer, Heidelberg (2006)

13. Mihaljević, M.J., Gangopadhyay, S., Paul, G., Imai, H.: Internal state recovery of Grain-v1 employing normality order of the filter function. IET Inform. Secur. **6**(2), 55–64 (2006)

14. Nyberg, K.: On the construction of highly nonlinear permutations. In: Rueppel, R.A. (ed.) EUROCRYPT 1992. LNCS, vol. 658, pp. 92–98. Springer, Heidelberg (1993)

15. Pasalic, E.: On guess and determine cryptanalysis of LFSR-based stream ciphers. IEEE Trans. Inform. Theor. **55**(7), 3398–3406 (2009)

16. Hawkes, P., Rose, G.: Primitive specification and supporting documentation for SOBER-t16 submission to NESSIE. In: Proceedings of the First Open NESSIE Workshop, KU-Leuven (2000)

17. Pasalic, E.: Probabilistic versus deterministic algebraic cryptanalysisa performance comparison. IEEE Trans. Inform. Theor. **55**(11), 2182–2191 (2009)

18. Wei, Y., Pasalic, E., Hu, Y.: Guess and determinate attacks on filter generators-revisited. IEEE Trans. Inform. Theor. **58**(4), 2530–2539 (2012)

19. Braeken, A., Lano, J., Mentens, N., Preneel, B., Verbauwhede, I.: SFINKS: A Synchronous Stream Cipher for Restricted Hardware Environments. eSTREAM, ECRYPT Stream Cipher Project, Report 2005/026 (2005)

Families of Pseudorandom Binary Sequences with Low Cross-Correlation Measure

Oğuz Yayla$^{(\boxtimes)}$

Department of Mathematics, Hacettepe University, Beytepe Campus, Ankara, Turkey
oguz.yayla@hacettepe.edu.tr

Abstract. Pseudorandom sequences are used in many areas of cryptography for instance as a key stream of stream ciphers. These sequences have to be unpredictable and resist to known attacks, hence they are supposed to satisfy some properties e.g., large linear complexity and low correlation. Since they are generated by a sequence generator, we also need to talk about a family of sequences and its properties. A family of sequences must have complex and rich structure e.g., large family size, large family complexity, strict avalanche property and low cross-correlation. In this study, we present two large families of pseudorandom binary sequences with low cross-correlation measure. In fact, we extend the family construction method given by K. Gyarmati, C. Mauduit and A. Sárközy and obtain larger families.

Keywords: Pseudorandomness · Family of binary sequences · Cross-correlation measure

1 Introduction

Pseudorandom binary sequences are used in many areas of modern cryptography. For instance they are used as the key stream in stream ciphers. Thus, the quality of a pseudorandom sequence generator has to be validated. Its quality is measured by statistical test packages (for example L'Ecuyer's TESTU01, Marsaglia's Diehard or the NIST battery) as well as by proving theoretical results on certain measures of pseudorandomness such as the correlation measure of order ℓ introduced by Mauduit and Sárközy [8]. In this study, we focus on theoretical results.

Consider a binary sequence

$$E_N = (e_1, e_2, \ldots, e_N) \in \{-1, +1\}^N.$$

In [8] Mauduit and Sárközy introduced the following measures of pseudorandomness: the *well distribution measure* of E_N is defined by

$$W(E_N) = \max_{a,b,t} \Big| \sum_{j=0}^{t-1} e_{a+bj} \Big|,$$

© Springer International Publishing Switzerland 2015
B. Ors and B. Preneel (Eds.): BalkanCryptSec 2014, LNCS 9024, pp. 31–39, 2015.
DOI: 10.1007/978-3-319-21356-9_3

where the maximum is taken over all $a \in \mathbb{N} \cup \{0\}, b, t \in \mathbb{N}$ such that $0 \leq a \leq a + b(t-1) \leq N - 1$, and the *correlation measure of order k* of E_N is defined as

$$C_k(E_N) = \max_{M,D} \left| \sum_{n=1}^{M} e_{n+d_1} e_{n+d_2} \cdots e_{n+d_k} \right|,$$

where the maximum is taken over all $D = (d_1, d_2, \ldots, d_k)$ and M such that $0 \leq d_1 < d_2 < \cdots < d_k \leq N - M$.

It was proved in [3] that $W(E_N)$ and $C_k(E_N)$ are "small" for a truly random sequence $E_N \in \{-1, +1\}$, i.e. if one chooses each sequence with probability 2^{-N} (for proof see also [2]). More precisely, the order of magnitude of $W(E_N)$ and $C_k(E_N)$ (for fixed k) is $N^{1/2}$ and $N^{1/2}(\log N)^{c(k)}$, respectively. Thus, a sequence E_N is called a "good" pseudorandom if both $W(E_N)$ and $C_k(E_N)$ (for small k) are small and ideally greater than $N^{1/2}$ only by at most a power of $\log N$. Hence, if a binary sequence $E_N \in \{-1, +1\}$ (after transforming it into bit representation) is used as a key stream in cryptographic applications, then E_N must be unpredictable, i.e. a "good" pseudorandom sequence. The most natural way of attacking to a cipher for recovering the key stream is the exhaustive search on the set of all possible binary sequences $E_N \in \{-1, +1\}$ with large $W(E_N)$ (or large $C_k(E_N)$). Since this set is much smaller than the set of all sequences in $\{-1, +1\}^N$, the attack recovers the key if the key is not a "good" pseudorandom sequence. Besides a fast method of exhaustive search, one also needs a fast algorithm to generate the set of sequences with large $W(E_N)$ (or large $C_k(E_N)$). For other applications of "good" pseudorandom sequences, we refer to [10].

It was shown in [8] that the Legendre symbol forms a "good" pseudorandom sequence. Since then new "good" pseudorandom sequences have been constructed. On the other hand, these "good" pseudorandom sequences are very few, and in cryptography we generally need large families of "good" pseudorandom sequences. Large families of "good" pseudorandom binary sequences with low well distribution and correlation measures were also constructed e.g. in [4,5,7]. In these constructions, only individual sequences are considered to be a "good" pseudorandom sequence. However, this is not enough to say that the family is good, and in many applications we need to show that the family has a complex and rich structure. For this purpose, *family complexity* [1], *collision and avalanche effect* [11] are introduced and widely studied. And recently, Gyarmati, Mauduit and Sárközy [6] introduced the *cross-correlation measure of order k* to characterize a family of sequences. Then, it was shown in [12] that the family complexity of a binary sequence can be estimated by the cross-correlation measure of its dual family. We note that in cryptographic applications the key streams with low family complexity are known to be weak, and one can exploit this weakness to recover the whole key with less complexity than exhaustive search, for details see [1]. Below we give the definition of the cross-correlation measure of a family of binary sequences.

Definition 1. *The cross-correlation measure of order k of a family $\mathcal{F}$ of binary sequences $E_{i,N} = (e_{i,1}, e_{i,2}, \ldots, e_{i,N}) \in \{-1 + 1\}^N$, $i = 1, 2, \ldots, |\mathcal{F}|$, is defined as*

$$\Phi_k(\mathcal{F}) = \max_{M,D,I} \left| \sum_{n=1}^{M} e_{i_1,n+d_1} \cdots e_{i_k,n+d_k} \right|$$

where D denotes a k tuple $(d_1, d_2, \ldots, d_k)$ of integers such that $0 \leq d_1 \leq d_2 \leq \cdots \leq d_k < M + d_k \leq N$ and $d_i \neq d_j$ if $E_{i,N} = E_{j,N}$ for $i \neq j$, and I denotes a k tuple $(i_1, i_2, \ldots, i_k)$ in $\{1, 2, \ldots, |\mathcal{F}|\}$.

If $\mathcal{F} = \{E_N\}$ consists of only one sequence E_N, then $\Phi_k(\mathcal{F}) = C_k(E_N)$. In [6], Gyarmati, Mauduit and Sárközy show the connection between the cross-correlation measure of order k and other measures. Then they present two families of pseudorandom binary sequences with small cross-correlation measure.

In this paper, we continue in this direction. We extend the families of pseudorandom binary sequences given in [6]. More precisely, we obtain larger families of pseudorandom binary sequences which have small cross correlation measure of order k (see Theorems 1 and 2). In addition, we prove an upper bound on the second order cross-correlation measure for families generated by the reducible quadratic polynomials (see Theorem 1 (iii)). We also present explicit examples of constructed families for cyrptographic applications (see Example 1).

The paper is organized as follows. In Sect. 2 we present the previous work mainly given in [6]. Then we extend the families given in [6] and present our main results in Sect. 3.

2   Background

Gyarmati, Mauduit and Sárközy [6] construct two families of binary sequences and prove that the sequences have low cross-correlation measure at certain orders. And, they show that the family size of the constructed binary sequences are large. They use a lemma based on Weil's theorem to prove an upper bound for cross-correlation of each constructed family of binary sequences. We first state their lemma and afterwards we present their families of sequences in the following theorems.

Lemma 1 *[[6] Lemma 1]. If p is a prime number, χ is a non-principal character modulo p of order t, $h(x) \in \mathbb{F}_p[x]$ has degree r and it is not of the form $h(x) = cg(x)^t$ with $c \in \mathbb{F}_p$, $g(x) \in \mathbb{F}_p[x]$, and X, Y are real numbers with $0 < Y \leq p$, then*

$$\left| \sum_{X < n \leq X+Y} \chi(h(n)) \right| < 9rp^{1/2} \log p.$$

Theorem A *[[6] Theorem 2]. Let d be a positive integer and p be a prime number such that $d < p$. Then we consider all polynomials of the form*

$$f(x) = (x - x_1)(x - x_2) \ldots (x - x_d)$$

where $x_1, x_2, \ldots, x_d$ are distinct elements of $\mathbb{F}_p$ and

$$x_1 + x_2 + \ldots + x_d = 0.$$

Let $\mathcal{F}_A$ be the family of binary sequences $E_p(f) = (e_1, e_2, \ldots, e_p)$ assigned to the polynomial f by the formula:

$$e_n = \begin{cases} \left(\frac{f(n)}{p}\right) & \text{if } p \nmid f(n) \\ +1 & \text{if } p \mid f(n) \end{cases} \tag{1}$$

for $n = 1, 2, \ldots, p$.

(i) We have $\phi_2(\mathcal{F}_A) < 20 dp^{1/2} \log p$.

(ii) If k and t are odd integers for $f \in \mathcal{F}$, then we have $\phi_k(\mathcal{F}_A) < 10 k dp^{1/2} \log p$.

Moreover, the family size is

$$|\mathcal{F}_A| = \frac{1}{d}\binom{p-1}{d-1}$$

if $d < p/(20 p^{1/2} \log p)$.

Theorem B [[6] Theorem 1]. Let d be a positive integer and p be a prime number such that $d < p$, consider all irreducible polynomials $f(x) \in \mathbb{F}_p[x]$ of the form

$$f(x) = x^d + a_2 x^{d-2} + a_3 x^{d-3} + \cdots + a_d$$

and let $\mathcal{F}_B$ denote the family of the binary sequences $E_p(f)$ assigned to the polynomials f by the formula (1). Then we have

$$\phi_k(\mathcal{F}_B) < 9 k dp^{1/2} \log p \tag{2}$$

for all $k = 2, 3, \ldots, p-1$. Moreover, the family size satisfies

$$|\mathcal{F}_B| \geq p^{\lceil d/3 \rceil - 1}$$

if $d < p^{1/2}/(18 \log p)$.

We note that the constant in the right hand side of (2) was given 10 in [6], however since the polynomials don't have roots over the ground field, we can replace it with 9. On the other hand, they are equivalent in terms of big-O notation.

3   Large Families of Binary Sequences with Low Cross-Correlation

In this section we present families of binary sequences with low cross-correlation measure. In fact, we extend the families given in [6] while keeping their cross-correlation measure low. We first present the extension of Theorem A.

Theorem 1. *Let p be a prime number and $d \in \mathbb{Z}^+$ such that $d < p^{1/2}/(20 \log p)$. Then consider all polynomials of the form*

$$f(x) = (x - x_1)(x - x_2) \ldots (x - x_t) \tag{3}$$

where $x_1, x_2, \ldots, x_t$ are distinct elements of $\mathbb{F}_p$ and

$$x_1 + x_2 + \ldots + x_t = 0 \tag{4}$$

such that $1 \leq t \leq d$. Let $\mathcal{F}_1$ be the family of binary sequences $E_p(f) = (e_1, e_2, \ldots, e_p)$ assigned to the polynomial f by the formula (1).

(i) We have $\phi_2(\mathcal{F}_1) < 20dp^{1/2} \log p$. If we consider only the second order cross-correlation measure, then the family size is

$$|\mathcal{F}_1| = \sum_{t=1}^{d} \frac{1}{t} \binom{p-1}{t-1}. \tag{5}$$

(ii) If k and t are odd integers for all $f \in \mathcal{F}_1$, then we have $\phi_k(\mathcal{F}_1) < 10kdp^{1/2} \log p$. In this case, the family size is

$$|\mathcal{F}_1| = \sum_{\substack{t=1 \\ t\text{-odd}}}^{d} \frac{1}{t} \binom{p-1}{t-1}.$$

(iii) If k is an odd integer and $t = 2$ for all $f \in \mathcal{F}$, then we have $\phi_k(\mathcal{F}_1) < 20kp^{1/2} \log p$. And, the family size is

$$|\mathcal{F}_1| = \frac{p-1}{2}.$$

Proof. We need to estimate

$$|V_k(E_p(f_1), \ldots, E_p(f_k), M, D)| := \left| \sum_{n=1}^{M} e_{1,n+d_1} \cdots e_{k,n+d_k} \right|$$

for $E_p(f_i) = (e_{i,1}, e_{i,2}, \ldots, e_{i,p})$ and $\deg(f_i) = t_i \leq d$. For an index i such that $1 \leq i \leq k$ we know that

$$f_i(n + d_i) \equiv 0 \mod p$$

has at most t_i solutions. Thus there exist $\sum_{i=1}^{k} t_i$ zeros for all $f_1, f_2, \ldots, f_k$. According to equation (1) we have

$$\left| \sum_{n=1}^{M} e_{1,n+d_1} \cdots e_{k,n+d_k} \right| \leq \left| \sum_{n=1}^{M} \left(\frac{f_1(n+d_1)}{p} \right) \cdots \left(\frac{f_k(n+d_k)}{p} \right) \right| + \sum_{i=1}^{k} t_i$$

$$\leq \left| \sum_{n=1}^{M} \left(\frac{f_1(n+d_1) \cdots f_k(n+d_k)}{p} \right) \right| + kd$$

We use Lemma 1 to prove the bounds on the cross correlation measure.

(i) If $t_1 \neq t_2$ then clearly $f_1(x+d_1) \neq f_2(x+d_2)$. In case $t_1 = t_2$, assume that $f_1(x+d_1) = f_2(x+d_2)$. Hence, we get $d_1 = d_2$ by comparing coefficients of the term x^{t_i-1}. So, we have $f_1(x+d_1) = f_2(x+d_1)$, but this contradicts to $f_1 \neq f_2$. Similarly we have $f(x+d_1) \neq f(x+d_2)$ if $d_1 \neq d_2$ by comparing coefficients of the term x^{t-1}. Therefore, there exists at least one distinct factor between $f_1(x+d_1)$ and $f_2(x+d_2)$. In other words, $f_1(x+d_1)f_2(x+d_2)$ is a non-square polynomial. By using Lemma 1 with the quadratic Legendre character, the polynomial $h(x) = f_1(x+d_1)f_2(x+d_2)$ and $t = 2$ we obtain that

$$|V_2(E_p(f_1), E_p(f_2), M, D)| < 18dp^{1/2}\log p + 2d < 20dp^{1/2}\log p.$$

This proves the first part of the case (i). Next, for the proof of (5) we first observe that

$$\left|\sum_{n=1}^{M} e_{1,n} e_{2,n}\right| \leq \left|\sum_{n=1}^{M}\left(\frac{f_1(n)f_2(n)}{p}\right)\right| + 2d$$
$$< 20dp^{1/2}\log p$$
$$< p$$

for $d < p/(20p^{1/2}\log p)$. Thus $E_p(f_1) \neq E_p(f_2)$. This shows that the family size $|\mathcal{F}_1|$ equals the number of polynomials satisfying (3) and (4) for all $t \leq d$.

It is shown in [6, Theorem 2] that the family size equals

$$\frac{1}{t_0}\binom{p-1}{t_0-1}$$

for some fixed $t_0 \leq d$. Thus by summing them up we obtain the family size (5).

(ii) Suppose that k is an odd integer and the degree of polynomials in the family $\mathcal{F}_1$ is an odd integer. The polynomial $h(x) = f_1(x+d_1)\ldots f_k(x+d_k)$ has degree

$$\deg(h) = \sum_{i=1}^{k} t_i$$

which is an odd integer. Thus h is a non-square polynomial. Therefore similar to case (i) we prove the result.

(iii) Suppose that k is an odd integer and the degree of polynomials in the family $\mathcal{F}_1$ is 2. Then we have $x_1 + x_2 = p$. Now we consider the sum of roots of the polynomial $h(x) = f_1(x+d_1)\cdots f_k(x+d_k)$

$$\sum_{i=1}^{k}(x_{i1} - d_i) + (x_{i2} - d_i) = kp + 2\sum_{i=1}^{k} d_i,$$

which is an odd integer. Thus h is a non-square polynomial. Therefore, similar to case (i) we prove the result.   □

One can think of extending Theorem 1 (iii) to the family consisting of polynomials whose roots sum up an odd integer for an even integer $t > 2$. We note that in this case the family size decreases rapidly.

Next, we present a direct extension of Theorem 1 (ii).

Corollary 1. *Let p be a prime number and $d \in \mathbb{Z}^+$ such that $d < p^{1/2}/(20 \log p)$. Then consider all polynomials of the form*

$$f(x) = (x - x_1)^{s_1}(x - x_2)^{s_2} \cdots (x - x_t)^{s_t}$$

where $x_1, x_2, \ldots, x_t$ are distinct elements of $\mathbb{F}_p$ such that $1 \leq s_1 + s_2 + \ldots + s_t \leq d$. Let $\mathcal{F}$ be the family of binary sequences $E_p(f) = (e_1, e_2, \ldots, e_p)$ assigned to the polynomial f by the formula given in (1). Let k and $\deg(f)$ be odd integers for $f \in \mathcal{F}$. Then we have $\phi_k(\mathcal{F}) < 10kdp^{1/2} \log p$.

Proof. It is very similar to proof of Theorem 1 (ii).   □

We note that the family of binary sequences given in Corollary 1 has the same upper bound on the cross-correlation measure like the family given in Theorem 1 (ii). And, it is larger than the family given in Theorem 1 (ii). On the other hand, there exist collisions in the family given in Corollary 1. For instance, consider two polynomials over $\mathbb{F}_p$ for some prime p:

$$f(x) = (x - x_1)^3(x - x_2)^5(x - x_3) \text{ and } g(x) = (x - x_1)(x - x_2)(x - x_3)^7$$

for some $x_1, x_2, x_3 \in \mathbb{F}_p$. Polynomials f and g are distinct, but they generate the same sequence, i.e. $E_p(f) = E_p(g)$. On the other hand, it is easy to see that there exist $x_1, x_2 \in \mathbb{F}_p$ such that the sequence $E_p(h)$ for $h(x) = (x - x_1)^2(x - x_2) \in \mathbb{F}_p[x]$ is included in the family given in Corollary 1, but not in the family given in Theorem 1 (ii).

Now we present another family of binary sequences with low cross-correlation and large family size. This family given below is an extension of the family given in Theorem B.

Theorem 2. *Let p be a prime number and $d \in \mathbb{Z}^+$ such that $d < p^{1/2}/(18 \log p)$. Then consider all irreducible polynomials $f(x) \in F_p[x]$ of the form*

$$f(x) = x^t + a_2 x^{t-2} + a_3 x^{t-3} + \cdots + a_t \tag{6}$$

for some integer $2 \leq t \leq d$ and let $\mathcal{F}_2$ denote the family of the binary sequences $E_p(f)$ assigned to the polynomials f by the formula (1). Then we have

$$\phi_k(\mathcal{F}_2) < 9kdp^{1/2} \log p \tag{7}$$

for all $k = 2, 3, \ldots, p - 1$. And the family size satisfies

$$|\mathcal{F}_2| \geq \sum_{t=2}^{d} p^{\lceil t/3 \rceil - 1}. \tag{8}$$

Proof. The proof is very similar to the proof of Theorem 1. We only note that

$$
\left| \sum_{n=1}^{M} e_{1,n+d_1} \cdots e_{k,n+d_k} \right| \leq \left| \sum_{n=1}^{M} \left(\frac{f_1(n+d_1) \cdots f_k(n+d_k)}{p} \right) \right|
$$

holds as each f_i is an irreducible polynomial for $i = 1, 2, \ldots, k$. The polynomial $h(x) = f_1(x + d_1) \cdots f_k(x + d_k)$ is non-square, and then by applying Lemma 1 we obtain the bound (7). Next, it is shown in [[6], Theorem 1] that for a fixed degree $t_0 \leq p$ the family size satisfies $\geq p^{\lfloor t_0/3 \rfloor - 1}$. Thus by summing them up we get the result (8).   □

We note that it is not easy to generate many irreducible polynomials. Thus the construction of the family given in Theorem 2 is not effective. On the other hand, the family given in Theorem 1 can be constructed easily, but we cannot measure its cross correlation for each k.

The size of family $\mathcal{F}_1$ is larger than the size of family $\mathcal{F}_A$, however they are asymptotically equal to each other. Similarly, the size of family $\mathcal{F}_2$ is larger than the size of family $\mathcal{F}_B$, however they are asymptotically equal to each other.

Remark 1. In cryptographic applications we need large key space, in other words family size has to be large so that the key becomes unpredictable. The family size of our constructed families in Theorems 1 and 2 increases exponentially by the degree d of the seed polynomial f. In order to guarantee the good pseudorandom properties of the constructed sequences we choose the degree from the interval $3 \leq d \leq p^{1/4}$, see [10, Section 8]. We choose d near to the lower end so that the sequences possess better pseudorandom properties. On the other hand, if one shortens the sequence at a position $M < p$, then the sequence may loose the pseudorandom properties. But, if $M \geq \lceil p^{\frac{1}{4\sqrt{e}}} \rceil$ we know that the sequence still preserves its pseudorandom properties, see [10, Section 7].

We now give an explicit example of constructed families under the facts given in Remark 1.

Example 1. We present explicit examples of families whose sizes are approximately equivalent to recommended key sizes of Advanced Encryption Standard (AES) [9]. Let us choose $p = 10^{10} + 19$. Then, the family size of $\mathcal{F}_1$ becomes at least 2^{125}, 2^{247}, and 2^{541} for $d = 5, 9$, and 19 respectively. Similarly, the family size of $\mathcal{F}_2$ becomes at least 2^{132}, 2^{265}, and 2^{532} for $d = 15, 27$, and 52 respectively. We note that if the sequence is shortened at a position $M \geq \lceil p^{\frac{1}{4\sqrt{e}}} \rceil \approx 100$, it still has the good properties. On the other hand, one can also use such sequences without shortening e.g. for an encryption of a video steam having block length p (≈ 1 gigabyte).

Acknowledgment. This paper was written when the author was visiting Johann Radon Institute for Computational and Applied Mathematics (RICAM), Linz. The hospitality of RICAM is gratefully acknowledged. The author has benefited from discussions with Arne Winterhof. The visit was supported by the Scientific and Technological Research Council of Turkey (TÜBİTAK) under Grant No. 2219. The author thanks anonymous referees for useful suggestions.

References

1. Ahlswede, R., Khachatrian, L.H., Mauduit, C., Sárközy, A.: A complexity measure for families of binary sequences. Period. Math. Hungar. **46**(2), 107–118 (2003)
2. Alon, N., Kohayakawa, Y., Mauduit, C., Moreira, C.G., Rödl, V.: Measures of pseudorandomness for finite sequences: typical values. Proc. Lon. Math. Soc. **95**, 778–812 (2007)
3. Cassaigne, J., Mauduit, C., Sárközy, A.: On finite pseudorandom binary sequences. VII. the measures of pseudorandomness. Acta Arith. **103**(2), 97–118 (2002)
4. Goubin, L., Mauduit, C., Sárközy, A.: Construction of large families of pseudorandom binary sequences. J. Number Theory **106**(1), 56–69 (2004)
5. Gyarmati, K.: On a family of pseudorandom binary sequences. Period. Math. Hungar. **49**(2), 45–63 (2004)
6. Gyarmati, K., Mauduit, C., Sárközy, A.: The cross correlation measure for families of binary sequences. In: Applied Algebra and Number Theory, pp. 126–143. Cambridge University Press (2014)
7. Liu, H.: A family of pseudorandom binary sequences constructed by the multiplicative inverse. Acta Arith. **130**(2), 167–180 (2007)
8. Mauduit, C., Sárközy, A.: On finite pseudorandom binary sequences. I. measure of pseudorandomness, the Legendre symbol. Acta Arith. **82**(4), 365–377 (1997)
9. NIST: Advanced encryption standard. Federal Information Processing Standard, FIPS-197 12 (2001)
10. Rivat, J., Sárközy, András: On pseudorandom sequences and their application. In: Ahlswede, Rudolf, Bäumer, Lars, Cai, Ning, Aydinian, Harout, Blinovsky, Vladimir, Deppe, Christian, Mashurian, Haik (eds.) General Theory of Information Transfer and Combinatorics. LNCS, vol. 4123, pp. 343–361. Springer, Heidelberg (2006)
11. Tóth, V.: Collision and avalanche effect in families of pseudorandom binary sequences. Period. Math. Hungar. **55**(2), 185–196 (2007)
12. Winterhof, A., Yayla, O.: Family complexity and cross-correlation measure for families of binary sequences. The Ramanujan Journal online first (2014). doi:10.1007/s11139-014-9649-5

Algebraic Attacks Using Binary Decision Diagrams

Håvard Raddum[1]([✉]) and Oleksandr Kazymyrov[2]

[1] Simula@UiB, Bergen, Norway
haavardr@simula.no
[2] University of Bergen, Bergen, Norway

Abstract. Algebraic attacks have been developed against symmetric primitives during the last decade. In this paper we represent equation systems using binary decision diagrams, and explain techniques for solving them. Next, we do experiments with systems describing reduced versions of DES and AES, as well as systems for the problem of determining EA-equivalence. We compare our results against Gröbner basis and CryptoMiniSat.

Keywords: Binary decision diagram · Block cipher · Algebraic attack · Symmetric primitives

1 Introduction

Comparing the complexity of finding the key to a cryptosystem with solving a system of equations were first mentioned by Claude Shannon [1], and is today known as algebraic attacks. The main idea is to describe an encryption scheme via a system of equations and solve it. However, algebraic attacks against cryptographic primitives began to develop actively only in the early 2000s. Several methods to attack hash functions, stream and block ciphers have been described [2–10].

In the middle of the 20th century, it was proposed to use binary decision diagrams (BDDs) for representing Boolean functions [11,12]. This representation has several advantages. Many logical operations on BDDs can be implemented by polynomial-time graph manipulation algorithms [12], and the memory consumption can be extremely low, even for very complex Boolean functions. Most modern cryptographic primitives are based on binary logic because of the large spread of binary computers. Therefore, the description of cryptographic transformations using Boolean or vectorial Boolean functions is an easy task.

Several attacks based on BDDs exist for stream ciphers. Their efficiency was demonstrated both for general methods and for particular cases on A5/1, E0 and Trivium [13,14]. In this paper we extend previous results on block ciphers and present new specific strategies and approaches for solving systems of equations based on BDDs.

We apply the proposed methods on DES with reduced number of rounds, on MiniAES (a small variant of Rijndael) and on the problem of determining EA-equivalence. Our experiments on DES allow us to break six rounds in

© Springer International Publishing Switzerland 2015
B. Ors and B. Preneel (Eds.): BalkanCryptSec 2014, LNCS 9024, pp. 40–54, 2015.
DOI: 10.1007/978-3-319-21356-9_4

approximately one minute on a MacBook Air 2013. This is a factor 2^{20} improvement over the best earlier algebraic attack on DES using MiniSAT [5]. There have been several earlier attempts to break MiniAES [7,15,16]. Approaches that exploit the short key in MiniAES (only 16 bits) succeed very quickly, but the general methods of F4 and XL/XSL failed to solve systems representing more than one round of MiniAES. The approach we use in this paper does not exploit the short key, while still solving systems representing 10 rounds of MiniAES using approximately 45 min and 8 GB of memory.

The rest of the paper is organized as follows. Section 2 explains BDDs and the fundamental operations we do on them. Section 3 describes our approach to solving BDD systems, and introduces some solving strategies. Section 4 gives the details and results of our algebraic attack against DES and MiniAES as well as the EA-equivalence problem, comparing complexities against SAT-solver and Gröbner base techniques. Finally, Sect. 5 concludes the paper and give some directions for further research.

2   Binary Decision Diagram Fundamentals

The literature discusses several variants of BDDs. For clarity we will always mean a *zero-suppressed, reduced,* and *ordered* BDD in this paper. A comprehensive treatment of BDDs can be found in [12]. In this section we only give a brief description with emphasis on visualization and our use of a BDD.

2.1   Binary Decision Diagrams

A BDD is a directed acyclic graph. Exactly one node in the graph, called the *source node,* has no incoming edges, and exactly one node in the graph, called the *sink node,* has no outgoing edges. All nodes except for the sink node are called *internal* nodes, and have one or two outgoing edges, called the 0-*edge* and/or the 1-*edge.* In most other descriptions of BDDs, each internal node is associated with a variable. In this paper each internal node will be associated with a **linear combination** of variables. There are no edges between nodes associated with the same linear combination.

When visualizing a BDD, we draw the graph from top to bottom, with the source node on top, the sink node at the bottom, and all edges directed downwards. All internal nodes are organized in horizontal *levels* between the sink and source nodes. One level consists of all nodes associated to one particular linear combination, and we write the linear combination to the left of the level. Dotted edges indicate 0-edges while solid lines indicate 1-edges. An example of a BDD with four levels associated with linear combinations in four variables is shown in Fig. 1.

In the literature there are various ways to understand a BDD. Some interpret a BDD to represent a family of sets while others see a BDD as an efficient encoding of a Boolean function. In this paper we put emphasis on the fact that a path from the source to the sink node assigns values to the linear combinations

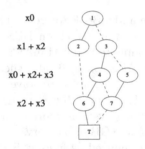

Fig. 1. Example of a BDD with four levels.

of the levels. If we choose the b-edge ($b \in \{0, 1\}$) out from a node, we assign the value b to the linear combination associated with the level of the node. Any path from the source to the sink node gives values to the linear combinations and can be regarded as a right-hand side in a system of linear equations.

2.2 Representing an S-Box as a BDD

We are interested in finding a BDD that represents a given S-box with n input bits and m output bits. Let the input bits and output bits of the S-box be $x_0, \ldots, x_{n-1}$ and $y_0, \ldots, y_{m-1}$, respectively. Let the first n levels be associated with $x_0, \ldots, x_{n-1}$ (x_0 for the source node and x_{n-1} for level n), and build a complete binary tree from x_0 to x_{n-1}. Next, assign $y_0, \ldots, y_{m-1}$ to the m lowest levels (with y_0 at the highest of these), and build a complete binary tree upwards from the sink node to the y_0-level, branching in 0-edges and 1-edges. Then there will be only one path from a given node at the y_0-level to the sink node. There will be 2^m nodes at the y_0-level, each representing a unique path to the sink node, assigning values to $y_0, \ldots, y_{m-1}$.

Any path from the source node down to level x_{n-1} will assign values to the input bits $x_0, \ldots, x_{n-2}$. Selecting a 0-edge or a 1-edge out of a node at the x_{n-1}-level will complete the assignment of input bits. This edge is connected to the node at the y_0-level whose unique path to the sink node will give the correct output of the S-box. Joining all nodes at the x_{n-1}-level to all nodes at the y_0-level in this way will complete the construction of the BDD. Figure 2 shows an example of a BDD representing a 4×4 S-box.

2.3 Basic Operations on a BDD

We must be able to run the *reduction* algorithm [17] on a BDD, bringing the BDD into a reduced state. The reduction algorithm basically merges nodes representing equivalent Boolean functions, thus minimizing the number of nodes in the BDD. For a fixed order of the linear combinations, a reduced BDD is unique. There are two other operations that forms the core of *linear absorption* (explained later). Both were described in [18], but we repeat them briefly here for completeness.

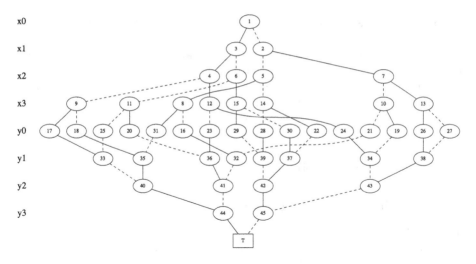

Fig. 2. BDD representing the S-box {5,C,8,F,9,7,2,B,6,A,0,D,E,4,3,1}.

Swapping Levels. This operation swaps the linear combinations at two adjacent levels, and was first described in [19], using single variables. When changing the order of the levels, nodes and edges must be re-arranged in the BDD to preserve the underlying function. Fortunately, swapping levels is a local operation, meaning that only nodes and edges at the two involved levels need to be touched while the rest of the BDD remains intact. The time complexity of swapping two levels is linear in the number of nodes on the highest level, but the number of nodes on the lowest level may double in the worst case.

After swapping two levels, the BDD may not be in the reduced state, and it may be necessary to run the reduction algorithm. Hence, the number of nodes in the BDD after swapping two levels may increase or decrease. By repeatedly swapping levels one may put the set of linear combinations for the levels into any desired order. Finding the order of levels that give the fewest nodes is an NP-complete problem [20].

Adding Levels. Traditionally, the levels in a BDD have been associated with single variables and not linear combinations. It has therefore not been natural to think of "adding" one level onto another. This changes when we have linear combinations associated with the levels. If l_1 and l_2 are two linear combinations associated to two adjacent levels (l_1 above l_2), we are interested in replacing l_2 with $l_1 + l_2$. The algorithm for adding levels was first described in [18], and follows the same logic as with swapping levels. Nodes and edges at the levels for l_1 and l_2 must be rearranged to preserve the underlying function, but the rest of the BDD remains the same. The complexity is similar to swapping, and the number of nodes at the new level associated to $l_1 + l_2$ may double in the worst case. The reduction algorithm should be run after adding levels to make sure the BDD remains in a reduced state.

3   Solving Systems of Equations with Linear Absorption

By repeatedly swapping and adding linear combinations, we can essentially do all linear operations on the linear combinations of the BDD. We can, for instance, perform Gaussian elimination on the set of linear combinations. As will become clear in the following, a barrier to find a solution to a system of equations arises when there are dependencies among the linear combinations of the levels in a BDD. We overcome this problem by using linear absorption. The technique was first described in [18], but we include an example of the procedure here as it is central in our approach to solve non-linear equation systems.

3.1   Absorbing One Linear Dependency

The attentive reader will have noticed that the linear combinations in the example BDD in Sect. 2.1 are not independent. If we label them l_0, l_1, l_2, l_3 from top to bottom we have $l_0 + l_2 + l_3 = 0$. Thus, when we select a path in the BDD and create the corresponding linear system of equations, we may or may not get a consistent system. If the values assigned to l_0, l_2 and l_3 sum to 0 we get a solution, if not, the system is inconsistent. We use linear absorption to remove all paths that yield inconsistent systems as follows.

First, swap l_0 and l_1 to obtain the BDD in Fig. 3a. Next, use addition of linear combinations to add l_0 onto l_2, and obtain the BDD in Fig. 3b. Finally, we use addition again to add $l_0 + l_2$ to l_3. This creates the **0**-vector as linear combination for the lowest level, resulting in the BDD shown in Fig. 3c.

When selecting a path in the BDD now, it does not make sense to choose a 1-edge out of a node on the level associated with **0**. Such a path would yield a "$0 = 1$"-assignment. Hence we can delete all outgoing 1-edges from the nodes at the **0**-level. Now we are certain that any remaining path will yield a system of linear equations that is consistent with the linear dependency $l_0 + l_2 + l_3 = 0$.

Moreover, the whole level associated with **0** can be removed. It is easy to show that the Boolean function represented by a node on this level is equal to the function for the node pointed to by the 0-edge. Hence, all nodes on the **0**-level can be merged with their children along the 0-edge, and the level disappears. We say that the linear dependency $l_0 + l_2 + l_3 = 0$ has been *absorbed*. The resulting BDD for our example is shown in Fig. 3d.

In general, the removal of 1-edges from a level associated with the **0**-vector may create internal nodes with no incoming edges. We call these *orphan* nodes as they have no parents. After absorbing one linear dependency, all orphan nodes, and subgraphs only reachable through an orphan node, should be removed as part of the reduction procedure.

If there are several dependencies among the linear combinations in a BDD, we can easily find all and absorb them one after another. When all dependencies have been absorbed, we know that *any* remaining path in the BDD will give a consistent linear system of equations, which in turn is solved to find the values of the actual variables.

3.2   Building and Solving Equation Systems as BDDs

It is rather straight-forward to build a system of equations representing a cryptographic primitive as a set of BDDs. For an encryption algorithm, the user-selected key bits become variables. We also look at the cipher blocks between the rounds of the primitive. We assign variable names to the bits between rounds, such that the input and output bits of all non-linear components can be written as linear combinations of variables.

For each non-linear component we then construct the corresponding BDD, like explained for S-boxes in Sect. 2.2. We replace the x_i and y_j with the linear combinations actually occuring in the cipher. After this we are left with a set of BDDs with linear combinations from the same pool of variables.

To proceed with finding a solution to the system we must join the BDDs together. There exist algorithms for joining two BDDs [17][12, p.16], but they are somewhat complex, and assume single variables associated with the levels. We do it in a much simpler way:

– To join two BDDs, just replace the sink node of one with the source node of the other.

With this simple operation, we can easily string together some or all BDDs in a system and get fewer, or only one, BDD(s) in the set. If we join all BDDs together, finding a solution is equivalent to finding a path in the joined BDD that gives a right hand side yielding a consistent linear system. As can be expected, for interesting systems there will be many dependencies among the linear combinations in a fully joined BDD, so finding a path respecting all these dependencies is not trivial. We can, however, try to handle this problem with linear absorption, and if we can absorb all linear dependencies in the BDD we know that any remaining path will give a consistent linear system. The algorithm for solving a system of BDDs can then be summed up as:

1. Join BDDs.
2. Absorb all linear dependencies.
3. Select path and solve resulting system of linear equations.

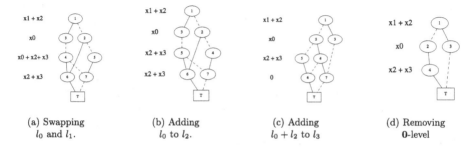

(a) Swapping l_0 and l_1.   (b) Adding l_0 to l_2.   (c) Adding $l_0 + l_2$ to l_3 (d) Removing **0**-level

Fig. 3. Absorbing one linear dependency.

3.3 Complexity

The first and third steps in the general solving algorithm are easy (assuming a modest number of BDDs and variables, which is the case even for full scale ciphers). Hence the second step must be hard if our cryptographic primitives are to remain secure. What we get when joining all BDDs together is a very long and very slim BDD, basically just a string of many small BDDs. The number of nodes at one level may double when adding or swapping two linear combinations, and after absorbing a whole linear dependency the total number of nodes may, in the worst case, double. This seems to lead to exponential growth in the number of dependencies absorbed, but in practice the number of nodes after absorbing a linear dependency is very far from doubling. Remember, the number of nodes may also *decrease* when applying a swap or an add operation.

If we expect a unique or only a few solutions, the BDD after absorbing all dependencies will have only one or a few paths. A BDD with only one path has only one node at each level, tied together with a string of 0- and 1-edges. Since all the systems we are interested in have very few solutions, we know that the number of nodes must decrease sharply before the last dependencies are absorbed. This means we will always reach some tipping point when absorbing dependencies, where the number of nodes in the BDD starts to decrease.

We take as our measure of complexity the largest number of nodes that a BDD contained during linear absorption. This is a measure of memory complexity, and is not equivalent to the time it takes to solve a system. On the other hand, there is no guessing involved in our solving method, and no operations that must be repeated an exponential number of times. Memory rather than time is the resource that constrains us. With 8 GB of RAM it is hard to find a system where our solver runs for over an hour without either finishing or running out of memory. Therefore, we believe the largest number of nodes we had during the solving process is the most meaningful measure of complexity.

3.4 Solving Strategies

When joining together many BDDs and absorbing all linear dependencies, the solving complexity depends heavily on the order the BDDs are joined. Finding the ordering of BDDs that gives the minimum complexity is probably a hard problem. During our experiments we have not found a strategy for ordering that is universally best. However, we describe here some strategies for how to join and absorb with the aim to keep the complexity down.

Automatic Ordering. This is a default strategy, that can be applied to any system and does not require any deeper understanding of how the BDDs have been made. The procedure is to look for the subset of BDDs with the smallest total number of nodes, that still contains some dependencies. When this subset is found, we join these BDDs and absorb all dependencies. The number of BDDs in the set will then decrease by at least one, and we repeat the procedure until there is only one BDD left and all dependencies have been absorbed.

Divide-and-Conquer. This strategy takes the approach that it is always easy to join a *few* BDDs together and absorb all dependencies. To solve the system though, one sooner or later has to join all BDDs, and absorb all remaining dependencies. The assumption is that the true complexity of solving the system will only appear when all BDDs are joined. Thus we would like to have only a minimum of dependencies left when we are forced to join all BDDs together.

The divide-and-conquer strategy is to split the system in two (roughly) equally large halves, such that there are many dependencies within each half but only a few that use linear combinations from BDDs in both halves. We can then attack each half independently, trying to absorb all dependencies. If we succeed, we are left with one BDD with only independent linear combinations in each half. These can now be joined, and we absorb the relatively few remaining dependencies in the full BDD. When attacking one half, we use the Divide-and-Conquer technique recursively, treating the half as a complete system. The recursion stops when a "system" only contains one or two of the original BDDs.

Finding the optimal way to split a system in two equally sized parts seems to be a hard problem in general. However, knowledge of how the system has been constructed can help in this regard, as we will see with DES.

Finding Good Joining Order by Cryptanalysis. When we are trying to solve a system representing a cryptographic primitive, analysis of the primitive may help in deciding a good order of how to join the BDDs. The strategy is simply to decide on an order for the original BDDs, join all of them into one long BDD, and absorb all linear dependencies. The order of the BDDs should be such that each linear dependency only involves linear combinations on levels that are relatively close to each other. Absorbing each linear combination then becomes a somewhat local operation that only affects a small part of the BDD, keeping the complexity down.

4   Application of the Algebraic Attack Based on BDDs

This section describes practical aspects and results of the proposed attack on DES and MiniAES as well as the time comparison of solving extended affine equivalence (EA) problem using Gröbner basis, CrytoMiniSat and BDD approaches.

4.1   A Practical Attack on Reduced des

Previous results on solving DES systems can be found in [5] where the authors solve a 6-round version, and in [21] where DES with 6, 7 and 8 rounds are attacked. In all papers it was necessary to fix 20+ of the key bits to their correct values for the attacks to work, reducing the effective key size to at most 36 bits. The actual solving of equation systems was done by MiniSAT [22].

Our best result is that we can solve a 6-round system using 8 chosen plaintext/ciphertext pairs without fixing or guessing any variables. The average complexity is $2^{20.571}$ nodes. Solving the system for 6-round DES with 8 chosen plaintexts takes approximately one minute on a MacBook Air 2013 with 8 GB of memory.

Constructing des System of Equations. We assume the reader is familiar with the operations of DES [23]. The only non-linear part of DES is the application of the eight 6×4 S-boxes in each round. We assign variables to the output of the S-boxes in each round, except for the last two whose output can be expressed as linear conbinations of other variables and ciphertext bits. The key schedule of DES is linear, so we only need to assign variables to the 56 user-selected key bits. After this the input and output bits of each S-box can be expressed as linear combinations of variables, and we construct a BDD for each S-box as described in Sect. 2.2. Each BDD contains approximately 185 nodes after reduction, the eight different S-boxes vary slightly in size.

Solving Strategy. The solving strategy we found to work best for DES is Divide-and-Conquer. We then need to divide our system in two equally big halves, and the key schedule of DES gives a clear hint on how to do this: One half of the 56 key bits *only* appears in the inputs to S-boxes $1 - -4$, while the other half only appears in the S-boxes $5 - -8$. This applies to all rounds. For each round, we put the BDDs representing S-boxes $1 - -4$ into the set A_0, and the BDDs for S-boxes $5 - -8$ into the set B_0. Then we try to solve A_0 and B_0 independently, using Divide-and-Conquer again. For dividing A_0, we have found (by exhaustive search) that the best division is to group together the same two S-boxes from odd-numbered rounds, i.e. S-boxes 1 and 2, and the other S-boxes (3 and 4) from even-numbered rounds, into set A_1. The other BDDs from A_0 go into the set B_1. See Fig. 4 for a sketch of the division used. B_0 is re-divided similarly, and further divisions are done by exhaustive search on the fly.

Several Plaintexts. When using several plaintext/ciphertext pairs, we build one DES system for each. These systems will have the same 56 key-bit variables, but variables representing internal state will, in general, be different for each plaintext. However, if we carefully choose the difference between the plaintexts we can reuse a lot of internal variables across different systems. For producing up to eight different plaintexts, we vary only three bits in the left half. Then the input to the first round will be equal for each text, and the difference in the input to the second round will only be in three bits. These bits are chosen so

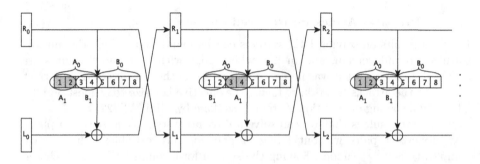

Fig. 4. Division used for Divide-and-Conquer strategy for DES.

they only affect one S-box each. In the experiments bits 1, 5 and 17 (numbering from 0 through 31) in the left half were used for generating differences, affecting S-boxes 1, 2 and 5 in the second round. Tracing differences further we find that we may reuse variables across systems as far as into the fourth round.

We merge the different systems by joining all BDDs arising from the same S-box in the same round. As these share the same key variables, and often many other variables as well, there are many linear dependencies among the levels in the joined BDD. These dependencies are absorbed, and after this pre-processing we are left with a system of $8r$ BDDs representing an r-round version of DES, regardless of the number of chosen plaintexts used.

Extracting Linear Equations. When using more than four plainetxts in the experiments, we observed that the heaviest step while solving did not occur when joining the sets A_0 and B_0, but rather when joining A_1 and B_1. After all dependencies in A_0 had been absorbed the resulting BDD was very slim, with many levels only containing one node.

If a level only has outgoing b-edges (which is often the case with one-node levels) we know that the associated linear combination is equal to b, ($b \in \{0, 1\}$). We can use this linear equation to eliminate a variable from the system. Extracting as many linear equations as possible and eliminating variables after all dependencies in A_0 had been absorbed, it became trivial to absorb all dependencies in B_0, and the full system.

Results for des Experiments. We have solved systems representing DES for $4, 5$ and 6 rounds, using $1 - 8$ plaintext/ciphertext pairs. For each choice of rounds and number of plaintexts we randomly generated and solved 100 systems, recording their complexities. The minimum, maximum and average (in bold) complexities observed are summarized in Table 1.

There are rather large variations in complexities inside most cells in Table 1. In each cell, the key and one plaintext were chosen at random for each of the 100 instances, and some choices give much lower complexity than others. We can not explain the differences, and have not been able to identify which choices lead to low solving complexity.

4.2 A Practical Attack on Scaled-Down Version of AES

There are many scaled-down versions of the AES cipher (MiniAES). The first one that follows Rinjdael's description was proposed in [24]. A few years later Cid et al. analyzed many small AES variants in [7], and Elizabeth Kleiman tried to attack MiniAES in her master and doctoral theses [15,25]. Also, an equation system representing MiniAES was solved in [16].

Description of MiniAES. The constants of our studied encryption model are the block length (16 bits) and the key size (16 bits). This scaled-down cipher corresponds to AES-128 [26]. In contrast to original AES, the mini version is a nibble (4 bits) oriented cipher with the state represented as a 2×2 matrix.

Table 1. Complexities for solving reduced-round DES-systems. Each cell shows the minimum, **average** and maximum complexity observed over 100 instances.

# texts rounds	1	2	3	4	5	6	7	8
4	$2^{22.651}$ $\mathbf{2^{22.715}}$ $2^{22.770}$	$2^{10.800}$ $\mathbf{2^{14.506}}$ $2^{17.473}$	$2^{9.281}$ $\mathbf{2^{10.606}}$ $2^{13.006}$	$2^{9.585}$ $\mathbf{2^{10.257}}$ $2^{12.029}$	$2^{9.748}$ $\mathbf{2^{9.805}}$ $2^{9.892}$	$2^{9.976}$ $\mathbf{2^{10.070}}$ $2^{10.412}$	$2^{10.103}$ $\mathbf{2^{10.203}}$ $2^{10.978}$	$2^{10.283}$ $\mathbf{2^{10.381}}$ $2^{10.446}$
5		$2^{19.472}$ $\mathbf{2^{22.110}}$ $2^{23.805}$	$2^{13.831}$ $\mathbf{2^{16.455}}$ $2^{19.329}$	$2^{11.440}$ $\mathbf{2^{13.526}}$ $2^{15.618}$	$2^{12.126}$ $\mathbf{2^{13.995}}$ $2^{16.633}$	$2^{12.289}$ $\mathbf{2^{14.212}}$ $2^{16.758}$	$2^{12.583}$ $\mathbf{2^{14.410}}$ $2^{16.882}$	$2^{12.749}$ $\mathbf{2^{14.704}}$ $2^{17.414}$
6						$2^{24.506}$ $\mathbf{2^{24.929}}$ $2^{25.352}$	$2^{22.206}$ $\mathbf{2^{22.779}}$ $2^{24.324}$	$2^{19.932}$ $\mathbf{2^{20.571}}$ $2^{21.915}$

The round function consists of four routines: AddroundKey (AK_k), SubBytes (SB), ShiftRows (SR) and MixColumns (MC). The encryption algorithm can be described as

$$E_K(M) = \prod_{i=1}^{r}(AK_{k_i} \circ MC \circ SR \circ SB) \circ AK_{k_0}(M),$$

where r is the number of rounds. The substitution and MDS matrix was taken from [24].

Constructing System of BDDs for MiniAES. Unlike DES, MiniAES has non-linear components in the key schedule. We assign variables to the output of the S-boxes in each round, except for the last one. Additionally, we have to add 8 extra variables for each round key, except the first one with 16 bits of the user-selected key. Then the number of BDDs and variables is equal to $2r + 4r = 6r$ and $(16 + 8r) + 16(r - 1) = 24r$, respectively.

Solving Strategy. The best strategy we found for solving the MiniAES systems was to determine a good order of BDDs by cryptanalysis, join all BDDs and do a full absorption of all dependencies.

The order was found by carefully studying which variables that appear in each BDD, both from the key schedule and the encryption function. Variables from the cipher state only appear in two consecutive rounds. It is therefore clear that the four BDDs from the same round should be joined close to each other, and also close to the two BDDs from the key schedule producing the round key used for the round. The BDDs were put together in groups of six this way, following the rounds of the cipher.

The order of the BDDs in each group was determined by looking at which variables that appear in each individual BDD. Two BDDs that share many variables should be adjacent in the final order. After doing this for the four, five and six round versions it became clear that a pattern emerged for the joining order. This pattern was followed for the higher number of rounds.

Results for MiniAES Experiments. The complexities for solving MiniAES systems for various rounds are summed up in Table 2. Of course, MiniAES only has a 16-bit key and can be broken very fast using for instance CryptoMiniSAT, which essentially does a very intelligent brute force on the key [27, p.250-251]. In [16], the authors create the polynomials for the ciphertext bits using only the user-selected key bits as variables. This results in 16 polynomials in 16 variables containing approximately 2^{15} terms each, that can be solved using PolyBoRi. Our algorithm does not take advantage of the short key, and should be compared to the earlier attacks in [7,15] that also does not exploit the short key.

For each number of rounds we solved 10 different instances, using 1 known plaintext/ciphertext pair. We were not able to reduce the complexities by using more pairs. The observed complexities for one particular number of rounds did not vary, so the minimum, maximum and average complexities are all the same. We have also changed the S-box and the MixColumn matrix to see if other choices affected the complexity, but we found the complexity remains the same for all variants tried.

It has been observed before that for one plaintext/ciphertext pair in scaled-down AES versions there may be more than one key that encrypts the given plaintext into the given ciphertext. This was shown in our experiments as well, often we had two, three or even four solutions to our systems.

Table 2. Complexities of solving MiniAES systems.

Rounds	4	5	6	7	8	9	10
Complexity	$2^{22.404}$	$2^{23.051}$	$2^{23.440}$	$2^{24.154}$	$2^{24.217}$	$2^{24.862}$	$2^{24.961}$

4.3   Problem of Determining EA-equivalence

To get a good comparison against other solvers we have chosen the problem of EA-equivalence [29]. This problem is interesting in cryptography, and it can be solved via non-linear systems of equations. There are no special variables in these systems, like key bits, so we get a fair comparison between CryptoMiniSAT, Gröbner bases and the BDD method.

Two functions are EA-equivalent if the following equation holds for all $\mathbf{x} \in GF(2)^n$

$$F(x) = M_1 \cdot G(M_2 \cdot x \oplus V_2) \oplus M_3 \cdot x \oplus V_1, \qquad (1)$$

where elements of $\{M_1, M_2, M_3, V_1, V_2\}$ have dimensions $\{m \times m, n \times n, m \times n, m, n\}$ and M_1 and M_2 are non-singular [29]. For simplicity, we set $n = m$. The EA-equivalence problem can then be formulated as follows:

For given functions $F, G : GF(2)^n \mapsto GF(2)^n$ find M_1, M_2, M_3, V_1, V_2 such that (1) holds or show that such vectors and matrices do not exist.

The variables in the system to be solved are the entries in M_1, M_2, M_3, V_1 and V_2, so the number of variables is $3n^2 + 2n$. The maximum number of equations and a system's degree can be calculated theoretically for given F and G [30]. However, for $n \leq 6$ the system can always be made quadratic by introducing the matrix $M_3' = M_1^{-1} \cdot M_3$ and the vector $V_1' = M_1^{-1} \cdot V_1$ and add them as additional equations and variables.

For $n = 4$ and $n = 5$ the problem of EA-equivalence is tractable, and the complexity comparison of Gröbner basis (GB), CryptoMiniSat (SAT) and proposed approach (BDD) is presented in Table 3 for five different instances. Unlike the two other methods, CryptoMiniSat only finds one solution by default. Therefore, we have used the option "n = +infinity" in CryptoMiniSat to force it to find all solutions and get a fair comparison. For GB we tested with several options for ordering, with or without using "faugere" option (turning linear algebra on or off), and with or without parallelization. The smallest observed times we could achieve are reported below.

Table 3. Time complexity for solving EA-equivalence problem

#	n	Number of solutions	Seconds used to solve		
			BDD	GB	SAT
1	4	2	$2^{4.05}$	$2^{1.30}$	$2^{13.71}$
2	4	60	$2^{4.86}$	†	$2^{16.77}$
3	4	2	$2^{3.92}$	$2^{1.01}$	$2^{12.08}$
4	5	1	$2^{10.20}$	$2^{11.43}$	-
5	5	155	$2^{10.48}$	†	-

In Table 3 "†" means that the Gröbner bases solver implemented in Sage crashes after several minutes with out-of-memory message, and "–" means that CryptoMiniSat spent more than 78 hours (2^{18} seconds) without finding a solution [28].

5   Conclusions

In this paper we have explained an approach to build and solve equation systems using binary decision diagrams and reported on experiments with the method. The best previous results on algebraic attacks against DES use guessing at least

20 of the key bits. We improved on these results using BDDs, breaking six rounds of DES without guessing any variables.

For MiniAES we have also received results which are better than the previous algebraic attacks described in [7] and [15]. According to our experiments a system representing 10 rounds of MiniAES can be solved in 45 min on a ordinary computer using the BDD approach. However, attacks exploiting the short key have lower complexities. At the same time, the BDD method is shown to be advantageous compared to Gröbner basis and CryptoMiniSat on solving the EA-equivalence problem.

These experiments indicate the BDD approach can compete with other methods in applications which require solving the non-linear equation systems. There are several open questions to address in future research. Does there exist a generic algorithm giving an order of BDDs that yield low complexity when applying linear absorption? Is it possible to analytically estimate the complexity of solving a BDD system of equations, or do we have to actually run the solver to find out? Which ciphers are most vulnerable against this type of algebraic attacks? We hope the potential of BDDs in cryptanalysis will be thoroughly examined in future research.

References

1. Shannon, C.E.: Communication theory of secrecy systems. Bell Syst. Tech. J. **28**(4), 656–715 (1949)
2. Raddum, H., Semaev, I.: Solving multiple right hand sides linear equations. Des. Codes Crypt. **49**(1–3), 147–160 (2008). Springer
3. Courtois, N.T.: Fast algebraic attacks on stream ciphers with linear feedback. In: Boneh, D. (ed.) CRYPTO 2003. LNCS, vol. 2729, pp. 176–194. Springer, Heidelberg (2003)
4. Courtois, N.T., Bard, G.V., Wagner, D.: Algebraic and slide attacks on KeeLoq. In: Nyberg, K. (ed.) FSE 2008. LNCS, vol. 5086, pp. 97–115. Springer, Heidelberg (2008)
5. Courtois, N.T., Bard, G.V.: Algebraic cryptanalysis of the data encryption standard. In: Galbraith, S.D. (ed.) Cryptography and Coding 2007. LNCS, vol. 4887, pp. 152–169. Springer, Heidelberg (2007)
6. Helleseth, T., Rønjom, S.: Simplifying algebraic attacks with univariate analysis, Information Theory and Applications Workshop (ITA), pp. 1–7. IEEE (2011)
7. Cid, C., Murphy, S., Robshaw, M.: Small scale variants of the AES. In: Gilbert, H., Handschuh, H. (eds.) FSE 2005. LNCS, vol. 3557, pp. 145–162. Springer, Heidelberg (2005)
8. Bard, G.V.: Algebraic Cryptanalysis. Springer, Heidelberg (2009)
9. Albrecht, M.: Algorithmic Algebraic Techniques and Their Application to Block Cipher Cryptanalysis, University of London, Thesis (2010). http://www.sagemath.org/files/thesis/albrecht-thesis-2010.pdf
10. Daum, M.: Cryptanalysis of Hash functions of the MD4-family, Ruhr University Bochum, Thesis (2005). http://www.cits.ruhr-uni-bochum.de/imperia/md/content/magnus/dissmd4.pdf
11. Lee, C.Y.: Representation of switching circuits by binary-decision programs. Bell Syst. Tech. J. **38**, 985–999 (1959)

12. Knuth, D.E.: The Art of Computer Programming Volume 4, Fascicle 1: Bitwise tricks and techniques; Binary Decision Diagrams, Addison-Wesley Professional (2009)
13. Krause, M.: BDD-Based cryptanalysis of keystream generators. In: Knudsen, L.R. (ed.) EUROCRYPT 2002. LNCS, vol. 2332, pp. 222–237. Springer, Heidelberg (2002)
14. Stegemann, D.: Extended BDD-based cryptanalysis of keystream generators. In: Adams, C., Miri, A., Wiener, M. (eds.) SAC 2007. LNCS, vol. 4876, pp. 17–35. Springer, Heidelberg (2007)
15. Kleiman, E.: High Performance Computing techniques for attacking reduced version of AES using XL and XSL methods, Graduate Theses and Dissertations (2010). http://lib.dr.iastate.edu/etd/11473
16. Bulygin, S., Brickenstein, M.: Obtaining and solving systems of equations in key variables only for the small variants of AES. Math. Comput. Sci. 3(2), 185–200 (2010). Birkhäuser-Verlag
17. Bryant, R.E.: Graph-based algorithms for boolean function manipulation. IEEE Trans. Comput. 35(8), 677–691 (1986)
18. Schilling, T.E., Raddum, H.: Solving compressed right hand side equation systems with linear absorption. In: Helleseth, T., Jedwab, J. (eds.) SETA 2012. LNCS, vol. 7280, pp. 291–302. Springer, Heidelberg (2012)
19. Rudell, R.: Dynamic variable ordering for ordered binary decision diagrams. In: IEEE/ACM International Conference on Computer-aided Design, vol. 12, pp. 42–47 (1993)
20. Bollig, B., Wegener, I.: Improving the variable ordering of OBDDs is NP-complete. IEEE Trans. Comput. 45(9), 993–1002 (1996)
21. Perret, J.C.F.L., Spaenlehauer, P.J.: Algebraic Differential Cryptanalysis of DES, Western European Workshop on Research in Cryptology (2009). http://www.pjspaenlehauer.net/data/papers/DESweworc.pdf
22. Eén, N., Sörensson, N.: An extensible SAT-solver. In: Giunchiglia, E., Tacchella, A. (eds.) SAT 2003. LNCS, vol. 2919, pp. 502–518. Springer, Heidelberg (2004)
23. Federal Information Processing Standards Publication (FIPS PUB) 46. National Bureau of Standards, Washington (1977)
24. Phan, R.C.-W.: Mini advanced encryption standard (Mini-AES): a testbed for cryptanalysis students. Cryptologia 26(4), 283–306 (2002). Taylor & Francis
25. Kleiman, E.: The XL and XSL attacks on Baby Rijndael, Master Thesis, Iowa State University (2005). https://orion.math.iastate.edu/dept/thesisarchive/MS/EKleimanMSSS05.pdf
26. Announcing the Advanced Encryption Standard (AES), Federal Information Processing Standards Publication 197, United States National Institute of Standards and Technology (NIST) (2001)
27. Soos, M., Nohl, K., Castelluccia, C.: Extending SAT solvers to cryptographic problems. In: Kullmann, O. (ed.) SAT 2009. LNCS, vol. 5584, pp. 244–257. Springer, Heidelberg (2009)
28. Stein, W., et al.: Sage mathematics software (version 6.2). The Sage Development Team (2014). http://www.sagemath.org
29. Budaghyan, L., Kazymyrov, O.: Verification of restricted EA-equivalence for vectorial boolean functions. In: Özbudak, F., Rodríguez-Henríquez, F. (eds.) WAIFI 2012. LNCS, vol. 7369, pp. 108–118. Springer, Heidelberg (2012)
30. Eilertsen, A.M., Kazymyrov, O., Kazymyrova, V., Storetvedt, M.: A Sage library for analysis of nonlinear binary mapping. In: Pre-proceedings of Central European Conference on Cryptology (CECC14), pp. 69–78 (2014)

Cryptographic Hardware

Cryptographic Hardware

Universally Composable Firewall Architectures Using Trusted Hardware

Dirk Achenbach[1]([✉]), Jörn Müller-Quade[1], and Jochen Rill[2]

[1] Karlsruhe Institute of Technology (KIT), Karlsruhe, Germany
{dirk.achenbach,joern.mueller-quade}@kit.edu
[2] FZI Forschungszentrum Informatik, Karlsruhe, Germany
rill@fzi.de

Abstract. Network firewalls are a standard security measure in computer networks that connect to the Internet. Often, ready-to-use firewall appliances are trusted to protect the network from malicious Internet traffic. However, because of their black-box nature, no one can be sure of their exact functionality.

We address the possibility of actively compromised firewalls. That is, we consider the possibility that a network firewall might collaborate with an outside adversary to attack the network. To alleviate this threat, we suggest composing multiple firewalls from different suppliers to obtain a secure firewall architecture. We rigorously treat the composition of potentially malicious network firewalls in a formal model based on the Universal Composability framework. Our security assumption is trusted hardware.

We show that a serial concatenation of firewalls is insecure even when trusted hardware ensures that no new packages are generated by the compromised firewall. Further, we show that the parallel composition of two firewalls is only secure when the order of packets is not considered. We prove that the parallel composition of three firewalls is insecure, unless a modified trusted hardware is used.

Keywords: Formal models · Firewalls · Universal composability · Network security

1 Introduction

The protection of computer networks against attackers from the Internet is crucial for companies to protect their intellectual property. Network firewalls are used to shield networks against threats from the Internet. The task of a firewall is to inspect the network packets that pass through it and then to decide whether to let them pass. Firewalls use a set of predefined rules to facilitate this decision. These rules may specify static filters, but may also be functions of the history of network traffic.

The protection from attacks from outside the network is a well understood problem and has become the business model of many companies. Firewalls are

© Springer International Publishing Switzerland 2015
B. Ors and B. Preneel (Eds.): BalkanCryptSec 2014, LNCS 9024, pp. 57–74, 2015.
DOI: 10.1007/978-3-319-21356-9_5

considered a secure *black box* which protects the network from attacks. However, since many firewall appliances are purchased from third-party vendors, people have no control and insight into their actual functionality. Companies and individuals alike rely on the trustworthiness of firewall appliances. Most firewalls are made of general-purpose hardware with just the same capabilities as any modern computer. In addition, firewalls are often equipped with update mechanisms which make their functionality completely replaceable. It seems naïve to see a firewall as a secure black box. Indeed, as the documents that were leaked by Edward Snowden in 2013 reveal, the National Security Agency has the capability to install backdoors in a number of commercial firewalls: JETPLOW, HALLUXWATER, FEEDTROUGH, GOURMETTROUGH, and SOUFFLETROUGH [1].

The serial concatenation of firewalls does not yield a secure solution if one considers the possibility of actively malicious firewalls. In this paper, we address this problem. We give solutions using trusted hardware. We model our solutions in the Universal Composability framework.

1.1 Related Work

To our knowledge, we are first to explicitly model network firewalls in the UC framework.

Network Firewalls. The purpose, aim and function of network firewalls is widely understood and agreed upon, e.g. [3,11,19]. The informational RFC 2979 [6] defines characteristics of firewalls. Since there is no globally agreed-on standard for what constitutes good and bad network packets however, there is also no complete specification of the function of a firewall.

The security of firewalls or systems of firewalls has mainly been studied under two aspects. One concern is verfiying the correctness and soundness of rule sets. Gouda et al. [8] develop a formal model for verification of distributed rule sets based on trees. They are able to check whether the firewall system accepts or denies a specific class of packets. Ingols et al. [12] check for conflicting or otherwise problematic rules with the aid of Binary Decision Diagrams.

We are not aware of any works that consider the firewall as being malicious.

Universal Composability. The Universal Composability (UC) framework [4] was proposed by Canetti in 2001. It follows the "real-world-ideal-world" paradigm and is inherently asynchronous. Katz et al. [14] recently proposed an extension for synchronous computation. Alternative approaches to the problem of composable security include the reactive simulatability framework [2,18], the GNUC framework [10]—which aims at being a drop-in replacement for UC—or the Abstract Cryptography paradigm [16,17]. The UC framework has been used to prove the security of a variety of protocols. An example of such a protocol is the OAuth protocol. Chari et al. [5] present a proof that the OAuth protocol is UC secure, given an ideal SSL functionality.

Secure Hardware. Katz [13] uses tamper-proof hardware to realise universally composable multi-party computation. He assumes tamper-proof tokens that can be programmed with an arbitrary program. Such a programmed token is then handed to another party in the protocol, which may then interact with the token. Goldwasser et al. [7] introduce the computational paradigm of one-time programs, i.e. programs that can only be run once, on one input. Of course, such programs cannot exist purely in software, as software can be copied indefinitely. Goldwasser et al. introduce "one-time-memory devices" to create a compiler for one-time programs.

Robust Combiners. The idea of mistrusting the implementation of a secure functionality has been studied in the scope of *robust combiners*. A (k, n)-robust combiner combines n candidate implementations of the secure functionality $\mathcal{P}$ in a way that the overall security still holds if at least k implementations are secure [9].

The notion of a robust combiner is not suited for our purposes. The very definition of robust combiners requires a specific and fixed functionality $\mathcal{P}$. However, in the case of firewalls, it is unclear what this functionality precisely is. Informally speaking, the functionality of a network firewall is "filtering all malicious packets". It is not possible to formalise this functionality in a protocol or a program, since, in general, it is not possible to decide whether an arbitrary packet is malicious or not.

Byzantine Fault Tolerance. Our constructions are reminiscent of problems in byzantine fault tolerance. However, we use a very different communication structure. In the original Byzantine Generals Problem [15], every party can communicate with every other party. This leads to specific bounds concerning the number of trusted parties needed to achieve fault tolerance. Even when signing messages is possible, in order to allow for m corrupted parties, one still needs at least $(2m + 1)$ trusted parties and $(m + 1)$ rounds of communication. In our case, we do not allow the parties to communicate freely, but only according to the specific structure of the network—we do not allow firewalls to exchange messages with each other. Thus, the results which byzantine fault tolerance research provides are not applicable to our scenario.

1.2 Our Contribution

In this paper we explore the idea of actively malicious firewalls. We present a novel methodology to analyse architectures of multiple firewalls based on the Universal Composability (UC) framework. The UC framework allows us to define security in a natural way while also providing us with a composition theorem. We assume trusted hardware to compose firewalls: modules with simple and fixed functionalities that can compare network packets. We rigorously analyse different approaches. Our analysis reveals subtle attacks on presumably secure architectures. We give ideal functionalities for these architectures which make these weaknesses explicit.

1.3   A Model for Firewalls

We assume a packet-switched local-area network (LAN) in which there are only uncompromised hosts. They are connected through a single uplink to the Internet, in which are potentially compromised hosts. To facilitate an easier discussion, we call machines in the LAN being "inside" and machines on the Internet being "outside". The "inside" is only connected to the "outside" through a firewall (network), whose job is to protect machines "inside" from machines "outside". For ease of exposition, we model communication in networks in one direction only (cf. Sect. 2).

We assume that each firewall can have any number of *network interfaces* for input and output. The output of a firewall then depends on the packet $p \in P$ it gets as input (where P is the set of all possible packets), its internal state $s \in S$ and the network interface $i \in I$ the packet arrived on.

After processing this information, the firewall then outputs a packet p' on a specific network interface i' and updates its internal state (e.g. outputs a new internal state s'). The functionality of a firewall is defined formally in Definition 1.

Definition 1 (The functionality of an ideal firewall F_j).

$$F_{\mathrm{fw}_j} : P \times I \times S \to (P \cup \bot) \times (I \cup \bot) \times S$$

$$F_{\mathrm{fw}_j}(p, i, s) = \begin{cases} (p', i', s') & \textit{if output is generated,} \\ (\bot, \bot, s') & \textit{else.} \end{cases}$$

We stress that our definition of a firewall functionality is universal. Because it is stateful—it receives its previous state as input, may use it for its computation and outputs an updated state—a firewall may base its output on an arbitrarily long history of incoming and outgoing packets. It may, for example, reconstruct a TCP session. Further, we do not restrict how its output depends on its input. A firewall might for example receive a packet, store it, transform it, and output it much later. Because the functionality processes whole packets including their payload, our definition covers the whole network protocol stack (e.g. Ethernet, IP, TCP, HTTP, HTML).

1.4   The Universal Composability Framework

In this chapter we give a brief review of the Universal Composability (UC) framework. It is a tool for proving the security of multi-party protocols by comparing their execution with an idealised version of the protocol. The framework allows us to model a system of firewalls as a protocol execution and underspecify the concrete functionality of the participating firewalls and only state what an ideal execution would look like.

In the UC framework, participants in a protocol are modeled as Interactive Turing Machines (ITMs). Since there are different definitions of ITMs in literature, we will briefly summarise the definition given by Canetti [4].

Definition 2 (Interactive Turing Machine). *An* Interactive Turing Machine *(ITM) is a multi-tape turing machine with the following tapes. A tape is externally writeable (EW), if it can be written by every other turing machine.*

- *an* identity tape *(EW)*
- *a* security parameter tape *(EW)*
- *an* input tape *(EW)*
- *a* communication tape *(EW)*
- *an* output tape
- *a* working tape
- *a* subprocess tape

We call an ITM probabilistic, *if it, in addition, has a* random tape, *which contains a random bitstring of a specific distribution.*

A protocol is a number of interacting ITMs. The execution of a protocol π in the UC framework happens in the context of two additional ITMs: the adversary $\mathcal{A}$ and the environment $\mathcal{Z}$. The adversary represents the party which wants to attack the protocol, the environment represents the perception of the execution from an outside point of view.

There are some general restrictions concerning the communication among the participating parties: the adversary and the environment are allowed to communicate freely. In addition, the adversary is allowed to write to the communication tapes of every participant and the environment can write to the input tapes and receive outputs of the parties of the protocol. This captures the notion that the environment represents the external input to the protocol but will not interfere with the protocol itself.

We realise protocol execution in the $\mathcal{F}$-hybrid model of computation: Parties cannot communicate directly, but must use a functionality $\mathcal{F}$ as a proxy, which is modeled as another ITM. $\mathcal{F}$ also communicates with the adversary. The exact behaviour of $\mathcal{F}$ is specified in advance and must reflect the exact nature of the communication link. For example, $\mathcal{F}$ might be set up in a Dolev-Yao fashion, so that $\mathcal{A}$ can intercept and send arbitrary network messages. We will setup $\mathcal{F}$ in a way that reflects our network architecture: The adversary cannot intercept all communication or inject messages into the network at will. It is only possible to send messages on established links as specified in the architecture diagram. However, the adversary can send a special message to the other parties: the *corruption message*. If a party receives a corruption message, it stops executing its own program and instead gives complete control of its functions to the adversary. This includes disclosing its internal state.

The execution of the protocol is turn-based. If an ITM is activated, it can perform computations and write to a tape of any other ITM based on the aforementioned restrictions. Then its turn ends. If an ITM receives input on one of its tapes, it is the next to be activated. The first ITM to be activated is the environment $\mathcal{Z}$.

The output of the whole protocol is the output of $\mathcal{Z}$ and we assume, without loss of generality, that it consists of one bit. The distribution of all outputs of

$\mathcal{Z}$ is a random ensemble based on the two parameters z (the input) and k (the security parameter).

Definition 3 (Ensemble of a protocol execution). *We denote the random variable which describes the execution of a protocol π with adversary $\mathcal{A}$, environment $\mathcal{Z}$, input z, security parameter k as* $\mathsf{EXEC}_{\pi,\mathcal{A},\mathcal{Z}}(k,z)$. *The set of random distributions* $\{\mathsf{EXEC}_{\pi,\mathcal{A},\mathcal{Z}}(k,z)\}_{k\in N, z\in\{0,1\}^*}$ *is denoted as* $\mathsf{EXEC}_{\pi,\mathcal{A},\mathcal{Z}}$.

The security of a protocol execution in the UC framework is based on a comparison with an execution of an idealised version of the protocol: the *ideal protocol*. The ideal protocol contains the *ideal functionality* $\mathcal{F}_{\mathsf{ideal}}$ which completely realises the properties of the analysed protocol. In the ideal protocol, all parties only act as dummies which directly give their input to the ideal functionality and receive back their output without performing any computation themselves. The ideal functionality may communicate with the adversary in order to model the influence $\mathcal{A}$ is allowed to have. We call this adversary the "adversary simulator" $\mathcal{S}$. Since the only instance which performs computations is $\mathcal{F}_{\mathsf{ideal}}$, which is ideal by definition, the whole protocol execution is ideal and thus secure. Note that this does not model an absolute security guarantee but a guarantee relative to the defined ideal functionality.

We model the ideal functionality as the same firewall network, but with the adversary removed. For example, when we combine two firewalls, of which one may be compromised, the ideal model we compare our protocol to is just one uncompromised firewall.

Definition 4 (Ideal protocol). *Let $\mathcal{F}_{\mathsf{ideal}}$ be an ideal functionality. Then, the ideal protocol which realises $\mathcal{F}_{\mathsf{ideal}}$ is denoted as* $\mathsf{IDEAL}_{\mathcal{F}}$.

Informally, a protocol π is UC secure if, for every adversary $\mathcal{A}$ and every environment $\mathcal{Z}$, $\mathcal{Z}$ can not distinguish if it is interacting with π or with the ideal protocol implementing π. To capture that notion formally, we define indistinguishability. Because parties may behave indeterministically, their outputs are modeled as distributions. Further, since protocol runs are parameterized (e.g. by the security parameter k), the following definition uses probability ensembles.

Definition 5 (Indistinguishablity). *Two binary ensembles X and Y are indistinguishable $(X \approx Y)$, if $\forall c, d \in N$ $\exists k_0 \in N$, so that for all $k > k_0$ and all $a \in \cup_{\kappa \le k^d}\{0,1\}^\kappa$ holds:*

$$|Pr(X(k,a)=1) - Pr(Y(k,a)=1)| < k^{-c}$$

Based on that notion, we now formalise the indistinguishability of two protocols in the UC framework. The simulator's job is to simulate the presence of $\mathcal{A}$ to the environment, so that it cannot distinguish the real protocol execution from the idealised version. The security notion requires that there is a successful simulator for every adversary.

Definition 6 (UC emulates). *Let π and ϕ be two protocols. Then π UC emulates the protocol ϕ, if $\forall \mathcal{A}\ \exists \mathcal{S}$, so that $\forall \mathcal{Z}$ holds:*

$$\mathsf{EXEC}_{\pi,\mathcal{A},\mathcal{Z}} \approx \mathsf{EXEC}_{\phi,\mathcal{S},\mathcal{Z}}$$

We can now formally state when a protocol *realises* a functionality.

Definition 7 (UC realises). *A protocol π (securely) UC realises an ideal functionality $\mathcal{F}_{\mathsf{ideal}}$, if π UC emulates the corresponding ideal protocol $\mathsf{IDEAL}_{\mathcal{F}}$.*

If a protocol π realises a given ideal functionality, then we say π is *UC secure*.

The UC framework is a powerful instrument for analyzing the security of protocols because it provides a composition theorem. Informally speaking, the composition theorem states that if π securely realises an ideal functionality $\mathcal{F}_{\mathsf{ideal}}$, one can use π instead of $\mathcal{F}_{\mathsf{ideal}}$ in other protocols without compromising security.

2 Composing Firewalls

In this section, we discuss different architectural solutions to the problem of maliciously acting firewalls and analyze their security in the Universal Composability (UC) framework. To simplify the exposition, we only discuss unidirectional networks. The easiest approach for extending the model to bidirectional communication would be using a independent instance of $\mathcal{F}_{\mathsf{ideal}}$ for each direction and deducing the security of the composed system by using the Composition Theorem. However, this approach would require the protocols for each direction to be independent of each other and not have a joint state. Actual firewall solutions base their decisions on all observed packets (not only those in one direction), however. Thus, the security of the bidirectional extensions of the architectures we discuss has to be proven manually.

We only discuss the security of a single atomic building block for complex firewall architectures. The Composition Theorem of the UC framework provides us with a strong guarantee for networks composed of several building blocks.

2.1 Adversarial Model

We assume an outside adversary who can statically corrupt exactly one firewall in the network. He gains full control over this firewall and can send and receive messages in its name (via a GSM link, for example). Because our constructions are symmetric, our corruption model is equivalent to an adaptive model.

2.2 Trusted Hardware

The UC framework gives strong security guarantees. It is difficult to obtain secure protocols in the plain UC model, however. This problem can be alleviated by using a set-up assumption like a Common Reference String, a Public-Key Infrastructure or trusted hardware. Secure hardware is often modeled as tokens that offer some black box functionality. They cannot be made to deviate from the specified functionality and parties may not learn the value of internally stored values if they are not allowed to do so.

We envision similar network devices for our task. They have two very simple functionalities depending on the direction of the packet flow. In one direction their job is to compare packets that come in from different sources and decide whether to let them pass. In the other direction their job is to split incoming packets and distribute them to several firewalls. Because these "packet comparators" offer only limited functionality, they could be manufactured easily, maybe even by the network owner himself. Also, it would be very hard to hide any backdoors or undocumented functionality in the device. Thirdly, because of its simple functionality, the device need not be able to download updates or even be freely programmable. We envision such a device to be realized as an Application-Specific Integrated Circuit (ASIC). In our security analysis, we assume that the specialized hardware we use cannot be compromised, i.e. is *trusted hardware*.

We formalize the functionality for comparison in Fig. 2 and the functionality for splitting in Fig. 1. This explicit distinction is solely for the purpose of simplifying the model in the case of uni-directional communication. Practically realizing the required functionality at wire speed is not impractical: The trusted device need only compare packets as fast as the slowest of the firewalls can analyze them.

We express the notion of "packet equivalence" with a relation $\equiv$ that we assume to be defined appropriately.

An idealised description of trusted hardware split
Upon receiving packet p on the interface connected to the outside:

- Output p to every interface connected to a firewall.

Fig. 1. The splitting functionality the trusted hardware must perform. We assume that there is a fixed interface for connecting with the outside network and a number of other interfaces to which the firewalls are connected.

An idealised description of trusted hardware hw
Keep a local cache realised as an unordered list.
Upon receiving packet p on interface i:

- If there is another input interface $j \neq i$, and a corresponding entry (j, q) with $p \equiv q$ in the cache:
  - Remove (j, q) from the cache,
  - output p.
- Otherwise, store (i, p) in the cache.

Fig. 2. The function the trusted hardware must perform. Because network packets may arrive at different times or in a different order, they must be cached in order to be available for comparison. We assume the relation $\equiv$ to be defined appropriately.

A firewall may change the order of the packets it delivers. Some packets might need to be inspected more closely (Deep Packet Inspection), while others would just be waved through—take for example packages from a voice-over-IP (VoIP) connection. Therefore, it is not sufficient for the trusted hardware to compare packets one-by-one in the order they arrive.

Formally analyzing availability is outside the scope of this work.

2.3   Serial Concatenation of Two Firewalls

An obvious idea is to concatenate two firewalls and compare whether packets that exit the network originally were sent from the outside. This way, no firewall can "make up" packets. This concatenation of firewalls is not secure. We formalize this claim in Appendix A. For the sake of brevity, we only state our result here.

Figure 3 shows a graphical representation of the network architecture of the serial concatenation. fw_1, fw_2, split and hw will be the parties in the corresponding UC protocol.

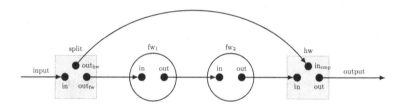

Fig. 3. The serial concatenation of firewalls using secure hardware to compare packets. hw compares whether "what goes in, comes out". split forwards the packet to two components. The connecting arrows represent network cables in a "real" network.

Packets from outside the network always arrive at split first. Parties cannot communicate directly. Instead, we provide them with an ideal functionality for communication. This functionality ensures that parties can only communicate in a way that is fixed by the structure of the network. This is justified, since in an "real" network, components can also only communicate along the network cables.

We omit session IDs from all descriptions of functionalities and protocols. Different instances behave independently. We use the notion of "public delayed output", introduced by Canetti [4]. This means that a message is given to the adversary prior to delivery. The adversary then decides when (or whether) it is delivered.

The main idea for the ideal functionality is that any firewall architecture, regardless of the amount of different firewalls or their specific rule set, should behave as if the corrupted firewall was not there (see Fig. 4).

We only state our result and the idea for the proof here. For details and a full proof, see Appendix A.

The ideal functionality of two firewalls $\mathcal{F}_{\text{ideal}}$

- Upon receiving (input, p):
  - Let fw_k be the non-corrupted party; compute $F_{\text{fw}_k}(p, \text{in}, s) = (p', i', s')$. Ask the adversary if p should be delivered. If yes, $p' \neq \bot$ and $i' \neq \bot$, write p' to the output tape of hw. Else, do nothing. Save the new internal state s'.

Fig. 4. The ideal functionality of two firewalls.

Theorem 1. π_{serial} *does* not *UC realise* $\mathcal{F}_{\text{ideal}}$ *in the* $\mathcal{F}_{\text{serial}}$-*hybrid model.*

The idea is that if fw_2 is corrupted, it could output a malicious packet just at the same time this packet arrives at split (sent by the environment). This would force hw to output the packet, even though it was blocked by fw_1.

2.4 Parallel Composition of Two Firewalls

The serial composition of two firewalls is not secure with regard to our envisioned ideal functionality. Better results can be achieved using parallel composition. The idea is that the trusted hardware only accepts a packet if both firewalls accept it. Figure 5 shows this composition. We will now discuss the security of this architecture.

The protocol of the parallel architecture is defined in Definition 8.

Definition 8 (Protocol of the parallel architecture π_{parallel}).

- split: *Upon receiving* (input, p): *Call* $\mathcal{F}_{\text{parallel}}(\text{send}, \text{out}_1, \text{out}_2, p)$.
- fw_k: *Upon receiving* (in, p): *Calculate*
  $F_{\text{fw}_k}(p, \text{in}, s) = (p', i', s')$. *If* $p' \neq \bot$ *and* $i' \neq \bot$, *call* $\mathcal{F}_{\text{parallel}}(\text{send}, p', i')$. *Save the new internal state* s'.
- hw: *Upon receiving* (in$_i$, p), *check if there is an entry* (in$_j$, q) *with* $i \neq j$ *and* $p \equiv q$ *in the internal storage. If so, write p to the output tape and remove both entries. Else, do nothing.*

The functionality describing the network structure is depicted in Fig. 6.

We will compare the protocol from Definition 8 with an ideal functionality. The ideal functionality is the same as in the serial case, since the natural approach of defining ideal functionalities only uses the uncorrupted firewall, which again leads to the functionality in Fig. 4. However, as in the serial case, the parallel architecture does not realise this functionality.

Theorem 2. π_{parallel} *does not UC realise* $\mathcal{F}_{\text{ideal}}$ *in the* $\mathcal{F}_{\text{parallel}}$-*hybrid model.*

We prove this by describing an attack which cannot be simulated.

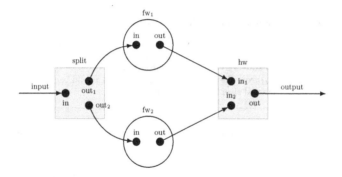

Fig. 5. The parallel composition of two firewalls with trusted hardware. hw only accepts packets that are output by both firewalls.

The ideal network function $\mathcal{F}_{\mathsf{parallel}}$
Initialise an empty queue (first-in-first-out) for both fw_1 and fw_2.

- Upon receiving (send, out_1, out_2, p) from split: Push p into the queue for both fw_1 and fw_2.
- Upon receiving (deliver, fw_k) from the adversary: Fetch the next packet p from fw_k's queue. Provide public delayed output of (p, in) to fw_k.
- Upon receiving (send, out, p) from fw_k: Provide a public delayed output of (p, in_k) to hw.

Fig. 6. The ideal network function representing the parallel concatenation of firewalls with trusted hardware.

Proof. Let, w.l.o.g., fw_1 be honest and fw_2 be corrupted. Also, let p_1 and p_2 be packets that are accepted by fw_1. The environment sends packets p_1 and p_2 to the architecture which the adversary delivers to fw_1. Both packets are accepted by fw_1 and forwarded to hw. Then, the adversary sends packets p_2 and p_1 from fw_2. Since both packets have been accepted and were sent to hw previously (but in reverse order), hw will send out p_2 and p_1—in this order. Thus, the adversary was able to reverse the order of packets. Since the adversary is not allowed to influence the order of packets in the ideal model, there exists no simulator which can simulate this attack. □

The Internet Protocol explicitly does not give any guarantees about the ordering of packets, since the correct order is encoded in the packet. The packet itself, however, can not be altered by the adversary. Thus, we modify our ideal functionality and explicitly grant the attacker the ability to reorder the outgoing packet stream. The new ideal functionality is described in Fig. 7.

Theorem 3. π_{parallel} *UC realises* $\mathcal{F}_{\mathsf{ideal}_2}$ *in the* $\mathcal{F}_{\mathsf{parallel}}$-*hybrid model.*

Proof. To prove the statement, we will give the description of a simulator and show that this simulator can simulate every adversary, so that no environment can distinguish between the real and ideal model. Let w.l.o.g. fw_1 be corrupted and fw_2 be honest. Let $\mathcal{S}$ be a simulator with the following functionality:

The ideal functionality of two firewalls with packet reordering $\mathcal{F}_{\mathsf{ideal}_2}$

- Upon receiving (input, p): Let w.l.o.g fw_1 be the non-corrupted party; compute $F_{\mathsf{fw}_1}(p, \mathsf{in}, s) = (p', i', s')$. If $p' \neq \perp$ and $i' \neq \perp$, save p' in an indexed memory structure m at the next free index. Save new internal state s'. Give p to the adversary.
- Upon receiving (deliver, j) from the adversary: If $m[j]$ contains a valid packet, write (out, $m[j]$) to the output tape of hw and clear $m[j]$; else do nothing.

Fig. 7. The ideal functionality of two firewalls with packet reordering.

- Upon activation, or when given a packet p, simulate the real model and observe its output. If the output of the real model is a packet p', calculate the position of p' in the internal memory structure of the ideal functionality and advise the functionality to deliver the packet on that index. (The case that p' is not found in the internal memory structure of the ideal functionality need not be covered, as is proven below.)

Note that the simulator receives exactly the same input as the adversary in the real model—it can perfectly simulate the communication between the adversary and the environment. Thus, the environment can only distinguish the models based on their output streams. We argue that the output of the real and ideal model are identical. Assume towards a contradiction that they are not.

Let $\{fw_2(S)\}$ denote the set of all packets fw_2 outputs when given the input stream S. There are two possibilities which would cause a difference in output streams:

Case 1. The adversary in the real model suppressed a packet which did not get suppressed in the ideal model. This is impossible however, since the simulator only advises the ideal functionality to deliver a packet if it observes it being output in its simulation of the real model.

Case 2. The real model outputs a packet which is not output in the ideal world. Assume that this was the case and let p be that packet. The following conditions have to hold: p has to be in $\{fw_2(S)\}$ and p has to be output by $\mathcal{A}$ (using fw_1). This is true because the trusted hardware will ensure that a packet is only output when both firewalls accept it. For a packet *not* to be output in the *ideal model*, one of the following conditions have to hold:

- p is not in $\{fw_2(S)\}$. This way, p will not be in the internal memory structure of the ideal functionality. Thus, the simulator can not advise the delivery of that packet. This is a contradiction, since we assumed that p was output in the real model, which in turn implies that $p \in \{fw_2(S)\}$.
- $p \in \{fw_2(S)\}$ *and* the simulator did not advise the functionality to deliver p. This is also a contradiction, since we assumed that p was output in the real model. This would cause the simulator to advise the output of p by definition.

We now have shown that the assumption that the environment can observe a difference in packet output stream in the real and the ideal world leads to a contradiction in all cases. This, together with the ability of the simulator to fully simulate the adversary, proves the indistinguishability of the models.   □

2.5 Parallel Composition of Three or More Firewalls

The parallel approach to compose firewalls described above does indeed improve security compared to one single and potentially malicious firewall. There is large class of attacks that become possible when the adversary can selectively suppress packets. Because the parallel architecture with two firewalls has this weakness, we extend the architecture to a quorum of three firewalls.

In the following section, we assume that uncorrupted firewalls in this architecture will have the same behaviour. However, we allow them to disagree on the order of packets.

There is a non-trivial attack on this architecture. When both uncorrupted firewalls both output the same packet p, the adversary can use clever timing to output p from the corrupted firewall directly after the first uncorrupted firewall. The trusted hardware would then observe two p packets on different interfaces and output p. However, a third p packet would arrive from the second uncorrupted firewall. Then, the adversary could output p again. This would cause hw to output p again and thus duplicate the packet. The natural extension of $\mathcal{F}_{\text{ideal}_2}$ to the case of three firewalls already covers this attack. This functionality is depicted in Fig. 8.

The other protocols and functionalities (π_{parallel_3} and $\mathcal{F}_{\text{parallel}_3}$) can easily be extended to the case of three firewalls by adding the third firewall as an additional party. We will omit their descriptions here.

The ideal functionality of three firewalls $\mathcal{F}_{\text{ideal}_3}$

- Upon receiving (input, p): Let w.l.o.g. fw_1 and fw_2 be the non-corrupted parties; compute $F_{\text{fw}_1}(p, \text{in}, s) = (p', i', s')$ and $F_{\text{fw}_2}(p, \text{in}, s) = (p'', i'', s'')$. If $p' \neq \bot$ and $i' \neq \bot$, save p' in an indexed memory structure m at the next free index. If $p'' \neq \bot$ and $i'' \neq \bot$, also save p'' in m at the next free index. Save the new internal states. Give p to the adversary.
- Upon receiving (deliver, j) from the adversary: If $m[j]$ contains a valid packet, write (out, $m[j]$) to the output tape of hw and clear $m[j]$; else do nothing.

Fig. 8. The ideal functionality of three firewalls.

The attack described above can also be performed in $\mathcal{F}_{\text{ideal}_3}$. When fw_1 and fw_2 both output the same packet, both will be saved in m. The adversary can now output both packets by giving the right indices.

Theorem 4. π_{parallel_3} UC realises $\mathcal{F}_{\text{ideal}_3}$ in the $\mathcal{F}_{\text{parallel}_3}$-hybrid model.

The proof is very similar to the proof of Theorem 3. We omit it here.

It is not acceptable to give an attacker the ability to duplicate packets. We alter the functionality of our trusted hardware slightly to prevent the attack. The

---

An idealised description of trusted hardware without packet duplication hw_3

Keep a local cache for each incoming interface realised as an unordered list. Upon receiving packet p on interface i:

- Check if the cache of interface i contains an entry $-q$ with $p \equiv q$. If so, delete $-q$ and halt.
- Check if there exists an interface $j \neq i$ with an entry q with $p \equiv q$ in the cache of that interface:
  - Remove q from the cache,
  - output p,
  - add an entry $-p$ to the cache of all other interfaces k with $k \neq i$ and $k \neq j$.
- Otherwise, store p in the cache of interface i.

Fig. 9. The updated functionality of the trusted hardware to prevent packet duplication. The hardware now marks a packet as "missing" if a firewall has not yet delivered it, but two others have.

The ideal functionality of three firewalls without packet duplication $\mathcal{F}_{ideal_4}$

Initialise three index-based memory structures m_1, m_2 and m_{out}.

- Upon receiving (input, p): Let w.l.o.g. fw_1 and fw_2 be the non-corrupted parties; compute $F_{fw_1}(p, in, s) = (p', i', s')$ and $F_{fw_2}(p, in, s) = (p'', i'', s'')$. Save the new internal states. Save p' in m_1 and p'' in m_2. Give p to the adversary.
- Upon receiving (deliver, j, k) ($k \in \{1, 2\}$): If $m_k[j]$ contains a valid packet p''':
  - Check how many times that packet (or an equivalent packet) is in m_{out}. Let that number be n.
  - Check if either m_1 or m_2 (or both) contain that packet at least $n + 1$ times.
  - If so, write (out, p''') to the output tape and to m_{out}.

Fig. 10. The ideal functionality of three firewalls without packet duplication. For every packet, at least one of the firewalls must have sent this packet at least as often as it got passed to hw.

functionality is depicted in Fig. 9. The idea is that at the moment the hardware outputs a packet, exactly two firewalls must have output this packet before. Then, the hardware can mark this packet as missing from the third firewall. If it arrives eventually, this mark will be removed and no further action will be taken.

The corresponding ideal functionality is depicted in Fig. 10. It now continuously checks whether the amount of identical packets being given to hw matches the amount of identical packets which either one of the uncorrupted firewalls sent. As previously however, we allow the reordering of packets.

Theorem 5. $\pi_{parallel_4}$ *UC realises* $\mathcal{F}_{ideal_4}$ *in the* $\mathcal{F}_{parallel_3}$*-hybrid model.*

Proof. The general technique is similar to the technique used in the proof of Theorem 3. See Appendix B for details.

3   Conclusion and Directions for Future Research

In this work, we consider the problem of actively malicious firewalls. We introduce a framework for analysing firewall networks consisting of multiple firewalls

---

The ideal network function $\mathcal{F}_{\text{serial}}$

Initialize an empty queue (first-in-first-out) for both hw and fw_1.

- Upon receiving $(\text{send}, \text{out}_{\text{fw}}, \text{out}_{\text{hw}}, p)$ from split:
  - Push p into the queue for hw and fw_1.
  - Give the adversary p and let him choose one of the queues. Pull the next packet from that queue. If the adversary chose hw's queue, send $(p, \text{in}_{\text{cmp}})$ to hw, otherwise send (p, in) to fw_1.
- Upon receiving $(\text{send}, \text{out}, p)$ from fw_1: Provide a public delayed output of (p, in) to fw_2.
- Upon receiving $(\text{send}, \text{out}, p)$ from fw_2: Provide a public delayed output of (p, in) to hw.

Fig. 11. The ideal network function representing the serial concatenation of firewalls with special hardware.

based on the Universal Composition framework. The serial concatenation of firewalls turns out to be insecure. The parallel composition of two firewalls using a trusted packet comparator is secure with regard to an ideal functionality which allows for packet reordering. We show that this positive result can not be directly extended to a 2-out-of-3 quorum decision, since the adversary would be able to duplicate packets. We give a solution for that by describing a slightly different trusted packet comparator. We gave an ideal functionality for the three firewall architecture and prove security with respect to this functionalitiy.

An important open research question is how to rigorously analyse the availability of the approaches we discussed. Intuitively, the parallel approach with three or more firewalls is more available than the one with two firewalls.

Firewall combination strategies other than those we discussed need further exploration. In extension to a generalised k-out-of-n quorum approach, one might consider complex firewall networks in the fashion of multiple parallel and serial stages. Also, how to deduce security guarantees for bidirectional communication (via a "Bidirection Theorem" similar to the Composition Theorem in UC) is an important open problem.

A   Serial Composition of Two Firewalls

We prove the previously stated Theorem 1 here. First, we provide the protocol of the serial architecture and define the ideal network function (Fig. 11).

Definition 9 (The protocol of the serial firewall architecture π_{serial}). *The protocol the parties are following is defined as follows:*

- split: *Upon receiving* (input, p): *Call* $\mathcal{F}_{\text{serial}}(\text{send}, \text{out}_{\text{fw}}, \text{out}_{\text{hw}}, p)$.
- fw_k: *Upon receiving* (in, p): *Calculate* $F_{fw_k}(p, \text{in}, s) = (p', i', s')$. *If* $p' \neq \bot$ *and* $i' \neq \bot$, *call* $\mathcal{F}_{\text{serial}}(\text{send}, i', p')$. *Save the new internal state* s'.
- hw: *Check whether there are two entries* (p, in) *and* $(q, \text{in}_{\text{cmp}})$ *in the local storage (with* $p \equiv q$). *If so, write* p *to the output tape and delete the entries.*

We now show that the serial concatenation of firewalls is not secure, even with a trusted comparator. To prove the statement, it suffices to show that there exists an attack which can not be simulated. We describe such an attack. The general idea is that if fw_2 is corrupted, it could output a malicious packet just at the same time this packet arrives at split (sent by the environment). This would force hw to output the packet, even though it was blocked by fw_1.

Theorem 1. π_{serial} *does* not *UC realise* $\mathcal{F}_{\text{ideal}}$ *in the* $\mathcal{F}_{\text{serial}}$-*hybrid model.*

Proof. Let fw_2 be corrupted and fw_1 be honest. Let p be a packet that is blocked by fw_1. The environment inputs p to split. This will cause $(p, \text{in}_{\text{cmp}})$ to be send to hw from split. In its next activation the adversary uses fw_2 to call $\mathcal{F}_{\text{serial}}(\text{send}, \text{out}, p)$ and advises the ideal functionality to deliver (p, in) to hw. hw will now have two identical packets on different interfaces (one from split and one from fw_2) in its storage and output p, even though p has been blocked by fw_1.

There is no simulator which can simulate this attack, since fw_1 will block the packet in the ideal model and the output of fw_2 will not be considered.   □

B   Parallel Composition of Three Firewalls

Theorem 5. π_{parallel_4} *UC realises* $\mathcal{F}_{\text{ideal}_4}$ *in the* $\mathcal{F}_{\text{parallel}_3}$-*hybrid model.*

Proof. The proof is similar to the proof of Theorem 3. We argue that the simulator behaves identically to the adversary and that the output of the ideal network is identical to the output of the real network. Let $\mathcal{S}$ be a simulator with the following functionality:

- Upon activation, or when given a packet p, simulate the real model and observe its output. If the output of the real model is a packet p', calculate (for the ideal functionality) the index of the memory structure in which p' is saved as well as its position within the memory. Advise the functionality to deliver the packet on that index. (The case that p' is not found in the internal memory structure of the ideal functionality need not be covered, as is proven below.)

The argument that $\mathcal{S}$ will never mistakenly suppress a packet in the ideal model is identical to Case 1 in the proof of Theorem 3. We need to argue Case 2: It is impossible that $\mathcal{S}$ is unable to schedule a packet it observes in the output of its internal simulation of the real network. Let p be such a packet that, after the input stream S is processed, is written to the output tape of hw in the real model but not to the internal memory structure of $\mathcal{F}_{\text{ideal}_4}$.

Let m_A, m_1 and m_2 be the lists the trusted hardware uses in the protocol for storing the packets output by the firewalls and marking the "negative" packets. Let m_{hw} be the list of all packets it has ever output. Let m'_1, m'_2, m'_{out} be the lists the ideal functionality uses for keeping track of the packets. Let $\|m\|_p$ denote the number of packets p the list m contains. We then define $|m|_p := \|m\|_p - \|m\|_{-p}$.

First, observe that $\mathcal{S}$ only schedules packets it observes in its simulation of the real model. Hence, by the description of hw: $|m_1|_p = |m_1'|_p - |m_{\mathrm{hw}}|_p$ and $|m_2|_p = |m_2'|_p - |m_{\mathrm{hw}}|_p$. Via the argument from Case 1 ($\forall p : |m_{out}'|_p \le |m_{\mathrm{hw}}|_p$) we have:

$$|m_1|_p \le |m_1'|_p - |m_{out}'|_p \tag{1}$$
$$|m_2|_p \le |m_2'|_p - |m_{out}'|_p \tag{2}$$

For p to be output in the real model, one of the following conditions has to hold:

$$|m_A|_p > 0 \text{ and } |m_1|_p > 0 \tag{3}$$
$$|m_A|_p > 0 \text{ and } |m_2|_p > 0 \tag{4}$$
$$|m_1|_p > 0 \text{ and } |m_2|_p > 0 \tag{5}$$

This is true because the trusted hardware will only forward packets which are in at least two of the packet lists. The functionality of hw can be restated in the following way: For every packet p which is output, insert a packet $-p$ into the lists of the three firewalls. If there are two packets p and $-p$ in the same list, both cancel each other out.

For p *not* to be written to the internal memory structure of $\mathcal{F}_{\mathrm{ideal}_4}$ in the ideal model, the following condition has to hold:

$$|m_{out}'|_p \ge |m_1'|_p \text{ and } |m_{out}'|_p \ge |m_2'|_p \tag{6}$$
$$\Leftrightarrow |m_1'|_p - |m_{out}'|_p \le 0 \text{ and } |m_2'|_p - |m_{out}'|_p \le 0 \tag{7}$$

This again describes the difference between the amount of packages p each individual firewall has output and the amount of packages p which got output in total after processing $\mathcal{S}$.

Concluding the argument, conditions (1) to (5) give us $|m_1'|_p - |m_{out}'|_p > 0$ and $|m_2'|_p - |m_{out}'|_p > 0$, which contradict condition (7). $\square$

References

1. Interactive graphic: The nsa's spy catalog. Spiegel Online International, December 2013. http://www.spiegel.de/international/world/a-941262.html
2. Backes, M., Pfitzmann, B., Waidner, M.: A general composition theorem for secure reactive systems. In: Naor, M. (ed.) TCC 2004. LNCS, vol. 2951, pp. 336–354. Springer, Heidelberg (2004)
3. Bellovin, S., Cheswick, W.: Network firewalls. IEEE Commun. Mag. **32**(9), 50–57 (1994)
4. Canetti, R.: Universally composable security: a new paradigm for cryptographic protocols. In: 2001 Proceedings of 42nd IEEE Symposium on Foundations of Computer Science, October 2001
5. Chari, S., Jutla, C.S., Roy, A.: Universally composable security analysis of oauth v2. 0. IACR Cryptology ePrint Archive 2011, 526 (2011)
6. Freed, N.: Behavior of and requirements for internet firewalls. RFC 2979 (2000)

7. Goldwasser, S., Kalai, Y.T., Rothblum, G.N.: One-time programs. In: Wagner, D. (ed.) CRYPTO 2008. LNCS, vol. 5157, pp. 39–56. Springer, Heidelberg (2008)
8. Gouda, M.G., Liu, A.X., Jafry, M.: Verification of distributed firewalls. In: 2008 IEEE GLOBECOM 2008 Global Telecommunications Conference, pp. 1–5. IEEE (2008)
9. Herzberg, A.: Folklore, practice and theory of robust combiners. J. Comput. Secur. **17**(2), 159–189 (2009)
10. Hofheinz, D., Shoup, V.: Gnuc: a new universal composability framework. Cryptology ePrint Archive, Report 2011/303 (2011). http://eprint.iacr.org/
11. Ingham, K., Forrest, S.: A history and survey of network firewalls. University of New Mexico, Technical report (2002)
12. Ingols, K., Chu, M., Lippmann, R., Webster, S., Boyer, S.: Modeling modern network attacks and countermeasures using attack graphs. In: 2009 Annual Computer Security Applications Conference, ACSAC 2009, pp. 117–126. IEEE (2009)
13. Katz, J.: Universally composable multi-party computation using tamper-proof hardware. In: Naor, M. (ed.) EUROCRYPT 2007. LNCS, vol. 4515, pp. 115–128. Springer, Heidelberg (2007). http://dx.doi.org/10.1007/978-3-540-72540-4_7
14. Katz, J., Maurer, U., Tackmann, B., Zikas, V.: Universally composable synchronous computation. In: Sahai, A. (ed.) TCC 2013. LNCS, vol. 7785, pp. 477–498. Springer, Heidelberg (2013). http://dx.doi.org/10.1007/978-3-642-36594-2_27
15. Lamport, L., Shostak, R., Pease, M.: The byzantine generals problem. ACM Trans. Program. Lang. Syst. **4**(3), 382–401 (1982). http://doi.acm.org/10.1145/357172.357176
16. Maurer, U.: Constructive cryptography – a new paradigm for security definitions and proofs. In: Mödersheim, S., Palamidessi, C. (eds.) TOSCA 2011. LNCS, vol. 6993, pp. 33–56. Springer, Heidelberg (2012)
17. Maurer, U., Renner, R.: Abstract cryptography. In: Chazelle, B. (ed.) The Second Symposium in Innovations in Computer Science, ICS 2011, pp. 1–21. Tsinghua University Press , January 2011
18. Pfitzmann, B., Waidner, M.: A model for asynchronous reactive systems and its application to secure message transmission. In: Proceedings of the 2001 IEEE Symposium on Security and Privacy, S&P 2001, pp. 184–200. IEEE (2001)
19. Schuba, C.L., Spafford, E.H.: A reference model for firewall technology. In: 1997 Proceedings of the 13th Annual Computer Security Applications Conference, pp. 133–145. IEEE (1997)

Higher-Order Glitch Resistant Implementation of the PRESENT S-Box

Thomas De Cnudde[1]([✉]), Begül Bilgin[1,2], Oscar Reparaz[1], and Svetla Nikova[1]

[1] ESAT-COSIC and iMinds, KU Leuven, Leuven, Belgium
{thomas.cnudde,begul.bilgin,oscar.reparaz,
svetla.nikova}@esat.kuleuven.be
[2] EEMCS-SCS, University of Twente, Enschede, The Netherlands

Abstract. Glitches, occurring from the unwanted switching of CMOS gates, have been shown to leak information even when side-channel countermeasures are applied to hardware cryptosystems. The polynomial masking scheme presented at CHES 2011 by Roche et al. is a method that offers provable security against side-channel analysis at any order even in the presence of glitches. The method is based on Shamir's secret sharing and its computations rely on a secure multi-party computation protocol. At CHES 2013, Moradi et al. presented a first-order glitch resistant implementation of the AES S-box based on this method. Their work showed that the area and speed overheads resulting from the polynomial masking are high. In this paper, we present a first-order glitch resistant implementation of the PRESENT S-box which is designed for lightweight applications, indicating less area and randomness requirements. Moreover, we provide a second-order glitch resistant implementation of this S-box and observe the increase in implementation requirements.

Keywords: Polynomial masking · Glitches · Sharing · PRESENT, S-box

1 Introduction

Radio frequency identification (RFID) systems, wireless sensor networks, smart cards and other compact mobile applications have become prevalent in everyday life. Their widespread deployment in applications ranging from supply chains to intelligent homes and even electronic body implants, has made their security a pressing issue. While block ciphers provide sufficient security against cryptanalysis for these applications, their hardware implementations are susceptible to side-channel leakage. By exploiting these leaks through side-channel analysis (SCA), a cryptosystem can be compromised more easily than promised by the cryptanalytic security. A common side-channel analysis is Differential Power Analysis (DPA) [12]. DPA exploits dependencies between the instantaneous power consumption of a device and the intermediate values arising in the computation of a cryptographic operation.

B. Ors and B. Preneel (Eds.): BalkanCryptSec 2014, LNCS 9024, pp. 75–93, 2015.
DOI: 10.1007/978-3-319-21356-9_6

Several countermeasures have been proposed to cope with these side-channels. Secure logic styles that balance the power consumption of different data values [23] can be used or noise can be increased in the form of random delays, random execution orders or by inserting dummy operations [24]. Even though an analysis becomes harder as this noise increases, these techniques do not provide provable security. A popular countermeasure that does provide provable security under certain assumptions is *masking* [4,8]. This method conceals *sensitive* information, such as key and plaintext related information, using random values. Compared to a naive implementation, a well implemented masked implementation typically offers more resistance against power analysis attacks, and makes the attack much more expensive as the order d of the masking increases. This masking order d in turn defines the order $d+1$ of the attack needed to retrieve the sensitive information. This attack order sets the number of shares that are jointly exploited by either analyzing the $(d+1)^{th}$-order statistical moment of the leakage at one point in time or by nonlinearly combining leakages from $d+1$ points in time. Such an attack is known as a $(d+1)^{th}$-order DPA attack. A dth-order secure implementation can consequently always be broken by a $(d+1)^{th}$-order attack. When the attack order is larger than one, this is known as a higher-order DPA (HO-DPA) attack [4,15].

Masking is however deteriorated by the switching behaviour of CMOS transistors, the so-called glitching effect [13,14]. Two masking schemes that show provable security against DPA in the presence of glitches, or glitch resistance for short, are the *polynomial masking scheme* [20] and *threshold implementations* [18]. While, at the time of writing, the latter achieves glitch resistance at the first-order only, the former provides this security also for higher orders. Therefore, we consider the polynomial masking scheme in this paper.

Masking introduces an overhead on the area and throughput. To avoid overly large and slow implementations, we will focus on lightweight, i.e. compact and power efficient, block ciphers. A popular lightweight block cipher is PRESENT [2] which, as of 2012, is part of the ISO/IEC 29192-2 standard [11], making its side-channel resistance relevant. Besides PRESENT, its S-box is also used in other lightweight cryptographic algorithms, including the LED block cipher [10], the GOST revisited block cipher [19] and the PHOTON lightweight hash function [9]. In this paper, we focus on glitch resistant implementations of the nonlinear part of PRESENT, the S-box, since this is typically the most challenging part of a masked implementation.

Related Work. An algorithmic description of a first-order glitch resistant Advanced Encryption Standard (AES) implementation using the polynomial masking scheme is given in [20]. In [16], this description is used to implement a first-order glitch resistant AES S-box on an FPGA. The PRESENT S-box has, to our knowledge, not yet been implemented using polynomial masking.

Contribution. In this paper, we present a first- and a second-order polynomially masked implementation of the 4-bit PRESENT S-box. To our knowledge, this is the first second-order PRESENT S-box implementation showing resistance against second-order DPA in the presence of glitches. The implementations are based on the guidelines for the first-order glitch resistant AES implementation proposed in [16]. We also present experimental confirmation showing that the implementations indeed achieve their claimed security. To this end, we applied univariate and bivariate leakage detection based on *Welch's t-test*.

Organization. Section 2 introduces the necessary background regarding the polynomial masking scheme and the PRESENT S-box. The design decisions, hardware implementations and their costs are presented in Sect. 3. The SCA results are shown in Sect. 4. Finally, the conclusion is drawn in Sect. 5.

2 Preliminaries

2.1 PRESENT Block Cipher

The PRESENT block cipher [2] is a symmetric key encryption algorithm designed considering the heavy constraints on performance, area and timing requirements of lightweight hardware applications. Its block length equals 64-bits. Key lengths of 80- and 128-bits are supported, which are referred to as PRESENT-80 and PRESENT-128 respectively. For lightweight applications, PRESENT-80 is recommended. The PRESENT cipher performs 31 rounds followed by a final key whitening stage. Each round consists of a binary addition with the round key and a substitution-permutation network. The permutation layer is bit oriented and can easily be implemented by wiring, making it very hardware friendly. The substitution layer applies 16 identical 4-bit S-boxes governed by the following table:

2.2 Polynomial Masking Scheme

Side-channel resistance in the presence of glitches can be achieved at any order by the polynomial masking scheme [20]. Sensitive variables are masked using Shamir's secret sharing scheme [22] and computations on the resulting shares are performed using the *BGW's* secure multi-party computation protocol [1].

In Shamir's scheme, a secret $Z \in K \equiv \mathbb{F}_{2^m}$ is shared among $n < 2^m$ players such that $d+1$ players are needed to reconstruct Z. To this end, a *dealer* generates a degree-d polynomial $P_Z(X) \in K[X]$ with constant term Z and secret, random coefficients a_i:

$$P_Z(X) = Z + \sum_{i=1}^{d} a_i X^i$$

When working in the field K, we will denote binary addition and field multiplication by $+$ and $.$ respectively.

Table 1. 4-bit to 4-bit substitution of the PRESENT S-box [2] in hexadecimal notation.

z	0	1	2	3	4	5	6	7	8	9	A	B	C	D	E	F
$S[z]$	C	5	6	B	9	0	A	D	3	E	F	8	4	7	1	2

This polynomial is then evaluated in n distinct, non-zero elements $\alpha_1, ..., \alpha_n \in K$, which are called the *public coefficients* and are available to all players. Lastly, each resulting value $Z_i = P_Z(\alpha_i)$ is distributed to its corresponding player i. The secret Z can be reconstructed using the first row $(\lambda_1, ..., \lambda_n)$ of the inverse of the $(n \times n)$ Vandermonde matrix $(\alpha_i^j)_{1 \leq i,j \leq n}$ as:

$$Z = \sum_{i=1}^{n} \lambda_i Z_i$$

This is exemplified for the second-order in Appendix B.

BGW's protocol defines how to securely operate on the shares. We can distinguish between operations that can be processed by all players independently and operations that need communication between the players. Multiplication of a share and a constant, addition of a share and a constant and addition of two shares can be processed by each player independently. As a result, these operations can be implemented straightforwardly. Multiplication of two shares, which is referred to as *shared multiplication*, requires the players to exchange information, which complicates its secure execution. This operation has to be performed in three steps [20]:

1. Each player multiplies its shares, resulting in a $2d$-degree polynomial
2. Each player masks the result of the previous multiplication and sends these shares to all other players
3. Each player reconstructs the result by interpolation and evaluation in the public coefficients

When the square of a share is desired, the shared multiplication can be omitted when following conditions are imposed [20]:

– The public coefficients α_i are distinct and non-zero
– The public coefficients α_i are stable over the Frobenius automorphism: for every α_i, there exists an α_j such that $\alpha_j = \alpha_i^2$

Each player can then independently perform the squaring on its own share but a reordering of the shares is needed between player i and player j when $i \neq j$ to keep the right public coefficient linked to its corresponding player.

To achieve glitch resistance with this masking scheme, two conditions need to be fulfilled. Firstly, the number of players has to exceed twice the degree of the polynomial, i.e. $n > 2d$. Secondly, each player has to leak independently of all other players.

2.3 Cyclotomic Classes

The masking complexity of an S-box is defined in [3] as the minimal number of nonlinear multiplications required to evaluate its polynomial. These nonlinear multiplications correspond to shared multiplications.

When calculating a power x^α from another power x^β, a nonlinear multiplication can be omitted if and only if α and β lie in the same *cyclotomic class*. A cyclotomic class is defined as follows.

Definition 1 (Cyclotomic Class). *With $m \in \mathbb{N}$ and $\alpha \in [0; 2^m - 2]$, the cyclotomic class C_α of α w.r.t. m is defined as:*

$$C_\alpha = \{\alpha \cdot 2^i \bmod 2^m - 1, i \in [0; m-1]\}$$

For the PRESENT S-box, we work in field $\mathbb{F}_{2^4}$. Its corresponding cyclotomic classes are:

$$C_0 = \{0\}, C_1 = \{1, 2, 4, 8\}, C_3 = \{3, 6, C, 9\}, C_5 = \{5, A\}, C_7 = \{7, E, D, B\} \tag{1}$$

An important property is that we can cycle through the elements of a cyclotomic class by squaring, which can be performed independently by all players when the conditions listed in Sect. 2.2 are fulfilled. As squaring is linear in $\mathbb{F}_{2^4}$, the S-box complexity equals the number of different transitions between these classes required to evaluate the S-box substitution function.

3   Hardware Implementation

In this section, the hardware implementations of the first-order and second-order glitch resistant PRESENT S-box are explained. First, the polynomial of the S-box and its evaluation order are established. Then the first-order glitch resistant implementation is discussed in detail. Afterwards, the modifications required to achieve second-order glitch resistance are given. This section is concluded with an overview of the implementation requirements.

3.1   Evaluation Order

The substitution of any 4-bit S-box can be expressed as a unique polynomial over $\mathbb{F}_{2^4}$ with a degree of at most $2^4 - 1 = 15$. This polynomial can be obtained by expanding the following expression [6]:

$$S(x) = \sum_{z \in \mathbb{F}_{2^4}} S(z)(1 + (x+z)^{15}) = \sum_{i=0}^{15} c_i x^i$$

Using the Mattson-Solomon polynomial, the coefficients c_i of $S(x)$ can directly be computed by:

$$c_i = \begin{cases} S(0), & \text{if } i = 0 \\ \sum_{k=0}^{2^4-2} S(\alpha^k)\alpha^{-ki}, & \text{if } i \le i \le 2^4 - 2 \\ S(1) + \sum_{i=0}^{2^4-2} c_i, & \text{if } i = 2^4 - 1 \end{cases}$$

where α is a primitive element in $\mathbb{F}_{2^4}$.

If we use $x^4 + x + 1$ as irreducible polynomial for the construction of $\mathbb{F}_{2^4}$, we get the following polynomial for the PRESENT S-box given in Table 1.

$$S(x) = Dx^{14} + Dx^{13} + Cx^{12} + Ex^{11} + 9x^{10} + 9x^9 + 7x^8$$
$$+ 4x^7 + Cx^6 + Ax^5 + Ex^4 + 7x^3 + 7x^2 + C$$

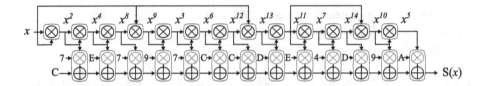

Fig. 1. Block diagram of the evaluation for the PRESENT S-box.

The evaluation order of this polynomial is an adaptation of the proposal by Carlet et al. in [3] to reduce the required memory and area by processing sequentially instead of in parallel. The block diagram of the PRESENT S-box evaluation is depicted in Fig. 1. The gray multipliers symbolize a field multiplication with a constant, while the black multipliers represent a shared multiplication. Starting from input x, squaring is consecutively carried out until all elements of the cyclotomic class C_1 from Eq. (1) are covered. The last element of that class is then multiplied with x to access cyclotomic class C_3, where all elements are again obtained by squaring. After a multiplication with x, squaring is performed again to reach all elements in C_7. To access the final cyclotomic class C_5, a multiplication with x^{11} is chosen, as multiplying our last obtained power with x would lead back to class C_1. This value will need to be stored separately.

From this discussion it is apparent that a shared multiplier cannot be omitted. As our primary design goal is low area, we choose to only implement a shared multiplier to handle all shared multiplications. However, by evaluating the polynomial this way, the designs can easily be extended with a dedicated squaring circuit and benefit from a significant reduction of required randomness. This extension is left as future work.

3.2 First-Order Glitch Resistant PRESENT S-Box

To achieve first-order glitch resistance, both conditions in Sect. 2.2 have to be fulfilled. Namely, our sensitive variables need to be masked by a first-order polynomial and need to be shared between three players with independent side-channel leakage. In order to achieve this independent leakage, we choose to temporally separate the players' operations. After each operation, the intermediate results are stored and left unaltered while another player is active. The design is shown in Fig. 2 and is similar to the AES S-box implementation from [16]. This design is compatible with all combinational finite field multipliers. The one used in our implementations is given in Appendix A.

Shared Multiplier. As pointed out in Sect. 2.2, the shared multiplication differs from the other operations in that it needs communication between the players. To achieve this, the computations are divided in two parts and the communicated intermediate values are stored in registers.

Step 1 and Step 2 (Sect. 2.2) of the shared multiplication are performed in the MULT_EL1$_i$ blocks. With every shared multiplication, each player receives a new random coefficient a_i to remask the multiplication of its input shares t_i. The reconstruction in Step 3 is handled by the MULT_EL2$_i$ blocks once all intermediate results are available.

The detailed working principle is described in *series* of clock cycles. Such a series consists of six clock cycles and is related to the control signals $em_{1 \leq i \leq 6}$, which can be seen in Fig. 2. During each series, a shared multiplication is realized.

– The first clock cycle of a series, enables signal em_1. The two required inputs for the shared multiplier are selected by $selm_1$. At the same time, a new random number a_1 is fed to the MULT_EL1$_1$ block. Together with this random number, the fixed public coefficients α_1, α_2 and α_3 are used to remask the multiplied input shares t_1.
– The same procedure is repeated on the second clock cycle using signal em_2 in block MULT_EL1$_2$and on the third clock cycle using em_3 in block MULT_EL1$_3$. After the third clock cycle, all intermediate results are available.
– In the fourth clock cycle, by activating signal em_4, the intermediate results related to the first public coefficient α_1 are stored in the registers $q_{1,1}, q_{2,1}, q_{3,1}$. The combinatorial logic in block MULT_EL2$_1$ then performs the reconstruction using λ_1, λ_2 and λ_3. This outputs the first share of the shared multiplication. The result is not saved in this clock cycle, but will be done at the start of the next series, with the activation of the select signal em_1.
– In the fifth and sixth clock cycles, the same principles as in the fourth clock cycle apply. The enable signal em_5 handles the reconstruction related to the second public coefficient α_2 in block MULT_EL2$_2$ and em_6 serves the reconstruction related to the third public coefficient α_3 in block MULT_EL2$_3$.

Note that, except for the registers, the shared multiplier is entirely combinational. Therefore, the MULT_EL1$_i$ andMULT_EL2$_i$ blocks are only active when a new value is assigned to their input registers. After one clock cycle, the intermediate values reach their stable states and the blocks stay idle until their input registers are changed again. By temporally separating the em_i signals with a carefully designed control unit, we achieve the required temporal separation.

Input Selection. The right inputs for the shared multiplier are selected by the multiplexers in the MULT_EL2$_i$ blocks. A glitch on the select signal of a multiplexer can temporarily change the inputs of the shared multiplier and induce processing in a player that is supposed to be idle. This would result in an overlap of leakages of different players and would eradicate the temporal separation. To avoid this, these $selm_i$ signals are synchronised. As was noted in Sect. 3.1, we need to store one extra intermediate value x^{11}. When the shares of this value are output at the MULT_EL2$_i$ blocks, the es_1, es_2 and es_3 signals follow the levels of the em_1, em_2 and em_3 signals to store the shares of x^{11} in separate registers.

Addition and Accumulation. To calculate the polynomial, the powers of x need to be multiplied with a constant and accumulated with the previously obtained results. This is handled by the ADD_ACC_EL$_i$ blocks. When the shares of a desired power of x are ready at the outputs of the shared multiplier, the

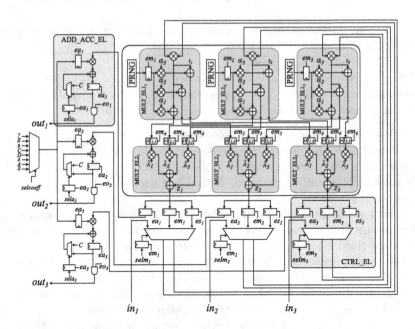

Fig. 2. Architecture diagram for the first-order PRESENT implementation.

ea_i signals activate with the corresponding em_i signals. With the activation of an ea_i signal, a new coefficient chosen by *selcoeff* is fed to an input of the ADD_ACC_EL$_i$ multiplier, resulting in the right multiplication of a constant and its corresponding power of x. In the first series of clock cycles, the constant value C of the polynomial is added to an empty register using the $sela_i$ signal, which activates with its corresponding em_i signal. In all following series of clock cycles, the register output is chosen to accumulate the results. The eo_i signal enables the output share of player i when the register holds the final value. This signal also activates with its corresponding em_i signal.

3.3   Second-Order Glitch Resistant PRESENT S-Box

We will now discuss how to extend our first-order design to the second-order. Again, both conditions in Sect. 2.2 need to be fulfilled. To provide second-order glitch resistance, our sensitive variables are now masked using a second-order polynomial and shared among five players. We again choose temporal separation to decouple the leakages of the different players. The operations in this (5,2)-sharing scheme are detailed in Appendix B. Figure 5 in Appendix C shows the resulting architecture diagram.

Shared Multiplier. The MULT_EL1$_i$ blocks now require two instead of one random coefficients to mask the multiplication of the inputs. Furthermore, the evaluation of the polynomial is done in five public coefficients and their squared value is needed. When hardcoding the public coefficients and their squares, we additionally require seven multiplications, seven additions and one register. Each player now requires five instead of three registers to share the intermediate results. The MULT_EL2$_i$ blocks need two extra multiplications and two extra additions to perform the reconstruction in the (5,2)-sharing scheme.

The control schedule is changed to incorporate five players. The same principles from Sect. 3.2 apply, but we need 10 em_i signals, the first five to control the MULT_EL2$_i$ blocks and the last five to store the intermediate values in the registers.

Input Selection, Addition and Accumulation. The only change made in these operations is the extension from three CTRL_EL (resp. ADD_ACC_EL) blocks to five.

The security against second-order DPA in the presence of glitches of this implementation can theoretically be explained as follows. As a second-order polynomial is used to divide the shares among five players, the shares of at least three players are required to interpolate the masked secret. Mixing up to two observations of intermediate variables will therefore not lead to enough information to reveal the secret variable. Furthermore, as the computations of each player are temporally separated, the information leaked by glitches is contained to the share of that player only and is not influenced by the shares of other players. This theoretical proof is valid for all orders when appropriate changes to the players are considered.

3.4 Implementation Requirements

The total area in NAND gate equivalents (GEs) covers 3594 GE and 8338 GE for the first- and second-order glitch resistant implementation respectively. The largest contributions come from the shared multiplier (37.8 % and 59.6 %) and the control unit (41.8 % and 25.7 %), both for the first- and second-order respectively). The detailed area requirements of the different blocks are given in Table 3 in Appendix D. The results are obtained from Synopsys 2010.03 using the NanGate 45 nm Open Cell Library [17].

The first-order implementation requires 89 clock cycles from the activation of the request signal to the output of all shares. For the second-order implementation, this number becomes 149 clock cycles. The secure evaluation of the first-order PRESENT S-box requires 156-bits of randomness. If a squaring module is used, this randomness can drop to 36-bits, trading off area. For secure evaluation of the second-order PRESENT S-box, the required randomness changes to 520-bits (resp. 120-bits when a squaring module is used). As all public coefficients should be distinct and non-zero, up to 15 players can be accommodated. By imposing the condition that $n > 2d$, this leads to a maximum of a seventh-order glitch resistant implementation for the PRESENT S-box. For all possible orders d of glitch resistance, the required number of randomness and clock cycles are summarized in Table 2.

Table 2. Number of clock cycles and randomness required for a dth-order glitch resistant PRESENT S-box implementation.

Number of Clock Cycles	$30(2d+1)-1$
Randomness (bits)	$52d(2d+1)$
Randomness with squaring module (bits)	$12d(2d+1)$

4   SCA Evaluation

In this section we provide experimental evidence that our implementations provide a reasonable guarantee against typical power analysis attacks. We perform leakage detection tests on the PRESENT S-box, implemented on a SASEBO-G board [21]. The board is externally clocked with a stable, relatively low-frequency clock source of 3.072MHz. All the randomness required for the computations is generated by an AES-based PRNG on the control FPGA. All the tests were performed with $1M$ traces unless explicitly stated otherwise.

For our evaluation, we use the non-specific fixed-vs-random methodology of [5,7]. In a nutshell, the leakage detection test assesses whether the means of power consumption traces, conditioned on any intermediate, are equal or not. In the context of first-order masking, this means whether the masking is sound or not. We stress that by using a non-specific test, we are targeting all intermediates appearing during the computation of an S-box. This allows us to test the implementation against a wide range of leakages, without assuming how the implementation may leak.

The original methodology starts by taking two sets of measurements corresponding to a fixed plaintext and random plaintexts. Then, a hypothesis test is applied time sample per time sample to test whether the means of the two populations are the same or not. Normally, a Student T-test is applied. Having set a significance level beforehand, the result of the test is directly interpretable in terms of probability. In our case, a value of the t-test statistic beyond 4.5 means that there is leakage with high probability. For details on the test, we refer to Appendix E. For our purposes of testing the higher-order security, we adapt the methodology to analyze higher-order moments in univariate and bivariate distributions (two time samples jointly analyzed). This is achieved by preprocessing the power traces through a suitable combination function. In our case, we use the centered product.

We begin with a univariate analysis of the first-order protected implementation. As a first sanity check of our experimental setup, we performed a univariate first-order test with the PRNG switched off, thus deliberately disabling the masking. The result of the t-test on the unmasked first-order implementation is given in Fig. 6 in Appendix E. This clearly shows that the implementation is leaking since the t-test statistic trace exceeds the confidence threshold $C = \pm 4.5$ in several clock cycles, which is expected as the masking is inactive. If we repeat the experiment with the PRNG enabled, the t-test statistic never exceeds the predefined threshold as the top left corner of Fig. 3 indicates.

We repeated the test on centered and squared traces. This is equivalent to test whether there is information leakage on the variances. Note that the first-order protected implementation is expected to leak in the second moment, as Fig. 3 indicates. This only provides us with the evidence that we indeed have enough traces to show that the first-order attack is more expensive in terms of traces than higher-order ones, and thus our goal of first-order security is attained.

We proceeded with a univariate analysis of the second-order glitch resistant implementation. The process follows the lines of the first-order protected implementations and the results are again shown in Fig. 3. We can see that the implementation is indeed first- and second-order univariate secure up to $1M$ traces. The implementation leaks in the third-order but this poses no problem to the security claims.

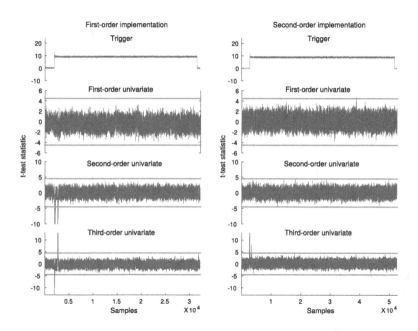

Fig. 3. Results of the first-, second- and third-order univariate analysis on the first- and second-order PRESENT S-box implementations.

We also performed a preliminary bivariate analysis. To this end, we preprocess each trace by first centering around a mean and then multiplying all possible pairs of time samples within a trace. This means that an m-sample trace is expanded into a $\binom{m}{2}$-sample trace, which results in a substantial increase in the computational and memory requirements. Then, a leakage test is performed on the preprocessed traces. To speed up the bivariate analysis, we opted for compressing the traces by a factor of 100.

As in the univariate case, we first carry out a sanity check to verify the soundness of this approach by performing a bivariate second-order analysis on the first-order secure implementation. This is expected to leak, and the results of Fig. 4 confirm this. We obtained t-test statistic values within the region of interest larger than 20, clearly indicating second-order bivariate leakage. These leakages are close to the diagonal, meaning that leakage occurs by combining samples from adjacent clock cycles. The leakage is visible with $200k$ traces.

We repeated the same experiment with the second-order secure implementation and found no value exceeding our confidence threshold of 4.5 with $1M$ traces. This provides some evidence that the second-order implementation indeed may be secure. However, we feel we cannot provide with a definite answer unless we exhaustively cover all possible pairs of time samples (without compression), something that is out of our current computational reach.

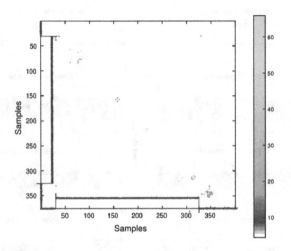

Fig. 4. Result of the second-order bivariate analysis on the first-order PRESENT S-box implementation.

5   Conclusions

We implemented a first- and second-order glitch resistant PRESENT S-box using the polynomial masking scheme presented in [20]. We verified these implementations with both univariate and bivariate attacks and confirmed the claimed SCA resistance. Our implementations resulted in 3594 GE for the first-order and in 8338 GE for the second-order implementation.

Acknowledgments. This work has been supported in part by the Research Council of KU Leuven (OT/13/071 and GOA/11/007), by the FWO (g.0550.12) and by the Hercules foundation (AKUL/11/19). Begül Bilgin was partially supported by the FWO project G0B4213N. Oscar Reparaz is funded by a PhD fellowship of the Fund for Scientific Research - Flanders (FWO).

Appendix A: Finite Field Multiplier

The combinational finite field multiplier in $\mathbb{F}_{2^4}$ used in our implementation is based on the algebraic normal form. The 4-bit inputs $A = (a_3, a_2, a_1, a_0)$ and $B = (b_3, b_2, b_1, b_0)$ result in output $C = (c_3, c_2, c_1, c_0)$ by following bitwise operations:

$$c_0 = (a_0 b_0) + (a_1 b_3) + (a_2 b_2) + (a_3 b_1)$$
$$c_1 = (a_0 b_1) + (a_1 b_0) + (a_1 b_3) + (a_2 b_2) + (a_2 b_3) + (a_3 b_1) + (a_3 b_2)$$
$$c_2 = (a_0 b_2) + (a_1 b_1) + (a_2 b_0) + (a_2 b_3) + (a_3 b_2) + (a_3 b_3)$$
$$c_3 = (a_0 b_3) + (a_1 b_2) + (a_2 b_1) + (a_3 b_0) + (a_3 b_3)$$

where A, B and C are in little-endian notation.

Appendix B: Polynomial Masking Scheme with (5,2)-sharing

This section lists the equations for the construction of, reconstruction from and operations on the shares when considering a (5,2)-sharing. We refer to [16] for a full coverage of the operations in the (3,1)-sharing scheme. In what follows, all additions and multiplications are in $\mathbb{F}_{2^4}$.

First, five distinct non-zero elements in $\mathbb{F}_{2^4}$ need to be chosen. These are referred to as the public coefficients $\alpha_{1 \leq i \leq 5}$. Together with these points, the first row $(\lambda_1, ..., \lambda_5)$ of the inverse Vandermonde matrix $(\alpha_i^j)_{1 \leq i,j \leq 5}$ is needed. These interpolation coefficients can be calculated as:

$$\lambda_1 = \alpha_2(\alpha_1 + \alpha_2)^{-1}\alpha_3(\alpha_1 + \alpha_3)^{-1}\alpha_4(\alpha_1 + \alpha_4)^{-1}\alpha_5(\alpha_1 + \alpha_5)^{-1}$$
$$\lambda_2 = \alpha_1(\alpha_2 + \alpha_1)^{-1}\alpha_3(\alpha_2 + \alpha_3)^{-1}\alpha_4(\alpha_2 + \alpha_4)^{-1}\alpha_5(\alpha_2 + \alpha_5)^{-1}$$
$$\lambda_3 = \alpha_1(\alpha_3 + \alpha_1)^{-1}\alpha_2(\alpha_3 + \alpha_2)^{-1}\alpha_4(\alpha_3 + \alpha_4)^{-1}\alpha_5(\alpha_3 + \alpha_5)^{-1}$$
$$\lambda_4 = \alpha_1(\alpha_4 + \alpha_1)^{-1}\alpha_2(\alpha_4 + \alpha_2)^{-1}\alpha_3(\alpha_4 + \alpha_3)^{-1}\alpha_5(\alpha_4 + \alpha_5)^{-1}$$
$$\lambda_5 = \alpha_1(\alpha_5 + \alpha_1)^{-1}\alpha_2(\alpha_5 + \alpha_2)^{-1}\alpha_3(\alpha_5 + \alpha_3)^{-1}\alpha_4(\alpha_5 + \alpha_4)^{-1}$$

Here, the multiplicative inverse in our field is represented by $.^{-1}$. Elements $\alpha_{1 \leq i \leq 5}$ and $\lambda_{1 \leq i \leq 5}$ are publicly available to all five players.

Sharing a value X requires two secret and random coefficients a_1, a_2 and the public coefficients $\alpha_{1 \leq i \leq 5}$. The resulting shares $X_{1 \leq i \leq 5}$ are calculated as:

$$X_i = X + (a_1\alpha_i) + (a_2\alpha_i^2), \text{ with } 1 \leq i \leq 5$$

Each player receives exactly one share X_i and has no access to any other share.

Reconstruction of the secret value X requires the interpolation coefficients $\lambda_{1 \leq i \leq 5}$:

$$X = (X_1\lambda_1) + (X_2\lambda_2) + (X_3\lambda_3) + (X_4\lambda_4) + (X_5\lambda_5)$$

To describe the operations, a constant value will be represented as c and two secret values as X and Y. Their (5,2)-sharings are given by $X_{1 \leq i \leq 5}$ and $Y_{1 \leq i \leq 5}$. Both are masked with the same public coefficients but use independent random secret coefficients a_1, a_2 and b_1, b_2.

Addition with a constant can be achieved by each player independently as:

$$\begin{aligned}
Z_i &= X_i + c \\
&= (X + (a_1\alpha_i) + (a_2\alpha_i^2)) + c \\
&= (X + c) + (a_1\alpha_i) + (a_2\alpha_i^2), \text{ with } 1 \leq i \leq 5
\end{aligned}$$

The resulting shares of the addition represent the correct new secret $Z = X + c$.

Multiplication with a constant is performed in a similar way and can again be achieved by each player independently:

$$\begin{aligned}
Z_i &= X_i c \\
&= (X + (a_1\alpha_i) + (a_2\alpha_i^2))c \\
&= (Xc) + (a_1 c\alpha_i) + (a_2 c\alpha_i^2), \text{ with } 1 \leq i \leq 5
\end{aligned}$$

Considering $(a_1\ c)$ and $(a_2\ c)$ as the new coefficients of the second-order polynomial, the shares $Z_{1 \leq i \leq 5}$ represent the desired output $Z = Xc$. Note that the reconstruction of the masked secret variable does not depend on the polynomial coefficients a_1, a_2, but on the interpolation coefficients $\lambda_{1 \leq i \leq 5}$, which only depend on the public coefficients $\alpha_{1 \leq i \leq 5}$.

Addition of two shared secrets is executed in following way:

$$\begin{aligned}
Z_i &= X_i + Y_i \\
&= (X + (a_1\alpha_i) + (a_2\alpha_i^2)) + (Y + (b_1\alpha_i) + (b_2\alpha_i^2)) \\
&= (X + Y) + (a_1 + b_1)\alpha_i + (a_2 + b_2)\alpha_i^2, \text{ with } 1 \leq i \leq 5
\end{aligned}$$

With $a_1 + b_1$ and $a_2 + b_2$ as the new polynomial coefficients, the resulting shares mask the desired new secret variable $Z = X + Y$.

Multiplication of two shared secrets consists of the following three steps:

1. Each player i first computes t_i

$$\begin{aligned}
t_i &= X_i Y_i \\
&= (XY) + (a_1 Y + b_1 X)\alpha_i + (a_1 b_1 + a_2 Y + b_2 X)\alpha_i^2 \\
&\quad + (a_1 b_2 + b_1 a_2)\alpha_i^3 + (a_2 b_2)\alpha_i^4, \text{ with } 1 \leq i \leq 5
\end{aligned}$$

2. Each player i then randomly selects two coefficients $a_{i,1}$, $a_{i,2}$ and remasks t_i:

$$q_{i,1} = t_i + (a_{i,1}\alpha_1) + (a_{i,2}\alpha_1^2)$$
$$q_{i,2} = t_i + (a_{i,1}\alpha_2) + (a_{i,2}\alpha_2^2)$$
$$q_{i,3} = t_i + (a_{i,1}\alpha_3) + (a_{i,2}\alpha_3^2)$$
$$q_{i,4} = t_i + (a_{i,1}\alpha_4) + (a_{i,2}\alpha_4^2)$$
$$q_{i,5} = t_i + (a_{i,1}\alpha_5) + (a_{i,2}\alpha_5^2)$$

Each $q_{i,\forall j\neq i}$ is subsequently send to the corresponding player j.
3. The outputs $q_{1,i}$, $q_{2,i}$, $q_{3,i}$ of each player i are then distributed and reconstructed as

$$Z_i = (q_{1,i}\lambda_1) + (q_{2,i}\lambda_2) + (q_{3,i}\lambda_3) + (q_{4,i}\lambda_4) + (q_{5,i}\lambda_5)$$

This sequence of operations gives the shares corresponding to the correct masked result $Z = XY$ in a secure way.

Square of a shared secret can only be computed in the straightforward way, i.e., as $Z = X^2$ or

$$Z_i = Z_i^2 = X^2 + (a_1^2\alpha_i^2) + (a_2^2(\alpha_i^2)^2), \text{ with } 1 \leq i \leq 5$$

when $\alpha_{1\leq i\leq 5}$ satisfy the conditions for frobenious stability. This means that for every α_i, there exists an α_j such that $\alpha_j = \alpha_i^2$. A reordering between every player i and player j satisfying $\alpha_j = \alpha_i^2$ is then required to keep the correct public coefficient linked to its player. When this reordering is not performed, the reconstruction of the correct masked secret $Z = X^2$ is not possible.

Appendix C: Second-order Hardware Architecture

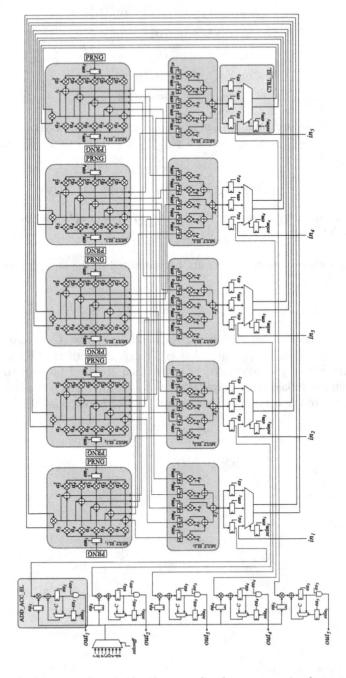

Fig. 5. Architecture diagram for the second-order PRESENT implementation.

Appendix D: Area Requirements for the First-Order and Second-Order present S-box Implementations

Table 3. Area in GE of the first-order and second-order PRESENT S-box implementations.

Component	Area (GE)	
	first-order	second-order
multiplier	47	47
mult_el1	233	639
mult_el2	148	252
shared_mult	1360	4969
add_acc_el	127	127
add_acc	379	630
ctrl_el	120	120
ctrl	352	592
Control unit	1503	2147
S-box	3594	8338

Appendix E: Welch's t-Test

An easy way to test for potential side-channel leakages, which might lead to a successful attack in a cryptographic system, is proposed by Goodwill et al. [7]. Due to its independence of a leakage model, this method is a convenient way to test whether or not the implementation of the device effectively counteracts SCA attacks. Although no single test can guarantee the revelation of all vulnerabilities against all possible SCA attacks, this test is designed to be sensitive enough to cover a wide range of potential problems. After acquisition of a sufficient amount of power traces, the traces are divided in two sets, A and B, based on an intermediate value in the computation. The problem of assessing whether there is potentially exploitable leakage or not is then formulated as an hypothesis test. The null hypothesis corresponds to the statement "the mean power curves of A and B are data-independent". The statistical test is *Welch's t-test*, a generalization of the *Student's t-test* allowing samples to have unequal variances [25]. For the first statistical moment, the t-test statistic is calculated as:

$$t = \frac{\overline{T_a} - \overline{T_b}}{\sqrt{\frac{s_a^2}{N_a} + \frac{s_b^2}{N_b}}}$$

where $\overline{T_i}$, s_i^2, N_i are the sample mean, sample variance and sample size of the set $T_{i \in a,b}$. This formula can easily be extended to higher statistical moments.

The t-test statistic is computed point-wise on the different sets of power traces. If no point exceeds a certain confidence threshold $\pm C$, then the null hypothesis holds, indicating that there is no relation between the processed intermediate value and the instantaneous power consumption. In case the threshold is crossed, another t-test is performed on an independent set of traces. When the t-test statistic exceeds $\pm C$ at the same points in time, the null hypothesis can be rejected with a significance level related to C. In that case, the alternate hypothesis holds, indicating that the power consumption and the intermediate values are related in a statistically significant way, making the device potentially vulnerable to SCA attacks.

Figure 6 shows the resulting t-test statistic in case the alternate hypothesis holds.

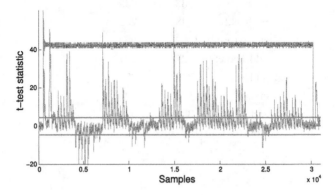

Fig. 6. Result of the t-test for the first-order PRESENT implementation with biased masks.

References

1. Ben-Or, M., Goldwasser, S., Wigderson, A.: Completeness theorems for non-cryptographic fault-tolerant distributed computation. In: Proceedings of the Twentieth Annual ACM Symposium on Theory of Computing, pp. 1–10. ACM, New York, NY, USA (1988)
2. Bogdanov, A., Knudsen, L.R., Leander, G., Paar, C., Poschmann, A., Robshaw, M., Seurin, Y., Vikkelsoe, C.: PRESENT: an ultra-lightweight block cipher. In: Paillier, P., Verbauwhede, I. (eds.) CHES 2007. LNCS, vol. 4727, pp. 450–466. Springer, Heidelberg (2007)
3. Carlet, C., Goubin, L., Prouff, E., Quisquater, M., Rivain, M.: Higher-order masking schemes for S-boxes. In: Canteaut, A. (ed.) FSE 2012. LNCS, vol. 7549, pp. 366–384. Springer, Heidelberg (2012)
4. Chari, S., Jutla, C.S., Rao, J.R., Rohatgi, P.: Towards sound approaches to counteract power-analysis attacks. In: Wiener, M. (ed.) CRYPTO 1999. LNCS, vol. 1666, pp. 398–412. Springer, Heidelberg (1999)
5. Cooper, J., De Mulder, E., Goodwill, G., Jaffe, J., Kenworthy, G., Rohatgi, P.: Test vector leakage assessment (TVLA) methodology in practice. In: International Cryptographic Module Conference (2013). http://icmc-2013.org/wp/wp-content/uploads/2013/09/goodwillkenworthtestvector.pdf
6. Crama, Y., Hammer, P.L.: Boolean Models and Methods in Mathematics, Computer Science, and Engineering, 1st edn. Cambridge University Press, New York (2010)

7. Goodwill, G., Jun, B., Jaffe, J., Rohatgi, P.: A testing methodology for side-channel resistance validation. In: NIST Non-Invasive Attack Testing Workshop (2011). http://csrc.nist.gov/news_events/non-invasive-attack-testing-workshop/papers/08_Goodwill.pdf

8. Goubin, L., Patarin, J.: DES and differential power analysis. In: Koç, Ç.K., Paar, C. (eds.) CHES 1999. LNCS, vol. 1717, pp. 158–172. Springer, Heidelberg (1999)

9. Guo, J., Peyrin, T., Poschmann, A.: The PHOTON family of lightweight hash. In: Rogaway, P. (ed.) CRYPTO 2011. LNCS, vol. 6841, pp. 222–239. Springer, Heidelberg (2011)

10. Guo, J., Peyrin, T., Poschmann, A., Robshaw, M.: The LED block cipher. In: Preneel, B., Takagi, T. (eds.) CHES 2011. LNCS, vol. 6917, pp. 326–341. Springer, Heidelberg (2011)

11. ISO/IEC: ISO/IEC 29192-2. Information technology - Security techniques - Lightweight cryptography - Part 2: Block ciphers. ISO/IEC (2012)

12. Kocher, P.C., Jaffe, J., Jun, B.: Differential power analysis. In: Wiener, M. (ed.) CRYPTO 1999. LNCS, vol. 1666, pp. 388–397. Springer, Heidelberg (1999)

13. Mangard, S., Popp, T., Gammel, B.M.: Side-channel leakage of masked CMOS gates. In: Menezes, A. (ed.) CT-RSA 2005. LNCS, vol. 3376, pp. 351–365. Springer, Heidelberg (2005)

14. Mangard, S., Pramstaller, N., Oswald, E.: Successfully attacking masked AES hardware implementations. In: Rao, J.R., Sunar, B. (eds.) CHES 2005. LNCS, vol. 3659, pp. 157–171. Springer, Heidelberg (2005)

15. Messerges, T.S.: Using Second-order power analysis to attack DPA resistant software. In: Paar, C., Koç, Ç.K. (eds.) CHES 2000. LNCS, vol. 1965, pp. 238–251. Springer, Heidelberg (2000)

16. Moradi, A., Mischke, O.: On the simplicity of converting leakages from multivariate to univariate. In: Bertoni, G., Coron, J.-S. (eds.) CHES 2013. LNCS, vol. 8086, pp. 1–20. Springer, Heidelberg (2013)

17. NanGate Open Cell Library. http://www.nangate.com/

18. Nikova, S., Rechberger, C., Rijmen, V.: Threshold implementations against side-channel attacks and glitches. In: Ning, P., Qing, S., Li, N. (eds.) ICICS 2006. LNCS, vol. 4307, pp. 529–545. Springer, Heidelberg (2006)

19. Poschmann, A., Ling, S., Wang, H.: 256 bit standardized crypto for 650 GE – GOST revisited. In: Mangard, S., Standaert, F.-X. (eds.) CHES 2010. LNCS, vol. 6225, pp. 219–233. Springer, Heidelberg (2010)

20. Prouff, E., Roche, T.: Higher-order glitches free implementation of the AES using secure multi-party computation. IACR Cryptology ePrint Arch. **2011**, 413 (2011)

21. Research Center for Information Security, National Institute of Advanced Industrial Science and Technology: Side-channel Attack Standard Evaluation Board SASEBO-G Specification

22. Shamir, A.: How to share a secret. Commun. ACM **22**(11), 612–613 (1979)

23. Tiri, K., Verbauwhede, I.: A logic level design methodology for a secure DPA resistant ASIC or FPGA implementation. In: Proceedings of the Conference on Design, Automation and Test in Europe DATE 2004, vol. 1, p. 10246. IEEE Computer Society, Washington, DC, USA (2004)

24. Tunstall, M., Benoit, O.: Efficient use of random delays in embedded software. In: Sauveron, D., Markantonakis, K., Bilas, A., Quisquater, J.-J. (eds.) WISTP 2007. LNCS, vol. 4462, pp. 27–38. Springer, Heidelberg (2007)

25. Welch, B.L.: The generalization of 'student's' problem when several different population variances are involved. Biometrika **34**(1/2), 28–35 (1947)

An Elliptic Curve Cryptographic Processor Using Edwards Curves and the Number Theoretic Transform

Nele Mentens[1], Lejla Batina[2], and Selçuk Baktır[3][✉]

[1] KU Leuven, ESAT/COSIC and IMinds,
Kasteelpark Arenberg 10, 3001 Leuven-heverlee, Belgium
nele.mentens@esat.kuleuven.be
[2] Radboud University Nijmegen, Institute for Computing and Information Sciences
(ICIS), 9010, 6500 GL Nijmegen, The Netherlands
lejla@cs.ru.nl
[3] Department of Computer Engineering, Bahçeşehir University,Istanbul, Turkey
selcuk.baktir@bahcesehir.edu.tr

Abstract. Hardware implementations of ECC processors based on
Edwards curves are very useful for various applications of security due
to the regularity of point operations. In this paper we explore one such
direction taking advantage of the DFT modular multiplication in a special composite field of a prime characteristic. Our results show potential
in terms of compactness while maintaining a feasible latency. We expect
this approach to be more beneficial for side-channel security.

Keywords: ECC · Edwards curves · Number theoretic transform · Side-
channel analysis

1 Introduction

Since its invention Elliptic Curve Cryptography (ECC) was recognized as a
proper alternative to classical public-key cryptosystems (such as RSA and other
discrete log-based systems) for constrained devices. In the past two decades,
both theoretical and practical research on ECC had many highlights and ECC-
based primitives are standardized and widely accepted for various applications.
Various trade-offs are also possible in the implementation of ECC. High-speed
implementations, as well as extremely low-cost architectures, have been designed
and implemented by taking advantage of the richness in the algorithm's mathematical structure and the various coordinates, representations and formulae
available.

Edwards curves were proposed for cryptography by Bernstein and Lange [4].
They built upon the work of Edwards who showed that this type of curves allow
for a unified formula replacing the two commonly used point operations i.e. add
and double. This solution is not just more elegant, in terms of feeding all inputs to
the same formula, but it is also more beneficial for side-channel security. Namely,

© Springer International Publishing Switzerland 2015
B. Ors and B. Preneel (Eds.): BalkanCryptSec 2014, LNCS 9024, pp. 94–102, 2015.
DOI: 10.1007/978-3-319-21356-9_7

it is known that using some sort of balanced approach in implementations i.e. side-channel atomicity [6], helps in preventing simple side-channel attacks. For this reason, various methods for balanced scalar multiplication algorithms such as Montgomery ladder, side-channel atomicity etc. were proposed.

In this work, we propose a hardware architecture for ECC using Edwards curves and the number theoretic transform. Our design is optimized on area and speed and it shows to be promising for exploring various trade-offs. For a first evaluation, we consider two architectures, one of which is based on the relevant previous work of Baktir et al. [3] and the other that is novel and improves on the former in terms of area. More precisely, our new architecture explores a way to come up with a more compact solution using this type of mathematical structure. Our results prove this approach to be a viable option for embedded security applications that require public-key solutions.

The remainder of this paper is organized as follows. Section 2 mentions the related work in literature on the implementation of ECC on FPGA. Section 3 provides necessary mathematical background on Edwards curves and the special modular multiplication used. In Sect. 4, we explain the details of our new hardware architecture. The results are given in Sect. 5 including a relevant comparison with some previous works. We conclude this paper in Sect. 6.

2   Related Work

There have been several FPGA implementations of ECC in literature. In [5], a pipelined architecture is implemented for ECC on FPGA. In [16], an ECC implementation is proposed using an optimized bit-parallel squarer and a digit-serial multiplier with a digit size of 16 bits. Another ECC implementation, proposed in [11], uses a digit-serial multiplier and an optimized squarer, with a digit size of 41 bits. In [12], ECC is implemented using a systolic array modular multiplier architecture with a word length of 8 bits. Finally, in [15], an ECC implementation is proposed using the affine coordinates, with an architecture that includes a divider, multiplier and an optimized squarer with a word length of 32 bits.

3   Mathematical Background

Elliptic Curve Cryptography is one of the most popular public-key cryptosystems nowadays. It is the top choice for public-key cryptography on platforms where resources in area, memory, power and energy are sparse such as smart cards, mobile phones and even RFIDs [10]. It was invented in the late 80's independently by N. Koblitz [8] and V. Miller [13] and ever since numerous research results on both, attacks and designs, were published. Yet, up to date no serious attack, for the cases of properly chosen curves and other parameters, is found. Side-channel security is also an active topic for ECC where mainly the work on countermeasures benefited from the richness of mathematical structures behind ECC. For an overview on both theoretical and practical work see [1].

The most straightforward algorithm for point multiplication on an elliptic curve, is the double-and-add algorithm, where a point double is executed for each bit of the scalar and a point addition is executed only if the scalar bit is equal to one. This algorithm has the disadvantage that the power consumption of the implementation reveals the presence of the point addition and thus the value of the scalar bits. To circumvent this, a dummy point addition can be inserted when the evaluated scalar bit is equal to zero. However, this countermeasure does not prevent safe-error attacks, where the attacker checks if the insertion of an error in the dummy operation causes the output to show errors. Another way to prevent Simple Power Analysis (SPA) attacks is the Montgomery ladder for point multiplication [14]. In this case, the operations are balanced for each scalar bit and there are no dummy operations. Another advantage of the Montgomery ladder for elliptic curves, is that the computation of the y-coordinate is not necessary because the difference between the intermediate points Q and S is always equal to P.

Both options above suggest solutions on the point multiplication level. Using Edwards coordinates (and curves) solves the problem on the group operation level i.e. it hinders the distinguishing of point operations (add and double). In addition, it does not bring implementation problems for special cases e.g. when an input or a result is the point at infinity.

3.1   Edwards Curves for Elliptic Curve Cryptography

Edwards curves are a new form of elliptic curves, introduced by Edwards [7] and proposed to be used for cryptographic purposes by Lange and Bernstein [4]. Edward curves allow for using the same arithmetic operations for performing both point addition and point doubling, which can simplify an implementation,

---

Algorithm 1. [2] DFT modular multiplication algorithm for $GF(p^m)$

Require: $(A) \equiv a(x) \in GF(p^m)$, $(B) \equiv b(x) \in GF(p^m)$, $(F) \equiv f(x) \in GF(p^m)$
Ensure: $(C) \equiv a(x) \cdot b(x) \cdot x^{-(m-1)} \bmod f(x) \in GF(p^m)$
1: **for** $i = 0$ to $d - 1$ **do**
2:     $C_i \leftarrow A_i \cdot B_i$
3: **end for**
4: **for** $j = 0$ to $m - 2$ **do**
5:     $S \leftarrow 0$
6:     **for** $i = 0$ to $d - 1$ **do**
7:         $S \leftarrow S + C_i$
8:     **end for**
9:     $S \leftarrow -S/d$
10:     **for** $i = 0$ to $d - 1$ **do**
11:         $C_i \leftarrow (C_i + F_i' \cdot S) \cdot X_i^{-1}$
12:     **end for**
13: **end for**
14: Return (C)

---

e.g. in hardware requiring a smaller control unit, and which can also result in an ECC implementation that is naturally resistant against SPA [9].

In this work, we use the Edwards curve defined by the equation $x^2 + y^2 = c^2(1+dx^2y^2)$ over the finite field $GF(p^m)$ for $c, d \neq 0$ and $dc^4 \neq 1$. On this curve, both elliptic curve point addition and elliptic curve point doubling operations can be performed using the same formula. For the two points $P_1(x_1, y_1), P_2(x_2, y_2)$, where $P_1 = P_2$ or $P_1 \neq P_2$, the point sum $P_3(x_3, y_3)$ can be found as follows:

$$x_3 = \frac{x_1 y_2 + y_1 x_2}{c(1 + dx_1 x_2 y_1 y_2)} \quad \text{and} \quad y_3 = \frac{y_1 y_2 - x_1 x_2}{c(1 - dx_1 x_2 y_1 y_2)} . \tag{1}$$

And the point $\infty = (0, c)$ is the point-at-infinity/identity element of the elliptic curve group defined on this Edwards curve.

3.2 Modular Multiplication Using the Number Theoretic Transform

The *discrete Fourier transform (DFT)* over a finite field $GF(p)$ is called the *number theoretic transform (NTT)* [17]. For a sequence (a) of length d, with coefficients a_i, for $0 \leq i \leq d-1$ in a finite field $GF(q)$, the NTT of (a), denoted

---

Algorithm 2. Pseudo-code for parallelized hardware implementation of DFT modular multiplication in $GF(p^m)$

Require: (A), (B)
Ensure: $(C) \equiv a(x) \cdot b(x) \cdot x^{-(m-1)} \bmod f(x)$
  1: $S \leftarrow 0$
  2: **for** $i = 0$ to $d/2 - 1$ **do**
  3:    $C_{2i} \leftarrow A_{2i} \cdot B_{2i}, \quad C_{2i+1} \leftarrow A_{2i+1} \cdot B_{2i+1}$
  4:    $S \leftarrow S + C_{2i} + C_{2i+1}$
  5: **end for**
  6: **for** $j = 0$ to $m - 2$ **do**
  7:    $S \leftarrow -S/d$
  8:    $S_{even} \leftarrow S \gg 1$
  9:    $S_{odd} \leftarrow (S \gg 1) + (S \gg 2)$
 10:    $S \leftarrow 0$
 11:    **for** $i = 0$ to $d/2 - 1$ **do**
 12:       $C_{2i} \leftarrow C_{2i} + S_{even}, \quad C_{2i+1} \leftarrow -(C_{2i+1} + S_{odd})$
 13:       $S_{even} \leftarrow S_{even} \gg 2$
 14:       $S_{odd} \leftarrow S_{odd} \gg 2$
 15:       **for** $k = i + 1$ to $d/2 - 1$ **do**
 16:          $C_{2k} \leftarrow C_{2k} \gg 2$
 17:          $C_{2k+1} \leftarrow C_{2k+1} \gg 2$
 18:       **end for**
 19:       $S \leftarrow S + C_{2i} + C_{2i+1}$
 20:    **end for**
 21: **end for**
 22: Return (C)

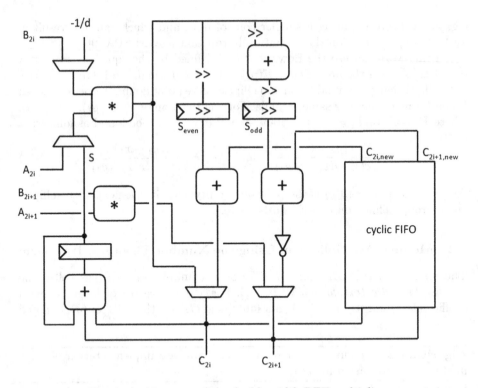

Fig. 1. Architecture of the double-width DFT multiplier

by (A), with coefficients A_i, for $0 \le i \le d-1$ also in $GF(p)$, can be computed by using a dth primitive root of unity $r \in GF(p)$ as follows:

$$A_j = \sum_{i=0}^{d-1} a_i r^{ij} \ , \ 0 \le j \le d-1 \ . \tag{2}$$

And the inverse NTT of (A) over $GF(p)$ can similarly be computed as

$$a_i = \frac{1}{d} \cdot \sum_{j=0}^{d-1} A_j r^{-ij} \ , \ 0 \le i \le d-1 \ . \tag{3}$$

We call the sequences (a) and (A) as the *time and frequency domain representations*, respectively, for the same sequence.

The *DFT Modular Multiplication* algorithm [2], given in Algorithm 1, performs Montgomery multiplication of elements in $GF(p^m)$ in the frequency domain. The inputs to the algorithm are the operands $a(x), b(x) \in GF(p^m)$ and the field polynomial $f(x)$, and the output is $c(x) = a(x) \cdot b(x) \cdot x^{-(m-1)}$ mod $f(x) \in GF(p^m)$, all in the frequency domain. In this work, we implement ECC over the finite field $GF((2^{13}-1)^{13})$ by utilizing Montgomery multiplication based on both Algorithm 1 and a parallelized version of Algorithm 1. Since our

Algorithm 3. Unified formula for elliptic curve point addition in projective coordinates using Edwards curves

---

Require: $P_1(X_1, Y_1, Z_1)$ and $P_2(X_2, Y_2, Z_2)$
Ensure: $P_3(X_3, X_3, X_3) = P_1 + P_2$
1: $R_1 \leftarrow X_1,\ R_2 \leftarrow Y_1,\ R_3 \leftarrow Z_1,\ R_4 \leftarrow X_2,\ R_5 \leftarrow Y_2,\ R_6 \leftarrow Z_2$
2: $R_3 \leftarrow R_3 \cdot R_6$
3: $R_7 \leftarrow R_1 + R_2$
4: $R_8 \leftarrow R_4 + R_5$
5: $R_1 \leftarrow R_1 \cdot R_4$
6: $R_2 \leftarrow R_2 \cdot R_5$
7: $R_7 \leftarrow R_7 \cdot R_8$
8: $R_7 \leftarrow R_7 - R_1$
9: $R_7 \leftarrow R_7 - R_2$
10: $R_7 \leftarrow R_7 \cdot R_3$
11: $R_8 \leftarrow R_1 \cdot R_2$
12: $R_8 \leftarrow d \cdot R_8$
13: $R_2 \leftarrow R_2 - R_1$
14: $R_2 \leftarrow R_2 \cdot R_3$
15: $R_3 \leftarrow R_3^2$
16: $R_1 \leftarrow R_3 - R_8$
17: $R_3 \leftarrow R_3 + R_8$
18: $R_2 \leftarrow R_2 \cdot R_3$
19: $R_3 \leftarrow R_3 \cdot R_1$
20: $R_1 \leftarrow R_1 \cdot R_7$
21: $R_3 \leftarrow c \cdot R_3$
22: $X_3 \leftarrow R_1,\ Y_3 \leftarrow R_2,\ Z_3 \leftarrow R_3$

---

base field is $GF(2^{13} - 1)$, we have a word length of 13-bits for the performed arithmetic operations.

4 Architecture of the ECC Processor

4.1 Modular Multiplier

The architecture of the NTT modular multiplication is based on the work of Baktir et al. [3]. We implemented two multiplier architectures. The first one corresponds to the architecture in [3], processing 13-bit words. The second architecture is new and has a bus width of 2 times 13 bits, following Algorithm 2. The new architecture is depicted in Fig. 1. In comparison to the architecture in [3], our new architecture needs an extra 13-bit multiplier, an extra 13-bit adder and a double-width cyclic FIFO. Note that we need less multiplexers than the architecture of Baktir et al. [3], which reduces the critical path of our architecture.

4.2 Control Logic

For our ECC implementations, we use Edwards curves in projective coordinates. The point operations are performed using the unified formula [4], given in Algorithm 3. Each operation is performed sequentially in time, which comes down to

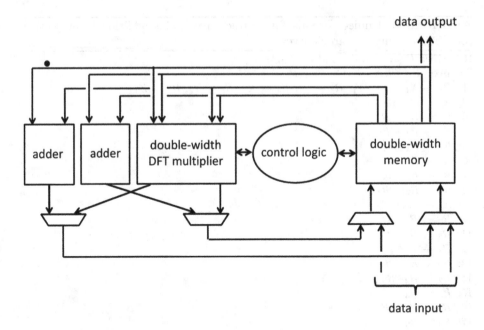

Fig. 2. Top-level architecture of the ECC processor

a finite state machine that fetches the inputs from the registers, initiates a point addition or subtraction, and writes back the result to the memory for each step of Algorithm 3.

4.3   Top-Level Architecture

In Fig. 2 the top-level architecture is depicted. It consists of the double-width multiplier and two parallel single-width adders. For each double-width addition, the two adders are used in parallel. The control logic implements the formulae for point multiplication on Edwards curves. The memory stores the intermediate results in words of $2 \cdot 13$ bits.

5   Implementation Results

As shown in Table 1, our architectures occupy far less slices than the other architectures in literature, although we must note that older Xilinx FPGAs consist of 4-input LUTs, while the Virtex-5 FPGA that we use, contains 6-input LUTs. In terms of latency, our architecture is slower than the others' results listed in the table. Comparing our architectures to each other shows that the double-width architecture operates at a higher frequency than the single-width architecture and uses less cycles to complete one point multiplication. The area of the double-width architecture is less than double of the area of the single-width architecture.

Table 1. Timing and area comparison for point multiplication of random points

Work	Platform	Freq. (MHz)	Key Length	Method	Slices	LUTs	Gates	Time (μs)
Ours 13 bits	XC5VFX70TF-FG1136	27	169	Binary	644	1981	–	42068
Ours 2 · 13 bits	XC5VFX70TF-FG1136	32	169	Binary	1001	2336	–	18425
Chelton [5]	Virtex-E	91	163	Montgomery	15368	–	–	33.05
Chelton [5]	Virtex-4	154	163	Montgomery	16209	–	–	19.55
Orlando [16]	XCV400E	76.7	167	Montgomery	–	3002	–	210
Lutz [11]	XCV2000E	66	163	Binary (Koblitz)	–	10017	–	264
Mentens [12]	XCV800	50.1	163	Binary	–	–	150678	3801
Morales [15]	Virtex-4	100	163	Binary	3528	–	–	1070

6   Conclusions and Future Work

In this work, we investigate the feasibility of hardware architectures for Elliptic Curve Cryptography using Edwards curves and the number theoretic transform. Our new architecture is optimized on both area and speed compared to a previously designed similar architecture and especially the compactness of our solution is very promising. Further on, the design exhibits some new trade-offs based on the specifics of the mathematical structure. For a first evaluation, we consider two architectures, one of which is based on the relevant previous work of Baktir et al. [3] and the other that is novel and improves on the former in terms of area. More in detail, our new architecture explores new avenues in finding compact ECC implementations for pervasive security that could provide an improved side-channel resistance. As future work, we will look into other architectural improvements and evaluate the side-channel security of the processor.

Acknowledgments. Dr. Baktır's work is supported by the grant EU FP7 Marie Curie IRG 256544.

References

1. Avanzi, R.M., Cohen, H., Doche, C., Frey, G., Lange, T., Nguyen, K., Vercauteren, F.: Handbook of Elliptic and Hyperelliptic Curve Cryptography. Chapman & Hall/CRC, Boca Raton (2005)
2. Baktır, S., Sunar, B.: Finite field polynomial multiplication in the frequency domain with application to elliptic curve cryptography. In: Levi, A., Savaş, E., Yenigün, H., Balcısoy, S., Saygın, Y. (eds.) ISCIS 2006. LNCS, vol. 4263, pp. 991–1001. Springer, Heidelberg (2006)
3. Baktır, S., Kumar, S., Paar, C., Sunar, B.: A state-of-the-art elliptic curve cryptographic processor operating in the frequency domain. Mob. Netw. Appl. **12**(4), 259–270 (2007)
4. Bernstein, D.J., Lange, T.: Faster addition and doubling on elliptic curves. In: Kurosawa, K. (ed.) ASIACRYPT 2007. LNCS, vol. 4833, pp. 29–50. Springer, Heidelberg (2007)
5. Chelton, W.N., Benaissa, M.: Fast elliptic curve cryptography on FPGA. IEEE Trans. Very Large Scale Integr. Syst. **16**(2), 198–205 (2008)

6. Chevallier-Mames, B., Ciet, M., Joye, M.: Low-cost solutions for preventing simple side-channel analysis: side-channel atomicity. IEEE Trans. Comput. **53**(6), 760–768 (2004)
7. Edwards, H.M.: A normal form for elliptic curves. Bull. Am. Math. Soc. **44**, 393–422 (2007)
8. Koblitz, N.: Elliptic curve cryptosystem. Math. Comp. **48**, 203–209 (1987)
9. Kocher, P.C., Jaffe, J., Jun, B.: Differential power analysis. In: Wiener, M. (ed.) CRYPTO 1999. LNCS, vol. 1666, p. 388. Springer, Heidelberg (1999)
10. Lee, Y.K., Sakiyama, K., Batina, L., Verbauwhede, I.: Elliptic curve based security processor for RFID. IEEE Transact. Comput. **57**(11), 1514–1527 (2008)
11. Lutz, J., Hasan, A.: High performance FPGA based elliptic curve cryptographic co-processor. In: Proceedings of the International Conference on Information Technology: Coding and Computing (ITCC 2004), vol. 2, p. 486. IEEE Computer Society (2004)
12. Mentens, N., ïrs, S.B., Preneel, B.: An FPGA implementation of an elliptic curve processor $GF(2^m)$. In: Proceedings of the 14th ACM Great Lakes Symposium on VLSI, GLSVLSI 2004, pp. 454–457. ACM (2004)
13. Miller, V.S.: Use of elliptic curves in cryptography. In: Williams, H.C. (ed.) CRYPTO 1985. LNCS, vol. 218, pp. 417–426. Springer, Heidelberg (1986)
14. Montgomery, P.: Speeding the pollard and elliptic curve methods of factorization. Math. Comput. **48**(177), 243–264 (1987)
15. Morales-Sandoval, M., Feregrino-Uribe, C., Cumplido, R., Algredo-Badillo, I.: A reconfigurable $GF(2^m)$ elliptic curve cryptographic coprocessor. In: 2011 VII Southern Conference on Programmable Logic (SPL), pp. 209–214, April 2011
16. Orlando, G., Paar, C.: A high-performance reconfigurable elliptic curve processor for $GF(2^m)$. In: Koç, Ç.K., Paar, C. (eds.) CHES 2000. LNCS, vol. 1965, p. 41. Springer, Heidelberg (2000)
17. Pollard, J.M.: The fast fourier transform in a finite field. Math. Comput. **25**, 365–374 (1971)

Preventing Scaling of Successful Attacks: A Cross-Layer Security Architecture for Resource-Constrained Platforms

Christian T. Zenger[1]([✉]), Abhijit Ambekar[2], Fredrik Winzer[1],
Thomas Pöppelmann[1], Hans D. Schotten[2], and Christof Paar[1]

[1] Horst Görtz Institute for IT-Security (HGI),
Ruhr-University Bochum, Bochum, Germany
{christian.zenger,fredrik.winzer,thomas.poeppelmann,
christof.paar}@rub.de
[2] Chair for Wireless Communications and Navigation,
University of Kaiserslautern, Kaiserslautern, Germany
{ambekar,schotten}@eit.uni-kl.de

Abstract. Key-establishment based on parameters of the communication channels is a highly attractive option for many applications that operate in a dynamic mobile environment with peer-to-peer association. So far, high usability and dynamic key management with the capability of perfect forward secrecy are very difficult to achieve for wireless devices which have to operate under strict resource constraints. Additionally, previous work has failed to address hybrid systems composed of physical layer security (PHYSEC) and asymmetric cryptography for key establishment. In this work we present the first hybrid system architecture suitable for resource-constrained platforms. As a result, long term deployment due to key diversity and forward/backward secrecy can be achieved while still satisfying the tight timing of an initial setup imposed by high user acceptance. Our design strongly focuses on reusing communication chip components for PHYSEC and makes use of efficient asymmetric cryptography (e.g., ECDH) augmented by physical layer security. Our prototype implementation demonstrates that our approach has the potential to dramatically reduce the cost of securing small embedded devices for the Internet of Things, and hence make mass production and deployment viable.

Keywords: Channel-based key establishment · Cross-layer protocol · Forward secrecy · Backward secrecy · Scaling of attacks · Internet of Things

1 Introduction

With increasing popularity of the wireless interconnection of small embedded systems, the so-called Internet of Things (IoT), new challenges regarding secu-

---

C. T. Zenger, A. Ambekar, F. Winzer and H.D. Schotten, and C. Paar — This author was supported in part by BMBF within the project Providing Physical Layer Security for the Internet of Things (PROPHYLAXE) (Grant 16KIS0008 and 16KIS0010).

B. Ors and B. Preneel (Eds.): BalkanCryptSec 2014, LNCS 9024, pp. 103–120, 2015.
DOI: 10.1007/978-3-319-21356-9_8

rity and privacy arise [13, 21, 42]. Due to limitations with regard to the available powerbudget and computational resources, established complex asymmetric protocols like the Transport Layer Security (TLS) protocol can often not be employed. Moreover, there are important economical and technical benefits resulting from minimal power consumption for security functions. As an example, a targeted lifetime of a battery-powered resource-constrained device in the order of 5–10 years would reduce maintenance costs and allow deployment at difficult to reach locations or unconventional application scenarios. Even though privacy and security properties are a fundamental requirement it is highly desirable that the energy consumed by a key establishment procedure should not lead to a significantly shorter energy lifetime and shall therefore be in the order of only a small percentage of the totally available energy. We would like to note that key establishment is fundamental operation in virtually every security solution. Therefore, several important IoT-related requirements are identified which can benefit from the system proposed in this paper, especially:

1. **Resource and cost constraints**. A central characteristic of many IoT systems is that they are cost-sensitive and thus, constrained with respect to computational resources and energy consumption without influencing usability. The latter is particularly pressing in the case of increasingly common wireless applications, which run on battery or energy harvesting [13]. Traditionally, small embedded systems are secured using (lightweight) symmetric cryptography even though this results in inflexible key distribution and management. Moreover, requirements like forward secrecy and backward secrecy (cf. [33]), also called perfect forward secrecy (PFS)[1], cannot be met using only symmetric cryptography. However, while asymmetric approaches allow for a much improved key management they result in long (sometimes unacceptably long) processing times, a large code size, and considerably energy consumption during encryption and transmission.

2. **Long term deployment**. Systems designed for a long life-cycle require stable parameters. While successful attacks on well-studied symmetric cryptography are rare the correct implementation of asymmetric systems is challenging on constrained devices [7, 27]. Overly loose security services, such as key diversity, leads to attacks, such as those illustrated by Eisenbarth et al. [19] and Strobel et al. [47]. Once they recovered the key, provided to all potential communication partners before deployment, the security posture of the entire system (maybe of the entire product batch) collapses. Given the lifespan of some decades of some Internet of Things application [13], it can be an advantage of have alternative solutions available.

---

[1] Locking previous traffic securely in the past is the main idea of perfect forward secrecy (PFS) [36]. The definition of PFS saying that compromising a long-term key does not compromise past session keys is, in our opinion, not complete. Our scheme does provide PFS without a long-term key, which leads additionally to long-term key independence of future traffic.

1.1   Physical Layer Security

Physical Layer Security (PHYSEC) introduced by Hershey et al. [28] is an alternative paradigm for generating shared secret keys. The approach is based on a common estimation of the wireless channel by the sender and receiver, whereby symmetric secret keys are derived from the common channel parameters. Without taking noise, interferences and non-linear components into account, the joint randomness of the symmetric key relies on the principle of *channel reciprocity* [31,44]. In other words, the radio channel from Alice to Bob is similar to the channel from Bob to Alice. For most practical channels this reciprocity property holds and the entropy of spatial, temporal, and spectral characteristics is sufficiently high due to unpredictable dynamics in the environment. Due to the *channel diversity* [22], security is established if an attacker's distance to the legitimate nodes is far enough so that the observed channel parameters to each node are uncorrelated and independent. Typically, in real environments this is given if the distance is greater than about half of the carrier wavelength [31]. For instance, for 2.4 GHz WiFi this translates to the relatively short distance of 6.25 cm. Because of the fact that eavesdropping PHYSEC strongly depends on the eavesdroppers position, most common attack vectors are not possible any more. As an example, for classical eavesdropping a directional antenna could be used from a greater distance. However, with PHYSEC it is ensured that from such a location no meaningful information can be obtained. This increases security as in many applications, e.g., Smart Factory systems [13].

1.2   Related Work

Most of the key establishment protocols that are used nowadays in wireless applications make use of manually configured symmetric keys [9]. However, those are not suitable for embedded devices without input options or displays as users have no means to enter or change keys easily. Also, pre-shared key solutions tend not to scale very well. Further, widely established are the IEEE 802.11 standards but they have serious security issues, e.g., in the WiFi Proteced Setup (WPS) standard [20,49]. Additionally, the aforementioned standards suffer from the lack of perfect forward secrecy [8] for an easy and efficient implementation. Furthermore, there exist many asymmetric protocols with PFS. Diffie et al. [15] presented the station-to-station protocol as key agreement with mutual entity authentication protocol with PFS. It performs a Diffie-Hellman key exchange with signed public keys. There are more asymmetric protocols with PFS [12,38,53]. However, all these protocols require asymmetric cryptography with cubic complexity regarding key size, which are not applicable on resource-constrained platforms.

1.3   Contribution

By focusing on resource-constraints and costs, this paper presents an evolutionary and energy efficient design of a *Channel-Based Key Establishment (CBKE)*

106 C.T. Zenger et al.

system for (wireless) IoT applications. For our PHYSEC design two design ideas are introduced: the passive salvaging of channel profile information provided by almost every wireless chip and the reusing of existing building blocks, and hardware modules of communication systems in order to profitably exploit the reciprocal variations of the wireless channel. Therefore, a novel methodology of enhancing channel reciprocity via Kalman filters is presented. Further, we show how errors in initial key material can be detected and corrected using BCH codes. To guarantee the security of the information reconciliation procedure we introduce the execution of an entropy estimator. Additionally, we evaluate how long it takes to establish a symmetric key with a security level of 128 bit. For the evaluation we implemented the Kalman filter and several PHYSEC quantization schemes from the literature as well as an information reconciliation scheme using BCH codes [41]. The duration of key generation via PHYSEC strongly depends on the channel and its entropy. Therefore, no guarantee of a fixed duration time for the key establishment can be made, which collides with the demand of a tight timing behavior of pairing protocols imposed by high user acceptance. We introduce the first hybrid security system, consisting of physical layer techniques and asymmetric cryptography. Our cross-layer protocol combines the advantages of both techniques to achieve *usable security*, which means fast individual pairing and highly efficient PFS and key diversity on resource-constrained platforms. Due to this hybrid approach the attack surface of using classical cryptanalysis is quite low and we can thus save a considerable amount of energy.

2 Adversary Model

We design a *PHYSEC for IoT*-architecture in a strong adversarial model that assumes the presence of an attacker during the initial authentication and key establishment session and during all further rekeying phases (at all times). We consider passive attackers eavesdropping the communication on the wireless channel and trying to reconstruct the channel measurements for gaining the initial key material and therefore the resulting secret key for encrypted communication. We also consider active attackers who are able to inject packages into the broadcast channel. The goal of the attacker in our scenario is to steal personal information and manipulate or fake internal information, e.g., provided by a sensor. Imagine a smart factory system where a single center node is communicating with multiple sensors and actuators. For this they are using a single fixed channel in time division duplex mode, which is a classical approach [11,23]. We do not consider hardware modification, Denial-of-Service attacks, or advanced active attacks, such as undetectable man-in-the-middle/masquerade attacks [43]. Those attackers require techniques to minimizes its risk of being detected. Therefore, an attacker has to be able to destroy only selected packets that are already on the air. Therefore, successful MITM-attacks requires reactive jamming and are difficult to achieve [52]. For the authentication of new small embedded systems without input options or display we recommend a user interactive authentication. Like the widely used push-button-method [1,6,14]. Here the user simply has to push a button, either on the node and the new sensor/actuator. This triggers the pairing protocol based on asymmetrical cryptography. After a short time period, the user gets a graphical feedback.

3 An Evolutionary Security Architecture for IoT

Shared secrets can be extracted by considering the framework as shown in Fig. 1. Initially the channel measurements are conducted within the so called coherence time, to obtain reciprocal channel profiles. The passive salvage of channel profiles is focused. Next we look for turning channel profiles into keys.

3.1 Passively Salvaging of Channel Profile Information

Due to the multi-path propagation of the transmitted signal, variations in amplitude and phase of the received signal occur. The variations of the channel are measured using various methods to construct the *channel profile*. Typically, such variations are characterized by the received signal strength indicator (RSSI) [2,32,34,40] and the Channel Impulse Response (CIR) [26,34,55] of the channel. All modern mobile communication systems estimate the channel profile in real-time for link adaptation. Thus by re-using the channel profile information either in form of impulse response or RSSI, variations of the channel can be obtained in real-time in existing systems. And by using these reciprocal variations, shared secrets can be established between legitimate nodes of wireless networks. Establishing bidirectional communication merely to mutually measure the channel is highly inefficient and inapplicable on mobile and resource-constrained devices. Therefore, we introduce channel measurement based on passively salvaging of channel profile information from independent application layer communication, without influencing those.

3.2 Turning Channel Profiles into Symmetric Keys

Our system for generating secret keys from channel profiles is based on [54]. These profiles are quantized into vector bits to obtain an initial preliminary key.

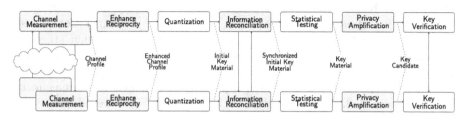

Fig. 1. Overview of the components involved in the evolutionary security architecture for IoT: Extracting shared secret keys from variations of the channel. The grey blocks are available in virtually every wireless communication chip and could be reused.

The non perfect reciprocity in measurement, half-duplexity, and noise, leads to errors in the vector bits of the preliminary key. These errors are detected and corrected in the information reconciliation stage by using error correcting techniques. Since information for error detection and correction is exchanged over the channel during the information reconciliation stage, further enhancement of entropy is done in the privacy amplification stage.

Enhancing Channel Reciprocity: Generally channel profiles are quantized directly to obtain preliminary keys. However channel measurements are not always perfectly reciprocal due to the half-duplex nature of measurements, hardware non-linearity, and noise in the circuitry. We consider the approach of pre-processing the channel profile first instead of quantizing them directly. We use *Kalman filtering* to process the channel profile and enhance its reciprocity [2]. The Kalman filter, also known as linear quadratic estimation, was first described in technical papers by Swerling in 1958, Rudolf Kalman in 1960, and Kalman and Bucy in 1961 [51]. Kalman filter recursively estimates the state of a process by using apriori and aposteriori estimations such that, the mean of the squared error is minimised [51]. Typical chip-sets using Kalman filter include [4].

Quantization: The constructed channel profiles are quantized into vector bits to obtain a *preliminary key*. Quantisation can be done either on the whole block of the profile or on smaller blocks of the profile. Typical quantisation algorithms include; ASBG [32], Adaptive quantisation [2], multi-bit adaptive quantisation [39], Channel Quantisation with Guard-band [50]. We apply several schemes and as part of our contribution we evaluate the efficiency later on.

Entropy Estimation/Statistical Testing: The radio channel changing over time is utilized as a common random number generator. A random number generator is a critical component in every cryptographic device. As introduced in [54], an important security feature of the PHYSEC system design is a statistical test to provide online entropy testing. In our opinion a statistical test is urgently needed especially to guarantee that possible biases of the channel profiles combined with the public transmitted reconciliation data do not reveal the entire key material. Additionally, with the entropy estimated of the initial key material the collection of the amount of entropy required can be verified. For system we chose the health test of *Intel's Ivy Bridge* random number generator [25].

Information Reconciliation: The non perfect reciprocity in measurement, half-duplexity, and noise, leads to errors in vector bits of preliminary key. These errors are detected and corrected in the information reconciliation stage by applying BCH codes [41]. For reconciliation we use the well known BCH codes since most of the present day communication systems are equipped with it [30,45]. We utilize the syndrome-based approach based in secure sketch as introduced by Dodis et al. [16] and applied for PHYSEC by Edman et al. [18].

Privacy Amplification: Uniformly distributed and precisely reproducible random strings are the initial requirement for cryptographic secrets. If those requirements are not entirely fulfilled for a random variable, privacy amplification is required [29]. Moreover, during the reconciliation phase the eavesdropper will also have access to the error correcting bits. To avoid the possibilities of key predictions and to collect the entropy estimated of the initial key material, we apply a universal hash function for privacy amplification (e.g., SHA-3 [10]).

Key Verification: In [46] protocol 9.4 a mutual challenge-and-response protocol is described. We use this protocol to determine, if both parties assure the other they know the same key.

4   Physical Layer Security Meets Asymmetric Cryptography

Management of keys is one of the most complicated issues in almost every secure communication system (see Sect. 1). Both, symmetric or asymmetrical approaches for resource-constrained platforms have proved either too energy consumptive in the actual key establishment (usually asymmetric) or inflexible in the key management procedures (usually symmetric) [36].

While a PHYSEC system is less complex than asymmetric approaches, the execution time strongly depends on the entropy rate gained of the individual channel. Therefore, key generation is not applicable for time-critical applications. As a consequence we propose and analyze a two staged approach. In stage (1) asymmetrical cryptography is used to authenticate a session with low latency and after time t_{PHY} the system enters stage (2) where a secret symmetric key is established using physical layer security. Thus in stage (1) we do not need security against an attacker with unbounded computation time as the asymmetric key establishment just has to hold till the system enters stage (2). This allows us to relax the parameters for the asymmetric schemes and thus saves energy and computation time. This is especially helpful due to the cubic complexity of RSA and ECC. The minimum key length then depends on the resources of a possible attacker and the time the system is deployed in order to take Moore's law into account. As an example, a device could perform an ECDH key exchange with roughly 100–130 bit (50–75 bit of symmetric security) and then switch after 12 h to stage (2) using the properties of the physical layer. We evaluate real-world duration times t_{PHY} of a channel-based key establishment later on.

4.1   Short Asymmetric Keys

Against conventional approaches, small platforms can perform an initial key exchange/pairing, e.g., ECDH, with very short keys, even if they operate under strict resource constraints. ECC has a cubic complexity regarding the key length, therefore the energy consumption and processing time decreases sharply by reducing the key length. The advantage of ECDH with very short keys is the usability of the very fast and deterministic (regarding execution time) authentication process on devices, which have to operate under strict resource constraints. The authentication process is based on a key agreement in trusted environment/time. The stage (1) with short keys adds a method to authenticate the devices without an impact on usability because of the long time for PHYSEC-based key establishment. Because of its shortness, the *key* k_0 is not long-term secure and does not provide confidentiality, although authentication. As described above, within a (budget-depending) predefined period of time, an attacker cannot impersonalize for instance a sensor for sending authenticated messages. Another feature of interest is that within this period of time the credentials for authentication can be inherited as we demonstrate later on.

We think that the role of asymmetric cryptographic in our approach has also a contribution to the security. Eberz et al. [17] presented an attack where he was able to manipulate a PHYSEC scheme by injecting unauthenticated packets. An asymmetric key used for preventing such active injection attacks.

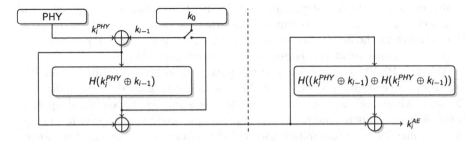

Fig. 2. The iterative key refreshing algorithm provides forward and backward secrecy by hashing the key k_{i-1} and the PHYSEC key k_i^{PHY} together to form later a new session key k_i^{AE}. Key k_0 may not be long-term secure, but its property of authentication is transferred to future keys.

4.2 Asymmetric Cryptography Meets Physical Layer Security

We propose a two stage approach to eliminate the problems introduced in the previous Sects. 1 and 4.1. In this subsection, we explain how to add long term security, such as PFS, on a resource-constrained platform. In the stages we will combine PHYSEC with an asymmetrical key establishment to reach a symbiotic gain shown in Fig. 2. In stage (1) asymmetrical cryptography is used to authenticate a session with low latency and after time t_{PHY} the system enters stage (2) where a secret is established using physical layer security. The key is refreshed periodically after entering stage (2) with PHYSEC. Time t_{PHY} depends on the amount of entropy commonly extracted out of the channel. According to the environment it can vary between seconds and days. In stage (1) an asymmetrical key establishment is used to establish a key k_0 fast and authenticated trough the user. As described above, we expect that after a budget dependent time period the key will be successfully attacked because of its shortness. An important point to mention is that this first step adds a method to establish a key k_0 while devices are assumed to be authentic without an impact on usability because of the non-determinable time needed by PHYSEC-based key establishment. In stage (2), started with the first established PHYSEC key k_1^{PHY}. For our scheme we extended the forward and enhanced backward secrecy construction for random number generator presented in [33] by repeatedly refreshing k_i^{PHY}. Key k_1^{PHY} adds confidentiality to the system by getting hashed with k_0 to output the first key $k_1^{AE} = (k_0 \oplus k_1^{PHY}) \oplus H(k_0 \oplus k_1^{PHY}) \oplus H((k_0 \oplus k_1^{PHY}) \oplus H(k_0 \oplus k_1^{PHY}))$. The right part of the equation (as well as of the Fig. 2) protects previous outputs against an adversary who knows the current key material k_{i-1} and k_i^{PHY} of the system and the current and future output k_i^{AE}. We assume, that H is a cryptographic hash function described above and k_1^{PHY} has a security level of at least 128 bit. We assume, that k_0 is only known by the devices and cannot be revealed in stage (1). So the user authenticates the devices by establishing k_0, e.g., by push-button-method. Accessing stage (2) combines the authenticated key k_0 with the PHYSEC key k_1^{PHY}, so an attacker cannot calculate k_1^{AE}, even if he later can reveal k_0. After entering stage (2) the devices generate continuously new keys $k_i^{AE} = (k_{i-1} \oplus k_{i-1}^{PHY}) \oplus H(k_{i-1} \oplus k_{i-1}^{PHY}) \oplus H((k_{i-1} \oplus k_{i-1}^{PHY}) \oplus H(k_{i-1} \oplus k_{i-1}^{PHY}))$ clocked by PHYSEC. This key history provides backward secrecy and forces an attacker to reveal a new k_i^{PHY} and knowing the old k_i to calculate k_{i+1}. So if H is preimage resistant, it is not possible to calculate new or old session keys from revealing a session key or the first key k_0. This is very important to prevent successful implementation attack, e.g., a side-channel attack on the authenticated-encryption (AE) scheme the key was generated for, from scaling.

Our system offers perfect forward secrecy (with regard to the lifetime of a key) without public key cryptography by continuously hashing and generating fresh keys, because the attacker shall not be able to determine the next random number provided by the channel. Keys are mutually independent between pairs of nodes and thus a compromise of a single node does not scale. In summary, the symbiotic combination of asymmetric key establishment methods and PHYSEC offers cheap PFS and provides authentication with usability for resource-constrained platforms.

5   Prototype Implementation

With focus on a real-world scenario, we chose two hardware platforms for our prototypical implementation. As a representative for an access point (as well as for further stationary nodes) we chose the *WRT54GL WiFi router* from Cisco-Linksys, equipped with open source firmware and the BCM2050 2.4 GHz radio chip. A very small and cheap platform is the *WiFi DipCortex* [35]. It is equipped with an NXP ARM Cortex M3 LPC1347 and a TI SimpleLink CC3000 WiFi module and represents the typical WiFi sensor or actuator. The key generation scheme is based on network management traffic generated by an independent application. Our prototype implementation utilizes the channel estimation provided by those transaction. We chose WiFi chips implementing the MAC-layer in software, thus we could extended the respective software drivers. We added an interface into the driver to read out the RSSI values of each IEEE 802.11

packet. For each experiment the platforms commonly measured the channel at least 30,000 times with a sampling rate of one RSSI value per second. Therefore, each set of measurement was achieved over a period of more than 8 h.

5.1   Experimental Measurement Setup

For evaluation of the duration time for generating keys with 128 bit security level, we present three experimental measurements setups, shown in Fig. 3. In *setup 1* Bob B_s is stationary placed 8 meter apart from Alice A, so channel variation is caused by movement in the environment, e.g., by moving people. In *setup 2* Bob B_d is cyclically moving on an ellipse with a constant velocity of 0.45 m/s. In *setup 3* Bob B_r is moving randomly within the area of the ellipse. Additionally, each setup introduces three eavesdropper E_1, E_2, and E_3 at different positions given in Fig. 3. Alice (A) and Bob (B_x), and Eves E_1, E_2, E_3 apply reciprocity enhancement, quantization, information reconciliation, health testing, and privacy amplification, as presented in Sect. 3. The passive attackers E_i applies its correlated observation in the same system configuration than Alice and Bob for achieving the secret key. To evaluate the impact of the pre-computation we evaluated the measurement with and without Kalman filter. For quantization we implemented and evaluated several schemes proposed by Tope et al. [48], Aono et al. [5], Mathur et al. [34], Jana et al. [32], and Ambekar et al. [3]. The information reconciliation is applied by $BCH(n, k, d)$ codes as presented by Edman et al. [18]. We apply all codes of length $n = 63$ to evaluate the best combination for quantizer and code-parameter.

5.2   Results

Unlike to previous work we evaluate the security level instead of simply the number of synchronized bits between Alice and Bob. Additionally, we focus on the establishment of secret symmetric keys with a security level of 128 bit (based on the on-line statistical testing). Next we evaluate the required duration time

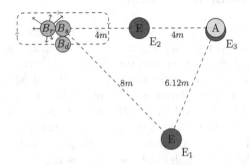

Fig. 3. Experimental measurement setups including access point Alice (A), wireless sensor node Bob stationary (B_s), cyclic moving (B_d), and randomly moving (B_r) and the eavesdropper Eve placed away from Alice and Bob (E_1), between Alice and Bob (E_2), and next to Alice (E_3).

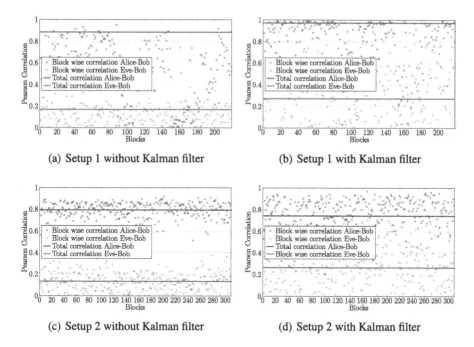

(a) Setup 1 without Kalman filter

(b) Setup 1 with Kalman filter

(c) Setup 2 without Kalman filter

(d) Setup 2 with Kalman filter

Fig. 4. The block wise Pearson correlation coefficient between (pre-processed) channel measurements of Alice-Bob and of Eve$_3$-Bob observation with a block size of 100 RSSI values for setup 1 (a-b) and for setup 2 (c-d). (The results of setup 2 are also representative for setup 3.)

of the PHYSEC system for all possible combinations of quantisation schemes and BCH codes. For all experiments we also present results of the attackers.

The correlation coefficients for the measurements of setup 1 and setup 2 of Alice-Bob and Eve$_3$-Bob are illustrated in Fig. 4. Here we also present a block wise analysis of the (pre-processed) channel profiles. For evaluation approaches, e.g., those presented by Guillaume et al. [24] or maybe for addressing block code performance evaluation, we recommend block wise analysis, because of the strong variance of these blocks.

Interestingly, there is a distinction on the performance of Kalman filter between the stationary setup and the setups where Bob is moving. For enhancing reciprocity, we make the following observation that when channel profiles from a mobile setup are measured, the Kalman filter does not improve the reciprocity. However with the same setup for a static channel, it enhances the reciprocity. This is because the Kalman filter enhances the reciprocity by predicting and estimating the values. Higher the correlation between the samples better would be the predictions. In a moving-channel scenario, the low sampling rate leads to decrease in correlation. As a result this leads to decreased prediction performance. However with the same setup in a static case, it leads to an increased performance. Such a behavior is also observed while estimating user position in navigation applications. Thus in case of enhancing reciprocity, for mobile-channel conditions, a higher degree of sampling is required to obtain better performance.

However in both the cases, Eve's correlation does not exceeds the one of both Alice and Bob. Our results show that the closer the position of the attacker to Alice, the higher correlated its eavesdropped channel measurement is. Whereby the correlation value over the hole measurement with the highest amount is 0.16 for E_3 in setup 1. Therefore, by applying the same system configurations than Alice and Bob, eavesdropping leads to a non-successful result. The bit error rate of Eve's and Bob's preliminary key material is ≈ 0.5.

Further we evaluate the performance of different quantizer and BCH code combinations. The above mentions quantization schemes as well as all BCH codes with $n = 63$ are applied. The required samples on average for establishing symmetric secret keys with a security level of 128-bit varies for the setups. With an amount of samples, equal to the duration time t_{PHY} in seconds, of 2200, 422, and 347 the variation margin between the three setups amounts to 634 %. By applying Kalman filtering the amount of samples is 512, 2370, and 642. The Kalman worse the results for *setup 2* and *setup 3*. But for the case of a stationary setup, which is can be very usually for sensors, it reduces the number of required samples down to 23 %. For more details we refer to the Appendix.

6   Conclusion

In the current paper, the first hybrid security architecture has been proposed, that combines PHYSEC with asymmetric cryptography. Both approaches are based on entirely different sets of security features. Asymmetric cryptography based on a mathematical framework while physical layer security is based on non-predictable features of the wireless channel. By combining both the orthogonal primitives, the security of the system is strengthened and the challenge for attacking it are increased. Further use of asymmetric cryptography *cheap* satisfies the tight timing requirements of embedded systems. Additionally our PHYSEC system provides key diversity with energy efficient PFS security by reuse hardware modules that are already deployed for non-security related perations. We present experimental measurements setups using resource-constrained devices. Further, we demonstrate the influences from Kalman filer and present evaluation results of applying the Kalman filter, several quatization schemes, and different BCH codes.

Appendix

Experimental Measurement Setup: The hardware platforms, WRT54GL WiFi router and WiFi DipCortex, for our prototypical implementation are illustrated in Fig. 5.

Evaluation Results: The required samples of a symmetric secret key with a security level 128 bit for *setup 1, 2* and *3* are evaluated. In *setup 1* the single

(a). WRT54GL Wi-Fi router: Alice & Eve   (b). WiFi DipCortex: Bob

Fig. 5. Experimental measurement setups including access point Alice (A), wireless sensor node Bob stationary (B_s), cyclic moving (B_d), and randomly moving (B_r) and the eavesdropper Eve placed away from Alice and Bob (E_1), between Alice and Bob (E_2), and next to Alice (E_3).

bit quantizer by Jana et al. [32] requires less time to generate 128-bit keys, the key generation is greatly improved by the precomputation by Kalman filter, as depicte in the required samples per key in Fig. 6. In *setup 2* also the single bit quantizer by Jana et al. [32] requires less time to generate 128-bit keys, moreover the key generation is harmed by the precomputation by Kalman filter, as depicte in the required samples per key in Fig. 7. Best key generation is performed in *setup 3* again by the single it quantizer by Jana et al. [32]. Also the other quantizer perform their best results in this setup, as shown in Fig. 8. But also in this setup the precomputation using a Kalman filter effects the key generation performance.

The results regarding quantizer and $BCH(n, k, d)$ code are summarized in Table 1. Usually the single bit quantizer by Jana et al. [32] requires least samples to generate a 128-bit key. In *setup 3* this quantizer requires 347 RSSI values without Kalman to generate a single key and in setup 1 the Kalman improves the result to a requirement from 2200 RSSI values to only 512 RSSI values. Therefore, it takes between 6 upto 9 min (without Kalman 36 min). Overall, the quantizer by Jana et al. [32] requires significantly less RSSI values than the other

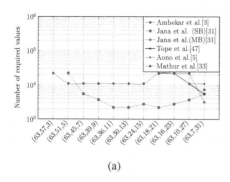   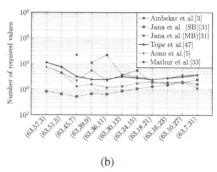

(a)   (b)

Fig. 6. Evaluation results of setup 1: Required samples per of 128-bit keys for stationary node, for different quantizerper evaluated $BCH(n, k, d)$ code, (a) without Kalman filter and (b) with.

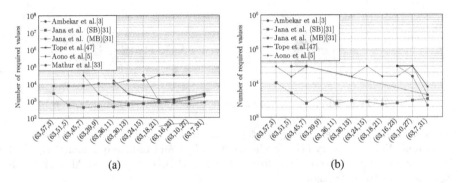

Fig. 7. Evaluation results of setup 2: Required samples per of 128-bit keys for stationary node, for different quantizerper evaluated $BCH(n, k, d)$ code, (a) without Kalman filter and (b) with.

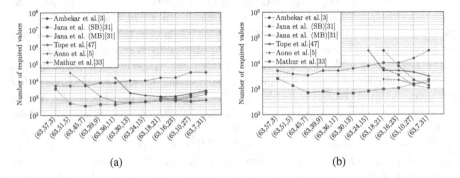

Fig. 8. Evaluation results of setup 3: Required samples per of 128-bit keys for stationary node, for different quantizerper evaluated $BCH(n, k, d)$ code, (a) without Kalman filter and (b) wit.

mentioned quantizer. Especially the quantizer by Mathur et al. [34] requires a high amount of samples to generate keys as this quantizer drops most of the samples and generates much shorter bit stream [34]. For some system parameter no key could be achieved.

Statistical Analysis: For statistical analysis we evaluated the preliminary key material offline by applying NIST suite [37]. As some these tests require large number of bits, we constrain the evaluated test to those which are able to execute blocks of 500 bit. The outputs of the NIST statistical tests are successful rates for each quantizer listed in Table 2. Most of quantizers output pass the tests with high rates. Note that this shall not apply to the multi-bit quantizer by Jana et al. [32], as the blocks by this quantizer do not have high pass rates. Moreover the results for the quantizer by Mathur et al. [34] are not reliable as the amount of quantized block is not representative.

Table 1. Minimum number of required samples for establishing symmetric keys with a security level of 128 bit, as well as the coresponding BCH(n,k,d) code.

| | Quantization schemes | Without Kalman filter | | With Kalman filter | |
		BCH(n,k,d)	(#Samples)	BCH(n,k,d)	(#Samples)
Setup 1	Ambekar et al.[3]	(63,7,31)	7334	(63,7,31)	1572
	Jana et al.(SB)[32]	(63,18,21)	**2200**	(63,45,7)	**512**
	Jana et al.(MB)[32]	(63,7,31)	3143	(63,7,31)	1100
	Tope et al.[48]	(63,7,31)	5500	(63,18,21)	2445
	Aono et al.[5]	(63,7,31)	11000	(63,36,11)	2200
	Mathur et al.[34]	(63,45,7)	11000	(63,45,7)	22000
Setup 2	Ambekar et al.[3]	(63,10,27)	656	(63,7,31)	**2200**
	Jana et al.(SB)[32]	(63,45,7)	**422**	(63,18,21)	**2370**
	Jana et al.(MB)[32]	(63,10,27)	670	(63,7,31)	4400
	Tope et al.[48]	(63,18,21)	1184	(63,7,31)	7700
	Aono et al.[5]	(63,36,11)	717	(63,7,31)	4400
	Mathur et al.[34]	(63,45,7)	7700	-	-
Setup 3	Ambekar et al.[3]	(63,10,27)	642	(63,7,31)	1340
	Jana et al.(SB)[32]	(63,45,7)	**347**	(63,36,11)	**642**
	Jana et al.(MB)[32]	(63,10,27)	604	(63,7,31)	1063
	Tope et al.[48]	(63,18,21)	1184	(63,7,31)	3080
	Aono et al.[5]	(63,30,13)	550	(63,10,27)	1467
	Mathur et al.[34]	(63,45,7)	5134	(63,45,7)	3423

Table 2. Pass rates of several NIST statistical tests for preliminary key material of the quatizations schemes by Tope et al. [48], Aono et al. [5], Mathur et al. [34], Jana et al. [32], and Ambekar et al. [3] (setup 2).

		[3]	[32]	MB [32]	[48]	[5]	[34]
	# Blocks	122	37	122	30	48	1
Statistical tests	Frequency	0.77444	0.62162	0.03279	0.73333	0.87500	1.00000
	Block Frequency	0.83459	0.94595	0.00820	0.86667	0.91667	1.00000
	Cum. Sums (fwd)	0.76692	0.70270	0.01639	0.73333	0.91667	1.00000
	Cum. Sums (rev)	0.78195	0.70270	0.03279	0.73333	0.91667	1.00000
	Runs	0.71429	0.18919	0.00000	0.43333	0.41667	1.00000
	Longest Run	0.74436	0.45946	0.05738	0.63333	0.79167	1.00000
	FFT	0.82707	0.89189	0.94262	1.00000	0.97917	1.00000
	App. Entropy	0.91729	1.00000	1.00000	1.00000	1.00000	1.00000
	Serial (1)	0.65414	0.94595	0.48361	0.73333	0.93750	1.00000
	Serial (2)	0.78947	0.97297	0.67213	0.83333	0.97917	1.00000
	Linear Complexity	0.78195	0.91892	0.94262	0.93333	0.95833	0.00000

118   C.T. Zenger et al.

References

1. Alliance, W.F.: Wi-Fi Simple Configuration Technical Specification, Version 2.0.2 (2011)
2. Ambekar, A., Schotten, H.: Enhancing channel reciprocity for effective key management in wireless ad-hoc networks. In: Proceedings of Vehicular Technology Conference, Spring, Seoul, South Korea, May 2014
3. Ambekar, A., Hassan, M., Schotten, H.D.: Improving channel reciprocity for effective key management systems. In: 2012 International Symposium on Signals, Systems, and Electronics (ISSSE), pp. 1–4. IEEE (2012)
4. Analog: ADIS16480 Kalman Data Sheet. http://www.analog.com/static/imported-files/data_sheets/ADIS16480.pdf
5. Aono, T., Higuchi, K., Ohira, T., Komiyama, B., Sasaoka, H.: Wireless secret key generation exploiting reactance-domain scalar response of multipath fading channels. IEEE Trans. Antennas Propag. **53**(11), 3776–3784 (2005)
6. Atkins, D., Stallings, W., Zimmermann, P.: PGP message exchange formats. RFC 1991 (Informational), August 1996. http://www.ietf.org/rfc/rfc1991.txt, obsoleted by RFC 4880
7. Bernstein, D.J., Chang, Y.-A., Cheng, C.-M., Chou, L.-P., Heninger, N., Lange, T., van Someren, N.: Factoring RSA keys from certified smart cards: Coppersmith in the wild. In: Sako, K., Sarkar, P. (eds.) ASIACRYPT 2013, Part II. LNCS, vol. 8270, pp. 341–360. Springer, Heidelberg (2013)
8. Bersani, F., Tschofenig, H.: The EAP-PSK protocol: A Pre-Shared Key Extensible Authentication Protocol (EAP) Method. RFC 4764 (Experimental), January 2007. http://www.ietf.org/rfc/rfc4764.txt
9. Bersani, F.: EAP shared key methods: a tentative synthesis of those proposed so far. http://tools.ietf.org/html/draft-bersani-eap-synthesis-sharedkeymethods-00
10. Bertoni, G., Daemen, J., Peeters, M., Assche, G.V.: Keccak sponge function family main document. Submission to NIST (Round 2) 3 (2009)
11. Beyer, S.: ZigBee Applications in sub-1 GHz Frequency Resuage. http://www.cambridgewireless.co.uk/docs/SB%20Atmel%20-%20ShortRangeWirelessSIG.pdf
12. Borisov, N., Goldberg, I., Brewer, E.: Off-the-record communication, or, why not to use PGP. In: Proceedings of the 2004 ACM Workshop on Privacy in the Electronic Society, WPES 2004, pp. 77–84. ACM, New York (2004). http://doi.acm.org/10.1145/1029179.1029200
13. Cisco: The Internet of Things - How the Next Evolution of the Internet is Changing Everything (2011). http://share.cisco.com/internet-of-things.html
14. Dierks, T., Rescorla, E.: The Transport Layer Security (TLS) Protocol Version 1.2. RFC 5246 (Proposed Standard), August 2008. http://www.ietf.org/rfc/rfc5246.txt, updated by RFCs 5746, 5878, 6176
15. Diffie, W., van Oorschot, P.C., Wiener, M.J.: Authentication and authenticated key exchanges. Des. Codes Cryptography **2**(2), 107–125 (1992). http://dblp.uni-trier.de/db/journals/dcc/dcc2.html
16. Dodis, Y., Katz, J., Reyzin, L., Smith, A.: Robust fuzzy extractors and authenticated key agreement from close secrets. In: Dwork, C. (ed.) CRYPTO 2006. LNCS, vol. 4117, pp. 232–250. Springer, Heidelberg (2006)
17. Eberz, S., Strohmeier, M., Wilhelm, M., Martinovic, I.: A practical man-in-the-middle attack on signal-based key generation protocols. In: Foresti, S., Yung, M., Martinelli, F. (eds.) ESORICS 2012. LNCS, vol. 7459, pp. 235–252. Springer, Heidelberg (2012)

18. Edman, M., Kiayias, A., Tang, Q., Yener, B.: On the security of key extraction from measuring physical quantities. arXiv preprint arXiv:1311.4591 (2013)
19. Eisenbarth, T., Kasper, T., Moradi, A., Paar, C., Salmasizadeh, M., Shalmani, M.T.M.: On the power of power analysis in the real world: a complete break of the KEELOQ code hopping scheme. In: Wagner, D. (ed.) CRYPTO 2008. LNCS, vol. 5157, pp. 203–220. Springer, Heidelberg (2008)
20. Fluhrer, S., Mantin, I., Shamir, A.: Weaknesses in the key scheduling algorithm of RC4. In: Proceedings of the 4th Annual Workshop on Selected Areas of Cryptography, pp. 1–24 (2001)
21. Forum, W.R.: User Scenarios2020 - A Worldwide Wireless Future, WWRF OUT-LOOK, July 2009
22. Goldsmith, A.: Wireless Communications. Cambridge University Press, Cambridge (2005)
23. Group, I.W., et al.: IEEE 802.11-2007: Wireless LAN Medium Access Control (MAC) and Physical Layer (PHY) Specifications. IEEE 802.11 LAN Standards 2007 (2007)
24. Guillaume, R., Zenger, C., Mueller, A., Paar, C., Czylwik, A.: Fair comparison and evaluation of quantization schemes for phy-based key generation. In: 19th International OFDM Workshop 2014 (InOWo 2014), pp. 1–5, August 2014
25. Hamburg, M., Kocher, P., Marson, M.E.: Analysis of Intel's Ivy Bridge digital random number generator (2012). http://www.cryptography.com/public/pdf/Intel_TRNG_Report_20120312.pdf
26. Hamida, S.T.B., Pierrot, J.B., Castelluccia, C.: An adaptive quantization algorithm for secret key generation using radio channel measurements. In: 2009 3rd International Conference on New Technologies, Mobility and Security (NTMS), pp. 1–5. IEEE (2009)
27. Heninger, N., Durumeric, Z., Wustrow, E., Halderman, J.A.: Mining your Ps and Qs: Detection of widespread weak keys in network devices. In: Proceedings of the 21st USENIX Security Symposium, August 2012
28. Hershey, J.E., Hassan, A.A., Yarlagadda, R.: Unconventional cryptographic keying variable management. IEEE Transact. Commun. **43**(1), 3–6 (1995)
29. Impagliazzo, R., Levin, L.A., Luby, M.: Pseudo-random generation from one-way functions. In: Proceedings of the twenty-first annual ACM symposium on Theory of computing, pp. 12–24. ACM (1989)
30. Instruments, T.: TI Data Sheetsl. http://www.ti.com/lit/ds/symlink/am3359.pdf
31. Jakes, W.C.: Microwave Mobile Communications. Wiley, New York (1974)
32. Jana, S., Premnath, S.N., Clark, M., Kasera, S.K., Patwari, N., Krishnamurthy, S.V.: On the effectiveness of secret key extraction from wireless signal strength in real environments. In: Proceedings of the 15th Annual International Conference on Mobile Computing and Networking (MobiCom), pp. 321–332. ACM (2009)
33. Killmann, W., Schindler, W.: A proposal for: functionality classes for random number generators (2011), BSI, AIS 20/AIS 31
34. Mathur, S., Trappe, W., Mandayam, N., Ye, C., Reznik, A.: Radio-telepathy: extracting a secret key from unauthenticated wireless channel. In: Proceedings of the 14th ACM international Conference on Mobile Computing and Networking, pp. 128–139. ACM (2008)
35. MBED: Wifi dipcortex datasheet. https://mbed.org/platforms/WiFi-DipCortex/
36. Menezes, A.J., Vanstone, S.A., Oorschot, P.C.V.: Handbook of Applied Cryptography. CRC Press Inc, Boca Raton (1997)
37. NIST, S.: 800–22. A Statistical Test Suite for Random and Pseudorandom Number Generators for Cryptographic Applications (2000)

38. Orman, H.: The OAKLEY Key Determination Protocol. RFC 2412 (Informational), November 1998. http://www.ietf.org/rfc/rfc2412.txt
39. Patwari, N., Croft, J., Jana, S., Kasera, S.: High-rate uncorrelated bit extraction for shared secret key generation from channel measurements. IEEE Transact. Mob. Comput. 9(1), 17–30 (2010)
40. Premnath, S., Jana, S., Croft, J., Gowda, P.L., Clark, M., Kasera, S.K., Patwari, N., Krishnamurthy, S.V.: Secret key extraction from wireless signal strength in real environments. IEEE Transact. Mob. Comput. 12(5), 917–930 (2013)
41. Proakis, J.G.: Digital Communications. Mcgraw-Hill, New York (2008)
42. Rivera, J., van der Meulen, R.: Gartner Says the Internet of Things Installed Base Will Grow to 26 Billion Units By 2020 (2013). http://www.gartner.com/newsroom/id/2636073
43. Shiu, Y.S., Chang, S.Y., Wu, H.C., Huang, S.C.H., Chen, H.H.: Physical layer security in wireless networks: a tutorial. IEEE Wirel. Commun. 18(2), 66–74 (2011)
44. Smith, G.S.: A direct derivation of a single-antenna reciprocity relation for the time domain. IEEE Transact. Antenna Propag. 52(6), 1568–1577 (2004)
45. Specification, G.: Global positioning systems directorate systems engineering and integration interface specification (2012)
46. Stinson, D.: Cryptography: Theory and Practice. Discrete Mathematics and Its Applications, 3rd edn. Taylor & Francis, Boca Raton (2005)
47. Strobel, D., Driessen, B., Kasper, T., Leander, G., Oswald, D., Schellenberg, F., Paar, C.: Fuming acid and cryptanalysis: handy tools for overcoming a digital locking and access control system. In: Canetti, R., Garay, J.A. (eds.) CRYPTO 2013, Part I. LNCS, vol. 8042, pp. 147–164. Springer, Heidelberg (2013)
48. Tope, M.A., McEachen, J.C.: Unconditionally secure communications over fading channels. In: Military Communications Conference, MILCOM 2001. Communications for Network-Centric Operations: Creating the Information Force, vol. 1, pp. 54–58. IEEE (2001)
49. Viehboeck, S.: Brute forcing Wi-Fi Protected Setup (2011). http://sviehb.files.wordpress.com/2011/12/viehboeck_wps.pdf
50. Wallace, J., Chen, C., Jensen, M.: Key generation exploiting MIMO channel evolution: algorithms and theoretical limits. In: 3rd European Conference on Antennas and Propagation, EuCAP 2009, pp. 1499–1503, March 2009
51. Welch, G., Bishop, G.: An Introduction to the Kalman Filter. Technical report, University of North Carolina at Chapel Hill, July 2006
52. Wilhelm, M., Martinovic, I., Schmitt, J.B., Lenders, V.: Short paper: reactive jamming in wireless networks: how realistic is the threat? In: Proceedings of the fourth ACM conference on Wireless network security, pp. 47–52. ACM (2011)
53. Ylonen, T., Lonvick, C.: The Secure Shell (SSH) Protocol Architecture. RFC 4251 (Proposed Standard), January 2006. http://www.ietf.org/rfc/rfc4251.txt
54. Dierks, T., Rescorla, E.: The Transport Layer Security (TLS) Protocol Version 1.2. RFC 5246 (Proposed Standard), August 2008. http://www.ietf.org/rfc/rfc5246.txt, updated by RFCs 5746, 5878, 6176
55. Zhang, J., Kasera, S.K., Patwari, N.: Mobility assisted secret key generation using wireless link signatures. In: Proceedings of International Conference on Computer Communications IEEE INFOCOM, pp. 1–5. IEEE (2010)

Cryptographic Protocols I

A Secure and Efficient Protocol for Electronic Treasury Auctions

Atilla Bektaş[1], Mehmet Sabır Kiraz[2](✉), and Osmanbey Uzunkol[2]

[1] IAM, Middle East Technical University, Ankara, Turkey
bektasatilla@gmail.com
[2] MCS Labs, TÜBİTAK BİLGEM, Kocaeli, Turkey
{mehmet.kiraz,osmanbey.uzunkol}@tubitak.gov.tr

Abstract. Auctions have become an important part of electronic commerce. Considering the gradually increasing importance of confidentiality and privacy in auction modeling, various designs have been proposed to ensure secure transmission especially in sealed-bid auctions. However, to the best of our knowledge there is no secure and privacy preserving Treasury Auction system. Looking at systems currently in use, many countries perform those auctions manually. Since all the bids are transferred to the system in clear form, confidentiality and privacy are not guaranteed. Therefore, the system is more vulnerable to potential threats especially due to the ongoing advances and developments in technology. In a secure electronic auction system, it is possible to determine the winner or the winners without revealing any private information. In this work, we propose a new, secure and efficient electronic auction protocol for Treasury Auctions based on secure multi-party computation, secret sharing and threshold homomorphic cryptosystem.

Keywords: Treasury auctions · Secure multi-party computation · Threshold homomorphic encryption · Confidentiality · Privacy

1 Introduction

Domestic debt refers to the money lent to the government as mandatory or voluntary from individuals, private institutions or public authorities for a specific maturity date and interest. The main tool that governments use to borrow in domestic markets is to hold regular auctions (also called as *Treasury auctions*) of Treasury securities. In this paper, we deal with the process of these auctions from a cryptographic point of view rather than their financial aspects.

In current practice, mainly three parties are involved in the Treasury auctions: *Treasury*, playing the role of the authority; *Central Bank*, acting as a fiscal agent of the Treasury; *Investor*, which is also called as *bidder*. Investors typically submit their bids that specify an amount and a price (or a yield) at which they wish to purchase the amount demanded. Here, the submission is carried out by means of conventional ways, e.g., EFT (Electronic Funds Transfer), fax or

© Springer International Publishing Switzerland 2015
B. Ors and B. Preneel (Eds.): BalkanCryptSec 2014, LNCS 9024, pp. 123–140, 2015.
DOI: 10.1007/978-3-319-21356-9_9

a special application[1]. Once submitted, these bids are sorted from the highest to the lowest price (or from the lowest to the highest yield). Since the submission and sorting steps are carried out by a system usually settled in the Central Bank, then the new ordered list is transmitted to the Treasury. The Treasury then examines and evaluates the submitted quotes, and finally determines the winners. The determination process is done manually.

While it is known that there have been almost no problems in the auction processes and the procedures have been operated successfully so far, letting all the bids be transferred in clear text and the operations be realized on clear text imply that confidentiality of all the submitted bids and privacy of the bidders are not guaranteed cryptographically. With the advances and developments in technology, this makes also the system vulnerable to potential threats. For example, a corrupted user on the Central Bank may share some of the bids with other parties or bidders since he/she can see all the submitted bids. Similarly, a corrupted user on the Treasury may change the order of the accepted/rejected bidders in the list, i.e., may replace the final result with another loser without being detected. Another example, in case of a corrupted fax channel, it also causes to be a security violation as all the transferred bids are in clear text. Thus, the manual system is completely insecure from the cryptographic point of view. Moreover, since the knowledge of individual bids is of great value to the others who may use this knowledge to better their own positions it becomes crucial that the confidentiality of all the submitted bids and privacy of the bidders should be satisfied.

1.1   Contributions

Current Treasury auction processes are usually performed manually. Despite the fact that there have been almost no problems in processes and the procedures have been operated successfully so far, confidentiality and privacy are not guaranteed in systems currently in use from the cryptographic point of view. In particular, this means that it is possible to manipulate the results in case of curious adversaries.

In this paper, we mainly focus on improving the security and privacy aspects of the current manual Treasury auction system by proposing a secure electronic system where all the bids (each specifying an amount and a price) and the corresponding name of the bidders are kept secret until the auction result is published. While the system can easily be used in other analogous scenarios, we examine the whole process from bid submission to auction award using the underlying cryptographic techniques which are secure multi-party computation (MPC), secret sharing and threshold homomorphic cryptosystem. We also use a secure sorting with a secure comparison subprotocol that can be found in Sect. 4 and Appendix A.

To the best of our knowledge, this is the first study applied on issuing Treasury securities via electronic auction method in which a secure electronic auction process is included and both confidentiality and privacy are satisfied.

---

[1] E.g., *Treasury Automated Auction Processing System* (in US); *Bloomberg Auction System* (in UK); *Deutsche Bundesbank Bund Bidding System* (in Germany).

Roadmap. The rest of the paper is organized as follows. Some related works about the subject are discussed in the following subsection. Section 3 outlines the most common and current manual Treasury auction process including some rules in offering mechanism. Section 4 introduces our proposed model in details, and security analysis and complexity analysis are presented in Sects. 5 and D, respectively. Lastly, Sect. 6 draws conclusion, summarizes the study and discusses the generalizations of our proposed model. Since we have a limited space, proofs of the theorems in Sect. 5 are added in the appendices.

1.2 Related Work

A number of contributions on secure auction have been made until now (e.g., [7,8]). In [21], an architecture for mechanism design including auctions is presented by using garbled circuit techniques. The aim of this mechanism is to preserve the inputs of the participating parties. In [6] the implementation of a secure system for trading quantities of a certain commodity among many buyers and sellers, a so-called double auction, is outlined.

Most of the protocols proposed so far have not been implemented until recently, and experience with real-life applications is highly limited. However, many business applications could benefit from secure computation and in recent years, many MPC projects started to use in practice by the results of [2,4,6,16]. Among these, [6] is the first large-scale and practical application of MPC. In Estonia, a secure system for jointly collecting and analyzing financial data for a consortium of ICT (Information and Communications Technology) companies was developed. In this system secret sharing and secure MPC techniques were used. This was the first time where the actual secure multi-party function evaluation was done over Internet using real data. The details are presented in [4,5].

MPC has been studied since the 1980s [3,9,14]. Until recently, it has been mostly academic work, because the related protocols add a fair amount of computational and network communication overhead [5]. An overview of the theoretical results known can be found in [10]. Also our work employs several techniques developed for multi-party secure function evaluation. In particular, we use secure sorting and comparison algorithms [12,17,18,20,25,28].

2 Security Model

We now give a formal security model of our system in the presence of malicious adversaries in the stand-alone model with random oracles assuming static adversary.

In our cryptographic protocols for Treasury Auction Model we suppose that there are n primary dealers (PD_i), one Treasury (T) and one Central Bank (CB). In particular, each PD_i has a private bid M_i engaging in a multi-party protocol with T and CB where $1 \leq i \leq n$. Security goals of our system consist of correctness (i.e., the output of the protocol is indeed correct) and full privacy (no malicious PD_i, T or CB cannot learn more information than what can be implied from the outcome). The main assumption is that T and CB do not maliciously collude. Taking this assumption into account, our main purpose is to ensure that privacy of honest bidders cannot be violated by any other illegal cooperation of third parties or primary dealers.

A malicious T is interested in learning the PD_i's bids and manipulating the output of the computation (i.e., changing the order of the sorted result in a malicious manner). T may also send a fake report to the PD_i in order to gain some advantage. Moreover, a malicious CB is also interested in changing the order of the result.

We further assume that every PD_i is curious, and can maliciously behave in arbitrary manner. A malicious PD_i aims to learn others' bids, and to maximize their own profits by means of manipulating the outcome. The system allows to collusion between PD_i and T, or between PD_i and CB or between different PD_i. Whenever a PD_i behaves maliciously by sending faulty messages, it will be fined and removed from the system and finally the protocol will be restarted. Note that a malicious PD_i can be easily detected in our system, therefore, there is no motivation for PD_i to behave maliciously.

3   Current Treasury Auction Processes

In this section, we summarize the most common and manually performed Treasury auction process currently in use. More details can be seen in [1]. Usually, the Central Bank runs all the operations related to the auction as the fiscal agent of the Treasury. Retail and corporate investors participate in the Treasury auctions through branches of the Central Bank, banks or brokers *via EFT, fax, or some special applications* [27]. Since there is a great competition here, the largest part of the participation is provided by the *primary dealers* as corporate investors. A primary dealer is a company or firm that wants to buy Treasury securities directly from the government with the intention of reselling them to others, thus acting as a market maker of Treasury securities. Many, but by no means all, industrial countries have a primary dealer system. For example, Canada, France, Italy, Spain, Turkey, the United Kingdom, and the United States have primary dealer system whereas Australia, New Zealand and Switzerland have no primary dealers.

Initially, the auction announcement is published on Internet at least one day before the auction by the Treasury. After the announcement, investors submit their bids (see Table 1 for an example bid information) in terms of price and nominal amount.

All submitted bids are final bids for investors. Furthermore, investors are bound to their bids until the deadline of bidding for the auction. There is no restriction for number of bids [27]. It means that an investor may submit more than one bid. After the bid submission stage, auction is closed and then all submitted bids are sorted from higher price to lower price (i.e., from lower interest

Table 1. An Example of bid information of an investor

Expected yield	5,69 %
Unit price offered	94,617 $
Nominal amount offered	1.000.000 $
Amount of payment to the Treasury on settlement date in case of being accepted	946.170 $
Amount of payment to the investor by the Treasury on maturity date	1.000.000 $

to higher interest). After the preparation of the ordered list, it is then forwarded to the Treasury for the evaluation process. The Treasury examines all offers within the framework of existing conditions and determines the lowest price that is accepted. The first m offers whose prices are higher than that point are accepted while the others are rejected. In fact, that cut-off point is the point where the required debt for the Treasury is also met. The following is the formula of finding cut-off point where p_i is the unit price and a_i is the nominal amount in i^{th} offer and δ is the amount of required debt of the Treasury.

$$\sum_{i=1}^{m+1} \frac{p_i \cdot a_i}{100} \geq \delta \text{ and } \sum_{i=1}^{m} \frac{p_i \cdot a_i}{100} < \delta.$$

After all operations and the calculations outlined below are done, the results are submitted to the Central Bank in order to inform the bidders. Assuming there are k bids in an ordered list, m is the cut-off point and d is the maturity in terms of days, then the following calculations are done by the Treasury corresponding to Table 2.

- Total Amount

  (Offered, Accepted) $= (\mu_1, \mu_2) = \left(\sum_{i=1}^{k} \frac{p_i \cdot a_i}{100} , \sum_{i=1}^{m} \frac{p_i \cdot a_i}{100} \right)$

- Total Nominal Amount

  (Offered, Accepted) $= (\mu_3, \mu_4) = \left(\sum_{i=1}^{k} a_i , \sum_{i=1}^{m} a_i \right)$

- Average Price

  (Offered, Accepted) $= (\mu_5, \mu_6) = \left(\frac{\mu_1}{\mu_3} \cdot 100 , \frac{\mu_2}{\mu_4} \cdot 100 \right)$

- Minimum Price
  (Offered, Accepted) $= (p_k, p_m)$
- Term Rate

  (Offered, Accepted) $= (\mu_7, \mu_8) = \left(\frac{100 - \mu_5}{\mu_5} \cdot 100 , \frac{100 - \mu_6}{\mu_6} \cdot 100 \right)$

- Annual Simple Rate

  (Offered, Accepted) $= (\mu_9, \mu_{10}) = \left(\frac{364 \cdot \mu_7}{d} , \frac{364 \cdot \mu_8}{d} \right)$

Auction results are announced to the public by the Central Bank, and a press release is issued by the Treasury on its website as in Table 2.

Table 2. Treasury auction result example

Amount (Net, $ Million)

	Offered	Accepted
Investor	2.534,0	380,1

Price ($)

	Offered	Accepted
Average Price	92,757	92,868
Minimum Price	92,560	92,850

Interest Rate (Average, %)

	Offered	Accepted
Term Rate	7,81	7,68
Annual Simple	6,34	6,24

4   Proposed Model

When the Treasury decides to hold an auction for issuing Treasury securities, it determines firstly the amount of debt; secondly it defines the auction time periods, i.e., open and close times, and announces these times to the public; thirdly the Treasury informs the Central Bank in order to open the electronic bid submission system to the bidders. After then the Central Bank starts the system with the Treasury's confirmation. Thus, the bidders who are willing to participate the auction prepare their offers and use the system by submitting their bids within a predetermined period. Note that our basic assumption is that *the Central Bank and the Treasury do not maliciously collude.*

Starting with the bid submission, our proposed model consists of two phases: Submission and Evaluation phase, Award phase. The Submission and Evaluation phase, as we outlined, starts with the bid submission of the bidders to the system where the bids are positive numbers. After bid submission deadline, secure function evaluation and secure MPC techniques are performed on those submitted (also encrypted) bids. This phase takes place between three parties: The Investor (we call them as The Primary Dealer), The Central Bank, The Treasury. In the Award phase, the auction results, i.e., the winners, are determined and subsequently announced. In this phase, a cryptographic protocol is run between the following two parties: The Investor (or The Primary Dealer) and The Treasury.

Before presenting the details of the two phases of our proposed system, necessary notations are given as follows: PD denotes Primary Dealer, T Treasury,

$\delta \in \mathbb{Z}^+$ Amount of required debt of the Treasury, $k \in \mathbb{Z}^+$ Number of bids in the auction, B_i i^{th} bid participated in the auction for $i = 1, \ldots, k$, PD_i Name of the Primary Dealer in B_i, $p_i \in \mathbb{Z}^+$ Unit price offered in B_i with $p_i \leq 100$, $1000 \leq a_i \leq 500000$ Nominal amount offered in B_i, $y_i = (p_i \cdot a_i)/100$ Amount of payment, pk_A Paillier public key of party A, sk_A Paillier secret key of party A, sk_A^j j^{th} shared part of the secret key of party A, Sign_A Process of time stamped RSA digital signing by party A conforming to the standard ETSI TS 101 733 (for example in CAdES-T format), Enc_{pk} Paillier encryption [22] under pk, Dec_{sk} Paillier decryption [22] under sk. Assume also that there are k bids for each auction. Paillier encryption/decryption and RSA signature can be used in our solution. All the parties have their own Paillier key pairs and Paillier private key of each Investor is shared between the Investor and the Treasury (note that the key distribution mechanism is assumed to be secure, see for instance [15]).

Let $\mathbb{Z}/n\mathbb{Z}$ denote the finite ring of integers modulo n with $n \in \mathbb{N}$. The multiplicative inverse of an element $x \in \mathbb{Z}/n\mathbb{Z}$ is denoted as usual by x^{-1} and equals to an element $y \in \mathbb{Z}/n\mathbb{Z}$, such that $x.y = 1$ in $\mathbb{Z}/n\mathbb{Z}$ if it exists. The representative of the element y is chosen such that $0 \leq y \leq n - 1$. As usual, the multiplicative inverse is efficiently computed by using the extended Euclidean algorithm. We form n as being the product of two different big primes p and q for our encryption/decryption purposes. We further note that the extended Euclidean algorithm is also used to negate an encrypted integer $\mathsf{Enc}_{pk}(-x) = \mathsf{Enc}_{pk}(x)^{-1}$ in $\mathbb{Z}/n\mathbb{Z}$ using the additive homomorphic property of Paillier encryption scheme.

4.1 Submission and Evaluation Phase

The steps of this phase are as follows (see Fig. 1 for the illustration).

1. Primary Dealer: (1) Determines the unit price p_i and nominal amount a_i to be submitted. (2) Computes the amount of payment $y_i = (p_i \cdot a_i)/100$. (3) Forms the bid array $B_i := (PD_i, p_i, a_i)$. (4) Calculates the hash value of B_i and then signs it. (5) Sets $S_{B_i} := \mathsf{Sign}_{PD_i}[\mathsf{Hash}(B_i)]$. (6) Encrypts the values p_i, a_i and y_i using pk_T, and encrypts S_{B_i} using pk_{PD_i}. (7) Sets $X_i := (\mathsf{Enc}_{pk_{PD_i}}(S_{B_i}), \mathsf{Enc}_{pk_T}(p_i), \mathsf{Enc}_{pk_T}(a_i), \mathsf{Enc}_{pk_T}(y_i))$. (8) Sends X_i to the system settled in the Central Bank.
2. Central Bank: Closes the system in order not to accept any new bids. Up to now, k four-tuple-bid values in the form

$$X_i = (\mathsf{Enc}_{pk_{PD_i}}(S_{B_i}), \mathsf{Enc}_{pk_T}(p_i), \mathsf{Enc}_{pk_T}(a_i), \mathsf{Enc}_{pk_T}(y_i))$$

   are collected on the system.
3. Treasury: (1) Encrypts the predetermined debt amount δ which is a secret value of the Treasury and then signs that encrypted value. (2) Sends $\mathsf{Sign}_T[\mathsf{Enc}_{pk_T}(\delta)]$ to the system settled in the Central Bank.
4. Central Bank: (1) Verifies the signature on $\mathsf{Sign}_T[\mathsf{Enc}_{pk_T}(\delta)]$. (2) Products all encrypted amount of payments, i.e., $\mathsf{Enc}_{pk_T}(y_i)$'s to obtain

$$\prod_{i=1}^{k} \mathsf{Enc}_{pk_T}(y_i) = \mathsf{Enc}_{pk_T}(\sum_{i=1}^{k} y_i) = \mathsf{Enc}_{pk_T}(\mu_1) = output_1.$$

(3) Products all encrypted nominal amounts, i.e., $\mathsf{Enc}_{pk_T}(a_i)$'s to obtain

$$\prod_{i=1}^{k} \mathsf{Enc}_{pk_T}(a_i) = \mathsf{Enc}_{pk_T}\left(\sum_{i=1}^{k} a_i\right) = \mathsf{Enc}_{pk_T}(\mu_3) = output_2.$$

(4) Runs **Subprotocols**.

– The collected k-many X_i's are considered as a list and these are subsequently sorted in terms of unit prices ($\mathsf{Enc}_{pk_T}(p_i)$) by using the insertion sorting method in reverse order, i.e., sorting from largest to smallest instead of sorting from smallest to largest (Insertion is a simple sorting algorithm that is efficient for small lists [24]). The following is the pseudo-code of this algorithm for our proposed system.

Input: Array X with unordered elements
Output: Array X with ordered elements

function insertionSort(array X)
for $index = 1 \rightarrow k - 1$ **do**
    $temp = X[index]$
    $pre = index - 1$
    while $pre \geq 0$ and Comparison($X[pre], temp$) **do**
        $X[pre + 1] \leftarrow X[pre]$
        $pre \leftarrow pre - 1$
    end while
    $X[pre + 1] = temp$
end for
return X

Unordered elements are X_i, $1 \leq i \leq k$. The items to be sorted are the second elements of X_i's which are $\mathsf{Enc}_{pk_T}(p_i)$'s. Thus, while sorting $\mathsf{Enc}_{pk_T}(p_i)$'s, the other components of X_i move together with $\mathsf{Enc}_{pk_T}(p_i)$. Ordered new list is composed of $X_{i,j}$'s where i is the old place of X_i and j is the new place of X_i in the list. In this new list, unit prices are sorted from largest to smallest.

Comparison ($X[pre], temp$) returns 1 if $\mathsf{Dec}_{sk_T}(X[pre]) \leq \mathsf{Dec}_{sk_T}(temp)$ and 0 otherwise. See Appendix A for the details.

Comparison function (see Appendix A) is a two-party protocol proposed by Veugen [28]. Although there are other methods for private comparison, the reason for choosing the Veugen's method is that the party A holds two secret (encrypted) values $\mathsf{Enc}_{pk_B}(a)$ and $\mathsf{Enc}_{pk_B}(b)$ of ℓ-bits and the party B holds the private key. They wish to compare the numbers a and b. The actual values of a and b are not known to A and B. At the end, as we slightly changed, both party will learn the result, i.e., will learn the result whether $a \leq b$ or not without knowing a and b explicitly. Whereas, most of the other methods have the property that there are two secret values and the party A holds one of them and the party B

holds the other, and the parties want to compare those secret values. At the end, both sides will learn whose value is greater than the other's. But in our case, despite we have two secret values, they are not held on two distinct parties, they both are held on one party, say on side A here. Hence, our choice became the newly proposed method (2012) of Veugen [28] which is based on DGK comparison protocol [11].

- Changes the numeration of X_i after sorting step as

$$X_{i,j} = (\mathsf{Enc}_{pk_{PD_{i,j}}}(S_{B_{i,j}}), \mathsf{Enc}_{pk_T}(p_{i,j}), \mathsf{Enc}_{pk_T}(a_{i,j}), \mathsf{Enc}_{pk_T}(y_{i,j}))$$

where j is the new place of X_i in the ordered new list. From now on it is useful to use X_j instead of $X_{i,j}$, i.e.,

$$X_j = (\mathsf{Enc}_{pk_{PD_j}}(S_{B_j}), \mathsf{Enc}_{pk_T}(p_j), \mathsf{Enc}_{pk_T}(a_j), \mathsf{Enc}_{pk_T}(y_j)).$$

- Takes the tuple X_k at the bottom of the list and on that tuple takes the encrypted unit price value $\mathsf{Enc}_{pk_T}(p_k) = output_3$.
- Uses all encrypted amount of payments in the ordered array, i.e., $\mathsf{Enc}_{pk_T}(y_i)$'s for $i = 1, \ldots, k$ as an input to the function FindCutoffPoint to find a positive integer m called cut-off point such that $m \leq k$. Namely, the algorithm takes $\mathsf{Enc}_{pk_T}(\delta)$ and $\mathsf{Enc}_{pk_T}(y_i)$'s with $i = 1, \ldots, k$ and m, where $m \leq k$, and outputs FindCutoffPoint($\mathsf{Enc}_{pk_T}(\delta), \mathsf{Enc}_{pk_T}(y_1), \ldots, \mathsf{Enc}_{pk_T}(y_k)$) (see Appendix A for the the algorithm.). Also note that because of the additive homomorphic property of Paillier encryption function Enc_{pk_T}, we have the equality

$$\prod_{i=1}^{t} \mathsf{Enc}_{pk_T}(y_i) = \mathsf{Enc}_{pk_T}(\sum_{i=1}^{t} y_i).$$

- Products the first m encrypted amount of payments in the list, i.e., $\mathsf{Enc}_{pk_T}(y_j)$'s to obtain

$$\prod_{j=1}^{m} \mathsf{Enc}_{pk_T}(y_j) = \mathsf{Enc}_{pk_T}(\sum_{j=1}^{m} y_j) = \mathsf{Enc}_{pk_T}(\mu_2) = output_4.$$

- Products the first m encrypted nominal amounts in the list, i.e., $\mathsf{Enc}_{pk_T}(a_j)$'s to obtain

$$\prod_{j=1}^{m} \mathsf{Enc}_{pk_T}(a_j) = \mathsf{Enc}_{pk_T}(\sum_{j=1}^{m} a_j) = \mathsf{Enc}_{pk_T}(\mu_4) = output_5.$$

- Takes the tuple X_m and on that tuple takes the encrypted unit price value

$$\mathsf{Enc}_{pk_T}(p_m) = output_6.$$

(6) Sends $\mathsf{Sign}_{CB}[\langle output_i, X_j \rangle : i = 1, \ldots, 6, \ j = 1, \ldots, m]$ to the Treasury.

5. Treasury: (1) Verifies the signature on $\mathsf{Sign}_{CB}[\langle output_i, X_j\rangle]$. (2) Decrypts the six encrypted values $\{output_i : i = 1, \ldots, 6\}$ and obtains the followings

$$\{\mu_1, \mu_2, \mu_3, \mu_4, p_k, p_m\}.$$

Here μ_1 is offered total amount of payment, μ_2 is accepted total amount of payment, μ_3 is offered total nominal amount, μ_4 is accepted total nominal amount, p_k is offered minimum price and p_m is accepted minimum price. (3) Calculates average price offered $\mu_5 = \left(\dfrac{\mu_1}{\mu_3} \cdot 100\right)$ and average price accepted $\mu_6 = \left(\dfrac{\mu_2}{\mu_4} \cdot 100\right)$. (4) Calculates term rate offered $\mu_7 = \left(\dfrac{100 - \mu_5}{\mu_5} \cdot 100\right)$ and term rate accepted $\mu_8 = \left(\dfrac{100 - \mu_6}{\mu_6} \cdot 100\right)$. (5) Calculates annual simple rate offered $\mu_9 = \left(\dfrac{364 \cdot \mu_7}{d}\right)$ and annual simple rate accepted $\mu_{10} = \left(\dfrac{364 \cdot \mu_8}{d}\right)$ with d being the maturity in terms of days. (6) Calculates the hash values of each accepted tuples, i.e., X_j's to get $H_j := \mathsf{Hash}(X_j)$ for all $j = 1, \ldots, m$ and then forms a look-up table with rows $\langle X_j, H_j\rangle$.

4.2 Award Phase

In this phase, the Primary Dealers learn exclusively the final decision on their corresponding submitted bids, i.e., they learn only whether the result is *Accept* or *Reject*. For this, we run the following two-party protocol steps (see Fig. 2 for the illustration).

1. Primary Dealer: Computes the hash value of X_i and sends $\mathsf{Hash}(X_i)$ with his certificate $cert_i$ to the Treasury.
2. Treasury: (1) Checks if $\mathsf{Hash}(X_i)$ matches one of H_j values in the look-up table $\langle X_j, H_j\rangle$. (2) Prepares the response res being either "Accept" or "Reject" and signs it as $\mathsf{Sign}_T[res]$. If $\mathsf{Hash}(X_i)$ is equal to one of H_j's then $res =$ "Accept", otherwise $res =$ "Reject". (3) Encrypts the signed response with the corresponding Primary Dealer's public key pk_{PD_i} as $\mathsf{Enc}_{pk_{PD_i}}(\mathsf{Sign}_T[res])$. (4) Decrypts that encrypted value with $sk_{PD_i}^{(2)}$ (the second shared part of the secret key of the Primary Dealer) as $\mathsf{Dec}_{sk_{PD_i}^{(2)}}(\mathsf{Enc}_{pk_{PD_i}}(\mathsf{Sign}_T[res]))$ and sends it to the Primary Dealer.
3. Primary Dealer: (1) Decrypts $\mathsf{Dec}_{sk_{PD_i}^{(2)}}(\mathsf{Enc}_{pk_{PD_i}}(\mathsf{Sign}_T[res]))$ with $sk_{PD_i}^{(1)}$ (the first shared part of the secret key of the Primary Dealer) and obtains the signed response

$$\mathsf{Dec}_{sk_{PD_i}^{(1)}} \mathsf{Dec}_{sk_{PD_i}^{(2)}} (\mathsf{Enc}_{pk_{PD_i}}(\mathsf{Sign}_T[res])) = \mathsf{Sign}_T[res].$$

(2) Verifies the signature on $\mathsf{Sign}_T[res]$. (3) If the response $res =$ "Reject", does nothing and terminates the protocol. Otherwise, i.e., if the response $res =$ "Accept" then gets the first component of the submitted tuple X_i, i.e., $\mathsf{Enc}_{pk_{PD_i}}(S_{B_i})$ and decrypts it with $sk_{PD_i}^{(1)}$ and sends $\mathsf{Dec}_{sk_{PD_i}^{(1)}}(\mathsf{Enc}_{pk_{PD_i}}(S_{B_i}))$ to the Treasury.

4. Treasury: (1) Decrypts $\mathsf{Dec}_{sk_{PD_i}^{(1)}}(\mathsf{Enc}_{pk_{PD_i}}(S_{B_i}))$ with $sk_{PD_i}^{(2)}$ and obtains S_{B_i}, i.e., $\mathsf{Sign}_{PD_i}[\mathsf{Hash}(B_i)]$. (2) Verifies the signature on $\mathsf{Sign}_{PD_i}[\mathsf{Hash}(B_i)]$. (3) Obtains the corresponding Primary Dealer's name PD_j and the corresponding unit price and nominal amount from look-up table to form the tuple $B_j = (PD_j, p_j, a_j)$. For this, decrypts $\mathsf{Enc}_{pk_T}(p_j)$ with secret key sk_T and obtains p_j where $j = 1, \ldots, m$ and decrypts $\mathsf{Enc}_{pk_T}(a_j)$ with secret key sk_T and obtains a_j where $j = 1, \ldots, m$. (4) Calculates the hash value $\mathsf{Hash}(B_j)$ of the formed tuple. (5) Checks whether $\mathsf{Hash}(B_i) \stackrel{?}{=} \mathsf{Hash}(B_j)$. (6) If confirmation occurs, then the formal contract is signed between the Treasury and each winner Primary Dealer. If confirmation does not occur, then there must be a problem with that Primary Dealer. If it is proven that there is an intended action then the penalty cases are concerned.

In this phase, if for example one winner remains silent, i.e., it does not start the protocol, one may consider various solutions, e.g., asking other users to prove that they really lose the auction. Note that for this case only, the Treasury can cooperate with the Central Bank to identify the silent winners, as the Central Bank receives all the bids, it publishes the list of all bidders to the Treasury. After detection of that silent winner, some penalty should be applied to it, e.g., banning from next few Treasury auctions, or imposing a fine. We underline that such a hiding player does not compromise privacy.

5   Security Analysis

In this section, we provide a security analysis of our proposed system in the presence of malicious parties from the Treasury, the Central Bank and the Primary Dealers. We assume that a key distribution or establishment procedure has been successfully performed. In particular, we focus on the malicious adversaries against the auction protocol. Ensuring communication privacy, message integrity and reliable digital signing process are some crucial policies. We show that our overall system satisfies these policies and leaks no private information in the presence of malicious parties under the assumption that the Treasury and the Central Bank do not collude. Firstly, we note that malicious parties cannot see private inputs of honest primary dealers. This is because each input is encrypted using a randomized encryption scheme (e.g., Paillier) and the transmission is done through a secure channel. Secondly, the message integrity of all the values are satisfied by using digital signatures.

Based on our security model in Sect. 2 we have the following theorems.

Theorem 1. *A malicious Investor (bidder) cannot manipulate the outcome.*

Proof. See Appendix E.

Theorem 2. *A malicious Treasury obtains no information about the bids except the winners.*

Proof. See Appendix F.

Theorem 3. *A malicious Central Bank obtains no information about the bids.*

Proof. See Appendix G.

We do not consider the fairness in our proposal (which can be for example solved by gradual release bit commitment schemes [13]). However, even if either the Central Bank or the Treasury attempts to abort the protocol, this does not satisfy any advantage to any of the participant because all the bids are encrypted and signed. Hence, they cannot manipulate the result. Moreover, even if the Treasury aborts the protocol during the Award phase this does not add any advantage since the encrypted bids remain anonymous. In practice, the Central Bank and the Treasury are two governmental bodies and they are the organizers of auctions, so their abortion of the protocol will affect the trusty of society. Therefore, it is better to focus on the abortion of the primary dealers. But, their abortion may realize only during the submission of their bids. Hence, this does not give any advantage to them except being out of the auction, i.e., no bids will be submitted to the Central Bank correctly.

6   Conclusion

In this paper, we describe the most common used and current Treasury auction procedure by pointing out the importance of security and privacy issues for the bids in the auctions. In Treasury auctions, there are more than one winners, say m, where m is also called cut-off point. During the determination step of m, the amount of required debt of the Treasury and the nominal amount offers of the primary dealers are needed. Focusing on this crucial point differs in some ways from other proposed auction models such as [6,19,21]. Therefore current auction schemes and protocols need significant modifications to be able to apply on the Treasury auctions.

Our proposed system securely collects the bids and analyzes them for determining the winners in a Treasury auction. Since the sensitive data of primary dealers (e.g., bid price and bid amount) is given to the system, the bids must be hidden until the end of the auction process. Except the winners, the rejected bidders' quotes are not disclosed. In our proposed model, all the participating parties do not have to trust each other and the sensitive data stays private throughout the whole process. To the best of our knowledge, our proposed treasury auction model is the first study on issuing Treasury securities.

A   Comparison Function

Assume that a party A has two encrypted values $\mathsf{Enc}_{pk_B}(a)$ and $\mathsf{Enc}_{pk_B}(b)$ of ℓ-bits and the party B has the private key. They want to compare the numbers a and b whose actual values are not known to A and B. By the following function the party A **outputs**

$$Comparison(\mathsf{Enc}_{pk_B}(a), \mathsf{Enc}_{pk_B}(b)) = \begin{cases} \mathsf{Enc}_{pk_B}(1) \text{ if } a \leq b \\ \mathsf{Enc}_{pk_B}(0) \text{ if } a > b. \end{cases}$$

If the result is decrypted by party B then the **output** becomes

$$Comparison(\mathsf{Enc}_{pk_B}(a), \mathsf{Enc}_{pk_B}(b)) = \begin{cases} 1 \text{ if } a \leq b \\ 0 \text{ if } a > b. \end{cases}$$

This protocol is proposed in Veugen's paper [28]. Note that we can use other methods for secure comparison as well, e.g., [12,17,18,23,26]. In our proposed system, the encrypted unit prices are to be compared pair by pair and the parties are the Central Bank (party A) and the Treasury (party B). According to Veugen [28], the following protocol shows how to adjust the DGK comparison protocol with encrypted inputs such that perfect security is achieved towards B requiring only a small increase in computational and communication complexity. The difference with DGK comparison protocol [11] is the modified subprotocol with private inputs. See [28] for the details.

Let $0 \leq a, b < 2^\ell < n$ and n be the Paillier public key component used in the main protocol. The notation $(a \leq b)$ is used to denote the bit such that

$$(a \leq b) = \begin{cases} 1 \text{ if } a \leq b \\ 0 \text{ if } a > b \end{cases}$$

and $\oplus$ denotes the exclusive or of two bits.

B   Submission and Evaluation Phase

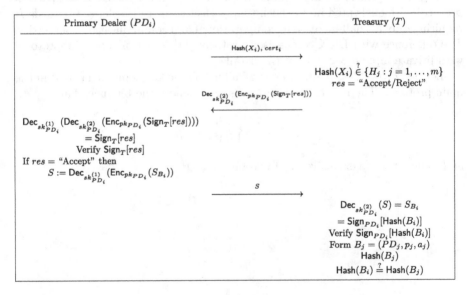

Fig. 1. Submission and evaluation phase of treasury auction process

C   Award Phase

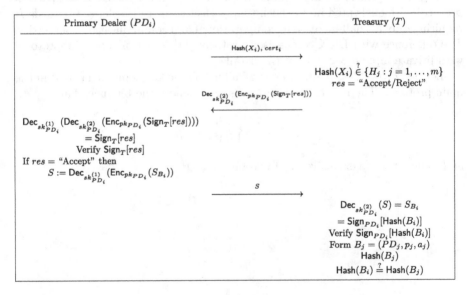

Fig. 2. Award phase of treasury auction process

D   Complexity Analysis

In this section, we present computational, communication and round complexity of our proposed system. For the computational complexity, we will only count expensive asymmetric operations. Since symmetric encryptions and hash functions are comparatively very cheap, these can be ignored in the analysis of overall complexity. Note that the submitted encrypted bid is a 4-tuple component. The Primary Dealers computes $4k$ encryptions where k denotes the number of bids. The Central Bank receives k four-tuple encrypted bids. After the bid submission deadline, subprotocol step will be run for k bids. We have $(k-1)k/2$ comparisons for k values in Sorting function and at most k comparisons for k values in FindCutoffPoint function. There are $(3\ell+10)$ public key encryptions in one Comparison function, then in total $(3\ell+10)(k^2+k)/2$ public key encryptions exist under the subprotocol step. Hence, in the Submission and Evaluation phase there are in total, with the $(8k+2+(3\ell+10)(k^2+k))/2$ public key encryptions and 3 additional signatures. There are only one public key operation and one signature in the Award phase. Hence, there are in total $(16k+24+(3\ell+10)(k^2+k))/2$ public key operations in our proposed model.

As for the communication complexity, there are in total $(4k+2\ell+4m+13)$ public key encryptions and 2 signatures transferred in the Submission and Evaluation phase, and one hashed value and 2 public key messages transferred in the Award phase. Hence, there are in total $(4k+2\ell+4m+15)$ public key operations, 2 signatures and one hashed value transferred.

Finally, we note that our proposed system have only constant rounds.

E   Proof of Theorem 1

For a primary dealer as an investor, the main privacy concern is secrecy of its name and anonymity of its bid values until end of the auction process. First of all, a malicious primary dealer cannot obtain any information during the Submission and Evaluation process because it only sends an encrypted and signed bid tuple $(\mathsf{Enc}_{pk_{PD_i}}(S_{B_i}), \mathsf{Enc}_{pk_T}(p_i), \mathsf{Enc}_{pk_T}(a_i), \mathsf{Enc}_{pk_T}(y_i))$. Therefore, it cannot change the other party's inputs since all the bid components are encrypted and signed. Moreover, nobody except the Treasury will be able to decrypt the values. Secondly, the name value PD_i is hashed and then encrypted using a $(2,2)$-threshold encryption scheme and the names of the winners are only revealed after the auction while the Treasury waits for the bidders to learn their own results. Finally, the response $res = $ "Accept/Reject" of the Treasury for the ith primary dealer can only be seen by that primary dealer because threshold decryption is performed $(\mathsf{Dec}_{sk_{PD_i}^{(2)}}(\mathsf{Enc}_{pk_{PD_i}}(\mathsf{Sign}_T[res])))$ by using the key share $sk_{PD_i}^{(2)}$ by the Treasury and needs decrypting with the other key share $sk_{PD_i}^{(1)}$ which is known only by the ith primary dealer.

At the beginning of the Award phase of the protocol, the bidder may refuse to send the related hash value $\mathsf{Hash}(X_i)$ to the Treasury. In this case both the bidder and the Treasury cannot learn the result of that bidder whether it is the accepted or rejected (because of anonymity of the bidders). In that case, the bidder must send the hash value $\mathsf{Hash}(X_i)$ in order to finalize the overall outcome. We can prevent this type of problem for example by penalty cases (e.g., banning of participation for future auctions). In order to find out that malicious bidder who did not send its hash value, the Treasury and all the primary dealers will meet and decrypt the related results. We underline that, such a hiding bidder does not compromise the privacy. Also no malicious party can submit a bid instead of an honest bidder for future auctions, by for example mounting a replay attack. Note that this is solved by means of time stamped signature schemes.   □

F   Proof of Theorem 2

A malicious Treasury gets no information during the Submission and Evaluation phase since the Central Bank sends encrypted values $\mathsf{Sign}_{CB}[\langle \text{output}_i, X_j \rangle]$ which are outputs of subprotocols. The Treasury obtains the encrypted ordered list $\langle X_j \rangle$ of the accepted bidders and cannot obtain any extra information about the bidders since the list is anonymised. Similarly, during the Award phase, Treasury obtains hashed values $\mathsf{Hash}(X_i)$ which do not give any useful information to him. Hence, a malicious Treasury cannot learn any additional information except the winners' bids.   □

G   Proof of Theorem 3

Firstly, the only privacy concern for the Treasury is the secrecy of δ. Since δ is encrypted with pk_T, nobody else but only the Treasury itself can open (decrypt) this encrypted value and therefore, a malicious Central Bank who computes homomorphic evaluations with $\mathsf{Enc}_{pk_T}(\delta)$ cannot learn any useful information about it. Secondly, the Central Bank cannot see the sum values $\sum_{i=1}^{k} a_i$, $\sum_{i=1}^{k} y_i$, $\sum_{i=1}^{m} a_i$ and $\sum_{i=1}^{m} y_i$ in clear form. Despite the Central Bank makes some evaluations and calculations with those values under encryption, it cannot extract the sum since it has no knowledge of the decryption key sk_T belonging to the Treasury. Note that our proposed model does not consider active collusion between dishonest parties in which secret keys are revealed. Hence, it may also be said that the privacy of the sums are also satisfied.

The Central Bank runs exclusively the subprotocols, and uses its secret key sk_{CB} for signing the subprotocol outputs $\{\langle \text{output}_i, X_j \rangle : i = 1, \ldots, 6, \ j = 1, \ldots, m\}$. Since the underlying subprotocols (sorting and comparing) are secure, a malicious Central Bank obtains no useful information. Therefore, privacy will not be compromised in the presence of a malicious Central Bank.   □

References

1. Bektaş, A.: On secure electronic auction process of government domestic debt securities in Turkey. Ph.D. thesis, Middle East Technical University, Ankara, Turkey, August 2013
2. Ben-David, A., Nisan, N., Pinkas, B.: FairplayMP: a system for secure multi-party computation. In: Proceedings of the 15th ACM Conference on Computer and Communications Security, CCS 2008, pp. 257–266. ACM, New York (2008)
3. Ben-Or, M., Goldwasser, S., Wigderson, A.: Completeness theorems for non-cryptographic fault-tolerant distributed computation. In: Proceedings of the Twentieth Annual ACM Symposium on Theory of Computing, STOC 1988, pp. 1–10. ACM, New York (1988)
4. Bogdanov, D., Laur, S., Willemson, J.: Sharemind: a framework for fast privacy-preserving computations. IACR Cryptology ePrint Archive 2008, 289 (2008). http://dblp.uni-trier.de/db/journals/iacr/iacr2008.html#BogdanovLW08
5. Bogdanov, D., Talviste, R., Willemson, J.: Deploying secure multi-party computation for financial data analysis. In: Keromytis, A.D. (ed.) FC 2012. LNCS, vol. 7397, pp. 57–64. Springer, Heidelberg (2012)
6. Bogetoft, P., Christensen, D.L., Damgård, I., Geisler, M., Jakobsen, T., Krøigaard, M., Nielsen, J.D., Nielsen, J.B., Nielsen, K., Pagter, J., Schwartzbach, M., Toft, T.: Secure multiparty computation goes live. In: Dingledine, R., Golle, P. (eds.) FC 2009. LNCS, vol. 5628, pp. 325–343. Springer, Heidelberg (2009)
7. Brandt, F., Sandholm, T.W.: Efficient privacy-preserving protocols for multi-unit auctions. In: S. Patrick, A., Yung, M. (eds.) FC 2005. LNCS, vol. 3570, pp. 298–312. Springer, Heidelberg (2005)
8. Brandt, F., Sandholm, T.: On the existence of unconditionally privacy-preserving auction protocols. ACM Trans. Inf. Syst. Secur. $11(2)$, 1–21 (2008)
9. Chaum, D., Crépeau, C., Damgård, I.: Multiparty unconditionally secure protocols. In: Proceedings of the Twentieth Annual ACM Symposium on Theory of Computing, STOC 1988, pp. 11–19. ACM, New York (1988)
10. Cramer, R., Damgård, I.: Multiparty computation, an introduction. In: Contemporary Cryptology. Advanced Courses in Mathematics CRM Barcelona. Birkhauser Verlag AG (2005)
11. Damgård, I., Geisler, M., Krøigaard, M.: Homomorphic encryption and secure comparison. Int. J. Appl. Crypt. $1(1)$, 22–31 (2008). doi:10.1504/IJACT.2008.017048
12. Garay, J.A., Schoenmakers, B., Villegas, J.: Practical and secure solutions for integer comparison. In: Okamoto, T., Wang, X. (eds.) PKC 2007. LNCS, vol. 4450, pp. 330–342. Springer, Heidelberg (2007)
13. Garay, J.A., Jakobsson, M.: Timed release of standard digital signatures. In: Blaze, M. (ed.) FC 2002. LNCS, vol. 2357. Springer, Heidelberg (2003)
14. Goldreich, O., Micali, S., Wigderson, A.: How to play ANY mental game or a completeness theorem for protocols with honest majority. In: Proceedings of the Nineteenth Annual ACM Symposium on Theory of Computing, STOC 1987, pp. 218–229. ACM, New York (1987)
15. Hazay, C., Mikkelsen, G.L., Rabin, T., Toft, T.: Efficient RSA key generation and threshold paillier in the two-party setting. In: Dunkelman, O. (ed.) CT-RSA 2012. LNCS, vol. 7178, pp. 313–331. Springer, Heidelberg (2012)
16. Henecka, W., Kögl, S., Sadeghi, A.R., Schneider, T., Wehrenberg, I.: TASTY: tool for automating secure two-party computations. In: Proceedings of the 17th ACM Conference on Computer and Communications Security, CCS 2010, pp. 451–462. ACM, New York (2010)

17. Jónsson, K.V., Kreitz, G., Uddin, M.: Secure multi-party sorting and applications (2011)
18. Katti, R.S., Ababei, C.: Secure comparison without explicit XOR. CoRR abs/1204.2854 (2012)
19. Lipmaa, H., Asokan, N., Niemi, V.: Secure vickrey auctions without threshold trust. In: Blaze, M. (ed.) FC 2002. LNCS, vol. 2357, pp. 87–101. Springer, Heidelberg (2003)
20. Lipmaa, H., Toft, T.: Secure equality and greater-than tests with sublinear online complexity. In: Fomin, F.V., Freivalds, R., Kwiatkowska, M., Peleg, D. (eds.) ICALP 2013, Part II. LNCS, vol. 7966, pp. 645–656. Springer, Heidelberg (2013)
21. Naor, M., Pinkas, B., Sumner, R.: Privacy preserving auctions and mechanism design. In: Proceedings of the 1st ACM Conference on Electronic Commerce, EC 1999, pp. 129–139. ACM, New York (1999)
22. Paillier, P.: Public-key cryptosystems based on composite degree residuosity classes. In: Stern, J. (ed.) EUROCRYPT 1999. LNCS, vol. 1592, p. 223. Springer, Heidelberg (1999)
23. Schoenmakers, B., Tuyls, P.: Practical two-party computation based on the conditional gate. In: Lee, P.J. (ed.) ASIACRYPT 2004. LNCS, vol. 3329, pp. 119–136. Springer, Heidelberg (2004)
24. Sedgewick, R., Wayne, K.: Algorithms, 4th edn. Addison-Wesley, Redwood City (2011)
25. Toft, T.: Sub-linear, secure comparison with two non-colluding parties. In: Catalano, D., Fazio, N., Gennaro, R., Nicolosi, A. (eds.) PKC 2011. LNCS, vol. 6571, pp. 174–191. Springer, Heidelberg (2011)
26. Toft, T.: Sub-linear, secure comparison with two non-colluding parties. In: Catalano, D., Fazio, N., Gennaro, R., Nicolosi, A. (eds.) PKC 2011. LNCS, vol. 6571, pp. 174–191. Springer, Heidelberg (2011)
27. Undersecretariat of Treasury: Annual Edns 200813. Technical report, Republic of Turkey Prime Ministry (2012)
28. Veugen, T.: Improving the DGK comparison protocol. In: 2012 IEEE International Workshop on Information Forensics and Security (WIFS), pp. 49–54. WIFS 2012, Tenerife, Spain, Dec 2012

Anonymous Data Collection System with Mediators

Hiromi Arai[1], Keita Emura[2(✉)], and Takahiro Matsuda[3]

[1] The University of Tokyo, Tokyo, Japan
[2] National Institute of Information and Communications Technology (NICT),
Tokyo, Japan
k-emura@nict.go.jp
[3] National Institute of Advanced Industrial Science and Technology (AIST),
Tokyo, Japan

Abstract. Nowadays, sensitive data is treated for a constellation of purposes, e.g., establishing the presence or absence of causal association among certain diseases. Then, statistics of sensitive data needs to be computed, and a number of methods for computing such statistics with concerning privacy so far have been investigated, e.g., secure computation, differential privacy, k-anonymity, etc. On the contrary, it seems not clear how to collect sensitive data with concerning privacy in the first place. Moreover, the cost for data collection should be considered if the number of data suppliers is relatively large.

In this paper, we propose an anonymous data collection system with mediators, where no mediator knows actual data, but simultaneously mediators can check a data format whether data belongs to a certain range. Then, data with the expected format can be collected in a "secure" and "efficient" way. For constructing this system, we employ public key encryption with an additional functionality which is called *restrictive public key encryption* (RPKE). Finally, we estimate the performance of the proposed system in which existing concrete constructions are used and confirm it is sufficiently efficient for practical use.

1 Introduction

There have been investigated a number of methods to obtain statistics of sensitive data with concerning privacy so far, e.g., secure computation [36], differential privacy [14], k-anonymity [30,31], etc. On the contrary, it seems not clear how to collect sensitive data with concerning privacy in the first place. In order to build databases containing sensitive data for a certain purpose, e.g., computing statistics of medical data, such data needs to be collected in the first place. Of course, utilization efficiency is one of the most important priorities for data mining whereas a data collector is not overly solicitous about privacy of data suppliers.

1.1 Anonymous Data Collection

Building on the earlier work by Yang et al. [35], Brickell and Shmatikov [12] proposed an anonymous data collection system by employing public key encryption

© Springer International Publishing Switzerland 2015
B. Ors and B. Preneel (Eds.): BalkanCryptSec 2014, LNCS 9024, pp. 141–160, 2015.
DOI: 10.1007/978-3-319-21356-9_10

(PKE) and digital signature as its building blocks. In the Brickell-Shmatikov system, there are a data collector and data suppliers. One drawback of their system is efficiency. Specifically, in their system, all data suppliers are required to be on-line during the data collection procedure, and the number of rounds (i.e. interaction between the data collector and data suppliers) is linear in the number of data suppliers. Moreover, since one data is sequentially encrypted n-times where n is the number of data suppliers, the ciphertext overhead becomes $O(n)$ (when hybrid encryption is employed) and thus the total communication overhead becomes $O(n^2)$. These situations are quite inefficient when a large number of data is treated. Subsequently, Ashrafi and Ng [4] improve the efficiency of the Brickell-Shmatikov system. However, still all data suppliers are required to be on-line, and the round complexity was not improved in the asymptotic sense. Moreover, though these systems [4,12] considered integrity and confidentiality in addition to anonymity, formal *cryptographic* definitions of integrity and confidentiality were not given in these works, though cryptographic tools are employed.

An alternative attempt for secure data collection may be using *mediators*, since the data collector can delegate the data collection task to them, and the costs of the data collector can be reduced. Moreover, in many practical situations in which sensitive data is collected, the data collector does not necessarily have to identify data suppliers. For example, managing an identity table causes a risk for data exposure, and unnecessary data should not be collected/managed/stored as much as possible. Of course, the data collector should not reveal data itself to mediators. One naive approach would be to use PKE, where the data collector has a public key and data suppliers encrypt their data using the public key, and the data collector checks collected data after decrypting these ciphertexts. However, this approach does not make sense since mediators do nothing, and no cost for data collection is reduced. Therefore, in order to reduce the costs of data arrangement, the data collector needs to be able to give format-check capabilities (e.g., check whether data belongs to a certain range) to mediators.

1.2   Our Contribution

In this paper, we propose a secure data collection system with mediators, where:

- The data collector can delegate data collection and data arrangement tasks to mediators in a "secure" way so that no mediator can know (unallowable information of) actual data.
- Mediators can check a data format without knowing data itself so that data belongs to a certain range (age, gender, disease, etc.), and can sort out (encrypted) data by regarding a range as a quasi-identifier.
- There is no interaction between data suppliers and data collector, i.e. no data supplier is required to be on-line during the data collection procedure. In this aspect, we significantly improve the efficiency of the Brickell-Shmatikov system [12] (albeit employing a different setting).

- The ciphertext overhead is independent from the number of data suppliers n (i.e., $O(1)$), and the total communication overhead is $O(n)$ which is the same as the case that all data are sent without any encryption, whereas that of the Brickell-Shmatikov system is $O(n^2)$.
- The data collector does not identify data suppliers. We remark that our anonymity definition also considers collusion resistance as is similar to the definition given by Brickell and Shmatikov [12], where even if the data collector and all data suppliers (except at least two honest data suppliers) collude, no one can link honest data suppliers and data provided by the honest suppliers.

We give formal *cryptographic* security definitions (*semantic security, anonymity, and format-check soundness*) for a secure data collection system with mediators, and prove that the proposed system is secure in the sense of our definitions. Our proposed secure data collection system employs a cryptographic primitive called *Restrictive Public Key Encryption* (RPKE) [27,28], which is a kind of public key encryption with non-interactive zero-knowledge (NIZK) range proof[1]. Roughly speaking, in RPKE, one can verify a ciphertext is an encryption of a plaintext that lies in a specific message space MS, but no other information is revealed from the ciphertext. See Sect. 2 (and Appendix A) for more details.

We also estimate the efficiency of the proposed system by using the PBC library [2]. We use the Sakai et al. RPKE scheme [27,28] (see Appendix A). We confirm that for each algorithm, its running time is at most millisecond order on a standard desktop PC, which seems sufficiently practical.

Our Scenario: A general scenario where our system is suitable and can be used is a situation in which there is a data collector who wants to use microdata and there are individuals with his or her private data. We furthermore suppose that (1) the individuals are willing to provide their private data if the microdata is not explicitly linkable to individuals, and (2) the data collector needs microdata but no identifier of individuals.

More concretely, the following scenario poses an intuitive and motivating example. Suppose a location-based service company wants to gather location data of its clients for services. The clients regard location information as highly sensitive and permit only their servicer to access their data. The company needs location data at micro level for data mining such as recommendation systems. However, each of the individuals need not to be identified in such a service. Moreover, the number of corresponding data suppliers is potentially large. Suppose the data collector wants to collect data of 20 s and 30 s only (e.g., the data collector wants to know data of relatively young people but not teenage). Then, the data collector just decrypts ciphertexts of 20 s and 30 s only, or mediators

---

[1] We remark that a naive combination of PKE and NIZK range proof is not enough. First, general NIZK is quite inefficient and an efficient instantiation is not trivial. Second, plaintexts (to be proved to belong to a range via NIZK) need to be recovered via a decryption procedure. On the contrary, RPKE supports both range proofs and decryption in an efficient way, and this is the reason why we adopt RPKE as a building block.

144   H. Arai et al.

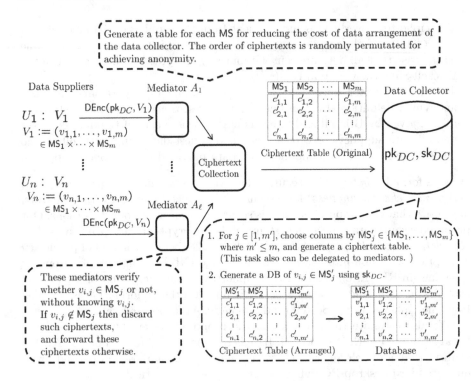

Fig. 1. Brief description of our secure data collection system

also can eliminate unnecessary data (i.e., ciphertexts encrypted by 10 s, 40 s,...) without knowing data itself. We remark that, as a naive way, the data collector also can eliminate unnecessary data after decrypting ciphertexts. However, this naive method is inefficient in the sense that the data collector needs to decrypt all ciphertexts containing unnecessary data, and this can be a problem when there are a large number of data suppliers. On the contrary, our system is effective to achieve an efficient and secure data collection. As another example, let the data collector be a drug company that wants to collect [age, gender, disease name] but does not want to identify data suppliers in order to avoid any exposure risk of unnecessary information. Then, our system is effective.

Brief Description of Our System: The procedure of our proposed system is briefly explained as follows (we illustrate a brief description of our system in Fig. 1). Suppose a data collector, who has a public key pk_{DC} and a secret key sk_{DC} of RPKE, wants to delegate the task of collecting data to mediators. The data collector specifies the domain MS from which data is expected to be sampled. When a data supplier U_i agrees to give his/her data, the data supplier encrypts data, say $V_i = (v_{i,j})_{j=1}^m$, using pk_{DC} and sends the ciphertext C to a mediator. The mediator checks whether $v_{i,j} \in \mathsf{MS}_j$ or not *without knowing $v_{i,j}$* by the verification algorithm of RPKE, stores it if $v_{i,j} \in \mathsf{MS}_j$, and discards it if $v_{i,j} \notin \mathsf{MS}_j$. The mediator can build a table for each MS when multiple domains are defined, since anyone can check the corresponding data belongs to MS_j from $c_{i,j}$ without knowing data itself. This can reduce the cost of data arrangement of the data collector. Note that the ordering of records/entries of data should be shuffled (as in MIX-net or secure multi-party shuffle protocols [10,13,16,17]) for hiding the information of who the actual data suppliers are, from the viewpoint of the data collector. Then the data collector can extract ciphertexts according to $MS'_j \in \{MS_1, \ldots, MS_m\}$ for $j \in [1, m']$, where $m' \leq m$, without verifying ciphertexts since the verification has been done by mediators. Then, the data collector does not have to decrypt all ciphertexts. This procedure corresponds to the case introduced as our scenario where the data collector wants to collect data of 20 s and 30 s only and the mediator eliminates unnecessary data (i.e., ciphertexts encrypted by 10s, 40s,...) without knowing data itself. Of course the arrangement task also can be delegated to mediators. But the data collector may later use the currently unnecessary data, and here we assume that the data collector generates the arranged table. Finally, the data collector decrypts ciphertexts and obtains data $v_{i,j}$.

Alternative Solution and its Limitation: One may think that using anonymous communication channels (e.g., Tor [3]) between a data supplier and a data collector is enough for secure data collection, since we assume that data does not contain any identifier that uniquely determines the corresponding data supplier[2]. Moreover, one may think that no encryption is employed since such data are no longer quite sensitive. Nevertheless, end-to-end encryption is necessary since some unexpected third party (including mediators) may obtain data and use it if no encryption is required. Even if data suppliers simply encrypt their own data by using a public key of the data collector, and send ciphertexts via anonymous channels, there is no way to reduce the cost for data collection (i.e., the data collector is required to decrypt all ciphertexts). On the contrary, our solution can delegate the cost to mediators in a secure way.

One may think that symmetric key cryptography should be employed for the fast decryption rather than RPKE. However, in order to use it, the data collector needs to somehow establish a shared key between the data collector and *each* data supplier. Though this issue might be solved by using hybrid encryption, the decryption cost of hybrid encryption is almost the same as that of usual PKE.

Related Work: The importance of sensitive data collection is discussed in ISO/IES 20732 [1]. But the concrete techniques are not given, and it is left to the data collector to consider it.

Yang et al. [35] proposed an anonymous data collection system, but this system was shown insecure by Brickell and Shmatikov [12]. Brickell and Shmatikov also proposed another anonymous data collection system, but as mentioned earlier, there is a room for improving efficiency of their system (and its improved version by Ashrafi and Ng [4] also) since all data suppliers are required to be on-line during the data collection procedure, and the number of rounds depends

---

[2] This assumption is the same as that of Brickell and Shmatikov [12]. They also assume that responses and respondents are not linkable by content.

linearly on the number of data suppliers. Ashrafi and Ng [5] also proposed an anonymous online data collection system which employs the onion route approach, but they estimate anonymity in the information theoretic sense (i.e., information entropy is used). Since computationally secure cryptographic tools (digital signature and PKE) are used in their system, we do not think that such an information-theoretic estimation of anonymity makes much sense.

2 Building Blocks

In this section, we give definitions of building blocks. Throughout the paper, we use the following notation: "PPT" stands for *probabilistic polynomial time*. The character "κ" always indicates *security parameter* which decides the length of keys. A function $f : \mathbb{N} \to \mathbb{N}$ is said to be *negligible* if for all positive polynomials p and for all sufficiently large $\kappa \in \mathbb{N}$, it holds that $f(\kappa) < 1/p(\kappa)$.

2.1 Restrictive Public Key Encryption (RPKE)

In RPKE [27,28], one can verify that a ciphertext is an encryption of a plaintext that lies in a specific message space MS but no other information is revealed from the ciphertext. RPKE can be a useful tool for format checking, e.g., one can verify the decryption result is either 0 or 1 without decryption.

We observe that the Sakai et al. RPKE scheme [27,28] can capture multiple message spaces $MS_1, \ldots, MS_m$. Therefore, in the following definition we explicitly capture multiple message spaces. Here, MRA stands for Message Restriction Authority that specifies message spaces.

Definition 1 (RPKE). *A restrictive public key encryption (RPKE) scheme* $\mathcal{RPKE}$ *consists of six algorithms* (MRASetup, RKeyGen, MSSetup, REnc, VerifyMS, RDec):

MRASetup: *This is the key generation algorithm (for the MRA) which takes as input a security parameter* $\kappa \in \mathbb{N}$, *and outputs a public key* pk_{MRA} *and a secret key* sk_{MRA}.

RKeyGen: *This is the user key generation algorithm which takes as input* pk_{MRA}, *and outputs a public encryption key* pk_d *and a secret decryption key* sk_d.

MSSetup: *This is the public verification key generation algorithm which takes as input* pk_{MRA}, sk_{MRA}, *and message spaces* $\mathcal{MS} := (MS_1, \ldots, MS_m)$, *and outputs a public verification key* $pk_{\mathcal{MS}} := (pk_{MS_1}, \ldots, pk_{MS_m})$.

REnc: *This is the encryption algorithm which takes as input* pk_{MRA}, pk_d, MS $\in \mathcal{MS}$, pk_{MS}, *and a message* M, *and outputs a ciphertext* C.[3]

---

[3] We can define the encryption algorithm so that the algorithm outputs $\perp$ if $M \notin$ MS, and a ciphertext C otherwise. Actually, the Sakai et al. scheme matches this definition. Nevertheless, the current definition makes sense since an RPKE scheme, where the encryption algorithm works for any plaintext but the verification algorithm can detect whether $M \in$ MS or not, could be constructed. See Appendix C for details.

VerifyMS: *This is the public verification algorithm which takes as input* pk_{MRA}, pk_d, $\mathsf{MS} \in \mathcal{MS}$, $\mathsf{pk}_{\mathsf{MS}}$, *and* C, *and outputs a bit 1 or 0. Here 1 means that the corresponding message belongs to* MS, *and 0 otherwise.*

RDec: *This is the decryption algorithm which takes as input* pk_{MRA}, pk_d, sk_d, $\mathsf{MS} \in \mathcal{MS}$, $\mathsf{pk}_{\mathsf{MS}}$, *and* C, *and outputs* M *or* $\perp$ *(meaning that* C *is invalid).*

We require the correctness property: for all $\kappa \in \mathbb{N}$, *all sets of message spaces* $\mathcal{MS}$, *all restricted message spaces* $\mathsf{MS} \in \mathcal{MS}$, *all messages* $M \in \mathsf{MS}$, *all* $(\mathsf{pk}_{MRA}, \mathsf{sk}_{MRA}) \leftarrow \mathsf{MRASetup}(1^\kappa)$, *all* $(\mathsf{pk}_d, \mathsf{sk}_d) \leftarrow \mathsf{RKeyGen}(\mathsf{pk}_{MRA})$, *all* $\mathsf{pk}_{\mathcal{MS}} \leftarrow \mathsf{MSSetup}(\mathsf{pk}_{MRA}, \mathsf{sk}_{MRA}, \mathcal{MS})$, *and all* $C \leftarrow \mathsf{REnc}(\mathsf{pk}_{MRA}, \mathsf{pk}_d, \mathsf{MS}, \mathsf{pk}_{\mathsf{MS}}, M)$, *it holds that* $\mathsf{RDec}(\mathsf{pk}_{MRA}, \mathsf{pk}_d, \mathsf{sk}_d, \mathsf{MS}, \mathsf{pk}_{\mathsf{MS}}, C) = M$ *and* $\mathsf{VerifyMS}(\mathsf{pk}_{MRA}, \mathsf{pk}_d, \mathsf{MS}, \mathsf{pk}_{\mathsf{MS}}, C) = 1$.

We require indistinguishability with restrictive message space under chosen plaintext attack (IND-MSR-CPA) and verification soundness. Briefly, IND-MSR-CPA captures confidentiality of RPKE, and guarantees that no adversary, who chooses two plaintexts that belong to the same message space and is given an encryption of one of the plaintexts, can guess which plaintext is encrypted significantly better than random guess. Verification soundness guarantees that $\mathsf{VerifyMS}(\mathsf{pk}_{MRA}, \mathsf{pk}_d, \mathsf{MS}, \mathsf{pk}_{\mathsf{MS}}, C) = 0$ if the decryption result of C does not belong to MS. The formal definitions are given in Appendix A due to the page limitation.

3   Definition of Our Secure Data Collection System

In this section, we give the syntax and the security definitions of our secure data collection system with mediators. In our system, there are three entities: Data collector, Data supplier(s), and Mediator(s). Data collector wants to collect certain data from Data suppliers in both a privacy-preserving and efficient way. Due to some reason (e.g., Data collector does not want to identify Data suppliers, wants to reduce the collection cost, etc.), Data collector requests Mediators to collect data from Data suppliers. Data suppliers encrypt data by using Data collector's public key, and give the corresponding ciphertext to Mediator. Though Mediator does not know the actual data, Mediator can check the format of encrypted data.

Definition 2 (Syntax of Data Collection System with Mediators).
A secure data collection system $\mathcal{SDCS}$ *consists of five algorithms* (KeyGen, DEnc, FormatCheck, TableGen, DDec):

KeyGen: *This is the key generation algorithm (for Data collector) which takes as input a security parameter* $\kappa \in \mathbb{N}$, *and outputs a set of message spaces* $\mathcal{MS} := (\mathsf{MS}_1, \ldots, \mathsf{MS}_m)$, *a public key* pk_{DC}, *and a secret key* sk_{DC}. *(This algorithm is supposed to be run by Data collector.)*

DEnc: *This is the data encryption algorithm which takes as input* pk_{DC} *and a set of data* $V = (v_1, \ldots, v_m) \in \mathsf{MS}_1 \times \cdots \times \mathsf{MS}_m$, *and outputs a ciphertext* $C_D := (c_1, \ldots, c_m)$. *(This algorithm is supposed to be run by each Data supplier.)*

FormatCheck: *Let* f-index $:= \{1, \ldots, m\}$. *This is the data format checking algorithm which takes as input* pk_{DC} *and a ciphertext* C_D, *and for each* $j \in [1, m]$ *changes* j-*th element of* f-index *to* ϵ *if the corresponding data* $v_j \notin \mathsf{MS}_j$, *and outputs* f-index. *(This algorithm is supposed to be run by Mediator.)*

TableGen: *This is the ciphertext table generation algorithm which takes as input* $\mathcal{MS}$, pk_{DC}, *and a set* $(C_{D,i})_{i=1}^{n}$ *of ciphertexts where* $C_{D,i} := (c_{i,1}, \ldots, c_{i,m})$, *and outputs a "permuted" set* $(C'_{D,i})_{i=1}^{n}$ *of ciphertexts. Namely, it is required that there is a permutation* $\phi : [1, n] \rightarrow [1, n]$ *such that* $C'_{D,i} = C_{D,\phi(i)}$ *holds for all* $i \in [1, n]$. *(This algorithm is supposed to be run by Mediator.)*

DDec: *This is the data decryption algorithm which takes as input* pk_{DC}, sk_{DC}, *and* C_D, *and outputs a table of data* $(v_1, \ldots, v_m)$ *or* $\bot$. *(This algorithm is supposed to be run by Data collector.)*

Besides the requirement of **TableGen** explained above, we require the following correctness property of the other algorithms: for all $\kappa \in \mathbb{N}$, all $(\mathcal{MS} := (\mathsf{MS}_1, \ldots, \mathsf{MS}_m), \mathsf{pk}_{DC}, \mathsf{sk}_{DC}) \leftarrow \mathsf{KeyGen}(1^\kappa)$, all data $V = (v_1, \ldots, v_m) \in \mathsf{MS}_1 \times \cdots \times \mathsf{MS}_m$, all $C_D \leftarrow \mathsf{DEnc}(\mathsf{pk}_{DC}, V)$, and all f-index $\leftarrow \mathsf{FormatCheck}(\mathsf{pk}_{DC}, C_D)$, it holds that $|\mathsf{f}\text{-index}| = m$ (i.e., no ϵ is contained in f-index) and $\mathsf{DDec}(\mathsf{pk}_{DC}, \mathsf{sk}_{DC}, C_D) = V$. Here, $|\cdot|$ denotes the number of elements which are not ϵ.

Next, we define *anonymity* which guarantees that Data collector obtains no information of Data suppliers. Mediators and Data suppliers are modeled as semi-honest parities that always follow the protocol description. The anonymity definition of Brickell and Shmatikov [12] and ours are the same in the sense that an adversary is allowed to choose two users but the adversary cannot distinguish which user is chosen by the challenger from the transcript of the protocol. In the following game, let n be the total number of Data suppliers. $\mathcal{A}$ chooses two Data suppliers α and β. Moreover, $\mathcal{A}$ chooses V_0^* and V_1^*. Here, we assume that V_0^* and V_1^* do not contain any identifier that uniquely determines α or β.

Definition 3 (Anonymity). *We say that* $\mathcal{SDCS}$ *has anonymity if for all PPT adversaries* $\mathcal{A}$ *the following advantage* $\mathsf{Adv}_{\mathcal{A},\mathcal{SDCS}}^{\mathrm{anon}}(\kappa)$ *is negligible.*

$$\mathsf{Adv}_{\mathcal{A},\mathcal{SDCS}}^{\mathrm{anon}}(\kappa) :=$$

$$\Pr \left[\begin{array}{l} (\mathcal{MS} := (\mathsf{MS}_1, \ldots, \mathsf{MS}_m), \mathsf{pk}_{DC}^*, \mathsf{sk}_{DC}^*) \leftarrow \mathsf{KeyGen}(1^\kappa) \\ (\alpha, \beta, V_0^*, V_1^*, (C_{D,i}^*)_{i \in [1,n] \setminus \{\alpha,\beta\}}, st) \leftarrow \mathcal{A}(\mathsf{pk}_{DC}^*, \mathsf{sk}_{DC}^*, \mathcal{MS}) \\ b \xleftarrow{\$} \{0,1\} \\ \textit{If } b = 0, \textit{ then} \\ \quad C_{D,\alpha}^* \leftarrow \mathsf{DEnc}(\mathsf{pk}_{DC}^*, V_0^*); \; C_{D,\beta}^* \leftarrow \mathsf{DEnc}(\mathsf{pk}_{DC}^*, V_1^*) \\ \textit{Else If } b = 1, \textit{ then} \\ \quad C_{D,\alpha}^* \leftarrow \mathsf{DEnc}(\mathsf{pk}_{DC}^*, V_1^*); \; C_{D,\beta}^* \leftarrow \mathsf{DEnc}(\mathsf{pk}_{DC}^*, V_0^*) \\ \textit{End If} \\ (C_{D,i}'^*)_{i=1}^{n} \leftarrow \mathsf{TableGen}(\mathcal{MS}, \mathsf{pk}_{DC}^*, (C_{D,i}^*)_{i=1}^{n}) \\ b' \leftarrow \mathcal{A}((C_{D,i}'^*)_{i=1}^{n}, st) : \; b = b' \end{array} \right] - 1/2$$

where it is required that $V_0^*, V_1^* \in \mathcal{MS}$.

Next, we define *semantic security* which guarantees that no information of data v is revealed from a ciphertext. That is, no Mediator can know v, except the fact that v belongs to some message space MS. Here, an adversary $\mathcal{A}$ is modeled as honest-but-curious Mediator.

Definition 4 (Semantic Security). *We say that $\mathcal{SDCS}$ is semantically secure if for all PPT adversaries $\mathcal{A}$ the following advantage $\mathsf{Adv}^{ss}_{\mathcal{A},\mathcal{SDCS}}(\kappa)$ is negligible.*

$$
\mathsf{Adv}^{ss}_{\mathcal{A},\mathcal{SDCS}}(\kappa) :=
$$

$$
\left| \Pr \left[\begin{array}{l} (\mathcal{MS} := (\mathsf{MS}_1,\ldots,\mathsf{MS}_m), \mathsf{pk}^*_{DC}, \mathsf{sk}^*_{DC}) \leftarrow \mathsf{KeyGen}(1^\kappa) \\ (V_0^*, V_1^*, st) \leftarrow \mathcal{A}(\mathcal{MS}, \mathsf{pk}^*_{DC}) \\ b \xleftarrow{\$} \{0,1\}; \ C_D^* \leftarrow \mathsf{DEnc}(\mathsf{pk}^*_{DC}, V_b^*) \\ b' \leftarrow \mathcal{A}(C_D^*, st) : \ b = b' \end{array} \right] - 1/2 \right|
$$

where it is required that $V_0^*, V_1^* \in \mathcal{MS}$.

We remark that the above definition does not capture chosen ciphertext security where $\mathcal{A}$ is allowed to issue decryption queries. For the sake of simplicity we do not consider chosen ciphertext security though it can be straightforwardly obtained.

Next, we define *format-check soundness* which guarantees that for all $C_j \in$ tbl if C_j passes the check by FormatCheck (i.e. it is not marked as "ϵ"), the decryption result of C_j belongs to MS_j. That is, Data collector can be sure of the validity of the result of the format checking executed by Mediators, without decryption.

Definition 5 (Format-check Soundness). *We say that $\mathcal{SDCS}$ has format-check soundness if for all PPT adversaries $\mathcal{A}$ the following advantage $\mathsf{Adv}^{fc}_{\mathcal{A},\mathcal{SDCS}}(\kappa)$ is negligible.*

$$
\mathsf{Adv}^{fc}_{\mathcal{A},\mathcal{SDCS}}(\kappa) :=
$$

$$
\Pr \left[\begin{array}{l} (\mathcal{MS} := (\mathsf{MS}_1,\ldots,\mathsf{MS}_m), \mathsf{pk}_{DC}, \mathsf{sk}_{DC}) \leftarrow \mathsf{KeyGen}(1^\kappa) \\ (C_D^* := (c_j^*)_{j=1}^m) \leftarrow \mathcal{A}(\mathsf{pk}_{DC}, \mathcal{MS}) \\ \mathsf{f\text{-}index}^* \leftarrow \mathsf{FormatCheck}(\mathsf{pk}_{DC}, C_D^*) \\ (v_1,\ldots,v_m) \leftarrow \mathsf{DDec}(\mathsf{pk}_{DC}, \mathsf{sk}_{DC}, C_D^*) \\ : \exists j \in [1,m] \ s.t. \ j \in \mathsf{f\text{-}index}^* \ and \ v_j \notin \mathsf{MS}_j \end{array} \right]
$$

4   Proposed Secure Data Collection System

In this section, we construct our secure data collection system by using RPKE. Security proofs are given in Appendix B. Let $\mathcal{RPKE} = (\mathsf{MRASetup}, \mathsf{RKeyGen}, \mathsf{MSSetup}, \mathsf{REnc}, \mathsf{VerifyMS}, \mathsf{RDec})$ be a RPKE scheme.

Table 1. Ciphertext Table (Generated by Mediator)

MS_1	MS_2	$\cdots$	MS_m
$c'_{1,1}$	$c'_{1,2}$	$\cdots$	$c'_{1,m}$
$c'_{2,1}$	$c'_{2,2}$	$\cdots$	$c'_{2,m}$
$\vdots$	$\vdots$	$\vdots$	$\vdots$
$c'_{n,1}$	$c'_{n,2}$	$\cdots$	$c'_{n,m}$

Table 2. Ciphertext Table with two identifiers "Age" and "Disease"

Age				Disease
MS_1	MS_2	$\cdots$	MS_9	MS_{10}
−	$c'_{1,2}$	$\cdots$	-	$c'_{1,10}$
−	−	$\cdots$	$c'_{2,9}$	$c'_{2,10}$
$\vdots$	$\vdots$	$\vdots$	$\vdots$	$\vdots$
$c'_{n,1}$	−	$\cdots$	−	$c'_{n,10}$

4.1 Our Construction

Protocol 1 (Proposed Secure Data Collection System)

KeyGen(1^κ): *Define* $\mathcal{MS} := (MS_1, \ldots, MS_m)$. *Run* (pk_{MRA}, sk_{MRA}) $\leftarrow$ MRASetup(1^κ), (pk_d, sk_d) $\leftarrow$ RKeyGen(pk_{MRA}), *and* $pk_{\mathcal{MS}} := (pk_{MS_1}, \ldots, pk_{MS_m})$ $\leftarrow$ MSSetup(pk_{MRA}, sk_{MRA}, MS). *Output* $pk_{DC} = (pk_{MRA}, pk_d, pk_{\mathcal{MS}})$ *and* $sk_{DC} = (sk_{MRA}, sk_d)$.

DEnc(pk_{DC}, V): *Let* $V = (v_1, \ldots, v_m) \in MS_1 \times \cdots \times MS_m$. *Run* $c_j \leftarrow$ REnc($pk_{MRA}, pk_d, MS_j, pk_{MS_j}, v_j$) *for* $j \in [1, m]$ *and output* $C_D := (c_j)_{j=1}^m$.

FormatCheck(pk_{DC}, C_D): *Let* $C_D = (c_j)_{j=1}^m$ *be a set of encrypted data. Set* f-index $= \{1, \ldots, m\}$. *For each* $j \in [1, m]$, *change* j-*th element of* f-index *to* ϵ *if* VerifyMS($pk_{MRA}, pk_d, MS_j, pk_{MS_j}, c_j$) $= 0$. *Output* f-index.

TableGen($\mathcal{MS}, pk_{DC}, (C_{D,i})_{i=1}^n$): *Pick a random permutation* $\phi : [1, n] \to [1, n]$, *and output a ciphertext table* tbl $= (C'_{D,i})_{i=1}^n = (C_{D,\phi(i)})_{i=1}^n$ *(see Table 1).*

DDec(pk_{DC}, sk_{DC}, C_D): $\qquad\qquad$ *For* $\qquad\qquad$ *all* $j \in [1, m]$, *run* $v_j \leftarrow$ RDec($pk_{MRA}, pk_d, sk_d, MS_j, pk_{MS_j}, c_j$), *and output the data* $V = (v_j)_{j \in [1, m]}$.

In Table 1, each MS is regarded as a quasi-identifier. We remark that multiple message spaces can also be regarded as a quasi-identifier. For example, for the identifier "Age", we can set Age $:= \{10\,s, 20\,s, \ldots, 90\,s\}$ and $MS_1 := 10\,s, \ldots, MS_9 := 90s$ and $MS_{10} :=$ Disease. In this case, we can add one more row "Age" in the corresponding ciphertext table. In the example of Table 2, a Data supplier corresponding to the ciphertext of the first row is 20 s, that corresponding to the ciphertext of the second row is 90 s, and that corresponding to the ciphertext of the n-th row is 10 s.

5 Performance Evaluation

In our system, cryptographic operations are the dominant factor. Therefore, in this section, we evaluate running time of algorithms in which the Sakai et al. RPKE scheme [28] is used as building blocks. We use the PBC library [2] (pbc-0.5.13). We compiled the benchmark program with gcc 4.4.7 and run it on a 3.10-GHz Intel(R) Xeon(R) Processor E3-1220 64-bits PC (CentOS release 6.4)

Table 3. Running time (basic operations)

Operation	Time(msec)
Pairing	1.146
Exp. ($\mathbb{G}$)	1.727
Exp. ($\mathbb{G}_T$)	0.149
Exp. ($\mathbb{G}'$)	0.617

Table 4. Running time (algorithms)

Algorithm	Time(msec)	Entity
DEnc	$59.822m$	Data supplier
FormatCheck	$68.708m/\ell$	Mediator
DDec	$0.617m'$	Data collector

with 8 GB memory. We use a (Type A) curve $y^2 = x^3 + x$, and use symmetric pairing settings. A base group element $g \in \mathbb{G}$ is 512 bits, and a target group element $G \in \mathbb{G}_T$ is 1024 bits. We remark that we use Barreto-Naehrig (BN) elliptic curves [7] as a DDH-hard group $\mathbb{G}'$, since the BN curve is Type III (asymmetric), and symmetric external Diffie-Hellman (SXDH) assumption is believed to hold. Here, a group element $\hat{f} \in \mathbb{G}'$ is 160 bits. In our evaluation, we ignore operations over a DDH-hard group (3 times exponentiations) since it is not a dominant factor. Moreover, we ignore multiplications over $\mathbb{G}$ and $\mathbb{G}_T$, computation of hash function, and operations over $\mathbb{Z}_p$ since these are relatively small compared to pairing and exponentiations (Exp.) over $\mathbb{G}$ and $\mathbb{G}_T$.

We give running times of basic operations and algorithms in Tables 3 and 4, respectively. Here, m is the number of data format, i.e., $\mathcal{MS} = (\mathsf{MS}_1, \ldots, \mathsf{MS}_m)$, ℓ be the number of mediators, and m' is the number of message spaces that the data collector wants to collect. We assume that each mediator handles the same number of ciphertexts. For example, in the example of Table 2, we can set $\mathsf{MS}_1 := 10\,\mathrm{s}, \mathsf{MS}_2 := 20\,\mathrm{s}, \ldots, \mathsf{MS}_9 := 90\,\mathrm{s}$, and $\mathsf{MS}_{10} := \mathrm{Disease}$, then $m = 10$. Let us assume that the data collector wants to collect data of 20 s and 30 s only (as introduced in our scenario). Then $m' = 2$. In this setting, we can confirm that for each algorithm, computation time is at most millisecond order, which seems sufficiently practical.

6   Discussion

Privacy-Preserved Outcome: We set multiple message spaces, and this setting is effective for indicating multiple data formats. For example, these spaces can be decided via k-anonymity [30,31]. We remark that it seems difficult to exactly capture k-anonymity, since message spaces are fixed *before* collecting data, and then it is difficult to correctly assume how many data will be collected for each format. That is, our setting does not guarantee k-anonymity in the strict sense, since table records might not be generalized so that each record is equal to at least $k - 1$ other records. However, we can expect some privacy-preserved outcome. For example, let each record be associated with a quasi-identifier such as age, gender, etc., and these quasi-identifiers can be message spaces of RPKE. For example, if we set $\mathsf{MS}_1 := 30\,\mathrm{s} := \{30, 31, \ldots, 39\}$ and $\mathsf{MS}_2 := \mathrm{Disease} := \{\mathrm{No\ Disease, Flu, Dyspepsia, Diabetes,\ Adiposeness}, \ldots\}$, then a Mediator can check whether data format is $(30\,\mathrm{s}, \mathrm{some\ disease})$ but the actual age and a disease name are not revealed. However, to formally argue any anonymity properties beyond our definition of anonymity, we would need to further study the effectiveness of such a data formatting, which may be related to k-anonymous data collection [37] and distributed privacy preserving data collection [34], and we leave it as a future work of this paper.

More Flexible Systems: In our system syntax, message spaces are fixed in the setup phase, i.e., before the data collection step. It seems desirable to allow the modification of message spaces even after the setup phase. We note that the MSSetup algorithm is defined in the syntax of RPKE. Thus, message spaces can be changed for each data mining/data processing by executing the MSSetup algorithm again, and Data Suppliers can use the new $\mathsf{pk_{MS}}$. As an alternative setting, one may consider the case in which a ciphertext is computed once, and this ciphertext is later checked whether its plaintext belongs to different ranges several times by Mediators for different purposes. However, a data collection system with such a functionality is not secure since Mediators can obtain additional information by checking whether the encrypted data belongs to different ranges multiple times.

More Efficient RPKE Construction: The Sakai et al. RPKE scheme requires to solve the discrete logarithm problem in the decryption algorithm (for constructing NIZK range proof and supporting decryption simultaneously) and the message space needs to be sufficiently small. That is, constructing a more efficient RPKE scheme could be an interesting future work since we give a *generic* construction of the system from RPKE and we can adopt *any* RPKE schemes.

Relations to Other Techniques: As shown in Tables 1 and 2, we can build an encrypted table which can be seen as a "k-type-anonymized" table by regarding MS as a quasi-identifier. However, Mediators may reveal the identity of Data suppliers from combinations of quasi-identifiers. Therefore, our k-type anonymization could be strengthened by considering ℓ-diversity [22], t-closeness [18], p-sensitivity [33], etc. Moreover, we cannot assume that records are unconditionally indistinguishable since PKE guarantees only computational indistinguishability of each record. Thus, our RPKE-based construction might be closer to computational anonymity [29] or k-concealment [32] where information-theoretic hiding property of k-anonymity is replaced with computational indistinguishability. Though it seems interesting to investigate a relation between these computational anonymization techniques and our RPKE-based construction, we leave it as a future work of this paper.

Acknowledgement. We would like to thank our colleagues, especially Hiroshi Nakagawa, Takeaki Uno, Toshihiro Kamishima, Shotaro Akaho, and Junpei Kawamoto. We also would like to thank the anonymous reviewers of BalkanCryptSec 2014 for their helpful comments and suggestions.

Appendix

A   Security Definitions of RPKE

Here, we give definitions of *indistinguishability with restrictive message space under chosen plaintext attack* (IND-MSR-CPA) and *verification soundness*. The former, *IND-MSR-CPA security*, captures confidentiality of RPKE, and guarantees that no adversary, who chooses two plaintexts that belong to the same message space and is given an encryption of one of the plaintexts, can guess which plaintext is encrypted significantly better than random guess. The security model allows an adversary to obtain sk_{MRA} in order to guarantee that even MRA cannot obtain information of plaintexts.

Definition 6 (IND-MSR-CPA). *We say that a RPKE scheme $\mathcal{RPKE}$ is IND-MSR-CPA secure if for all probabilistic polynomial-time (PPT) adversaries $\mathcal{A}$ the following advantage $\mathsf{Adv}^{\mathrm{ind}}_{\mathcal{A},\mathcal{RPKE}}(\kappa)$ is negligible.*

$$\mathsf{Adv}^{\mathrm{ind}}_{\mathcal{A},\mathcal{RPKE}}(\kappa) :=$$

$$\Pr \left[\begin{array}{l} (\mathsf{pk}_{MRA}, \mathsf{sk}_{MRA}) \leftarrow \mathsf{MRASetup}(1^{\kappa}) \\ (\mathsf{pk}_d, \mathsf{sk}_d) \leftarrow \mathsf{RKeyGen}(\mathsf{pk}_{MRA}) \\ (M_0^*, M_1^*, \mathsf{MS}^*, \mathcal{MS}^*, st) \leftarrow \mathcal{A}(\mathsf{pk}_{MRA}, \mathsf{sk}_{MRA}, \mathsf{pk}_d) \\ b \xleftarrow{\$} \{0,1\} \\ \mathsf{pk}_{\mathcal{MS}^*} := (\mathsf{pk}_{\mathsf{MS}_1}, \ldots, \mathsf{pk}_{\mathsf{MS}_m}) \leftarrow \mathsf{MSSetup}(\mathsf{pk}_{MRA}, \mathsf{sk}_{MRA}, \mathcal{MS}^*) \\ C^* \leftarrow \mathsf{REnc}(\mathsf{pk}_{MRA}, \mathsf{pk}_d, \mathsf{MS}^*, \mathsf{pk}_{\mathsf{MS}^*}, M_b^*) \\ b' \leftarrow \mathcal{A}(st, C^*) : \ b = b' \end{array} \right] - 1/2$$

where it is required that $\mathsf{MS}^* \in \mathcal{MS} = (\mathsf{MS}_1, \ldots, \mathsf{MS}_m)$, and $M_0^*, M_1^* \in \mathsf{MS}^*$.

Next, we define *verification soundness* which guarantees that $\mathsf{VerifyMS}$ $(\mathsf{pk}_{MRA}, \mathsf{pk}_d, \mathsf{MS}, \mathsf{pk}_{\mathsf{MS}}, C) = 0$ if the decryption result of C does not belong to MS. The following definition is exactly the same as that of Sakai et al.'s. However, it captures multiple message spaces since an adversary $\mathcal{A}$ can prepare multiple message spaces via the $\mathsf{MSSetup}$ oracle.

Definition 7 (Verification Soundness). *We say that a RPKE scheme $\mathcal{RPKE}$ has verification soundness if for all PPT adversaries $\mathcal{A}$ the following advantage $\mathsf{Adv}^{\mathrm{vs}}_{\mathcal{A},\mathcal{RPKE}}(\kappa)$ is negligible.*

$$\mathsf{Adv}^{\mathrm{vs}}_{\mathcal{A},\mathcal{RPKE}}(\kappa) :=$$

$$\Pr \left[\begin{array}{l} (\mathsf{pk}_{MRA}, \mathsf{sk}_{MRA}) \leftarrow \mathsf{MRASetup}(1^{\kappa}); \\ (\mathsf{pk}_d, \mathsf{sk}_d) \leftarrow \mathsf{RKeyGen}(\mathsf{pk}_{MRA}); \\ (\mathsf{MS}^*, \mathsf{pk}_{\mathsf{MS}^*}, C^*) \leftarrow \mathcal{A}^{\mathsf{MSSetup}(\mathsf{pk}_{MRA}, \mathsf{sk}_{MRA}, \cdot)}(\mathsf{pk}_{MRA}, \mathsf{pk}_d, \mathsf{sk}_d) \\ : \mathsf{VerifyMS}(\mathsf{pk}_{MRA}, \mathsf{pk}_d, \mathsf{MS}^*, \mathsf{pk}_{\mathsf{MS}^*}, C^*) = 1 \land \\ \quad \mathsf{RDec}(\mathsf{pk}_{MRA}, \mathsf{pk}_d, \mathsf{sk}_d, \mathsf{MS}^*, \mathsf{pk}_{\mathsf{MS}^*}, C^*) \notin \mathsf{MS}^* \end{array} \right]$$

where $\mathsf{pk}_{\mathsf{MS}^*}$ is required to be one of the public verification keys that $\mathcal{A}$ has received from the $\mathsf{MSSetup}$ oracle by querying MS^*.

B   Security Analysis

Theorem 1. *Our system is semantically secure if the underlying RPKE scheme is IND-MSR-CPA secure.*

Proof. We prove Theorem 1 using the standard hybrid argument. Let $\mathcal{A}$ be an adversary that attacks the semantic security of our system. For $i \in [1, m]$, let Game i be the semantic security game in which $C_D^* = (c_{D,1}^*, \ldots, c_{D,m}^*)$ is generated in such a way that the first i elements are generated by encrypting the elements in V_1^*, and the rest of $m - i$ elements are generated by encrypting the elements in V_0^*. Let p_i be the probability that $\mathcal{A}$ outputs 1 in Game i. By definition, Game 0 is equivalent to the semantic security game in which elements in V_0^* are encrypted, while Game m is equivalent to the semantic security game in which elements in V_1^* are encrypted. Therefore, $\mathcal{A}$'s semantic security advantage is upperbounded by the difference between the probability that $\mathcal{A}$ outputs 1 in Game 0 and that in Game 1, namely, $|p_0 - p_m|$. Note that by the triangle inequality, we have $|p_0 - p_m| \leq \sum_{i \in [1,m]} |p_{i-1} - p_i|$. Then, we show that for every $i \in [1, m]$, we can construct an algorithm $\mathcal{B}$ that breaks IND-MSR-CPA security with the advantage $(1/2)|p_{i-1} - p_i|$. The description of $\mathcal{B}$ that runs in the IND-MSA-CPA game is as follows:

The first stage algorithm $\mathcal{B}(\mathsf{pk}_{MRA}, \mathsf{sk}_{MRA}, \mathsf{pk}_d)$**:** $\mathcal{B}$ specifies $\mathcal{MS} :=$ $(\mathsf{MS}_1, \ldots, \mathsf{MS}_m)$, runs $\mathsf{MSSetup}(\mathsf{pk}_{MRA}^*, \mathsf{sk}_{MRA}^*, \mathcal{MS})$, and obtains $\mathsf{pk}_{\mathcal{MS}}^* :=$ $(\mathsf{pk}_{\mathsf{MS}_1}, \ldots, \mathsf{pk}_{\mathsf{MS}_m})$. $\mathcal{B}$ sets $\mathsf{pk}_{DC}^* := (\mathsf{pk}_{MRA}^*, \mathsf{pk}_d^*, \mathsf{pk}_{\mathcal{MS}}^*)$, and runs $\mathcal{A}$ on input $(\mathsf{pk}_{DC}^*, \mathcal{MS})$. When $\mathcal{A}$ outputs the challenge data (V_0^*, V_1^*) and its state information st, where $V_0^*, V_1^* \in \mathcal{MS}$, $\mathcal{B}$ parses $V_0^* = (v_{0,1}^*, \ldots, v_{0,m}^*) \in$ $\mathsf{MS}_1 \times \cdots \times \mathsf{MS}_m$ and $V_1^* = (v_{1,1}^*, \ldots, v_{1,m}^*) \in \mathsf{MS}_1 \times \cdots \times \mathsf{MS}_m$. Then $\mathcal{B}$ outputs $(v_{0,i}^*, v_{1,i}^*)$ as $\mathcal{B}$'s challenge and st' as its state information, where st' is the entire view of $\mathcal{B}$ so far.

The second stage algorithm $\mathcal{B}(st', c^*)$**:** If $i \geq 2$, then $\mathcal{B}$ runs $c_j^* \leftarrow$ $\mathsf{REnc}(\mathsf{pk}_{MRA}, \mathsf{pk}_d, \mathsf{MS}_j, \mathsf{pk}_{\mathsf{MS}_j}, v_{1,j})$ for $j \in [1, i-1]$. Furthermore, if $i \leq m-1$, then $\mathcal{B}$ runs $c_j^* \leftarrow \mathsf{REnc}(\mathsf{pk}_{MRA}, \mathsf{pk}_d, \mathsf{MS}_j, \mathsf{pk}_{\mathsf{MS}_j}, v_{0,j})$ for $j \in [i+1, m]$. Then $\mathcal{B}$ sets $C_D^* := (c_j^*)_{j=1}^m$, and runs $\mathcal{A}$ on input (C_D^*, st). When $\mathcal{A}$ terminates with output its guess bit b', $\mathcal{B}$ output this b' and terminates.

It is easy to see that if $\mathcal{B}$'s challenge bit is 0, then $\mathcal{B}$ simulates Game $i-1$ perfectly for $\mathcal{A}$, and thus the probability that $\mathcal{B}$ outputs 1 is exactly p_{i-1}. On the other hand, if $\mathcal{B}$'s challenge bit is 1, then $\mathcal{B}$ simulates Game i perfectly for $\mathcal{B}$, and thus the probability that $\mathcal{B}$ outputs 1 in this case is exactly p_i. Therefore, $\mathcal{B}$'s IND-MSR-CPA advantage is $(1/2)$ times $|p_{i-1} - p_i|$. This means that $|p_{i-1} - p_i|$ is negligible due to our assumption that the RPKE scheme is IND-MSR-CPA security. We can show this for every $i \in [1, m]$, which means that $\mathcal{A}$'s semantic security advantage is upper-bounded to be negligible.

Theorem 2. *Assume that data does not contain any identifier that uniquely determines the corresponding Data supplier. Then, our system is anonymous.*

It is straightforward to see that Theorem 2 holds, because TableGen uses a random permutation, and thus the distributions of $(C'_{D,i})_{i=1}^n$ in case $b = 0$ and $b = 1$ are identical.

Theorem 3. *Our system has format-check soundness if the underlying RPKE scheme has verification soundness.*

Proof. Let $\mathcal{A}$ be an adversary that breaks format-check soundness of our system. Then, we construct an algorithm $\mathcal{B}$ that, using $\mathcal{A}$ as a building block, breaks the verification soundness of the underlying RPKE scheme as follows:

$\mathcal{B}^{\mathsf{MSSetup}(\mathsf{pk}_{MRA},\mathsf{sk}_{MRA},\cdot)}(\mathsf{pk}_{MRA},\mathsf{pk}_d,\mathsf{sk}_d)$: $\mathcal{B}$ specifies $\mathcal{MS} := (\mathsf{MS}_1,\ldots,\mathsf{MS}_m)$, and for each $j \in [1,m]$ submits a MSSetup query MS_j to the oracle, and obtains $\mathsf{pk}_{\mathsf{MS}_j}$. Then $\mathcal{B}$ sets $\mathsf{pk}_{\mathcal{MS}} := (\mathsf{pk}_{\mathsf{MS}_1},\ldots,\mathsf{pk}_{\mathsf{MS}_m})$ and $\mathsf{pk}_{DC} := (\mathsf{pk}_{MRA},\mathsf{pk}_d,\mathsf{pk}_{\mathcal{MS}})$, and runs $\mathcal{A}$ on input $(\mathsf{pk}_{DC},\mathcal{MS})$. When $\mathcal{A}$ outputs $(C_D^* := (c_j^*)_{j=1}^m)$, $\mathcal{B}$ runs f-index$^* \leftarrow$ FormatCheck $(\mathsf{pk}_{DC}, C_D^*)$. $\mathcal{B}$ guesses $j \in [1,m]$ uniformly at random, sets $\mathsf{MS}^* := \mathsf{MS}_j$, $\mathsf{pk}_{\mathsf{MS}^*} := \mathsf{pk}_{\mathsf{MS}_j}$, and $c^* := c_j^*$, and terminates with output $(\mathsf{MS}^*, \mathsf{pk}_{\mathsf{MS}^*}, c^*)$.

It is easy to see that $\mathcal{B}$ perfectly simulates the format-check soundness game for $\mathcal{A}$, and conditioned on the event that $\mathcal{A}$ succeeds in breaking the format-check soundness of our system, $\mathcal{B}$ succeeds in breaking the verification soundness of the underlying RPKE scheme with probability at least $1/m$. Therefore, if $\mathcal{A}$ succeeds in breaking the format-check soundness of our system with non-negligible advantage, $\mathcal{B}$ succeeds in breaking the verification soundness of the RPKE scheme also with non-negligible advantage.

C   A Concrete RPKE Scheme

In this section, we review the Sakai et al. RPKE scheme [28]. They apply the revocation technique of the Nakanishi et al. group signature scheme [23]. Briefly, a plaintext is regarded as a user in the group signature context, and the revocation functionality is used to exclude the case in which prohibited plaintexts are encrypted. We remark that there are two types of revocable group signature: (1) any users can generate a valid group signature, but anyone can check whether the signer has been revoked or not [11,21,24,25], and (2) no revoked user can generate a valid group signature [6,19,20,23,26]. The former type usually has the feature that the signing or verification costs that are dependent on the number of revoked users. On the contrary, the latter type can achieve constant signing/verification costs. Thus, from the viewpoint of efficiency, the Sakai et al. RPKE scheme employs the latter type revocation technique. We remark that we may construct an RPKE scheme, where the encryption algorithm works for any plaintext but the verification algorithm can detect whether $M \in$ MS or not, by applying the former type revocation technique.

We note that the message space $[1, N]$ must be small so that M can be computed from $(\hat{f}, \hat{f}^M)$. In our usage, such a small message space is acceptable, e.g., if $30\,\mathrm{s} := \{30, 31, \ldots, 39\}$, then the size of the message space is just 10. Moreover, we can assume that the number of disease name is also fairly small. So, under such an assumption, we can ignore the computation cost of solving discrete logarithm. Without loss of generality, we assume that all message spaces MS $\in \mathcal{MS}$ can be represented as $[1, N] \setminus \{m_1, \ldots, m_r\}$, i.e., for $i \in [1, r]$, $m_i \in [1, N]$ is excluded from the message space. We describe the REnc algorithm and the RDnc algorithm for each message space MS $\in \mathcal{MS}$, and in our system these algorithms are run for all MS $\in \mathcal{MS}$ separately.

MRASetup(1^κ): Let $(\mathbb{G}, \mathbb{G}_T)$ be a bilinear group with a κ-bit prime order p and $e : \mathbb{G} \times \mathbb{G} \to \mathbb{G}_T$ be a bilinear map. In addition, let $\mathbb{G}'$ be a DDH-hard group with the same order p. Let $H : \{0, 1\}^* \to \mathbb{Z}_p$ be a cryptographic hash function (such as SHA-series) that will be modeled as a random oracle in the security proofs. Choose generators $g, \tilde{g}, \hat{g}, g_1, \tilde{g}_1, g_2, g_3, g_4, g_5 \xleftarrow{\$} \mathbb{G}$, $\hat{f} \xleftarrow{\$} \mathbb{G}'$, a signing key of BBS+ signatures [9,15] $X_1 \xleftarrow{\$} \mathbb{Z}_p$, and signing keys of BB signatures [8] $X_2, X_3 \xleftarrow{\$} \mathbb{Z}_p$, and compute the a verification key of BBS+ signatures $Y_1 = g^{X_1}$, and verification keys of BB signatures $Y_2 = g^{X_2}$ and $Y_3 = g^{X_3}$. For $k \in [1, \lfloor \sqrt{N} \rfloor]$, compute $F_{1,k} = \tilde{g}^{\frac{1}{X_2+k}}$. For $k \in [0, \lfloor 2\sqrt{N} \rfloor]$, compute $F_{2,k} = \hat{g}^{\frac{1}{X_3+k}}$. Output $\mathsf{pk}_{MRA} = (p, e, \mathbb{G}, \mathbb{G}_T, \mathbb{G}', H, Y_1, Y_2, Y_3, \{F_{1,k}\}_{k=1}, \{F_{2,k}\}_{k=0}^{\lfloor 2\sqrt{N} \rfloor}, \hat{f})$, and $\mathsf{sk}_{MRA} = (X_1, X_2, X_3)$.

RKeyGen(pk_{MRA}): Choose $\hat{g}_1, \hat{g}_2 \xleftarrow{\$} \mathbb{G}'$ and $z \xleftarrow{\$} \mathbb{Z}_p$, and compute $\hat{h} = \hat{g}_1^z$. Output $\mathsf{pk}_d = (\hat{g}_1, \hat{g}_2, \hat{h})$ and the corresponding secret key $\mathsf{sk}_d = z$.

MSSetup($\mathsf{pk}_{MRA}, \mathsf{sk}_{MRA}, \mathcal{MS}$): For all MS $\in \mathcal{MS}$, run the following procedure: Let MS $:= [1, N] \setminus \{m_1, m_2, \ldots, m_r\}$. Set $m_0 = 0$, and $m_{r+1} = N+1$. Choose a current serial number $t \in \mathbb{Z}_p$. For $\ell \in [0, r]$, compute (B_ℓ, y_ℓ, z_ℓ), where $B_\ell = (g_1^t g_2^{m_\ell} g_3^{m_{\ell+1}} g_4^{y_\ell} g)^{\frac{1}{X_1+z_\ell}}$, and $y_\ell, z_\ell \in \mathbb{Z}_p$. Output $\mathsf{pk}_{MS} = (t, \{(m_\ell, m_{\ell+1}, B_\ell, y_\ell, z_\ell)\}_{\ell=0}^r)$.

REnc($\mathsf{pk}_{MRA}, \mathsf{pk}_d, \mathsf{MS}, \mathsf{pk}_{MS}, M$): For $M \in$ MS, find the position j such that $m_j < M < m_{j+1}$. If there is no such m_j (which means $M \notin$ MS), output $\perp$. Choose $\alpha, \beta_{1,1}, \beta_{1,2}, \beta_{2,1}, \beta_{2,2}, u, \xi_1, \xi_1', \xi_2, \xi_2' \xleftarrow{\$} \mathbb{Z}_p$, compute $C_1 = B_j g_5^\alpha$, $C_2 = F_{1,\delta_{1,1}} g_5^{\beta_{1,1}}$, $C_3 = F_{2,\delta_{1,2}} g_5^{\beta_{1,2}}$, $C_4 = F_{1,\delta_{2,1}} g_5^{\beta_{2,1}}$, $C_5 = F_{2,\delta_{2,2}} g_5^{\beta_{2,2}}$, $C_6 = \tilde{g}^{\delta_{1,1}} \tilde{g}_1^{\xi_1}$, $C_7 = \tilde{g}^{\delta_{1,1}^2} \tilde{g}_1^{\xi_1'}$, $C_8 = \tilde{g}^{\delta_{2,1}} \tilde{g}_1^{\xi_2}$, $C_9 = \tilde{g}^{\delta_{2,1}^2} \tilde{g}_1^{\xi_2'}$, $\xi_1'' := \xi_1' - \xi_1 \delta_{1,1}$, $\xi_2'' := \xi_2' - \xi_2 \delta_{2,1}$, $C_{10} = \hat{g}_1^u$, $C_{11} = \hat{g}_2^u$, $C_{12} = \hat{f}^M \hat{h}^u$, $\zeta = \alpha z_j$, $\theta_{1,1} := \beta_{1,1} \delta_{1,1}$,

$\theta_{1,2} := \beta_{1,2}\delta_{1,2}$, $\theta_{2,1} := \beta_{2,1}\delta_{2,1}$, and $\theta_{2,2} := \beta_{2,2}\delta_{2,2}$. In addition, compute

$$\pi = NIZK \left\{ \begin{array}{l} \exists (M, \zeta, \alpha, y_j, z_j, m_j, m_{j+1}, \delta_{1,1}, \delta_{1,2}, \delta_{2,1}, \delta_{2,2}, \theta_{1,1}, \theta_{1,2}, \theta_{2,1}, \\ \theta_{2,2}, \beta_{1,1}, \beta_{1,2}, \beta_{2,1}, \beta_{2,2}, \xi_1, \xi_1', \xi_1'', \xi_2, \xi_2', \xi_2'', u) \\ : e(C_1, Y_1)/e(g,g) = e(g_5, Y_1)^\alpha e(g_5, g)^\zeta e(g_1^t, g) e(g_2, g)^{m_j} \\ \quad e(g_3, g)^{m_{j+1}} e(g_4, g)^{y_j}/e(C_1, g)^{z_j} \\ \wedge e(C_2, Y_2)/e(\tilde{g}, g) = e(g_5, Y_2)^{\beta_{1,1}} e(g_5, g)^{\theta_{1,1}}/e(C_2, g)^{\delta_{1,1}} \\ \wedge e(C_3, Y_3)/e(\dot{g}, g) = e(g_5, Y_3)^{\beta_{1,2}} e(g_5, g)^{\theta_{1,2}}/e(C_3, g)^{\delta_{1,2}} \\ \wedge e(C_4, Y_2)/e(\tilde{g}, g) = e(g_5, Y_2)^{\beta_{2,1}} e(g_5, g)^{\theta_{2,1}}/e(C_4, g)^{\delta_{2,1}} \\ \wedge e(C_5, Y_3)/e(\dot{g}, g) = e(g_5, Y_3)^{\beta_{2,2}} e(g_5, g)^{\theta_{2,2}}/e(C_5, g)^{\delta_{2,2}} \\ \wedge C_6 = \tilde{g}^{\delta_{1,1}} \tilde{g}_1^{\xi_1} \wedge C_7 = C_6^{\delta_{1,1}} \tilde{g}_1^{\xi_1''} \wedge C_7 = \tilde{g}^{-\delta_{1,2}+M-m_j} \tilde{g}_1^{\xi_1'} \\ \wedge C_8 = \tilde{g}^{\delta_{2,1}} \tilde{g}_1^{\xi_2} \wedge C_9 = C_8^{\delta_{2,1}} \tilde{g}_1^{\xi_2''} \wedge C_9 = \tilde{g}^{-\delta_{2,2}+m_{j+1}-M} \tilde{g}_1^{\xi_2'} \\ \wedge C_{10} = \hat{g}_1^u \wedge C_{11} = \hat{g}_2^u \wedge C_{12} = \hat{f}^M \hat{h}^u \end{array} \right\}$$

Concretely, π is computed as follows. Note that all pairing values are pre-computable.

1. Choose r_M, r_ζ, r_α, r_{y_j}, r_{z_j}, r_{m_j}, $r_{m_{j+1}}$, $r_{\delta_{1,1}}$, $r_{\delta_{1,2}}$, $r_{\delta_{2,1}}$, $r_{\delta_{2,2}}$, $r_{\theta_{1,1}}$, $r_{\theta_{1,2}}$, $r_{\theta_{2,1}}$, $r_{\theta_{2,2}}$, $r_{\beta_{1,1}}$, $r_{\beta_{1,2}}$, $r_{\beta_{2,1}}$, $r_{\beta_{2,2}}$, r_{ξ_1}, $r_{\xi_1'}$, $r_{\xi_1''}$, r_{ξ_2}, $r_{\xi_2'}$, $r_{\xi_2''}$, $r_u \xleftarrow{\$} \mathbb{Z}_p$.
2. Compute

$$R_1 = e(g_5, Y_1)^{r_\alpha} e(g_5, g)^{r_\zeta - \alpha r_{z_j}} e(g_1, g)^t e(g_2, g)^{r_{m_j}} e(g_3, g)^{r_{m_{j+1}}}$$
$$e(g_4, g)^{r_{y_j}}/e(B_j, g)^{r_{z_j}},$$

$$R_2 = e(g_5, Y_2)^{r_{\beta_{1,1}}} e(g_5, g)^{r_{\theta_{1,1}} - \beta_{1,1} r_{\delta_{1,1}}}/e(F_{1,\delta_{1,1}}, g)^{r_{\delta_{1,1}}},$$

$$R_3 = e(g_5, Y_3)^{r_{\beta_{1,2}}} e(g_5, g)^{r_{\theta_{1,2}} - \beta_{1,2} r_{\delta_{1,2}}}/e(F_{2,\delta_{1,2}}, g)^{r_{\delta_{1,2}}},$$

$$R_4 = e(g_5, Y_2)^{r_{\beta_{2,1}}} e(g_5, g)^{r_{\theta_{2,1}} - \beta_{2,1} r_{\delta_{2,1}}}/e(F_{1,\delta_{2,1}}, g)^{r_{\delta_{2,1}}},$$

$$R_5 = e(g_5, Y_3)^{r_{\beta_{2,2}}} e(g_5, g)^{r_{\theta_{2,2}} - \beta_{2,2} r_{\delta_{2,2}}}/e(F_{2,\delta_{2,2}}, g)^{r_{\delta_{2,2}}},$$

$$R_6 = \tilde{g}^{r_{\delta_{1,1}}} \tilde{g}_1^{r_{\xi_1}}, R_7 = C_6^{r_{\delta_{1,1}}} \tilde{g}_1^{r_{\xi_1''}}, R_8 = \tilde{g}^{-r_{\delta_{1,2}}+r_M-r_{m_j}} \tilde{g}_1^{r_{\xi_1'}},$$

$$R_9 = \tilde{g}^{r_{\delta_{2,1}}} \tilde{g}_1^{r_{\xi_2}}, R_{10} = C_8^{r_{\delta_{2,1}}} \tilde{g}_1^{r_{\xi_2''}}, R_{11} = \tilde{g}^{-r_{\delta_{2,2}}+r_{m_{j+1}}-r_M} \tilde{g}_1^{r_{\xi_2'}},$$

$$R_{12} = \hat{g}_1^{r_u}, R_{13} = \hat{g}_2^{r_u}, R_{14} = \hat{f}^{r_M} \hat{h}^{r_u}.$$

3. Compute $c = H(R_1, \ldots, R_{14}, C_1, \ldots, C_{12}, \mathsf{pk}_{MRA}, \mathsf{pk}_{MS}, \mathsf{pk}_d)$
4. Compute $s_M = r_M + cM$, $s_\zeta = r_\zeta + c\zeta$, $s_\alpha = r_\alpha + c\alpha$, $s_{y_j} = r_{y_j} + cy_j$, $s_{z_j} = r_{z_j} + cz_j$, $s_{m_j} = r_{m_j} + cm_j$, $s_{m_{j+1}} = r_{m_{j+1}} + cm_{j+1}$, $s_{\delta_{1,1}} = r_{\delta_{1,1}} + c\delta_{1,1}$, $s_{\delta_{1,2}} = r_{\delta_{1,2}} + c\delta_{1,2}$, $s_{\delta_{2,1}} = r_{\delta_{2,1}} + c\delta_{2,1}$, $s_{\delta_{2,2}} = r_{\delta_{2,2}} + c\delta_{2,2}$, $s_{\theta_{1,1}} = r_{\theta_{1,1}} + c\theta_{1,1}$, $s_{\theta_{1,2}} = r_{\theta_{1,2}} + c\theta_{1,2}$, $s_{\theta_{2,1}} = r_{\theta_{2,1}} + c\theta_{2,1}$, $s_{\theta_{2,2}} = r_{\theta_{2,2}} + c\theta_{2,2}$, $s_{\beta_{1,1}} = r_{\beta_{1,1}} + c\beta_{1,1}$, $s_{\beta_{1,2}} = r_{\beta_{1,2}} + c\beta_{1,2}$, $s_{\beta_{2,1}} = r_{\beta_{2,1}} + c\beta_{2,1}$, $s_{\beta_{2,2}} = r_{\beta_{2,2}} + c\beta_{2,2}$, $s_{\xi_1} = r_{\xi_1} + c\xi_1$, $s_{\xi_1'} = r_{\xi_1'} + c\xi_1'$, $s_{\xi_1''} = r_{\xi_1''} + c\xi_1''$, $s_{\xi_2} = r_{\xi_2} + c\xi_2$, $s_{\xi_2'} = r_{\xi_2'} + c\xi_2'$, $s_{\xi_2''} = r_{\xi_2''} + c\xi_2''$, and $s_u = r_u + cu$.
5. Output $C = (C_1, \ldots, C_{12}, \pi)$, where $\pi = (c, s_M, s_\zeta, s_\alpha, s_{y_j}, s_{z_j}, s_{m_j}, s_{m_{j+1}}, s_{\delta_{1,1}}, s_{\delta_{1,2}}, s_{\delta_{2,1}}, s_{\delta_{2,2}}, s_{\theta_{1,1}}, s_{\theta_{1,2}}, s_{\theta_{2,1}}, s_{\theta_{2,2}}, s_{\beta_{1,1}}, s_{\beta_{1,2}}, s_{\beta_{2,1}}, s_{\beta_{2,2}}, s_{\xi_1}, s_{\xi_1'}, s_{\xi_1''}, s_{\xi_2}, s_{\xi_2'}, s_{\xi_2''}, s_u)$.
   Output a ciphertext $C = (C_1, \ldots, C_{12}, \pi)$.

$\mathsf{VerifyMS}(\mathsf{pk}_{MRA}, \mathsf{pk}_d, \mathsf{MS}, \mathsf{pk}_{MS}, C)$: Note that all pairing values are pre-computable, except $e(C_1, g^{s_{z_j}} Y_1^c)$, $e(C_2, g^{s\delta_{1,1}} Y_2^c)$, $e(C_3, g^{s\delta_{1,2}} Y_3^c)$, $e(C_4, g^{s\delta_{2,1}} Y_2^c)$, and $e(C_5, g^{s\delta_{2,2}} Y_3^c)$.

1. Compute

$$R_1' = e(g_5, Y_1)^{s_\alpha} e(g_5, g)^{s_\zeta} e(g_1, g)^t e(g_2, g)^{sm_j} e(g_3, g)^{sm_{j+1}} e(g_4, g)^{sy_j}$$
$$e(g, g)^c / e(C_1, g^{s_{z_j}} Y_1^c),$$
$$R_2' = e(g_5, Y_2)^{s\beta_{1,1}} e(g_5, g)^{s\theta_{1,1}} e(\tilde{g}, g)^c / e(C_2, g^{s\delta_{1,1}} Y_2^c),$$
$$R_3' = e(g_5, Y_3)^{s\beta_{1,2}} e(g_5, g)^{s\theta_{1,2}} e(\dot{g}, g)^c / e(C_3, g^{s\delta_{1,2}} Y_3^c),$$
$$R_4' = e(g_5, Y_2)^{s\beta_{2,1}} e(g_5, g)^{s\theta_{2,1}} e(\tilde{g}, g)^c / e(C_4, g^{s\delta_{2,1}} Y_2^c),$$
$$R_5' = e(g_5, Y_3)^{s\beta_{2,2}} e(g_5, g)^{s\theta_{2,2}} e(\dot{g}, g)^c / e(C_5, g^{s\delta_{2,2}} Y_3^c),$$
$$R_6' = \tilde{g}^{s\delta_{1,1}} \tilde{g}_1^{s\xi_1} C_6^{-c}, R_7' = C_6^{s\delta_{1,1}} \tilde{g}_1^{s\xi_1''} C_7^{-c}, R_8' = \tilde{g}^{-s\delta_{1,2} + s_M - sm_j} \tilde{g}_1^{s\xi_1'} C_7^{-c},$$
$$R_9' = \tilde{g}^{s\delta_{2,1}} \tilde{g}_1^{s\xi_2} C_8^{-c}, R_{10}' = C_8^{s\delta_{2,1}} \tilde{g}_1^{s\xi_2''} C_9^{-c},$$
$$R_{11}' = \tilde{g}^{-s\delta_{2,2} + sm_{j+1} - s_M} \tilde{g}_1^{s\xi_2'} C_9^{-c}, R_{12}' = \hat{g}_1^{s_u} C_{10}^{-c}, R_{13}' = \hat{g}_2^{s_u} C_{11}^{-c},$$
$$R_{14}' = \hat{f}^{s_M} \hat{h}^{s_u} C_{12}^{-c}.$$

2. Output 1 if $c = H(R_1', \ldots, R_{14}', C_1, \ldots, C_{12}, \mathsf{pk}_{MRA}, \mathsf{pk}_{MS}, \mathsf{pk}_d)$, and 0 otherwise.

$\mathsf{RDec}(\mathsf{pk}_{MRA}, \mathsf{pk}_d, \mathsf{sk}_d, \mathsf{MS}, \mathsf{pk}_{MS}, C)$: Compute $\hat{f}^M = C_{12}/C_{10}^z$, solve the DL problem $(\hat{f}, \hat{f}^M)$, and output M. If the verification fails, output $\bot$.

References

1. ISO/IES 20732. http://www.iso.org/iso/catalogue_detail?csnumber=44375
2. The PBC (pairing-based cryptography) library. http://crypto.stanford.edu/pbc/
3. Tor Project. https://www.torproject.org/
4. Ashrafi, M.Z., Ng, S.K.: Collusion-resistant anonymous data collection method. In: KDD, pp. 69–78 (2009)
5. Ashrafi, M.Z., Ng, S.K.: Efficient and anonymous online data collection. In: Zhou, X., Yokota, H., Deng, K., Liu, Q. (eds.) DASFAA 2009. LNCS, vol. 5463, pp. 471–485. Springer, Heidelberg (2009)
6. Attrapadung, N., Emura, K., Hanaoka, G., Sakai, Y.: A revocable group signature scheme from identity-based revocation techniques: achieving constant-size revocation list. In: Boureanu, I., Owesarski, P., Vaudenay, S. (eds.) ACNS 2014. LNCS, vol. 8479, pp. 419–437. Springer, Heidelberg (2014). http://dx.doi.org/10.1007/
7. Barreto, P.S.L.M., Naehrig, M.: Pairing-friendly elliptic curves of prime order. In: Preneel, B., Tavares, S. (eds.) SAC 2005. LNCS, vol. 3897, pp. 319–331. Springer, Heidelberg (2006)
8. Boneh, D., Boyen, X.: Short signatures without random oracles and the SDH assumption in bilinear groups. J. Cryptol. 21, 149–177 (2008)
9. Boneh, D., Boyen, X., Shacham, H.: Short group signatures. In: Franklin, M. (ed.) CRYPTO 2004. LNCS, vol. 3152, pp. 41–55. Springer, Heidelberg (2004)
10. Boneh, D., Golle, P.: Almost entirely correct mixing with applications to voting. In: ACM Conference on Computer and Communications Security, pp. 68–77 (2002)

11. Boneh, D., Shacham, H.: Group signatures with verifier-local revocation. In: ACM Conference on Computer and Communications Security, pp. 168–177 (2004)
12. Brickell, J., Shmatikov, V.: Efficient anonymity-preserving data collection. In: KDD, pp. 76–85 (2006)
13. Chaum, D.: Untraceable electronic mail, return addresses, and digital pseudonyms. Commun. ACM **24**(2), 84–88 (1981)
14. Dwork, C.: Differential privacy. In: Bugliesi, M., Preneel, B., Sassone, V., Wegener, I. (eds.) ICALP 2006. LNCS, vol. 4052, pp. 1–12. Springer, Heidelberg (2006)
15. Furukawa, J., Imai, H.: An efficient group signature scheme from bilinear maps. IEICE Trans. **89**(A(5)), 1328–1338 (2006)
16. Jakobsson, M., Juels, A., Rivest, R.L.: Making mix nets robust for electronic voting by randomized partial checking. In: USENIX Security Symposium, pp. 339–353 (2002)
17. Laur, S., Willemson, J., Zhang, B.: Round-efficient oblivious database manipulation. In: Lai, X., Zhou, J., Li, H. (eds.) ISC 2011. LNCS, vol. 7001, pp. 262–277. Springer, Heidelberg (2011). http://dx.doi.org/10.1007/
18. Li, N., Li, T., Venkatasubramanian, S.: t-closeness: Privacy beyond k-anonymity and ℓ-diversity. In: ICDE, pp. 106–115 (2007). http://dx.doi.org/10.1109/ICDE. 2007.367856
19. Libert, B., Peters, T., Yung, M.: Group signatures with almost-for-free revocation. In: Safavi-Naini, R., Canetti, R. (eds.) CRYPTO 2012. LNCS, vol. 7417, pp. 571–589. Springer, Heidelberg (2012)
20. Libert, B., Peters, T., Yung, M.: Scalable group signatures with revocation. In: Pointcheval, D., Johansson, T. (eds.) EUROCRYPT 2012. LNCS, vol. 7237, pp. 609–627. Springer, Heidelberg (2012)
21. Libert, B., Vergnaud, D.: Group signatures with verifier-local revocation and backward unlinkability in the standard model. In: Garay, J.A., Miyaji, A., Otsuka, A. (eds.) CANS 2009. LNCS, vol. 5888, pp. 498–517. Springer, Heidelberg (2009)
22. Machanavajjhala, A., Gehrke, J., Kifer, D., Venkitasubramaniam, M.: ℓ-diversity: privacy beyond k-anonymity. In: ICDE, p. 24 (2006). http://dx.doi.org/10.1109/ ICDE.2006.1
23. Nakanishi, T., Fujii, H., Hira, Y., Funabiki, N.: Revocable group signature schemes with constant costs for signing and verifying. In: Jarecki, S., Tsudik, G. (eds.) PKC 2009. LNCS, vol. 5443, pp. 463–480. Springer, Heidelberg (2009)
24. Nakanishi, T., Funabiki, N.: Verifier-local revocation group signature schemes with backward unlinkability from bilinear maps. In: Roy, B. (ed.) ASIACRYPT 2005. LNCS, vol. 3788, pp. 533–548. Springer, Heidelberg (2005)
25. Nakanishi, T., Funabiki, N.: A short verifier-local revocation group signature scheme with backward unlinkability. In: Yoshiura, H., Sakurai, K., Rannenberg, K., Murayama, Y., Kawamura, S. (eds.) IWSEC 2006. LNCS, vol. 4266, pp. 17–32. Springer, Heidelberg (2006)
26. Nakanishi, T., Funabiki, N.: Revocable group signatures with compact revocation list using accumulators. In: Lee, H.-S., Han, D.-G. (eds.) ICISC 2013. LNCS, vol. 8565, pp. 435–451. Springer, Heidelberg (2014). http://dx.doi.org/10.
27. Sakai, Y., Emura, K., Hanaoka, G., Kawai, Y., Omote, K.: Towards restricting plaintext space in public key encryption. In: Iwata, T., Nishigaki, M. (eds.) IWSEC 2011. LNCS, vol. 7038, pp. 193–209. Springer, Heidelberg (2011)
28. Sakai, Y., Emura, K., Hanaoka, G., Kawai, Y., Omote, K.: Methods for restricting message space in public-key encryption. IEICE Trans. **96**(A(6)), 1156–1168 (2013)

29. Stokes, K.: On computational anonymity. In: Domingo-Ferrer, J., Tinnirello, I. (eds.) PSD 2012. LNCS, vol. 7556, pp. 336–347. Springer, Heidelberg (2012)
30. Sweeney, L.: Achieving k-anonymity privacy protection using generalization and suppression. Int. J. Uncertainty, Fuzziness Knowl.-Based Syst. **10**(5), 571–588 (2002)
31. Sweeney, L.: k-anonymity: A model for protecting privacy. Int. J. Uncertainty Fuzziness Knowl.-Based Syst. **10**(5), 557–570 (2002)
32. Tassa, T., Mazza, A., Gionis, A.: k-concealment: an alternative model of k-type anonymity. Trans. Data Priv. **5**(1), 189–222 (2012)
33. Truta, T.M., Campan, A., Meyer, P.: Generating microdata with p-sensitive k-anonymity property. In: Jonker, W., Petković, M. (eds.) SDM 2007. LNCS, vol. 4721, pp. 124–141. Springer, Heidelberg (2007). http://dx.doi.org/10.1007/978-3-540-75248-6_9
34. Xue, M., Papadimitriou, P., Raïssi, C., Kalnis, P., Pung, H.K.: Distributed privacy preserving data collection. In: Yu, J.X., Kim, M.H., Unland, R. (eds.) DASFAA 2011, Part I. LNCS, vol. 6587, pp. 93–107. Springer, Heidelberg (2011)
35. Yang, Z., Zhong, S., Wright, R.N.: Anonymity-preserving data collection. In: KDD, pp. 334–343 (2005)
36. Yao, A.C.C.: Protocols for secure computations (extended abstract). In: FOCS 1982, pp. 160–164 (1982)
37. Zhong, S., Yang, Z., Chen, T.: k-anonymous data collection. Inf. Sci. **179**(17), 2948–2963 (2009)

A Multi-Party Protocol for Privacy-Preserving Cooperative Linear Systems of Equations

Özgür Dagdelen[1]([⊠]) and Daniele Venturi[2]

[1] Technical University of Darmstadt, Darmstadt, Germany
oezguer.dagdelen@cased.de
[2] Sapienza University of Rome, Rome, Italy

Abstract. The privacy-preserving cooperative linear system of equations (PPC-LSE) problem is an important scientific problem whose solutions find applications in many real-word scenarios, such as banking, manufacturing, and telecommunications. Roughly speaking, in PPC-LSE a set of parties want to jointly compute the solution to a linear system of equations without disclosing their own inputs. The linear system is built through the parties' inputs.

In this paper we design a novel protocol for PPC-LSE. Our protocol has simulation-based security in the semi-honest model, assuming that one of the participants is not willing to collude with other parties. Previously to our work, the only known solutions to PPC-LSE were for the two-party case, and the only known other protocol for the multi-party case was less efficient and proven secure in a weaker model.

1 Introduction

Secure multi-party computation (MPC) is an important area of research in cryptography that started with the seminal work of Yao [37,38]. Generally speaking, MPC allows multiple (possibly untrusted) parties to evaluate any polynomial-time function on their inputs, while ensuring correctness of the output and privacy of parties' inputs. That is, no information about other parties' inputs is revealed to each party after a protocol run, besides what can be inferred given the output.

There exist general solutions for secure MPC. Yao [37] shows that any two-party function can be securely computed in the semi-honest adversarial model. Semi-honest adversaries follow faithfully the protocol specifications but can save intermediate computations. Any multi-party function can be securely computed in the malicious model, where dishonest parties behave arbitrarily, for any number of corrupted parties [19]. While those protocols constitute fundamental feasibility results, and despite recent progress in improving their efficiency over the last years (see, e.g., [4,9–13], general purpose MPC is not a panacea, as it generally relies on computationally-heavy building blocks such as garbled circuits, zero-knowledge proofs, and more. For this reason, designing secure protocols for *specific* tasks (even in weaker security models) is an important research direction.

© Springer International Publishing Switzerland 2015
B. Ors and B. Preneel (Eds.): BalkanCryptSec 2014, LNCS 9024, pp. 161–172, 2015.
DOI: 10.1007/978-3-319-21356-9_11

1.1 This Work

In this paper we focus on a particular such case, dealing with privacy-preserving cooperative scientific computations. As in generic MPC, in this setting multiple parties seek to jointly conduct computation tasks based on their private inputs. The main difference is that the set of functions considered typically admits a mathematical formulation.

One of the most prominent examples is the *privacy-preserving cooperative linear system of equations* (PPC-LSE) problem [15]. Here, a set of parties $P_1, \ldots, P_\ell$ each holding an $n \times n$ matrix $\mathbf{M}_i$ and vector $\mathbf{b}_i$ of size n want to privately compute the solution of a linear system of the form $(\mathbf{A}_1 + \ldots + \mathbf{A}_\ell)\mathbf{x} = (\mathbf{b}_1 + \ldots + \mathbf{b}_\ell)$. If privacy is not of concern, all parties could broadcast their inputs and the solution vector $\mathbf{x}$ can be computed by Gaussian elimination. However, PPC-LSE is interested in a solution where neither party is willing to disclose its own input. Solutions to PPC-LSE find application in many contexts, such as banking, manufacturing and telecommunications [27].

The versatility of PPC-LSE becomes apparent if one observes that many important problems can be stated as special cases of PPC-LSE. Consider, for instance, a related problem, called *privacy-preserving cooperative linear least-square* (PPC-LLS) problem which is defined as PPC-LSE but where no solution $\mathbf{x}$ typically exists. Here, one is interested in a vector $\mathbf{x}$ which approximates the linear system as best as possible. Existing literature shows that given a solution to PPC-LSE one can easily construct a solution to PPC-LLS. Another application of PPC-LSE is in *privacy-preserving polynomial interpolation* (PPPI), see e.g., [7,20,21,36]. In PPPI, each party holds a point (x_i, y_i) and wants to find the unique polynomial interpolating all points. To see the relation with PPC-LSE, think of each participant holding a matrix $\mathbf{A}_i$ and a vector $\mathbf{b}_i$, as follows:

$$\mathbf{A}_i = \begin{pmatrix} 0 & \cdots & & 0 \\ \vdots & \ddots & & 0 \\ 1 & x_i & x_i^2 & \ldots & x_i^n \\ 0 & \cdots & & 0 \\ \vdots & & \ddots & 0 \end{pmatrix} \qquad \mathbf{b}_i = \begin{pmatrix} 0 \\ \vdots \\ y_i \\ 0 \\ \vdots \end{pmatrix}.$$

Note that by adding all matrices $\mathbf{A}_i$ together, we get the Vandermonde matrix; thus a solution vector $\mathbf{x}$ to $(\mathbf{A}_1 + \ldots + \mathbf{A}_n)\mathbf{x} = (\mathbf{b}_1 + \ldots + \mathbf{b}_n)$ yields the coefficients of the polynomial the players are after. An application of PPPI can be found, for instance, in secure cloud storage [2].

Our main contribution is a novel and efficient MPC protocol for PPC-LSE. Our construction makes use of a 1-out-of-p oblivious transfer protocol, a common light-weight building block for secure multi-party computation, and improves the only previously known solution [26] in terms of both security and efficiency (see Sect. 1.2). Our protocol has simulation-based security in the semi-honest model [22], under the assumption that at least one party is not willing to collude with the other participants and all messages to this party are sent over a private channel.[1] Although this is a strong assumption, we believe it might still make sense for some applications, as it allows us to design a very efficient protocol. We leave it as an open problem to remove this further assumption, and find a light-weight MPC protocol for PPC-LSE in the semi-honest model.

1.2 Related Work

All previously known solutions for PPC-LSE deal only with the two-party case [15,33,35,36], and it is unknown whether those protocols can be easily and efficiently upgraded to the multi-party scenario. The only exception is the work by Kang and Hong [26] who proposed a protocol for PPC-LSE in the multi-party case. The security of their protocol is proven in the so-called "commodity-server model" [16], where parties derive the solution to a PPC-LSE instance with the help of a (possibly untrusted) commodity server. This server is not allowed to collude with any participant. Moreover, their analysis requires that the maximum number of colluding parties is upper bounded by some a priori-fixed threshold t.

In contrast, our scheme does not introduce a third party and in addition remains secure as long as a single party is not willing to collude. All other parties are allowed to collude in an arbitrary way. We stress that all known efficient protocols for PPC-LSE are proven secure in the semi-honest model.

1.3 Outline

We start by introducing some notation, and stating our model for simulation-based security with and without collusions (cf. Sect. 2). We turn to formally define the problem of PPC-LSE in Sect. 3. Our MPC protocol is presented in Sect. 4, and its efficiency is discussed in Sect. 5.

2 Preliminaries

2.1 Notation

Throughout the paper, we denote the security parameter by k. A function $negl(k)$ is negligible in k (or just negligible) if it decreases faster than the inverse of every polynomial in k. An algorithm is said to run in polynomial time (or is simply "efficient") if its number of steps is polynomial in the security parameter. We write vectors in lower-case boldface (e.g. v) and matrices in upper-case boldface (e.g. M).

Let $X = \{X_k\}_{k \in \mathbb{N}}$ and $Y = \{Y_k\}_{k \in \mathbb{N}}$ be two distribution ensembles. We say X and Y are computationally indistinguishable (and we write $X \equiv_c Y$) if for every polynomial-time algorithm $\mathcal{A}$ there exists a negligible function $negl$ such that $|\Pr(\mathcal{A}(X) = 1) - \Pr(\mathcal{A}(Y) = 1)| \leq negl(k)$.

---

[1] We note that a private channel can be straightforwardly established by means of encryption.

2.2 1-out-of-p Oblivious Transfer

A 1-out-of-p oblivious transfer (OT) protocol [6,18] is a two-party protocol generalizing the well-known 1-out-of-2 OT for $p > 2$. The protocol is run between a sender and a receiver, where the sender has p values $x_1, \ldots, x_p$ and a receiver obtains one of those values x_i of his choice. The receiver's input $i \in [p]$ is oblivious to the sender, and the receiver learns only x_i and nothing else about the sender's other inputs. Efficient 1-out-of-p oblivious transfer protocols can be found in [29,34].

Our construction makes use of 1-out-of-p OT. Nonetheless, an instantiation with $p = 2$ is preferable due to performance reasons; see Sect. 5. The security of standard OT has been very rigorously studied, and known constructions are fine-tuned with respect to communication and computation complexity. The reason is that OT is used massively as a building block for MPC, e.g., in the protocols based on garbled circuits [3,5,23,28,37].

2.3 Secure MPC and Collusions

All our security definitions are in the simulation-based model. In this section we recall the standard notion of simulation-based security in the context of multi-party computation.

Let $\phi : (\{0,1\}^*)^n \rightarrow (\{0,1\}^*)^n$ be a functionality, where $\phi_i(x_1, \ldots, x_n)$ denotes the i-th element of $\phi(x_1, \ldots, x_n)$ for $i \in [n]$. The input-output behavior of ϕ is denoted $(x_1, \ldots, x_n) \mapsto (y_1, \ldots, y_n)$. Consider a multi-party protocol Π for computing ϕ. Roughly, we say that Π is secure if the view of any adversary $\mathcal{A}$ involved in the protocol Π can be simulated by ideal adversary $\mathcal{S}$, sometimes called simulator, who interacts only with an ideal functionality $\mathcal{I}_\phi$. More precisely, in the *real world*, parties $P_1, \ldots, P_n$ execute protocol Π in order to compute the functionality $\phi(x_1, \ldots, x_n)$ in the presence of an (efficient) adversary $\mathcal{A}$. In the *ideal world*, the computation of ϕ is performed by an ideal functionality $\mathcal{I}_\phi$ which receives all inputs by parties $P_1, \ldots, P_n$ and returns to the parties their respective outputs $\phi_i(x_1, \ldots, x_n)$. Clearly, the parties do not learn any information other than their input/output given by $\mathcal{I}_\phi$ in an execution in the ideal world.

We only allow static corruptions, that is, adversaries determine the parties to corrupt at the beginning of the protocol execution. The adversary is called *passive* if it follows faithfully the protocol specifications but can save intermediate computations; on the other hand an *active* adversary can behave arbitrarily during a protocol execution. If the model considers only passive adversaries, we call it the semi-honest model.

Let $\mathbf{REAL}_{\Pi,\mathcal{A}(z)}(k, (x_1, \ldots, x_n))$ denote the joint output of adversary $\mathcal{A}$ (holding auxiliary input z) and parties $P_1, \ldots, P_n$ in an execution of protocol Π on inputs $(x_1, \ldots, x_n)$ and security parameter k. Similarly, let $\mathbf{IDEAL}_{\mathcal{I}_\phi,\mathcal{S}(z)}(k, (x_1, \ldots, x_n))$ denote the joint output of ideal-world adversary $\mathcal{S}$ and parties $P_1, \ldots, P_n$ in an execution with ideal functionality $\mathcal{I}_\phi$ and inputs $(x_1, \ldots, x_n)$ with security parameter k. Then, protocol Π securely realizes $\mathcal{I}_\phi$ if for every (efficient) active/passive adversary $\mathcal{A}$, there exists an (efficient) simulator $\mathcal{S}$ such that $\mathbf{IDEAL}_{\mathcal{I}_\phi,\mathcal{S}(z)}(k, (x_1, \ldots, x_n)) \equiv_c \mathbf{REAL}_{\Pi,\mathcal{A}(z)}(k, (x_1, \ldots, x_n))$.

The view in the presence of private channels. Our protocol will make use of private channels between parties. The messages sent over those channels, by definition, look truly random to outsiders (i.e., parties other than the sender and the receiver). Such random values can be easily simulated by an ideal adversary, and hence, for sake of simplicity, are not included in the view of a party that only consists of all his inputs, random coins, and messages that are sent explicitly to him.

The case of collusion. In the standard definition of secure computation the adversary $\mathcal{A}$ is considered as *monolithic*. This automatically models collusion between parties and gives strong security guarantees. For some protocols one may be able to prove security in a more restricted setting where some of the parties are not willing to collude. This needs to be defined explicitly; here we adopt the formalism of [25].

Instead of considering a single adversary which gets to see the state and all the messages exchanged by the corrupted parties, we consider a set of non-monolithic adversaries, each corrupting at most one (non-colluding) party and having access only to the view of that party. A different (monolithic) adversary controls the set of colluding parties. Security is defined by requiring that indistinguishability between the real and ideal world distributions hold with respect to the honest parties' outputs and a single adversary's view. In other words, for each independent adversary $\mathcal{A}_i$, the joint distribution composed of the honest parties' outputs and $\mathcal{A}_i$'s view in the real world—denoted $\mathbf{REAL}^{(i)}_{\Pi,\mathcal{A}(z)}(k,(x_1,\ldots,x_n))$— should be indistinguishable from the joint distribution composed of the honest parties' outputs and the simulator $\mathcal{S}_i$'s output in the ideal world—denoted $\mathbf{IDEAL}^{(i)}_{\mathcal{I}_\phi,\mathcal{S}(z)}(k,(x_1,\ldots,x_n))$. We refer the reader to [25, Definition 4.1] for the details.

3 Problem Statement

In this section we formally define the problem of PPC-LSE. Typically, this problem is stated as a two-party problem; here we consider its generalization to the multi-party setting. Roughly speaking, in PPC-LSE parties hold private inputs consisting of a matrix $\mathbf{A}_i$ and a vector $\mathbf{b}_i$, and look for a solution to a linear equation system defined by combining all parties inputs. It is, however, a-priori not clear how this combination of inputs should take place. Depending on the combination, one classifies three basic models [15] which we review below.

Model 1 (Homogeneous Model). *Consider a set of parties* $P_1,\cdots,P_\ell$. *Every party* P_i *holds an* $n_i \times n$ *matrix* $\mathbf{A}_i$ *and a* $1 \times n_i$ *vector* $\mathbf{b}_i$ *where* $n = n_1 + \ldots + n_\ell$. *The parties* $P_1,\cdots,P_\ell$ *want to privately solve*

$$\begin{pmatrix} \mathbf{A}_1 \\ \mathbf{A}_2 \\ \vdots \\ \mathbf{A}_\ell \end{pmatrix} \cdot x = \begin{pmatrix} \mathbf{b}_1 \\ \mathbf{b}_2 \\ \vdots \\ \mathbf{b}_\ell \end{pmatrix}$$

without disclosing their inputs $\mathbf{A}_i, \mathbf{b}_i$.

Model 2 (Heterogeneous Model). *Consider a set of parties $P_1, \cdots, P_\ell$. Every party P_i holds an $n \times n_i$ matrix A_i and all parties share the knowledge of a $1 \times n$ vector b where $n = n_1 + \ldots + n_\ell$. The parties $P_1, \cdots, P_\ell$ want to privately solve*

$$(A_1 \quad A_2 \quad \ldots \quad A_\ell) \cdot x = b$$

without disclosing their inputs A_i. The vector b should remain unknown to anyone besides the parties $P_1, \cdots, P_\ell$.

Model 3 (Hybrid Model). *Consider a set of parties $P_1, \cdots, P_\ell$. Every party P_i holds an $n \times n$ matrix A_i and a $1 \times n$ vector b_i. The parties $P_1, \cdots, P_\ell$ want to privately solve*

$$(A_1 + A_2 + \ldots + A_\ell) \cdot x = (b_1 + b_2 + \ldots + b_\ell)$$

without disclosing their inputs A_i, b_i.

Note that the homogeneous and heterogeneous models are special cases of the hybrid model. Therefore, we focus only on the latter in the sequel. We also note that one could change the dimensions of the inputs having possibly no solution or many solutions to the underlying linear system of equations. In the "no solution" case, one might ask to find the best possible solution. This problem is also called the "linear least-squares problem". The literature shows that one can generically derive a protocol for the linear least-squares problem given a protocol for PPC-LSE.

Ideal functionality for (multi-party) PPC-LSE. Recall that we prove the security of our protocols in the simulation-based model described in Sect. 2.3. To this end, we describe the ideal functionality $\mathcal{I}_{\mathsf{LSE}}$ capturing the functionality for secure PPC-LSE in the hybrid model. The ideal functionality $\mathcal{I}_{\mathsf{LSE}}$ receives as input A_i and b_i of party P_i and outputs to the parties P_i the value x such that $(A_1 + \ldots + A_\ell)x = (b_1 + \ldots, b_\ell)$ if x exists; else it returns $\perp$ to every party. In other words, we define the functionality ϕ for PPC-LSE as follows:

$$\phi((A_1, b_1), \ldots, (A_\ell, b_\ell)) = \begin{cases} A^{-1}b & \text{if } A^{-1} \text{ exists} \\ \perp & \text{otherwise} \end{cases}$$

where $A = A_1 + \ldots + A_\ell$ and $b = b_1 + \ldots, b_\ell$. Any protocol Π which privately computes the ideal functionality $\mathcal{I}_{\mathsf{LSE}}$ guarantees that the inputs of parties remain oblivious to other parties and outsiders who eavesdrop the communication in a protocol execution of Π.

4   An OT-Based Protocol

In this section we describe our protocol for multi-party PPC-LSE. Similarly to [26] (the only other known protocol for the multi-party setting), we make an assumption restricting the way dishonest parties may collude. Our assumption is weaker in that we only require that a single party is not willing to collude; all other players can collude arbitrarily. In contrast, [26] requires an explicit external non-colluding party acting as a distributor of shared data that is independent of other parties data; additionally their protocol tolerates only an a-priori fixed number $t < \ell$ of colluding players. We prove security of our protocol in the semi-honest model.

4.1 Protocol Description

We assume a finite field $\mathbb{F}$, and all operations and computations are performed over this finite field. In addition, we assume that there exists private channels between all parties. This can be easily realized by encrypting all messages sent to one party under his public key.[2]

The following two sub-protocols Π_1 and Π_2 will serve as building blocks for the final construction.

– The first sub-protocol Π_1 allows party P_1, called initiator, to privately retrieve $\widehat{\mathbf{A}} := \mathbf{P}(\mathbf{A}_1 + \ldots + \mathbf{A}_\ell)\mathbf{Q}$ where $\mathbf{P}, \mathbf{Q}$ are randomly chosen matrices.
– The second sub-protocol Π_2 allows the initiator P_1 to obtain privately $\widehat{\mathbf{b}} := \mathbf{P}(\mathbf{b}_1 + \ldots + \mathbf{b}_\ell)$.

The initiator P_1 solves the linear equation $\widehat{\mathbf{A}} \cdot \widehat{\mathbf{c}} = \widehat{\mathbf{b}}$ and sends $\widehat{\mathbf{c}}$ to party P_2 (called the assembler). P_2 derives $\mathbf{c} = \mathbf{Q} \cdot \widehat{\mathbf{c}}$ as the final solution to the equation $(\mathbf{A}_1 + \ldots + \mathbf{A}_\ell) \cdot \mathbf{c} = (\mathbf{b}_1 + \ldots + \mathbf{b}_\ell)$. Recall that privacy and security hold with respect to semi-honest parties $P_1, \ldots, P_\ell$. In all (sub)protocols, we merely assume party P_1 does not collude to ensure privacy of parties' inputs. The collusion of any (subset of) parties excluding P_1 does not harm privacy.

First sub-protocol. Π_1 is described in Fig. 1. We prove that protocol Π_1 privately computes $\mathcal{I}_{\mathsf{LSE}_1}$ in the semi-honest model. The ideal functionality $\mathcal{I}_{\mathsf{LSE}_1}$ receives as input $\mathbf{A}_i$ of party P_i and outputs to party P_1 the value $\mathbf{P}(\mathbf{A}_1 + \ldots + \mathbf{A}_\ell)\mathbf{Q}$, where $\mathbf{P}, \mathbf{Q} \xleftarrow{\$} \mathbb{F}^{n \times n}$. All other parties $P_2, \ldots, P_\ell$ receive the empty string.

Second sub-protocol. Π_2 is quite similar to Π_1 and is described in Fig. 2. Basically, protocol Π_2 privately computes $\mathcal{I}_{\mathsf{LSE}_2}$ in the semi-honest model, where ideal functionality $\mathcal{I}_{\mathsf{LSE}_2}$, upon input $\mathbf{b}_i$ of party P_i, outputs to party P_1 the value $\widehat{\mathbf{b}} := \mathbf{P}(\mathbf{b}_1 + \ldots + \mathbf{b}_\ell)$, with $\mathbf{P} \xleftarrow{\$} \mathbb{F}^{n \times n}$. All other parties $P_2, \ldots, P_\ell$ receive the empty string.

Final protocol. Now, given both sub-protocols Π_1 and Π_2, we build protocol Π_{LSE} for PPC-LSE as follows. All parties $P_1, \ldots, P_\ell$ hold as input a matrix $\mathbf{A}_i \in \mathbb{F}^{n \times n}$ and a vector $\mathbf{b}_i \in \mathbb{F}^n$. The parties proceed as follows:

1. Parties $P_1, \ldots, P_\ell$ execute protocol Π_1 such that only P_1 privately computes $\widehat{\mathbf{A}} = \mathbf{P}(\mathbf{A}_1 + \ldots + \mathbf{A}_\ell)\mathbf{Q}$. Parties $P_2, \ldots, P_\ell$ have no knowledge about $\widehat{\mathbf{A}}$.

---

[2] Clearly, this will introduce a requirement of a public key infrastructure.

Protocol Π_1

Steps performed by parties $P_1, \ldots, P_\ell$. Each P_i holds $\mathbf{A}_i \in \mathbb{F}^{n \times n}$.
Parameters p, m are chosen such that $\log(p)m = O(k)$.
All messages are sent over a private channel.

1. Parties P_1 and P_2 decompose $\mathbf{A}_1$ (resp. $\mathbf{A}_2$) by sampling random matrices $\mathbf{X}_1^{(1)}, \ldots, \mathbf{X}_m^{(1)}$ satisfying $\mathbf{A}_1 = \mathbf{X}_1^{(1)} + \ldots + \mathbf{X}_m^{(1)}$ (resp. $\mathbf{A}_2 = \mathbf{X}_1^{(2)} + \ldots + \mathbf{X}_m^{(2)}$).
2. For each $j = 1, \ldots, m$, party P_1 and P_2 perform the following sub-steps:
   (a) P_1 sends $(\mathbf{H}_1, \ldots, \mathbf{H}_p)$ to party P_2 where $\mathbf{H}_l = \mathbf{X}_j^{(1)}$ for a secretly chosen index $l \in [p]$ and $\mathbf{H}_i$ (with $i \neq l$) sampled uniformly.
   (b) P_2 chooses random matrices $\mathbf{P}, \mathbf{Q}$ and computes $\mathbf{P}(\mathbf{H}_i + \mathbf{X}_j^{(2)})\mathbf{Q} + \mathbf{R}_j$ for each $i = 1, \ldots, p$, where $\mathbf{R}_j$ is a random matrix.
   (c) P_1 executes 1-out-of-p OT and learns $\mathbf{P}(\mathbf{H}_l + \mathbf{X}_j^{(2)})\mathbf{Q} + \mathbf{R}_j = \mathbf{P}(\mathbf{X}_j^{(1)} + \mathbf{X}_j^{(2)})\mathbf{Q} + \mathbf{R}_j$.
3. Party P_2 sends to parties P_i (with $i = 3, \ldots, \ell$) the matrices $\mathbf{P}$ and $\mathbf{Q}$, and $\sum_{j=1}^{m} \mathbf{R}_j$ to P_1.
4. Parties P_i with $i = 3, \ldots, \ell$ send $\mathbf{P}\mathbf{A}_i\mathbf{Q}$ to party P_1.
5. Party P_1, after receiving all values, computes:

$$\widehat{\mathbf{A}} = \sum_{j=1}^{m}(\mathbf{P}(\mathbf{X}_j^{(1)} + \mathbf{X}_j^{(2)})\mathbf{Q} + \mathbf{R}_j) - \sum_{j=1}^{m}\mathbf{R}_j + \mathbf{P}\mathbf{A}_3\mathbf{Q} + \ldots + \mathbf{P}\mathbf{A}_\ell\mathbf{Q}$$

$$= \mathbf{P}(\mathbf{A}_1 + \mathbf{A}_2)\mathbf{Q} + \mathbf{P}\mathbf{A}_3\mathbf{Q} + \ldots + \mathbf{P}\mathbf{A}_\ell\mathbf{Q}$$

$$= \mathbf{P}(\mathbf{A}_1 + \mathbf{A}_2 + \mathbf{A}_3 + \ldots + \mathbf{A}_\ell)\mathbf{Q}.$$

Fig. 1. Description of protocol Π_1

2. Parties $P_1, \ldots, P_\ell$ execute protocol Π_2 such that only P_1 privately computes $\widehat{\mathbf{b}} = \mathbf{P}(\mathbf{b}_1 + \ldots + \mathbf{b}_\ell)$. Parties $P_2, \ldots, P_\ell$ have no knowledge about $\widehat{\mathbf{b}}$. Here, P_2 chooses the same matrix $\mathbf{P}$ as in the previous step.
3. P_1 solves the linear equation $\widehat{\mathbf{A}} \cdot \widehat{\boldsymbol{x}} = \widehat{\mathbf{b}}$. If a solution $\widehat{\boldsymbol{x}}$ exists, hands it over to party P_2. Otherwise, P_1 forwards $\perp$ to all parties.
4. P_2 computes $\boldsymbol{x} = \mathbf{Q} \cdot \widehat{\boldsymbol{x}}$ and broadcasts solution vector $\boldsymbol{x}$ to all parties $P_1, P_3, \ldots, P_\ell$.

4.2 Security Analysis

The theorems below state security of protocols Π_1 and Π_2, and of the final protocol Π_{LSE}. For space reasons, the proofs are deferred to the full version of this paper [8].

Theorem 4 (Privacy of Protocol Π_1). *Assuming the parties $P_1, \ldots, P_\ell$ are semi-honest, and P_1 does not collude, the protocol Π_1 securely realizes $\mathcal{I}_{\mathsf{LSE}_1}$.*

Theorem 5 (Privacy of Protocol Π_2). *Assuming the parties $P_1, \ldots, P_\ell$ are semi-honest, and P_1 does not collude, the protocol Π_2 enables $P_1, \ldots, P_\ell$ to privately compute functionality $\mathcal{I}_{\mathsf{LSE}_2}$.*

Protocol Π_2

Steps performed by parties $P_1, \ldots, P_\ell$. Each P_i holds a vector $\mathbf{b}_i \in \mathbb{F}^n$.
Parameters p, m are chosen such that $\log(p)m = O(k)$.
All messages are sent over a private channel.

1. Parties P_1 and P_2 decompose $\mathbf{b}_1$ (resp. $\mathbf{b}_2$) by sampling random vectors $\mathbf{x}_1^{(1)}, \ldots, \mathbf{x}_m^{(1)}$ satisfying $\mathbf{b}_1 = \mathbf{x}_1^{(1)} + \ldots + \mathbf{x}_m^{(1)}$ (resp. $\mathbf{b}_2 = \mathbf{x}_1^{(2)} + \ldots + \mathbf{x}_m^{(2)}$).
2. For each $j = 1, \ldots, m$ party P_1 and P_2 perform the following sub-steps:
   (a) P_1 sends $(\mathbf{h}_1, \ldots, \mathbf{h}_p)$ to party P_2 where $\mathbf{h}_l = \mathbf{x}_j^{(1)}$ for a secretly chosen index $l \in [p]$ and $\mathbf{h}_i$ (with $i \neq l$) sampled uniformly.
   (b) P_2 chooses random matrices $\mathbf{P}$ and computes $\mathbf{P}(\mathbf{h}_i + \mathbf{x}_j^{(2)}) + \mathbf{r}_j$ for each $i = 1, \ldots, p$, where $\mathbf{r}_j$ is a random vector.
   (c) P_1 executes 1-out-of-p OT and learns $\mathbf{P}(\mathbf{h}_l + \mathbf{x}_j^{(2)}) + \mathbf{r}_j = \mathbf{P}(\mathbf{x}_j^{(1)} + \mathbf{x}_j^{(2)}) + \mathbf{r}_j$.
3. Party P_2 sends to parties P_i (with $i = 3, \ldots, \ell$) the matrix $\mathbf{P}$, and $\sum_{j=1}^{m} \mathbf{r}_j$ to P_1.
4. Parties P_i with $i = 3, \ldots, \ell$ send $\mathbf{Pb}_i$ to party P_1.
5. Party P_1, after receiving all values, computes:

$$\widehat{\mathbf{b}} = \sum_{j=1}^{m}(\mathbf{P}(\mathbf{x}_j^{(1)} + \mathbf{x}_j^{(2)}) + \mathbf{r}_j) - \sum_{j=1}^{m}\mathbf{r}_j + \mathbf{Pb}_3 + \ldots + \mathbf{Pb}_\ell$$
$$= \mathbf{P}(\mathbf{b}_1 + \mathbf{b}_2) + \mathbf{Pb}_3 + \ldots + \mathbf{Pb}_\ell$$
$$= \mathbf{P}(\mathbf{b}_1 + \mathbf{b}_2 + \mathbf{b}_3 + \ldots + \mathbf{b}_\ell).$$

Fig. 2. Description of protocol Π_2

Theorem 6 (Privacy of Protocol Π_{LSE}). *Assuming parties $P_1, \ldots, P_\ell$ are semi-honest, and P_1 does not collude, the protocol Π_{LSE} enables $P_1, \ldots, P_\ell$ to privately compute functionality $\mathcal{I}_{\mathsf{LSE}}$. That is, it allows parties P_i with input $(\mathbf{A}_i, \mathbf{b}_i) \in (\mathbb{F}^{n \times n} \times \mathbb{F}^n)$ to privately compute vector $\boldsymbol{x} \in \mathbb{F}^n$ such that $(\mathbf{A_1} + \mathbf{A_2} + \ldots + \mathbf{A_\ell}) \cdot \boldsymbol{x} = (\boldsymbol{b_1} + \boldsymbol{b_2} + \ldots + \boldsymbol{b_\ell})$.*

To prove the last theorem we need to provide simulators $\mathcal{S}_1, \mathcal{S}_2$ whose output is computationally indistinguishable from the view of parties P_1 and $P_2, \ldots, P_\ell$ in a real execution of protocol Π_{LSE}. This is straightforward through the simulators of the sub-protocols Π_1 and Π_2.

5   Efficiency Considerations

When estimating computational and communication costs, we must take into consideration that some parties assume specific roles (e.g., P_1 as initiator and P_2 as assembler). Table 1 provides an overview for sub-protocol Π_1. Protocol Π_2 has similar complexity with the exception that computations are performed on vectors of size n rather than on matrices of size n^2. Regardless, all operations are performed in the finite field $\mathbb{F}$.

Note also that parties P_1 and P_2 execute two instances of 1-out-of-p OT [6]. Choosing $p = 2$ and $m = O(k)$, where k denotes the security parameter, allows us to instantiate our protocol with the usage of the well-investigated 1-out-of-2

170 170   Ö. Dagdelen and D. Venturi

Table 1. Efficiency estimates for Π_1 w.r.t. matrices of size n^2

Parties	Receiving	Sending	Additions	Multiplications
P_1	$\ell + 1$	$m \cdot p$	$m + \ell - 1$	0
P_2	$m \cdot p$	$1 + 2$ (broadcast)	$(2p + 1) + m$	$2m \cdot p$
$P_3, \ldots, P_\ell$	2	1	0	2

OT [32]. Efficient constructions for OT can be found, for instance, in [1,14,17, 24,30,31]. Note that our construction's security holds against semi-honest adversaries. For this reason we merely need an OT scheme secure against such adversaries.

Party P_1 solves also one linear equation, and P_2 executes one multiplication before the solution vector is broadcast to every party. The overall complexity for P_1 is $O(\ell + k)$, and $O(k)$ for P_2 while being constant for parties $P_3, \ldots, P_\ell$. Thus, we have $O(\ell n^2 + k n^2)$ in terms of computational complexity since operations are performed on either matrices of size n^2 or vectors of size n.

We compare the efficiency of our protocol with previous solutions for PPC-LSE. Given the two-party protocols of [15,33,35,36], one can obtain a scheme for the case of ℓ parties by running the underlying two-party solution $\binom{\ell}{2}$ times; this approach results in a high communication complexity due to the high number of OT executions. A related work [26] addresses PPC-LSE in the multi-party setting in the so-called "commodity-server model". Here, parties derive the solutions to a PPC-LSE instance with the help of a (possibly untrusted) commodity-server. The solution of [26] has a lower communication complexity of $O(t \cdot \ell)$, where $1 \leq t \leq \ell - 1$ is a bound on the number of parties allowed to collude. (We stress that, in any case, the commodity-server is never allowed to collude so there must be at least 2 non-colluding parties.) In contrast, our scheme yields communication complexity $O(\ell + k)$ and needs to assume a single non-colluding party. Moreover, due to the asymmetric structure of our construction, resource-limited parties may be in favor of playing the roles of $P_3, \ldots, P_\ell$. We stress that all messages are sent over a private channel, and encrypting messages before sending them entails a certain computational and communication blow-up. Nonetheless, asymptotically the cost of our protocol remains the same; which protocol performs better in practice depends on the number of parties involved and on the size of the equations.

We conclude by pointing out that generic solutions to PPC-LSE can also be obtained using linear secret sharing schemes or homomorphic encryption, as done in [33] for the two-party case, but the computation and communication complexity of the resulting protocol is much worse.

Acknowledgments. Özgür Dagdelen was supported by the German Federal Ministry of Education and Research (BMBF) within EC-SPRIDE.

References

1. Asharov, G., Lindell, Y., Schneider, T., Zohner, M.: More efficient oblivious transfer and extensions for faster secure computation. In: ACM Conference on Computer and Communications Security, pp. 535–548 (2013)
2. Ateniese, G., Dagdelen, Ö., Damgård, I., Venturi, D.: Entangled cloud storage. IACR Cryptology ePrint Arch. **2012**, 511 (2012)
3. Bellare, M., Hoang, V.T., Rogaway, P.: Foundations of garbled circuits. In: ACM Conference on Computer and Communications Security, pp. 784–796 (2012)
4. Bendlin, R., Damgård, I., Orlandi, C., Zakarias, S.: Semi-homomorphic encryption and multiparty computation. In: Paterson, K.G. (ed.) EUROCRYPT 2011. LNCS, vol. 6632, pp. 169–188. Springer, Heidelberg (2011)
5. Boneh, D., Gentry, C., Gorbunov, S., Halevi, S., Nikolaenko, V., Segev, G., Vaikuntanathan, V., Vinayagamurthy, D.: Fully key-homomorphic encryption, arithmetic circuit ABE and compact garbled circuits. In: Nguyen, P.Q., Oswald, E. (eds.) EUROCRYPT 2014. LNCS, vol. 8441, pp. 533–556. Springer, Heidelberg (2014)
6. Brassard, G., Crépeau, C., Robert, J.M.: All-or-nothing disclosure of secrets. In: Odlyzko, A.M. (ed.) CRYPTO 1986. LNCS, vol. 263, pp. 234–238. Springer, Heidelberg (1987)
7. Dagdelen, Ö., Mohassel, P., Venturi, D.: Rate-limited secure function evaluation: definitions and constructions. In: Public Key Cryptography, pp. 461–478 (2013)
8. Dagdelen, Ö., Venturi, D.: A multi-party protocol for privacy-preserving cooperative linear system of equations. In: BalkanCryptSec (2014)
9. Damgård, I.B., Ishai, Y.: Scalable secure multiparty computation. In: Dwork, C. (ed.) CRYPTO 2006. LNCS, vol. 4117, pp. 501–520. Springer, Heidelberg (2006)
10. Damgård, I., Ishai, Y., Krøigaard, M.: Perfectly secure multiparty computation and the computational overhead of cryptography. In: Gilbert, H. (ed.) EUROCRYPT 2010. LNCS, vol. 6110, pp. 445–465. Springer, Heidelberg (2010)
11. Damgård, I., Ishai, Y., Krøigaard, M., Nielsen, J.B., Smith, A.: Scalable multiparty computation with nearly optimal work and resilience. In: Wagner, D. (ed.) CRYPTO 2008. LNCS, vol. 5157, pp. 241–261. Springer, Heidelberg (2008)
12. Damgård, I.B., Nielsen, J.B.: Scalable and unconditionally secure multiparty computation. In: Menezes, A. (ed.) CRYPTO 2007. LNCS, vol. 4622, pp. 572–590. Springer, Heidelberg (2007)
13. Damgård, I., Pastro, V., Smart, N., Zakarias, S.: Multiparty computation from somewhat homomorphic encryption. In: Safavi-Naini, R., Canetti, R. (eds.) CRYPTO 2012. LNCS, vol. 7417, pp. 643–662. Springer, Heidelberg (2012)
14. Damgrd, I., Nielsen, J.B., Orlandi, C.: Essentially optimal universally composable oblivious transfer. In: Cryptology ePrint Archive, Report 2008/220 (2008)
15. Du, W., Atallah, M.J.: Privacy-preserving cooperative scientific computations. In: CSFW, pp. 273–294 (2001)
16. Du, W., Zhan, J.Z.: A practical approach to solve secure multi-party computation problems. In: Proceedings of the 2002 Workshop on New Security Paradigms, Virginia Beach, VA, USA, September 23–26, 2002, pp. 127–135 (2002)
17. Dubovitskaya, M., Scafuro, A., Visconti, I.: On efficient non-interactive oblivious transfer with tamper-proof hardware. In: Cryptology ePrint Archive, Report 2010/509 (2010)
18. Even, S., Goldreich, O., Lempel, A.: A randomized protocol for signing contracts. Commun. ACM **28**(6), 637–647 (1985)

19. Goldreich, O., Micali, S., Wigderson, A.: How to play any mental game or a completeness theorem for protocols with honest majority. In: STOC, pp. 218–229 (1987)
20. Hazay, C.: Oblivious polynomial evaluation and secure set-intersection from algebraic PRFs. IACR Cryptology ePrint Arch. **2015**, 004 (2015)
21. Hazay, C.: Lindell, yehuda: efficient oblivious polynomial evaluation with simulation-based security. IACR Cryptology ePrint Arch. **2009**, 459 (2009)
22. Hazay, C., Lindell, Y.: Efficient Secure Two-Party Protocols - Techniques and Constructions. Information Security and Cryptography. Springer, Heidelberg (2010)
23. Huang, Y., Evans, D., Katz, J., Malka, L.: Faster secure two-party computation using garbled circuits. In: USENIX Security Symposium (2011)
24. Ishai, Y., Kilian, J., Nissim, K., Petrank, E.: Extending oblivious transfers efficiently. In: Boneh, D. (ed.) CRYPTO 2003. LNCS, vol. 2729, pp. 145–161. Springer, Heidelberg (2003)
25. Kamara, S., Mohassel, P., Raykova, M.: Outsourcing multi-party computation. IACR Cryptology ePrint Arch. **2011**, 272 (2011)
26. Kang, J.-S., Hong, D.: A practical privacy-preserving cooperative computation protocol without oblivious transfer for linear systems of equations. JIPS **3**(1), 21–25 (2007)
27. Mishra, D.K., Trivedi, P., Shukla, S.: A glance at secure multiparty computation for privacy preserving data mining. Int. J. Comput. Sci. Eng. **1**(3), 171–175 (2009)
28. Mohassel, P., Riva, B.: Garbled circuits checking garbled circuits: more efficient and secure two-party computation. In: Canetti, R., Garay, J.A. (eds.) CRYPTO 2013, Part II. LNCS, vol. 8043, pp. 36–53. Springer, Heidelberg (2013)
29. Naor, M., Pinkas, B.: Oblivious transfer and polynomial evaluation. In: STOC pp. 245–254 (1999)
30. Nielsen, J.B., Nordholt, P.S., Orlandi, C., Burra, S.S.: A new approach to practical active-secure two-party computation. In: Safavi-Naini, R., Canetti, R. (eds.) CRYPTO 2012. LNCS, vol. 7417, pp. 681–700. Springer, Heidelberg (2012)
31. Peikert, C., Vaikuntanathan, V., Waters, B.: A framework for efficient and composable oblivious transfer. In: Wagner, D. (ed.) CRYPTO 2008. LNCS, vol. 5157, pp. 554–571. Springer, Heidelberg (2008)
32. Michael O. Rabin. How to exchange secrets with oblivious transfer. Cryptology ePrint Archive, Report 2005/187, 2005
33. Troncoso-Pastoriza, J.R., Comesana, P., Pérez-González, F.: Secure direct and iterative protocols for solving systems of linear equations. In: Proceedings of the First International Workshop Signal Processing in the Encrypted Domain (SPEED), pp. 122–141 (2009)
34. Tzeng, W.-G.: Efficient 1-out-n oblivious transfer schemes. In: Naccache, D., Paillier, P. (eds.) PKC 2002. LNCS, vol. 2274, pp. 159–171. Springer, Heidelberg (2002)
35. Wu, N., Zhang, J., Ning, L.: Discovering multivariate linear relationship securely. In: Proceedings from the Sixth Annual IEEE SMC, Information Assurance Workshop, IAW 2005, pp. 436–437 (2005)
36. Yang, X., Yu, Z., Kang, B.: Privacy-preserving cooperative linear system of equations protocol and its application. In: WiCOM, pp. 1–4 (2008)
37. Yao, A.C.: Protocols for secure computations (extended abstract). In: FOCS, pp. 160–164 (1982)
38. Yao, A.C.: How to generate and exchange secrets (extended abstract). In: FOCS, pp. 162–167 (1986)

Public Key Cryptography

Key-Policy Attribute-Based Encryption
for Boolean Circuits from Bilinear Maps

Ferucio Laurenţiu Ţiplea[1]($\boxtimes$) and Constantin Cătălin Drăgan[2]

[1] Department of Computer Science, "Al.I.Cuza" University of Iaşi,
700506 Iaşi, Romania
fltiplea@info.uaic.ro
[2] CNRS, LORIA, 54506 Vandoeuvre-lès-Nancy Cedex, France
catalin.dragan@loria.fr

Abstract. We propose a Key-policy Attribute-based Encryption (KP-ABE) scheme for (monotone) Boolean circuits based on bilinear maps. The construction is based on secret sharing and just one bilinear map, and it is a proper extension of the KP-ABE scheme in [7] in the sense that it is practically efficient for a class of Boolean circuits which strictly includes all Boolean formulas. Selective security of the proposed scheme in the standard model is proved, and comparisons with the scheme in [5] based on leveled multilinear maps, are provided. Thus, for Boolean circuits representing multilevel access structures, our KP-ABE scheme is more efficient than the one in [5].

1 Introduction

Attribute-based encryption (ABE) is a new paradigm in cryptography, where messages are encrypted and decryption keys are computed in accordance with a given set of attributes and an access structure on the set of attributes. There are two forms of ABE: *key-policy ABE* (KP-ABE) [7] and *ciphertext-policy ABE* (CP-ABE) [2]. In a KP-ABE, each message is encrypted together with a set of attributes and the decryption key is computed for the entire access structure; in a CP-ABE, each message is encrypted together with an access structure while the decryption keys are given for specific sets of attributes.

In this paper we focus only on KP-ABE. The first KP-ABE scheme was proposed in [7], where the access structures were specified by monotone Boolean formulas (monotone Boolean circuits of fan-out one, with one output wire). An extension to the non-monotonic case has later appeared in [9]. Both approaches [7,9] take into consideration only access structures defined by Boolean formulas. However, there are access structures of practical importance that cannot be represented by Boolean formulas, such as multilevel access structures [12,13]. In such a case, defining KP-ABE schemes for access structures defined by Boolean circuits becomes a necessity. The first solution to this problem was proposed in [5] by using leveled multilinear maps (sets of bilinear maps with some special property). A little later, a lattice-based construction was also proposed [6].

© Springer International Publishing Switzerland 2015
B. Ors and B. Preneel (Eds.): BalkanCryptSec 2014, LNCS 9024, pp. 175–193, 2015.
DOI: 10.1007/978-3-319-21356-9_12

Contribution. The KP-ABE schemes for Boolean circuits proposed so far are either based on leveled multilinear maps or on lattices. Direct extensions of the scheme in [7] to Boolean circuits face the *backtracking attack* [5]. Moreover, it was conjectured in [5] that such extensions cannot be realized using bilinear maps.

In this paper we show that an extension of the KP-ABE scheme in [7] to accommodate the case of (monotone) Boolean circuits is possible. The scheme we propose is practically efficient for a subclass of Boolean circuits which strictly extends the class of Boolean formulas (and, therefore, it can be considered as a proper extension of the scheme in [7]). In order to reach this objective, the Boolean circuits are endowed with explicit *fanout-gates* (FO-gates). This is not really necessary, but it is quite helpful in describing the secret sharing procedure used by the scheme. The secret sharing procedure works top-down as in [7]. The outputs of FO-gates are encrypted and the encryption keys are "transmitted" to their input wires in order to be further processed by the sharing procedure. This prevents the backtracking attack because it is not possible to compute the value at an output wire (of a FO-gate) by knowing the value at the other output wire, without computing bottom-up the value at the input wire.

The selective security of our KP-ABE scheme is proved in the standard model under the decisional bilinear Diffie-Hellman assumption.

We then discuss the complexity of our scheme and compare it with the scheme in [5]. Thus, if the FO-gates are not path-connected in the Boolean circuit, our scheme may perform better than the one in [5]. We prove this by considering Boolean circuits representing conjunctive and disjunctive multilevel access structures, and we show that our scheme distributes shorter decryption keys than the one in [5]. Whatever the considered Boolean circuit, our KP-ABE scheme has the advantage of using just one bilinear map while the scheme in [5] uses leveled multilinear maps whose size quadratically depends on the Boolean circuit depth.

Paper organization. The paper is organized into eight sections. The next section fixes the basic terminology and notation used throughout the paper. The third section discusses the scheme in [7], illustrates the backtracking attack, discussed the solution in [5] which thwarts the backtracking attack, and gives an informal overview of our solution. It also fixes the terminology on the Boolean circuits we use. Our construction is presented in the fourth section, its security is discussed in the fifth one, while the sixth section presents some comparisons between our scheme and the one in [5]. The seventh section shows that our scheme performs better than the one in [5] for Boolean circuits representing multilevel access structures. We conclude in the last section.

2 Preliminaries

Access structures. Recall first that [11], given a non-empty finite set $\mathcal{U}$ whose elements are called *attributes* in our paper, an *access structure* over $\mathcal{U}$ is any set $\mathcal{S}$ of non-empty subsets of $\mathcal{U}$. $\mathcal{S}$ is called *monotone* if it contains all subsets $B \subseteq \mathcal{U}$ with $A \subseteq B$ for some $A \in \mathcal{S}$. The subsets (of $\mathcal{U}$) that are in $\mathcal{S}$ are called *authorized sets*, while those not in $\mathcal{S}$, *unauthorized sets*. An authorized set A is *minimal* if there is no $B \in \mathcal{S}$ such that $B \subset A$.

It is customary to represent access structures by Boolean circuits (for more details about Boolean circuits the reader is refereed to [1]). A Boolean circuit has a number of input wires (which are not gate output wires), a number of output wires (which are not gate input wires), and a number of OR-, AND-, and NOT-gates. The OR- and AND-gates have two input wires, while NOT-gates have one input wire. All of them may have more than one output wire. That is, the fan-in of the circuit is at most two, while the fan-out may be arbitrarily large but at least one. A Boolean circuit is *monotone* if it does not have NOT-gates, and it is of *fan-out one* if all gates have fan-out one. In this paper all Boolean circuits have exactly one output wire. Boolean circuits of fan-out one correspond to *Boolean formulas*.

If the input wires of a Boolean circuit $\mathcal{C}$ are in a one-to-one correspondence with the elements of $\mathcal{U}$, we will say that $\mathcal{C}$ is a Boolean circuit over $\mathcal{U}$. Each $A \subseteq \mathcal{U}$ evaluates the circuit $\mathcal{C}$ to one of the Boolean values 0 or 1 by simply assigning 1 to all input wires associated to elements in A, and 0 otherwise; then the Boolean values are propagated bottom-up to all gate output wires in a standard way. $\mathcal{C}(A)$ stands for the Boolean value obtained by evaluating $\mathcal{C}$ for A. The access structure defined by $\mathcal{C}$ is the set of all A with $\mathcal{C}(A) = 1$.

Figure 1a pictorially represents a Boolean circuit $\mathcal{C}$ over $\mathcal{U} = \{1, 2, 3, 4\}$. For $A = \{1, 2\}$ we have $\mathcal{C}(A) = 1$ and for $B = \{2, 4\}$ we have $\mathcal{C}(B) = 0$.

Attribute-based encryption. A KP-ABE scheme consists of four probabilistic polynomial-time (PPT) algorithms [7]:

Setup(λ): this is a PPT algorithm that takes as input the security parameter λ and outputs a set of public parameters PP and a master key MSK;

Enc(m, A, PP): this is a PPT algorithm that takes as input a message m, a non-empty set of attributes $A \subseteq \mathcal{U}$, and the public parameters, and outputs a ciphertext E;

KeyGen($\mathcal{C}, MSK$): this is a PPT algorithm that takes as input an access structure $\mathcal{C}$ (given as a Boolean circuit) and the master key MSK, and outputs a decryption key D (for the entire Boolean circuit $\mathcal{C}$);

Dec(E, D): this is a deterministic polynomial-time algorithm that takes as input a ciphertext E and a decryption key D, and outputs a message m or the special symbol $\perp$.

The following correctness property is required to be satisfied by any KP-ABE scheme: for any $(PP, MSK) \leftarrow Setup(\lambda)$, any Boolean circuit $\mathcal{C}$ over a set $\mathcal{U}$ of attributes, any message m, any $A \subseteq \mathcal{U}$, and any $E \leftarrow Enc(m, A, PP)$, if $\mathcal{C}(A) = 1$ then $m = Dec(E, D)$, for any $D \leftarrow KeyGen(\mathcal{C}, MSK)$.

Security models. We consider the standard notion of selective security for KP-ABE [7]. Specifically, in the *Init* phase the *adversary* (PPT algorithm) announces the set A of attributes that he wishes to be challenged upon, then in the *Setup* phase he receives the public parameters PP of the scheme, and in *Phase 1* oracle access to the decryption key generation oracle is granted for the adversary.

In this phase, the adversary issues queries for decryption keys for access structures defined by Boolean circuits $\mathcal{C}$, provided that $\mathcal{C}(A) = 0$. In the *Challenge* phase the adversary submits two equally length messages m_0 and m_1 and receives the ciphertext associated to A and one of the two messages, say m_b, where $b \leftarrow \{0,1\}$. The adversary may receive again oracle access to the decryption key generation oracle (with the same constraint as above); this is *Phase 2*. Eventually, the adversary outputs a guess $b' \leftarrow \{0,1\}$ in the *Guess* phase.

The *advantage* of the adversary in this game is $P(b' = b) - 1/2$. The KP-ABE scheme is *secure* (in the selective model) if any adversary has only a negligible advantage in the selective game described above.

Bilinear maps and the decisional BDH assumption. Given G_1 and G_2 two multiplicative cyclic groups of prime order p, a map $e : G_1 \times G_1 \rightarrow G_2$ is called *bilinear* if it satisfies:

- $e(x^a, y^b) = e(x,y)^{ab}$, for any $x, y \in G_1$ and $a, b \in \mathbb{Z}_p$;
- $e(g,g)$ is a generator of G_2, for any generator g of G_1.

G_1 is called a *bilinear group* if the operation in G_1 and e are both efficiently computable.

The *Decisional Bilinear Diffie-Hellman.* (DBDH) problem in the bilinear group G_2 is the problem to distinguish between $e(g,g)^{abc}$ and $e(g,g)^z$ given g, g^a, g^b, and g^c, where g is a generator of G_1 and a, b, c, and z are randomly chosen from $\mathbb{Z}_p$. The *DBDH assumption* for G_2 states that no PPT algorithm $\mathcal{A}$ can solve the DBDH problem in G_2 with more than a negligible advantage.

3   The Backtracking Attack

The closest approaches to, and the starting point of, our paper are [5,7]. Goyal et al. [7] introduces the first KP-ABE scheme. The main idea here is quite elegant and simple, and can be summarized as follows:

- let $e : G_1 \times G_1 \rightarrow G_2$ be a bilinear map and g a generator of G_1, where G_1 and G_2 are of prime order p;
- to encrypt a message $m \in G_2$ by a set A of attributes, just multiply m by $e(g,g)^{ys}$, where y is a random integer chosen in the setup phase and s is a random integer chosen in the encryption phase. Moreover, an attribute dependent quantity is also computed for each attribute $i \in A$;
- the decryption key is generated as follows. The integer y is shared to all attributes so that it can be recovered only by authorized sets of attributes (the authorized sets are defined by monotone Boolean formulas). The sharing procedure is based on linear secret sharing schemes because linear combinations can be efficiently obtained as exponents of the bilinear map e. The shares associated to attributes are then used to compute the decryption key (which consists of a key component for each attribute);
- in order to decrypt $me(g,g)^{ys}$, one has to compute $e(g,g)^{ys}$. This can be done only if A is an authorized set of attributes. The computation of $e(g,g)^{ys}$ is bottom-up, starting from the key components associated to the attributes in A.

It was pointed out in [5] that the construction in [7] cannot be used to design a KP-ABE scheme for Boolean circuits. The reason is that, in case of OR-gates, any value computed at an input wire should be the same with the value computed at the other input wire. Therefore, knowing the value at one of the input wires of an OR-gate implicitly leads to the knowledge of the value at the other input wire (although these values are computed by different workflows). This aspect leads to the possibility of computing the value at the output wire of the circuit starting from values associated to some unauthorized set of attributes. In order to illustrate this attack, called the *backtracking attack* in [5], we consider the monotone Boolean circuit in Fig. 1a (remark that it has a fan-out of two). As we can easily see, the minimal authorized sets are $\{1, 2\}$, $\{1, 3\}$, and $\{3, 4\}$. Consider now the following scenario. Assume that a given message is encrypted by the authorized set of attributes $\{2, 3, 4\}$ and a user with the set of attributes $\{1, 2, 4\}$ asks for a decryption key. His set of attributes is authorized and, therefore, he has the right to obtain a decryption key. According to the definition of a KP-ABE, the decryption key for the set $\{1, 2, 4\}$ of attributes must not be valid to decrypt a message encrypted by the attributes $\{2, 3, 4\}$. However, the user can do as follows. The value computed at the input wire 2 "migrates" to the input wire 3 due to the existence of the OR-gate Γ_1. Corroborating this with the values at the input wires 1 and 4, a valid value will be computed at the output wire. This value is the same as the value computed by the set $\{2, 3, 4\}$ and, therefore, it allows the decryption of the message. Remark also that $\{2, 4\} = \{1, 2, 4\} \cap \{2, 3, 4\}$ is unauthorized.

The backtracking attack illustrated above cannot occur in case of access structures defined by Boolean formulas as in [7] because, in such a case, the input wires of OR-gates are not used by any other gates (the circuit is of fan-out one).

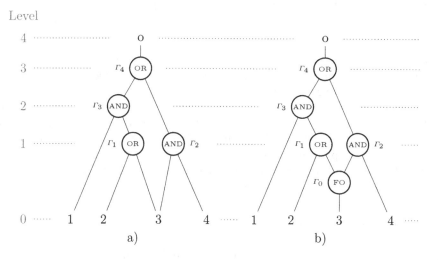

Fig. 1. (a) The backtracking attack; (b) Boolean circuit with FO-gates

To avoid the backtracking attack, [5] uses a "one-way" construction in evaluating monotone Boolean circuits. The idea is the next one:

- consider a *leveled multilinear map*, consisting of k groups $G_1, \ldots, G_k$ of prime order p, k generators $g_1, \ldots, g_k$ of these groups, respectively, and a set $\{e_{i,j} : G_i \times G_j \rightarrow G_{i+j} | i, j \geq 1, \ i + j \leq k\}$ of bilinear maps satisfying $e_{i,j}(g_i^a, g_j^b) = g_{i+j}^{ab}$, for all i and j and all $a, b \in \mathbb{Z}_p^*$, where k is the circuit depth plus one;
- the key components are associated to the circuit input wires and to each gate output wire (in [5], each gate has one output wire which may be used by more than one gate);
- the circuit is evaluated bottom-up and the values associated to output wires of gates on level j are powers of g_{j+1};
- as the mappings $e_{i,j}$ work only in the "forward" direction, it is not feasible to invert values on the level $j + 1$ in order to obtain values on the level j, defeating thus the backtracking attack.

As with respect to the existence of leveled multilinear, [5] shows how this scheme can be translated into the GGH graded algebra framework [4].

Looking more carefully at the example in Fig. 1a, we remark that the value obtained at the wire 3 via the input wire 1 and the OR-gate Γ_1 is then used at the AND-gate Γ_2. The backtracking attack illustrated above would be thwarted if the two outputs from 3 (one leading to Γ_1 and one leading to Γ_2) were different. This is in fact the starting point of our proposal. That is, we use explicit *fanout-gates* (FO-gates) with encrypted outputs to multiply input wires and gate output wires. Therefore, the Boolean circuits we use in the rest of the paper have FO-gates too. A FO-gate has one input wire and at least two output wires, and its role is to propagate its input to all outputs. In this way, the fan-out of all logic gates will be restricted to one. Moreover, as FO-gates may have arbitrary fanout, we assume that no two FO-gates are directly connected. Figure 1b pictorially represents the Boolean circuit in Fig. 1a using FO-gates.

We close this section by informally describing our solution and why it thwarts the backtracking attack (details will be given in the next sections):

- the information at the output wires of OR-gates are simple passed to the input wires, while the information at the output wires of AND-gates are shared as in the Karnin-Greene-Hellman scheme [8];
- the FO-gates, which are not present in [7], are processed by associating random keys to their input wires in order to deal with the output wires. In this way, the value computed at one of the output wires cannot be used to derive values at the other output wires. For instance, the value computed at the input wire 2 in Fig. 1b can "migrate" to the left output wire of the FO-gate Γ_0, but cannot be used as an input value for the AND-gate Γ_2.

4   Our Construction

In this section we propose a KP-ABE scheme for monotone Boolean circuits based on bilinear maps. The restriction to Boolean circuits that are monotone does not constitute a loss of generality (see page 7 in [5]). However, recall from the previous section that our Boolean circuits have FO-gates and all the logic gates have fan-out one. Assuming that the wires are labeled, we may write the gates as tuples (w_1, w_2, OR, w), (w_1, w_2, AND, w), and $(w, FO, w_1, \ldots, w_j)$, where $j \geq 2$. The elements before (after) the gate name are the input (output) wires of the gate. The output wire of a Boolean circuit will always be denoted by o, and the input wires by $1, \ldots, n$ (assuming that the circuit has n input wires).

Before describing our KP-ABE scheme assume that two multiplicative cyclic groups G_1 and G_2 of prime order p are given, together with a generator g of G_1 and a bilinear map $e : G_1 \times G_1 \to G_2$. As our KP-ABE scheme is based on secret sharing, we will define two procedures, one for secret sharing and the other one for secret reconstruction.

The sharing procedure, denoted $Share(y, C)$, inputs a Boolean circuit C and a value $y \in \mathbb{Z}_p$, and outputs two functions S and P with the following meaning:

1. S assigns to each wire of C a list of values in $\mathbb{Z}_p$;
2. P assigns to each output wire of a FO-gate a list of pairs in $G_1 \times G_1$.

By a *list of length n* of elements over a set X we understand any vector $L \in X^n$. $|L|$ stands for the length of L, $L_1 L_2$ for the *concatenation* of two lists L_1 and L_2, and $pos(L) = \{1, \ldots, |L|\}$ for the *set of positions* in the list L. $L(i)$ denotes the ith element of L. If L is a list of lists, then $L(i, j)$ denotes the jth element of the list $L(i)$.

Now, the sharing procedure is the following one.

Share(y, C)

1. Initially, all gates of C are unmarked;
2. $S(o) := (y)$;
3. If $\Gamma = (w_1, w_2, OR, w)$ is an unmarked OR-gate and $S(w) = L$, then mark Γ and assign $S(w_1) := L$ and $S(w_2) := L$;
4. If $\Gamma = (w_1, w_2, AND, w)$ is an unmarked AND-gate and $S(w) = L$, then mark Γ and do the followings:
   (a) for each $i \in pos(L)$ choose uniformly at random $x_i^1 \in \mathbb{Z}_p$ and compute x_i^2 such that $L(i) = (x_i^1 + x_i^2) \mod p$;
   (b) compute $L_1 = (x_i^1 | 1 \leq i \leq |L|)$ and $L_2 = (x_i^2 | 1 \leq i \leq |L|)$;
   (c) assign $S(w_1) := L_1$ and $S(w_2) := L_2$;
5. If $\Gamma = (w, FO, w_1, \ldots, w_j)$ is an unmarked FO-gate and $S(w_k) = L_k$ for all $1 \leq k \leq j$, then mark Γ and, for each $1 \leq k \leq j$, do the followings:
   (a) for each $i \in pos(L_k)$ choose uniformly at random $a_i \in \mathbb{Z}_p$ and compute b_i such that $L_k(i) = (a_i + b_i) \mod p$;
   (b) compute $L_k' = (a_i | 1 \leq i \leq |L_k|)$ and $P(w_k) := (g^{b_i} | 1 \leq i \leq |L_k|)$;
   (c) Assign $S(w) := L_1' \cdots L_j'$;
6. repeat the last three steps above until all gates get marked.

We will write $(S, P) \leftarrow Share(y, C)$ to denote that (S, P) is an output of the probabilistic algorithm $Share$ on input (y, C). $S(i)$ will be called the *list of shares* of the input wire i associated to the secret y ($1 \leq i \leq n$). Figure 2a generically illustrates the procedure *Share*.

We define now a reconstruction procedure $Recon(\mathcal{C}, P, V, g^s)$ which reconstructs a "hidden form" of the secret y from "hidden forms" of shares associated to some set A of attributes. This procedure is deterministic and outputs an evaluation function R which assigns to each wire a list of values in $G_2 \cup \{\perp\}$. The notation and conventions here are as follows:

- $\mathcal{C}$ is a monotone Boolean circuit with n input wires;
- (S, P) is an output of $Share(y, \mathcal{C})$, for some secret y;
- $s \in \mathbb{Z}_p$;
- $V = (V(i) | 1 \leq i \leq n)$, where $V(i)$ is either a list $(e(g, g)^{\alpha_i} | 1 \leq j \leq |S(i)|)$ for some $\alpha_i \in \mathbb{Z}_p$, or a list of $|S(i)|$ undefined values $\perp$, for all $1 \leq i \leq n$;
- $\perp$ is an *undefined value*, not in G_2, for which the following conventions are adopted:
  - $\perp < x$, for all $x \in G_2$;
  - $\perp \cdot z = \perp$, $z/\perp = \perp$, and $\perp^z = \perp$, for all $z \in G_2 \cup \{\perp\}$.

The reconstruction procedure can now be described as follows.

$\underline{Recon(\mathcal{C}, P, V, g^s)}$

1. Initially, all gates of $\mathcal{C}$ are unmarked;
2. $R(i) := V(i)$, for all $i \in \mathcal{U}$;
3. If $\Gamma = (w_1, w_2, OR, w)$ is an unmarked OR-gate and both $R(w_1)$ and $R(w_2)$ were defined, then mark Γ and assign

$$R(w, i) := sup\{R(w_1, i), R(w_2, i)\},$$

   for all $1 \leq i \leq |R(w_1)|$ (remark that $|R(w_1)| = |R(w_2)|$ and, for any i, if $R(w_1, i) \neq R(w_2, i)$ then either $R(w_1, i) = \perp$ or $R(w_2, i) = \perp$);
4. If $\Gamma = (w_1, w_2, AND, w)$ is an unmarked AND-gate and both $R(w_1)$ and $R(w_2)$ were defined, then mark Γ and assign $R(w, i) := R(w_1, i) \cdot R(w_2, i)$, for all $1 \leq i \leq |R(w_1)|$ (remark that $|R(w_1)| = |R(w_2)|$);
5. If $\Gamma = (w, FO, w_1, \ldots, w_j)$ is an unmarked FO-gate and $R(w)$ was defined, then mark Γ and do the followings:
   (a) split $R(w)$ into j lists $R(w) = R_1 \cdots R_j$ with $|R_k| = |P(w_k)|$ for all $1 \leq k \leq j$ (see the sharing algorithm for correctness);
   (b) $R(w_k, i) := R_k(i) \cdot e(P(w_k, i), g^s)$, for all $1 \leq k \leq j$ and for all $1 \leq i \leq |R_k|$;
6. repeat the last three steps above until all gates get marked.

We are now in a position to define our KP-ABE scheme, called *KP-ABE_Scheme*.

$\underline{KP\text{-}ABE\_Scheme}$

$Setup(\lambda, n)$: the setup algorithm uses the security parameter λ to choose a prime p, two multiplicative groups G_1 and G_2 of prime order p, a generator g of G_1, and a bilinear map $e : G_1 \times G_1 \to G_2$. Then, it defines the set of attributes

$\mathcal{U} = \{1, \ldots, n\}$, chooses $y \in \mathbb{Z}_p$ and, for each attribute $i \in \mathcal{U}$, chooses $t_i \in \mathbb{Z}_p$. Finally, the algorithm outputs the public parameters

$$PP = (p, G_1, G_2, g, e, n, Y = e(g,g)^y, (T_i = g^{t_i} | i \in \mathcal{U}))$$

and the master key $MSK = (y, t_1, \ldots, t_n)$;

$Encrypt(m, A, PP)$: the encryption algorithm encrypts a message $m \in G_2$ by a non-empty set $A \subseteq \mathcal{U}$ of attributes as follows:

- $s \leftarrow \mathbb{Z}_p$;
- output $E = (A, E' = mY^s, (E_i = T_i^s = g^{t_i s} | i \in A), g^s)$;

$KeyGen(\mathcal{C}, MSK)$: the decryption key generation algorithm generates a decryption key D for the access structure defined by a monotone Boolean circuit $\mathcal{C}$ with n input wires as follows:

- $(S, P) \leftarrow Share(y, \mathcal{C})$;
- output $D = ((D(i) | i \in \mathcal{U}), P)$, where $D(i) = (g^{S(i,j)/t_i} | 1 \leq j \leq |S(i)|)$, for all $i \in \mathcal{U}$;

$Decrypt(E, D)$: given E and D as above, the decryption works as follows:

- compute $V_A = (V_A(i) | i \in \mathcal{U})$, where

$$V_A(i,j) = e(E_i, D(i,j)) = e(g^{t_i s}, g^{S(i,j)/t_i}) = e(g,g)^{S(i,j)s}$$

for all $i \in A$ and $1 \leq j \leq |S(i)|$, and $V_A(i)$ is a list of $|S(i)|$ symbols $\perp$, for all $i \in \mathcal{U} - A$;
- $R := Recon(\mathcal{C}, P, V_A, g^s)$;
- $m := E'/R(o, 1)$ (recall that o is the output wire of $\mathcal{C}$).

Theorem 1. *The KP-ABE_Scheme above satisfies the correctness property. That is, for any encryption $E = (A, mY^s, (E_i | i \in A), g^s)$, any circuit $\mathcal{C}$ with n inputs and $\mathcal{C}(A) = 1$, and any $(S, P) \leftarrow Share(y, \mathcal{C})$, the valuation R returned by $Recon(\mathcal{C}, P, V_A, g^s)$ satisfies $R(o, 1) = Y^s$.*

Proof. By a simple inspection of the *Share* and *Recon* procedures. $\square$

5   Security Issues

We begin by showing that our scheme is resistant to the backtracking attack. This will be achieved by associating an access tree $\mathcal{T}_\mathcal{C}$ to a Boolean circuit $\mathcal{C}$ and showing that the backtracking attack succeeds on $\mathcal{C}$ if and only if it succeeds on $\mathcal{T}_\mathcal{C}$. Then, our claim will follow because the backtracking attack does not work in access trees.

The construction of $\mathcal{T}_\mathcal{C}$ consists of multiplying each wire of $\mathcal{C}$ as many times as paths are from the wire to the output wire (the number of such paths gives the numbers of shares the wire receives in the sharing process performed by the procedure *Share*). Then, each wire is labeled in order to distinguish the path associated to it. This is done by splitting up each FO-gate Γ with j ouput wires into j pseudo-gates $\Gamma^1, \ldots, \Gamma^j$, each with one input and one output wire (the kth output wire of Γ is the output wire of Γ^k, for all $1 \leq k \leq j$). If we collect all

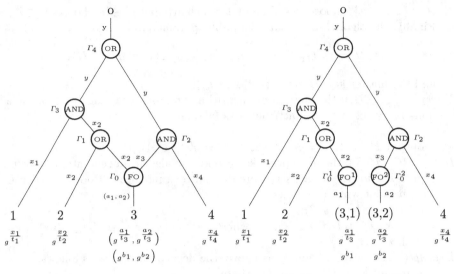

a) A Boolean circuit $\mathcal{C}$ b) The access tree $\mathcal{T}_{\mathcal{C}}$

Fig. 2. The construction of $\mathcal{T}_{\mathcal{C}}$

these exponents on the path from an wire to the output wire, we obtain a label which uniquely identifies the wire. The wires with an empty label have exactly one path from them to the output wire. For instance, the two wires 3 in Fig. 2b have, one of them the label 1 and the other one the label 2. The wires 1, 2, and 4 in the same figure have all an empty label.

If a wire w of $\mathcal{C}$ receives a list $S(w)$ of shares by the *Share* procedure applied to $\mathcal{C}$, then it is straightforward to see that each share $S(w, j)$ uniquely corresponds to some label $u_{w,j}$ as defined above. In the tree $\mathcal{T}_{\mathcal{C}}$, the wire $(w, u_{w,j})$ will receive the share $S(w, j)$.

This technique "unfolds" $\mathcal{C}$ with its lists of shares into a tree $\mathcal{T}_{\mathcal{C}}$ which has exactly one share for each wire. Now, it is straightforward to see that the backtracking attack succeeds on $\mathcal{C}$ if and only if it succeeds on $\mathcal{T}_{\mathcal{C}}$. As the backtracking attack does not work in access trees, our claim above follows.

Theorem 2. *The KP-ABE_Scheme is secure in the selective model under the decisional bilinear Diffie-Hellman assumption.*

Proof. In Appendix A.   □

6 Complexity of the Construction

We will discuss in this section the complexity of our construction (KP-ABE_Scheme) and we will compare it with the complexity of the construction provided in [5].

As our scheme uses just one bilinear map, the only question we have to answer with respect to the complexity of our construction is about the size of the decryption key. Assume that the Boolean circuit has n input wires and r FO-gates of fanout at most j. Two cases are to be considered:

Case 1: there is no path between any two FO-gates. In this case, by the sharing procedure, exactly r input wires will receive at most j shares (but at least two), and the other input wires will receive exactly one share. This leads to at most $n + r(j - 1)$ key components, and this is the minimum size of the decryption key (remark also that $r \leq n$ in this case);

Case 2: there are paths between FO-gates. In this case, the FO-gates on the highest level in the circuit may transmit the j shares collected at their input wires to FO-gates on the previous level. The sharing procedure will associate now at most j^2 shares to the input wires of these gates. This reasoning shows that the maximum number of shares some input wires of the circuit may receive is at most j^α, where α is the number of levels that contain FO-gates (α is less than or equal to miminum of r and the circuit depth).

The approach in [5] associates keys to the input wires of the circuit and to its output gates. Each input wire gets two keys, each OR-gate output wire gets four keys, and each AND-gate output wire gets three keys. The approach does not use explicit FO-gates, but an output wire of some gate may be used as an input wire for more than one gate. Therefore, the total number of keys is bounded from below by $2n + 3q$ and from above by $2n + 4q$, where q is the number of gates. The Boolean circuits in [5] can be transformed into our formalism if we replace each wire which is used by $j \geq 2$ gates by a FO-gate with j outputs. In this way, one can easily remark that q depends on both the number r of FO-gates and on the maximum number j of outputs of these FO-gates.

Another main difference between our scheme and the one in [5] consists of the number of bilinear maps used by them. While ours uses just one bilinear map, the one in [5] uses a leveled multilinear map with $\ell(\ell+1)/2$ bilinear map components interrelated with each other (see Sect. 3), where ℓ is the circuit depth.

7 Extensions and Applications

The above section shows that our KP-ABE_Scheme may be more efficient than the one in [5] when the Boolean circuits do not have FO-gates connected between them by paths. We will show in this section that the Boolean circuits representing multilevel access structures [10,12] fulfill this property. For a compact representation of multilevel access structures we need Boolean circuits with *threshold gates* (as in [7]). An (a, b)-*threshold gate*, where a and b are integers satisfying $1 \leq a \leq b$ and $b \geq 2$, is a logic gate with b input wires and one output wire. The output wire of such a gate is evaluated to the truth value 1 whenever at least a input wires of the gate are assigned to the truth value 1. OR-gates are $(1, 2)$-threshold gates, while AND-gates are $(2, 2)$-threshold gates.

A *disjunctive multilevel access structure* [10] over a set $\mathcal{U}$ of attributes is a tuple $(\bar{a}, \overline{\mathcal{U}}, \mathcal{S})$, where $\bar{a} = (a_1, \ldots, a_k)$ is a vector of positive integers satisfying $0 < a_1 < \cdots < a_k$, $\overline{\mathcal{U}} = (\mathcal{U}_1, \ldots, \mathcal{U}_k)$ is a partition of $\mathcal{U}$ (that is, all $\mathcal{U}_i$ are non-empty and their union is $\mathcal{U}$), and $\mathcal{S}$ is defined by:

$$\mathcal{S} = \{A \subseteq \mathcal{U} | (\exists 1 \leq i \leq k)(|A \cap (\cup_{j=1}^{i} \mathcal{U}_j)| \geq a_i)\}.$$

If we replace "$\exists$" by "$\forall$" in the above definition, we obtain the concept of *conjunctive multilevel access structure* [12]. It is well-known, and not difficult to prove (see Appendix B), that disjunctive and conjunctive multilevel access structures cannot be represented by Boolean formulas. Using Boolean circuits, these access structures can be easily represented as in Fig. 3. Moreover, the FO-gates are in between the first two levels.

Our KP-ABE_Scheme can be easily adapted to accommodate threshold gates. Assume that LSSS is a probabilistic linear secret sharing scheme [7] such that, given a and b as above, and given a master secret $x \in \mathbb{Z}_p$, the scheme outputs b shares $x_1, \ldots, x_b$ such that x can be uniquely reconstructed from any a shares. Moreover, assume that there exists an associated and efficient deterministic procedure $LSSS^{-1}$ such that

$$LSSS^{-1}(e(g, g)^{x_{i_1} s}, \ldots, e(g, g)^{x_{i_a} s}) = e(g, g)^{xs},$$

for any a shares $x_{i_1}, \ldots, x_{i_a}$ and any $s \in \mathbb{Z}_p$.

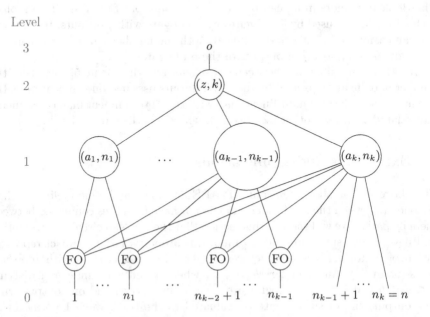

Fig. 3. Boolean circuit representation of multilevel access structure: z is 1 for the disjunctive case, and k for the conjunctive case.

Shamir's threshold secret sharing scheme satisfies this property and it was used in [7] exactly with this purpose.

Define now a procedure $Share'$ obtained from $Share$ by replacing the steps 3 and 4 by just one step:

3'. If $\Gamma = (w_1, \ldots, w_b, (a, b), w)$ is an unmarked (a, b)-threshold gate and $S(w) = L$, then mark Γ and do the followings:

(a) for each $i \in pos(L)$, run $LSSS$ and obtain the shares $x_i^1, \ldots, x_i^b$;
(b) for each $1 \leq j \leq b$ compute the list L_j from L by replacing $L(i)$ by x_i^j;
(c) assign $S(w_j) := L_j$, for all $1 \leq j \leq b$;

The corresponding reconstruction procedure $Recon'$ is obtained by replacing the steps 3 and 4 in $Recon$ by just one step:

3'. If $\Gamma = (w_1, \ldots, w_b, (a, b), w)$ is an unmarked (a, b)-threshold gate and $R(w_j)$ was defined for all $1 \leq j \leq b$, then mark Γ and assign $R(w)$ by

$$R(w, i) := sup\{LSSS^{-1}(R(w_{i_1}, i), \ldots, R(w_{i_a}, i))|i_1, \ldots, i_a \in \{1, \ldots, b\}\},$$

for all $1 \leq i \leq |R(w_1)|$;

The new ABE scheme, denoted KP-ABE_Scheme', is obtained from KP-ABE_Scheme by replacing $Share$ and $Recon$ by $Share'$ and $Recon'$, respectively. Its security can be proved as for the KP-ABE_Scheme.

The number of key components distributed by our KP-ABE_Scheme' when applied to a multilevel access structure as in Fig. 3 is

$$n_1 \cdot k + (n_2 - n_1) \cdot (k - 1) + \cdots + (n_k - n_{k-1}) \cdot 1$$

If we approximate n_1 and $n_i - n_{i-1}$ by the average value n/k, for all $2 \leq i \leq k$, the average number of the decryption key components is $n(k + 1)/2$.

The KP-ABE scheme in [5] can be easily adapted to accommodate $(1, b)$- and (b, b)-threshold gates. In the first case $2b$ key components are associated to the gate, while in the second case $b + 1$ key components are associated to the gate. However, there is no direct way to accommodate (a, b)-threshold gates when $1 < a < b$. The indirect way is to consider $C(b, a)$ threshold gates of type (a, a) and one threshold gate of type $(1, C(b, a))$ ($C(b, a)$ stands for the number of combinations of b taken a). Therefore, the number of decryption key components in case of a multilevel access structure can be approximated as follows:

Case 1: $a_i = n_i$, for all i. In this case, the number of key components is

$$2n + \sum_{i=1}^{k}(C(n_i, n_i) + 1) + (2k + 1 - z) = 2n + \sum_{i=1}^{k}(n_i + 1) + (2k + 1 - z)$$

If we write each n_i in the form $n_i = n_1 + (n_2 - n_1) + \cdots + (n_i - n_{i-1})$ and approximate n_1 and $n_j - n_{j-1}$ by the average value n/k, for all $2 \leq j \leq i$, we obtain the average number of the decryption key components as being $n(k + 5)/2 + (3k + 1 - z)$, where $z = 1$ for the disjunctive case and $z = k$ for conjunctive case;

Case 2: $a_i < n_i$, for all i. In this case, $a_i \geq i$ for all i. Using the inequality $C(n_i, a_i) \geq n_i$, we can bound from below the number of key components by

$$2n + \sum_{i=1}^{k} (a_i + 1)C(n_i, a_i) + \sum_{i=1}^{k} 2C(n_i, a_i) + (2k + 1 - z)$$

$$\geq 2n + \sum_{i=1}^{k} (i + 3)n_i + (2k + 1 - z).$$

If we apply the same reasoning as in the previous case to the right hand side of this inequality, we obtain the average estimate $(2 + (k + 1)(k + 5)/3)n + (2k + 1 - z)$ (z is as above).

Moreover, the leveled multilinear map has six bilinear map components, but only three of them are used (the approach in [5] counts three levels).

Our discussion so far, summarized in Table 1 below, shows clearly that our approach is more efficient than the one in [5] for multilevel access structures.

Table 1. Comparisons between the scheme in [5] and our scheme for multilevel access structures

Scheme	Average no. of keys		No. of bilinear maps
KP-ABE scheme in [5]	Case 1: $n\frac{k+5}{2} + 3k + 1 - z$		3
	Case 2: $\geq \left(2 + \frac{(k+1)(k+5)}{3}\right)n + 2k + 1 - z$		
Our KP-ABE Scheme/	$n\frac{k+1}{2}$		1

8   Conclusions

We have proposed in this paper a KP-ABE scheme for monotone Boolean circuits. The scheme is based on secret sharing and just one bilinear map, and can be viewed as an extension of the scheme in [7]. It is in fact the first KP-ABE scheme for monotone circuits based on bilinear maps.

The efficiency of our scheme depends on the number of FO-gates and their positions in the circuit. Thus, for Boolean circuits representing multilevel access structures our scheme performs better than the one in [5]. For more "complex" Boolean circuits, the KP-ABE scheme in [5] may have a better complexity than ours with respect to the number of decryption keys. However, it faces the problem of computing leveled multilinear maps. Although some progress has recently been achieved along this direction [3, 4], working with leveled multilinear maps is far more expensive than working with just one bilinear map.

Our KP-ABE Scheme associates at least two keys to each input wire of a FO-gate. Finding ways to reduce the number of keys would be extremely helpful in order to reduce the complexity of the scheme.

A Appendix

In this appendix to prove the security of our KP-ABE_Scheme.

Theorem 2. *The KP-ABE_Scheme is secure in the selective model under the decisional bilinear Diffie-Hellman assumption.*

Proof. It is sufficient to prove that for any adversary $\mathcal{A}$ with an advantage η in the selective game for KP-ABE_Scheme, a PPT algorithm $\mathcal{B}$ can be defined, with the advantage $\eta/2$ over the DBDH problem. The algorithm $\mathcal{B}$ plays the role of challenger for $\mathcal{A}$ in the selective game for KP-ABE_Scheme.

The algorithm $\mathcal{B}$ is given an instance of the DBDH problem, that is: two groups G_1 and G_2 of prime order p, a generator g of G_1, a bilinear map $e : G_1 \times G_1 \to G_2$, the values g^a, g^b, g^c, and $Z_v \leftarrow \{Z_0, Z_1\}$, where $Z_0 = e(g, g)^{abc}$, $Z_1 = e(g, g)^z$, and $a, b, c, z \leftarrow \mathbb{Z}_p$.

Now, the algorithm $\mathcal{B}$ runs $\mathcal{A}$ acting as a challenger for it.

Init. Let A be a non-empty set of attributes the adversary $\mathcal{A}$ wishes to be challenged upon.

Setup. $\mathcal{B}$ chooses at random $r_i \in \mathbb{Z}_p$ for all $i \in \mathcal{U}$, and computes $Y = e(g^a, g^b) = e(g, g)^{ab}$ and $T_i = g^{t_i}$ for all $i \in \mathcal{U}$, where

$$t_i = \begin{cases} r_i, & \text{if } i \in A \\ br_i, & \text{otherwise} \end{cases}$$

($\mathcal{B}$ can compute T_i because it knows r_i and g^b). Then, $\mathcal{B}$ publishes the public parameters

$$PP = (p, G_1, G_2, g, e, n, Y, (T_i | i \in \mathcal{U})).$$

The choice of T_i in this way will be transparent in the next step.

Phase 1. The adversary is granted oracle access to the decryption key generation oracle for all queries $\mathcal{C}$ with $\mathcal{C}(A) = 0$. Given such a query, the decryption key is computed as follows. The algorithm $\mathcal{B}$ uses first a procedure *FakeShare* which will share g^a as the procedure *Share* shares $y = ab$ (remark that $\mathcal{B}$ does not know ab). Then, $\mathcal{B}$ delivers decryption keys based on g^b. The following requirements are to be fulfilled:

1. from the adversary's point of view, the secret sharing and distribution of decryption keys should look as in the original scheme;
2. the reconstruction procedure *Recon*, starting from the decryption keys and an authorized set of attributes, should return $e(g, g)^{abc}$.

In order to easily describe the procedure *FakeShare* we adopt the notation $\mathcal{C}_w(A)$ for the truth value at the wire w when the circuit $\mathcal{C}$ is evaluated for A. The main idea in *FakeShare* is the following:

1. if the output wire w of a logic gate $\Gamma = (w_1, w_2, X, w)$ satisfies $C_w(A) = 0$, where X stands for "OR" or "AND", then the value to be shared at this wire is of the form g^x, for some $x \in \mathbb{Z}_p$; otherwise, the value to be shared at this wire is an element $x \in \mathbb{Z}_p$;

2. the shares obtained by sharing the value associated to w, and distributed to the input wires of Γ, should satisfy the same constraints as above. For instance, if $C_{w_1}(A) = 0$ and $C_{w_2}(A) = 1$, then the share distributed to w_1 should be of the form g^{x_1} while the share distributed to w_2 should be of the form x_2;

3. the same policy applies to FANOUT-gates as well.

The procedure *FakeShare* is as follows:

FakeShare(g^a, $\mathcal{C}$)

1. Initially, all gates of $\mathcal{C}$ are unmarked;
2. $S(o) := (g^a)$;
3. If $\Gamma = (w_1, w_2, OR, w)$ is an unmarked OR-gate and $S(w) = L$, then mark Γ and do the followings:
   (a) if $C_w(A) = C_{w_1}(A) = C_{w_2}(A)$, then $S(w_1) := L$ and $S(w_2) := L$;
   (b) if $C_w(A) = 1 = C_{w_1}(A)$ and $C_{w_2}(A) = 0$, then $S(w_1) := L$ and $S(w_2) := (g^{L(i)} | 1 \leq i \leq |L|)$;
   (c) if $C_w(A) = 1 = C_{w_2}(A)$ and $C_{w_1}(A) = 0$, then $S(w_2) := L$ and $S(w_1) := (g^{L(i)} | 1 \leq i \leq |L|)$.
   Remark that, in the last two cases (b) and (c), all the elements in L are from $\mathbb{Z}_p$;
4. If $\Gamma = (w_1, w_2, AND, w)$ is an unmarked AND-gate and $S(w) = L$, then mark Γ and do the followings:
   (a.) if $C_w(A) = 1$, then:
      i. for each $i \in pos(L)$ choose x_i^1 uniformly at random from $\mathbb{Z}_p$ and compute $x_i^2 = (L(i) - x_i^1) \mod p$. Define L_1 (L_2, resp.) as being the list obtained from L by replacing $L(i)$ by x_i^1 (x_i^2, resp.), for all $i \in pos(L)$;
      ii. assign $S(w_1) := L_1$ and $S(w_2) := L_2$;
   (b) if $C_w(A) = 0 = C_{w_2}(A)$ and $C_{w_1}(A) = 1$ then:
      i. for each $i \in pos(L)$ choose x_i^1 uniformly at random from $\mathbb{Z}_p$ and compute $g^{x_i^2} = L(i)/g^{x_i^1}$. Define L_1 (L_2, resp.) as being the list obtained from L by replacing $L(i)$ by x_i^1 ($g^{x_i^2}$, resp.), for all $i \in pos(L)$;
      ii. assign $S(w_1) := L_1$ and $S(w_2) := L_2$;
   (c) if $C_w(A) = 0 = C_{w_1}(A)$ and $C_{w_2}(A) = 1$ then do as above by switching w_1 and w_2;
   (d) if $C_w(A) = C_{w_1}(A) = C_{w_2}(A) = 0$ then:
      i. for each $i \in pos(L)$ choose x_i^1 uniformly at random from $\mathbb{Z}_p$ and compute $g^{x_i^2} = L(i)/g^{x_i^1}$. Define L_1 (L_2, resp.) as being the list obtained from L by replacing $L(i)$ by $g^{x_i^1}$ ($g^{x_i^2}$, resp.), for all $i \in pos(L)$;
      ii. assign $S(w_1) := L_1$ and $S(w_2) := L_2$;
5. If $\Gamma = (w, FANOUT, w_1, \ldots, w_j)$ is an unmarked FANOUT-gate and $S(w_k) = L_k$ for all $1 \leq k \leq j$, then mark Γ and do the followings:

(a) if $C_w(A) = C_{w_1}(A) = \cdots = C_{w_j}(A) = 1$ then
    i. for each $i \in pos(L_1)$ choose uniformly at random $a_i \in \mathbb{Z}_p$ and compute b_i such that $L_1(i) = (a_i + b_i) \mod p$;
   ii. compute $L_1' = (a_i | 1 \leq i \leq |L_1|)$ and $P(w_1) := (g^{b_i} | 1 \leq i \leq |L_1|)$;
   iii. compute L_k' and $P(w_k)$ in a similar way to L_1' and $P(w_1)$, for all $2 \leq k \leq j$;
   iv. Assign $S(w) := L_1' \cdots L_j'$;
(b) if $C_w(A) = C_{w_1}(A) = \cdots = C_{w_j}(A) = 0$ then
    i. for each $i \in pos(L_1)$ choose uniformly at random $a_i \in \mathbb{Z}_p$ and compute $g^{b_i} = L_1(i)/g^{a_i}$;
   ii. compute $L_1' = (g^{a_i} | 1 \leq i \leq |L_1|)$ and $P(w_1) := (g^{b_i} | 1 \leq i \leq |L_1|)$;
   iii. compute L_k' and $P(w_k)$ in a similar way to L_1' and $P(w_1)$, for all $2 \leq k \leq j$;
   iv. Assign $S(w) := L_1' \cdots L_2'$;
6. repeat the last three steps above until all gates get marked.

Let $(S, P) \leftarrow FakeShare(g^a, C)$. The algorithm $\mathcal{B}$ will deliver to $\mathcal{A}$ the decryption key $D = ((D(i)|i \in \mathcal{U}), P')$, where

$$D(i) = \begin{cases} ((g^b)^{S(i,j)/r_i} | 1 \leq j \leq |S(i)|), & \text{if } i \in A \\ (S(i,j)^{1/r_i} | 1 \leq j \leq |S(i)|), & \text{if } i \notin A \end{cases}$$

for any $i \in \mathcal{U}$. Remark that the key component $D(i)$ for $i \in A$ is of the form

$$(g^{bS(i,j)/r_i} | 1 \leq j \leq |S(i)|)$$

while for $i \notin A$ it is of the form

$$(g^{y_{i,j}/r_i} | 1 \leq j \leq |S(i)|) = (g^{by_{i,j}/br_i} | 1 \leq j \leq |S(i)|)$$

(for some $y_{i,j} \in \mathbb{Z}_p$) because the shares of i are all powers of g.

    The distribution of this decryption key is identical to that in the original scheme. Moreover, it is easy to see that the reconstruction procedure $Recon$, applied to $V_A(i,j) = e(g,g)^{S(i,j)bc}$ for all $i \in A$ and $1 \leq j \leq |S(i)|$, returns $e(g,g)^{abc}$.

Challenge. The adversary $\mathcal{A}$ selects two messages m_0 and m_1 (of the same length) and sends them to $\mathcal{B}$. The algorithm $\mathcal{B}$ encrypts m_u with Z_v, where $u \leftarrow \{0,1\}$, and sends it back to the adversary (recall that Z_v was randomly chosen from $\{Z_0, Z_1\}$). The ciphertext is

$$E = (A, E' = m_u Z_v, \{E_i = T_i^c = g^{cr_i}\}_{i \in A})$$

If $v = 0$, E is a valid encryption of m_u; if $v = 1$, E' is a random element from G_2.

Phase 2. The adversary may receive again oracle access to the decryption key generation oracle (with the same constraint as in *Phase 1*).

Guess. Let u' be $\mathcal{A}$'s guess. If $u' = u$, then $\mathcal{B}$ outputs $v' = 0$; otherwise, it outputs $v' = 1$.

We compute now the advantage of $\mathcal{B}$. Clearly,

$$P(v' = v) - \frac{1}{2} = P(v' = v|v = 0) \cdot P(v = 0) + P(v' = v|v = 1) \cdot P(v = 1) - \frac{1}{2}$$

Both $P(v = 0)$ and $P(v = 1)$ are 1/2. Then, remark that

$$P(v' = v|v = 0) = P(u' = u|v = 0) = \frac{1}{2} + \eta$$

and $P(v' = v|v = 1) = P(u' \neq u|v = 1) = \frac{1}{2}$. Putting all together we obtain that the advantage of $\mathcal{B}$ is $P(v' = v) - \frac{1}{2} = \frac{1}{2}\eta$.   □

B   Appendix

We will show here, by means of an example, that disjunctive multilevel access structures cannot be represented by Boolean formulas (Boolean circuits without FANOUT-gates).

Let $\mathcal{U} = \{1, 2, 3, 4\}$, $\mathcal{U}_1 = \{1, 2\}$, $\mathcal{U}_2 = \{3, 4\}$, $a_1 = 2$, and $a_2 = 3$. The minimal authorized sets are $\{1, 2\}$, $\{1, 3, 4\}$, and $\{2, 3, 4\}$. If this disjunctive multilevel access structure would be representable by a Boolean formula, then the following would hold:

1. 1 and 2 cannot be connected by an OR-gate because then $\{1\}$ would be authorized;
2. 1 and 2 cannot be connected by an AND-gate because $\{1, 3, 4\}$ is authorized and $\{3, 4\}$ would become authorized too, which is a contradiction;
3. 1 and 3 cannot be connected by an OR-gate because $\{1, 2, 3\}$ is authorized and $\{2, 3\}$ would become authorized too, which is a contradiction. Similarly, 1 and 4 cannot be connected by an OR-gate;
4. 1 and 3 cannot be connected by an AND-gate because $\{1, 2\}$ is authorized and $\{2, 3\}$ would become authorized too, which is a contradiction. Similarly, 1 and 4 cannot be connected by an AND-gate;
5. 2 and 3 (2 and 4) cannot be connected by OR- or AND-gates by similar reasons as above;
6. 3 and 4 cannot be connected by an OR-gate because $\{1, 3, 4\}$ is authorized and $\{1, 3\}$ would become authorized too, which is a contradiction;
7. according to the above items, 3 and 4 can be connected only by an AND-gate Γ. But then, it is easy to see that there is no way to connect 1, 2, and Γ to obtain this access structure (the discussion is similar to the one above).

Similarly, conjunctive multilevel access structures cannot be represented by Boolean formulas.

References

1. Bellare, M., Hoang, V.T., Rogaway, P.: Foundations of garbled circuits. In: Proceedings of the 2012 ACM Conference on Computer and Communications Security. CCS 2012, pp. 784–796. ACM, New York (2012)

2. Bethencourt, J., Sahai, A., Waters, B.: Ciphertext-policy attribute-based encryption. In: IEEE Symposium on Security and Privacy, S&P 2007, pp. 321–334. IEEE Computer Society (2007)
3. Coron, J.-S., Lepoint, T., Tibouchi, M.: Practical multilinear maps over the integers. In: Canetti, R., Garay, J.A. (eds.) CRYPTO 2013, Part I. LNCS, vol. 8042, pp. 476–493. Springer, Heidelberg (2013)
4. Garg, S., Gentry, C., Halevi, S.: Candidate multilinear maps from ideal lattices. In: Johansson, T., Nguyen, P.Q. (eds.) EUROCRYPT 2013. LNCS, vol. 7881, pp. 1–17. Springer, Heidelberg (2013)
5. Garg, S., Gentry, C., Halevi, S., Sahai, A., Waters, B.: Attribute-based encryption for circuits from multilinear maps. In: Canetti, R., Garay, J.A. (eds.) CRYPTO 2013, Part II. LNCS, vol. 8043, pp. 479–499. Springer, Heidelberg (2013)
6. Gorbunov, S., Vaikuntanathan, V., Wee, H.: Attribute-based encryption for circuits. In: Boneh, D., Roughgarden, T., Feigenbaum, J. (eds.) STOC, pp. 545–554. ACM (2013), preprint on IACR ePrint 2013/337
7. Goyal, V., Pandey, O., Sahai, A., Waters, B.: Attribute-based encryption for fine-grained access control of encypted data. In: ACM Conference on Computer and Communications Security, pp. 89–98. ACM (2006), preprint on IACR ePrint 2006/309
8. Karnin, E.D., Greene, J.W., Hellman, M.E.: On secret sharing systems. IEEE Trans. Inf. Theor. **29**(1), 35–41 (1983)
9. Ostrovsky, R., Sahai, A., Waters, B.: Attribute-based encryption with non-monotonic access structures. In: ACM Conference on Computer and Communications Security, pp. 195–203. ACM (2007), preprint on IACR ePrint 2007/323
10. Simmons, G.J.: How to (really) share a secret. In: Goldwasser, S. (ed.) CRYPTO 1988. LNCS, vol. 403, pp. 390–448. Springer, Heidelberg (1990)
11. Stinson, D.: Cryptography: Theory and Practice, 3rd edn. Chapman and Hall/CRC, Boca Raton (2005)
12. Tassa, T.: Hierarchical threshold secret sharing. J. Cryptology **20**(2), 237–264 (2007)
13. Tassa, T., Dyn, N.: Multipartite secret sharing by bivariate interpolation. J. Cryptology **22**(2), 227–258 (2008)

On the Anonymization of Cocks IBE Scheme

Gheorghe A. Schipor[✉]

Faculty of Computer Science,
"Alexandru Ioan Cuza" University of Iaşi, 700506 Iaşi, România
adrian.schipor@info.uaic.ro

Abstract. Identity based encryption is a relative new method of encryption in which the public key is calculated using an identity. Cocks proposed such a scheme, but his scheme doesn't provide anonymity. In this paper is proposed an extended version of the Cocks IBE scheme that provides anonymity. The ciphertext expansion and the computational time of the scheme proposed here is very close to that of the Cocks IBE scheme, and like the Ateniese-Gasti scheme, it provides universal anonymity.

Keywords: Identity based encryption · Anonymity · Identity · Public-key cryptography

1 Introduction

Until 1976, all known cryptographic algorithms were symmetric, the key used for encryption was the same as the key used for decryption. Whitfield Diffie and Martin Hellman laid the foundations of public key cryptography by their key exchange protocol, even if, in 1997, the British Government revealed that a similar scheme was created, in secret and independently, a few years earlier by James H. Ellis, Clifford Cocks and Malcolm J. Williamson.

The first who mentioned about an asymmetric scheme in which the public key can be calculated using the identity of the intended recipient was Adi Shamir, in 1984 [7], although he was unable to develop such a system. The problem remained opened until 2001, when Boneh and Franklin developed an IBE scheme based on elliptic curves [2]. Soon after, Cocks managed to develop another IBE scheme based on quadratic residuosity problem [8].

The scheme proposed by Cocks encrypts the plaintext bit by bit, every bit being mapped into a pair of two big integers, so it's very bandwidth consuming. However, as mentioned in [8] by Cocks, his scheme can be used in practice to encrypt short session keys.

We say that a cryptographic scheme is anonymous if nobody can say who is the recipient only by having the ciphertext and the public key. If anyone can anonymize the ciphertext using only the public key, the scheme is universally anonymous [12]. Galbraith showed that the Cocks IBE scheme is not anonymous, so the question that came was if the Cocks IBE scheme can be extended to provide anonymity but to not be much more expensive than the original scheme. Di Crescenzo and

© Springer International Publishing Switzerland 2015
B. Ors and B. Preneel (Eds.): BalkanCryptSec 2014, LNCS 9024, pp. 194–202, 2015.
DOI: 10.1007/978-3-319-21356-9_13

Saraswat were the first who extended the Cocks IBE scheme to support anonymity. However, their scheme is impractical to use when large data must be encrypted because it requires a large number of keys [6]. In 2009, Ateniese and Gasti proposed another scheme that extends Cocks IBE scheme and provides anonymity. More, only the public key is used to anonymize the ciphertext so their scheme is universally anonymous. However, every bit of plaintext is mapped into two lists of big integers [1], so the ciphertext expansion is very big.

In this paper I propose a more efficient scheme that extends the Cocks IBE scheme to provide anonymity. The ciphertext expansion of the scheme proposed here is very close to that of the Cocks IBE scheme, sending for a bit, besides the two big integers required by Cocks IBE scheme, only two small integers who usually can be represented on 8 bits. Also, the computational time of the scheme proposed in this paper is close to that of the original scheme, reducing the time to (de)anonymize the ciphertext with more than half of the amount of time required by Ateniese-Gasti scheme to realise these operations.

2   Cocks IBE Scheme

The Cocks IBE scheme requires a big integer n, which is the product of two primes numbers p and q, each of them congruent to 3 modulo 4. Also, it requires a hash function $H : \{0,1\}^* \mapsto \mathbb{Z}_n$. n is the public parameter, and (p,q) represents the master key.

Key Generation: The public key for an identity ID is $a = H(ID)$, with the Jacobi symbol $(\frac{a}{n}) = 1$. The private key corresponding to the public key a is calculated as

$$r = a^{(\phi(n)+4)/8} \mod n.$$

Encryption: A bit b is first encoded in $x = (-1)^b$. Two independent values $t, v \in \mathbb{Z}_n^*$ are chosen at random such that $(\frac{t}{n}) = (\frac{v}{n}) = x$, and the ciphertext is computed as

$$(s_1, s_2) = (t + \frac{a}{t} \mod n, v - \frac{a}{v} \mod n).$$

Decryption: To decrypt the pair (s_1, s_2) the recipient must decide which of the two choices he needs to decrypt, choosing s_1 if $r^2 \equiv a \mod n$ and s_2 if $r^2 \equiv -a \mod n$. The decrypted text is

$$x = (\frac{s_i + 2r}{n}), i \in \{1, 2\}.$$

3   Cocks IBE Anonymization

3.1   Galbraith's Test

Galbraith showed that Cocks IBE does not provide anonymity. Let $a \in \mathbb{Z}_n$ be the private key and $M_a[n] = \{(t + \frac{a}{t}) \mod n | t \in \mathbb{Z}_n^* \wedge (t/n) = (-1)^b\}$ be the set of all ciphertext values sampled using the public key $a \in \mathbb{Z}_n^*$. He proposed the following test:

$$GT(a, c, n) = (\frac{c^2 - 4a}{n}), c \in \mathbb{Z}_n$$

If c is sampled from $M_a[n]$, the test will return 1 always, because $c^2 - 4a$ is a square in $\mathbb{Z}_n$. If c is not sampled from $M_a[n]$ the test will return 1 with probability negligibly close to $1/2$ [1]. This holds because Perron showed that for a prime p, the difference between the squares and non squares from $\mathbb{Z}_p$ is just 1 if $p \equiv 3 \mod 4$.

For two public keys $a, b \in \mathbb{Z}_n^*$ and $c \in \mathbb{Z}_n$ a value of the ciphertext sampled using one of the two keys, the Galbraith's test over the public key a can be summarized as

$$GT(a, c, n) = \begin{cases} +1 \implies Prob[c \in M_a[n]] = 1/2 \\ -1 \implies c \notin M_{(a,n)}. \end{cases}$$

An adversary can apply Galbraith's test for multiple ciphertext values to determine whether the given ciphertext is intended for a or b [1].

In [1], Ateniese and Gasti proved that is no better test against anonymity over an encrypted bit, so the scheme proposed in this paper, like that of Ateniese and Gasti, is based on the Galbraith's test.

3.2   Ateniese-Gasti Scheme

The scheme proposed by Ateniese and Gasti in [1] extends Cocks IBE to provide anonymity. Also, their scheme is the first universally anonymous IBE, so anyone can anonymize the ciphertext using only the public key of the recipient.

Anoymization: Let (s_1, s_2) be the corresponding ciphertext of a bit b encrypted with the public key $a \in \mathbb{Z}_n^*$. To anonymize a component $s_i, i \in \{1, 2\}$ of the pair (s_1, s_2) one must proceed as follows:

1. choose k from the geometric distribution over the set $\{1, 2, 3, ...\}$ with the probability parameter $\frac{1}{2}$;
2. choose T random and set $Z = T + s_i \mod n$;
3. compute the mask as

$$(Z, T_1, T_2, ..., T_{k-1}, \boldsymbol{T}, T_{k+1}, ..., T_m),$$

$$GT(a_i, Z - T_j, n) = -1, 1 \leq j < k$$

$$GT(a_i, Z - T_j, n) = \pm 1, k < j \leq m,$$

$$i \in \{1, 2\}, a_1 = a, a_2 = -a.$$

The pair $((Z_1, T_{1_1}, T_{1_2}, ..., T_{1_k}, ..., T_{1_m}), (Z_2, T_{2_1}, T_{2_2}, ..., T_{2_k}, ..., T_{2_m}))$ represents the anonymized ciphertext.

Deanonymization: Given the anonymized ciphertext

$$((Z_1, T_{1_1}, T_{1_2}, ..., T_{1_k}, ..., T_{1_m}), (Z_2, T_{2_1}, T_{2_2}, ..., T_{2_k}, ..., T_{2_m})),$$

the recipient must first discard one of the two tuples based on whether a or $-a$ is a square in $\mathbb{Z}_n$, and find the smallest index $1 \leq j \leq m$ such that $GT(a_i, Z_i - T_{i_j}, n) = 1, i \in \{1, 2\}$. The initial value of ciphertext is $Z_i - T_{i_j}$.

Security: Ateniese and Gasti showed that their scheme does not reveal any information about the plaintext and an adversary cannot determine which public key was used to encrypt the plaintext, even thought the adversary selects the public keys and the plaintext.

4 A New Method of Anonymization

Like the scheme proposed by Ateniese and Gasti, the scheme proposed bellow is based on the Cocks IBE scheme and is universally anonymous. Also, the ciphertext expansion and the computational time of this scheme is very close to that of the Cocks IBE scheme.

Anonymization: To anonymize a component $s_i, i \in \{1, 2\}$ of the pair (s_1, s_2) with the public key $a \in \mathbb{Z}_n^*$, one must proceed as follows:

1. choose a bit d random;
2. if d is 1 then:
   (a) choose k from the geometric distribution over the set $\{1, 2, 3, ...\}$ with the probability parameter $\frac{1}{2}$;
   (b) $plus_i \leftarrow 1, j \leftarrow 0, s_{anon_i} \leftarrow s_i$;
   (c) $s_{anon_i} = s_{anon_i} + 1 \mod n$;
   (d) if $GT(a_i, s_{anon_i}, n) = 1$, then $plus_i \leftarrow plus_i + 1$, else $j \leftarrow j + 1$;
   (e) if $j = k$, then output $(s_{anon_i}, plus_i)$, else jump to (c);
3. else, $s_{anon_i} \leftarrow s_i$, choose $plus_i$ random from the geometric distribution over the set $\{1, 2, 3, ...\}$ with the probability parameter $\frac{1}{2}$ and output $(s_{anon_i}, plus_i)$.

The pair $((s_{anon_1}, plus_1), (s_{anon_2}, plus_2))$ represents the ciphertext anonymized.

Deanonymization: Given the anonymized ciphertext

$$((s_{anon_1}, plus_1), (s_{anon_2}, plus_2)),$$

the recipient must first choose the valid component based on whether a or $-a$ is a square in $\mathbb{Z}_n$. After that, the recipient must test if $GT(a, s_{anon_i}, n)$ equals -1 or 1. If $GT(a, s_{anon_i}, n) = 1$, then the component was not anonymized, so he can jump to decryption. Else, the component was anonymized so he must substract 1 from s_{anon_i} until he reaches the $plus_i$-th element such that $GT(a_i, s_{anon_i} - 1 - ..., n) = 1$. That value represents the initial ciphertext.

4.1   Security

At the base of the security of this scheme is the fact that the probability to anonymize a component is $\frac{1}{2}$. Let $a, b \in \mathbb{Z}_n^*$ be two public keys, and $s_{anon} \in M_a[n]$ be a component of the anonymized ciphertext. The probability that $GT(a, s_{anon}, n) = 1$ is $\frac{1}{2}$. The probability that $GT(b, s_{anon}, n) = 1$ is also $\frac{1}{2}$ because of the distribution of the Jacobi symbols in $\mathbb{Z}_n$. So an adversary cannot say what public key was used to encrypt the plaintext because for him each of the public keys has the same probability to be used. An adversary can be in one of the following four cases:

Case 1:
$$\begin{cases} GT(a, s_{anon}, n) = 1 \\ GT(b, s_{anon}, n) = 1 \end{cases}$$

The adversary cannot say what public key was used to encrypt the plaintext. For each of the two public keys, the ciphertext seems to not be anonymized. The adversary can suppose that the plaintext was encrypted with the public key a and not anonymized(the probability to be so is $\frac{1}{2}$) and $GT(b, s_{anon}, n)$ is 1 because of the distribution of the Jacobi symbols in $\mathbb{Z}_n$. Also, the adversary can suppose that the plaintext was encrypted with the public key b and not anonymized(the probability to be so is $\frac{1}{2}$) and $GT(a, s_{anon}, n)$ is 1 because of the distribution of the Jacobi symbols in $\mathbb{Z}_n$. It can be easily seen that the adversary cannot say with probability greater than $1/2$ which case is the good one.

Case 2:
$$\begin{cases} GT(a, s_{anon}, n) = -1 \\ GT(b, s_{anon}, n) = 1 \end{cases}$$

The adversary can suppose that the plaintext was encrypted with the public key a and anonymized(the probability to be so is $\frac{1}{2}$) and $GT(b, s_{anon}, n)$ is 1 because of the distribution of the Jacobi symbols in $\mathbb{Z}_n$. Also, the adversary can suppose that the plaintext was encrypted with the public key b and not anonymized(the probability to be so is $\frac{1}{2}$) and $GT(a, s_{anon}, n)$ is -1 because of the distribution of the Jacobi symbols in $\mathbb{Z}_n$. Therefore, the adversary cannot say with probability greater than $1/2$ which case is the good one.

Case 3:
$$\begin{cases} GT(a, s_{anon}, n) = 1 \\ GT(b, s_{anon}, n) = -1 \end{cases}$$

Similar with the **Case 2**.

Case 4:

$$\begin{cases} GT(a, s_{anon}, n) = -1 \\ GT(b, s_{anon}, n) = -1 \end{cases}$$

For each of the two public keys, the ciphertext seems to be anonymized. The adversary can suppose that the plaintext was encrypted with the public key a and anonymized(the probability to be so is $\frac{1}{2}$) and $GT(b, s_{anon}, n)$ is -1 because of the distribution of the Jacobi symbols in $\mathbb{Z}_n$. Also, the adversary can suppose that the plaintext was encrypted with the public key b and anonymized(the probability to be so is $\frac{1}{2}$) and $GT(a, s_{anon}, n)$ is -1 because of the distribution of the Jacobi symbols in $\mathbb{Z}_n$. Therefore, the adversary cannot say with probability greater than $1/2$ which case is the good one.

Anonymization Method: The method to anonymize a component should not reveal any informations about the used public key, so an adversary must find a valid deanonymized ciphertext for every public key $p_k \in \mathbb{Z}_n^*$ and to not make distinction between these ciphertexts.

It is easy to prove that the method used to anonymize the ciphertext doesn't reveal informations about the used public key. If an adversary has two public keys $a, b \in \mathbb{Z}_n^*$ and an anonymized(for both keys) component $(s_{anon}, plus_i)$, he can subtract 1 from s_{anon} until he reach the k-th element with $GT(a, s_{anon} - 1 - ..., n)$ $= 1$ or until he reach the k-th elemenet with $GT(b, s_{anon} - 1 - ..., n) = 1$. With both public keys he can determine a valid value. When a component is not anonymized, it is chosen $plus_i$ from the geometric distribution with the probability parameter $\frac{1}{2}$. This is because the Jacobi symbols are uniformly distributed in $\mathbb{Z}_n$, so we can consider that until we reach at the k-th element for that the value of Galbraith's test is -1(when the component is anonymized), we pass over same number of elements for that the value of Galbraith's test is 1. So the method used to anonymize a component does not reveal any information about the pubic key used to encrypt the plaintext.

Choosen Plaintext Attack: An IBE scheme is ANON-IND-ID-CPA-secure if is IND-ID-CPA-secure and an adversary cannot determine the key used for encryption even if he selects the plaintext and the identities and receives the plaintext encrypted with the public key corresponding to one of the chosen identities [13,14].

The scheme presented is IND-ID-CPA-secure because extends Cocks IBE scheme, which is IND-ID-CPA-secure, and the anonymization is done using only the public key and the ciphertext.

It remains to prove that an adversary cannot determine the key used for encryption when he selects the keys and the plaintext. In [13] is presented an experiment for this. The adversary has access to a random oracle H and to an oracle $KeyDer$ that returns the private key corresponding to any identity ID, but cannot request the private keys [1,13]:

Experiment $Exp_{IBE,A}^{ibe-ano-cpa}(n)$:

pick random oracle H;

$(ID_0, ID_1, msg, state) \leftarrow A^{KeyExtr(.),H}(find, PKG_{pub})$;

$b \leftarrow \{0,1\}$;

$W \leftarrow \{0,1\}^{|msg|}$;

$c \leftarrow Enc^H(ID_b, W, PKG_{pub})$;

$b' \leftarrow A^{KeyExtr(.),H}(guess, c, state)$;

if $b' = b$ return 1, else return 0.

The advantage of A is defined as

$$Adv_{IBE,A}^{ibe-ano-cpa}(n) =$$

$$Prob[Exp_{IBE,A}^{ibe-ano-cpa-1}(n) = 1] - Prob[Exp_{IBE,A}^{ibe-ano-cpa-0}(n) = 1].$$

We say that a scheme is IBE-ANO-CPA-secure if $Adv_{IBE,A}^{ibe-ano-cpa}(n)$ is a negligible function in n for all polynomial-time adversaries A [13].

In the proposed scheme every component from the pair corresponding to an encrypted bit is anonymized independently and even if both components encrypts the same value, since the Cocks IBE scheme is IND-ID-CPA-secure, the advantage of an adversary to win the experiment is only negligibly, even if he choose the plaintext and the keys. An adversary will be in one of the four cases presented, so he cannot find the key used for encryption because the components are anonymized independently and for every key he can find a valid value of ciphertext. To summarize,

$$Adv_{new-ibe-cocks,A}^{ibe-ano-cpa}(n) = \frac{1}{2} + negl(n)$$

for every adversary A, where *new-ibe-cocks* is the scheme presented.

Because is IBE-ANO-CPA-secure and IND-ID-CPA-secure, *new-ibe-cocks* is ANON-IND-ID-CPA-secure.

4.2   Practical Aspects

If Cocks IBE scheme is used to encrypt a 128 bits session key, the ciphertext length is only $128*2*1024$ bits, but the ciphertext is not anonymized. Using the Ateniese-Gasti scheme, the ciphertext length is $128*2*m*1024$ bits. However, using the scheme presented in this paper, the ciphertext length is only $128*2*(1024 + l)$ bits, where l is the number of bits required to represent the second component from an anonymized component. The $plus_i$ component is chosen from the geometric distribution over the set $\{1, 2, 3, ...\}$ with the probability parameter $\frac{1}{2}$, so l can be usually 8. It can be seen that the ciphertext expansion of this scheme is much smaller than the ciphertext expansion of the Ateniese-Gasti scheme, being closer to the Cocks IBE scheme.

Implementation: I implemented all three schemes and compared the results. The implementation was done using the C programming language and the big numbers library *GMP*. In all three implementations, I used 512 bits numbers for p and q. Every essential step of the schemes was executed 1000 times. The operating system under I tested the schemes is *Elementary OS, Linux Kernel 3.2* and the machine consists of 4GB RAM memory and an Intel Core i5 processor. The results are summarized in the Table 1.

Table 1. Average execution times

	Setup	Extraction	Encryption	Decryption
Cocks	26.77 ms	3.58 ms	18.7 ms	7.45 ms
Ateniese-Gasti	26.77 ms	3.58 ms	33.46 ms	24.46 ms
Proposed scheme	26.77 ms	3.58 ms	23.19 ms	14.38 ms

As you can see, the scheme proposed in this paper is more efficient than the scheme proposed by Ateniese and Gasti, reducing the (de)anonymization time with more than half of the time needed by their scheme. Also, like their scheme, this scheme is universally anonymous because only the public key is used to anonymize the ciphertext, so one could write an algorithm that has as input the ciphertext and the public key and outputs the anonymized ciphertext.

Overall, I propose a universally anonymous IBE scheme that is almost as efficient as Cocks IBE scheme.

References

1. Ateniese, G., Gasti, P.: Universally anonymous IBE based on the quadratic residuosity assumption. In: Fischlin, M. (ed.) CT-RSA 2009. LNCS, vol. 5473, pp. 32–47. Springer, Heidelberg (2009)
2. Boneh, D., Franklin, M.: Identity-based encryption from the weil pairing. SIAM J. Comput. **32**(3), 586–615 (2003)
3. Martin, L.: Introduction to Identity-Based Encryption. Artech House, Norwood (2008)
4. Tiplea, F.L.: Algebric Foundation of Computer Science. Polirom, Algebric Foundation of Computer Science. Polirom, Romanian (2006)
5. Damgård, I.B.: On the randomness of legendre and jacobi sequences. In: Goldwasser, S. (ed.) CRYPTO 1988. LNCS, vol. 403, pp. 163–172. Springer, Heidelberg (1990)
6. Di Crescenzo, G., Saraswat, V.: Public key encryption with searchable keywords based on jacobi symbols. In: Srinathan, K., Rangan, C.P., Yung, M. (eds.) INDOCRYPT 2007. LNCS, vol. 4859, pp. 282–296. Springer, Heidelberg (2007)
7. Shamir, A.: Identity-based cryptosystems and signature schemes. In: Blakely, G.R., Chaum, D. (eds.) CRYPTO 1984. LNCS, vol. 196, pp. 47–53. Springer, Heidelberg (1985)

8. Benachour, P., Farrell, P.G., Honary, B.: A line code construction for the adder channel with rates higher than time-sharing. In: Honary, B. (ed.) Cryptography and Coding 2001. LNCS, vol. 2260, p. 166. Springer, Heidelberg (2001)
9. Satoh, A., Morioka, S., Takano, K., Munetoh, S.: A compact rijndael hardware architecture with S-Box optimization. In: Boyd, C. (ed.) ASIACRYPT 2001. LNCS, vol. 2248, p. 239. Springer, Heidelberg (2001)
10. Spiegel, M.: Theory and Problems of Statistics. McGraw-Hill, New York (1992)
11. Boneh, D., Gentry, C., Hamburg, M.: Space-Efficient Identity Based Encryption Without Pairings. In: Proceedings FOCS 2007 (2007)
12. Hayashi, R., Tanaka, K.: Universally anonymizable public-key encryption. In: Roy, B.(ed.) ASIACRYPT 2005. LNCS, vol. 3788, pp. 293–312. Springer, Heidelberg (2005)
13. Abdalla, M., Bellare, M., Catalano, D., Kiltz, E., Kohno, T., Lange, T., Malone-Lee, J., Neven, G., Paillier, P., Shi, H.: Searchable encryption revisited: consistency properties, relation to anonymous IBE, and extensions. In: Shoup, V. (ed.) CRYPTO 2005. LNCS, vol. 3621, pp. 205–222. Springer, Heidelberg (2005)
14. Halevi, S.: A Sufficient Condition for Key-Privacy. Cryptology ePrint Archive, Report 2005/05 (2005)

Nearest Planes in Practice

Christian Bischof[1], Johannes Buchmann[1], Özgür Dagdelen[1],
Robert Fitzpatrick[2], Florian Göpfert[1](✉), and Artur Mariano[1]

[1] Technische Universität Darmstadt, Darmstadt, Germany
fgoepfert@cdc.informatik.tu-darmstadt.de
[2] Academia Sinica, IIS, Taipei City, Taiwan

Abstract. The learning with errors (LWE) problem is one of the most attractive problems that lattice-based cryptosystems base their security on. Thus, assessing the hardness in theory and practice is of prime importance. Series of work investigated the hardness of LWE from a theoretical point of view. However, it is quite common that in practice one can solve lattice problems much faster than theoretical estimates predict.

The most promising approach to solve LWE is the decoding method, which converts an LWE instance to an instance of the closest vector problem (CVP). The latter instance can then be solved by a CVP solver. In this work, we investigate how the nearest planes algorithm proposed by Lindner and Peikert (CT-RSA 2011) performs in practice. This algorithm improves an algorithm by Babai, and is a state-of-the-art CVP solver.

We present the first parallel version of the nearest planes algorithm. Our implementation achieves speedup factors of more than 11x on a machine with four CPU-chips totaling 16 cores. In fact, to the best of our knowledge, there is not even a single parallel implementation publicly available of any LWE solver so far. We also compare our results with heuristics on the running time of a single nearest planes run claimed by Lindner and Peikert and subsequently used by others for runtime estimations.

Keywords: Cryptanalysis · Lattices · Decoding attack · Nearest planes · Implementation

1 Introduction

The Learning with Errors (LWE) problem has attracted a considerable amount of attention since its introduction by Regev [26]. Along with its 'sister problem', the Short Integer Solutions (SIS) problem, LWE enjoys currently unique security guarantees, in effect asserting that 'weak' instances do not exist. Additional reasons for the current popularity of LWE and its more efficient variant (Ring-LWE) lie in their asymptotic efficiency, conjectured invulnerability to solution by large-scale quantum computers, the relatively 'lightweight' atomic operations required for their implementation and, lastly, the remarkable flexibility of LWE as a

B. Ors and B. Preneel (Eds.): BalkanCryptSec 2014, LNCS 9024, pp. 203–215, 2015.
DOI: 10.1007/978-3-319-21356-9_14

basis for cryptographic constructions. In consequence, a wide variety of schemes based on LWE have been proposed in recent years, ranging from basic public key encryption [19,22,25,26] and signature schemes [6,11,14,21] to advanced schemes like fully and somewhat homomorphic encryption, e.g., [8,9,12].

In contrast to strong theoretical results, however, the hardness of concrete LWE instances (and of lattice problems in general) in practice is still a remarkably unexplored and, at times, bewildering area. Obviously, this comparative neglect of practical hardness considerations presents a (arguably the principal such) potential problem with respect to the practical adoption of lattice-based cryptography in the future.

Restricting our attention to LWE, there are essentially three approaches to solve LWE instances known at present. The indirect way of solving LWE is by reducing LWE to a unique Shortest Vector Problem (uSVP) instance, and solve this derived instance using an (approximate) SVP solver, such as LLL and BKZ (2.0). This approach is also called the embedding attack [13,17]. Dedicated algorithms for solving LWE such as the combinatorial BKW algorithm [7] and the *decoding algorithm* [19] have been subsequently proposed. Except for the BKW algorithm, all of these algorithms for LWE rely on strong lattice reduction (i.e., BKZ 2.0). We will not consider BKW in the following, since it requires exponentially many samples and is therefore not practical in realistic scenarios.

While there are a series of works analyzing the embedding attack and the BKW algorithm in practice [1–3,5,15,23,24], the practical behavior of the decoding algorithm is still unexplored. In this work, we endeavor to enlighten this area a little further by showing experiments with a parallel version of the nearest planes attack proposed by Lindner and Peikert [19] following the decoding approach.

1.1 Our Contribution

In [19], a brief discussion is given with regard to the parallelization of the nearest planes algorithm, however, this consisted of largely high-level heuristic observations with no practical experiments or detailed consideration of such being made (to the best of our knowledge).

Since the decoding attack is widely believed to be the currently optimal method of attacking LWE in practice, we believe that a concrete instantiation and concrete consideration of such issues is of significant importance. We present experimental and theoretical results with regard to the performance of the nearest planes algorithm for LWE, with an emphasis on the parallel implementation. This includes exhaustive experiments with a concrete parallel implementation of nearest planes that scales very well on multi-core machines. The results from our experiments are used as a basis to predict the running time of nearest planes on concrete LWE instances (here we follow the approach by Lindner and Peikert [19]). We compare the results with other attacks and show that nearest planes is in fact the most promising known attack (in practice and theory) on those LWE instances.

Our sequential implementation can find up to 2^9 close lattice vectors per second. Since the parallel version scales quite well, we can conclude that it should be possible to find more than 2^{16} close lattice vectors per second, which is the bound given by Lindner and Peikert [19].

1.2 Related Work

Lindner and Peikert [19] proposed the nearest planes algorithm and showed (to some extent) how to simulate its performance. Albrecht et al. [2] evaluated the performance of the BKW algorithm on LWE instances. BKW is a combinatorial attack on LWE that is very suitable for parallelization, but only the sequential variant was considered in [2]. Another attack on LWE is the embedding approach by Kannan [17], the application of which was examined by Albrecht, Fitzpatrick and Göpfert [1], but there is no natural way to parallelize the implementation. To the best of our knowledge, there are no other studies on the parallelization of an LWE solver.

Liu and Nguyen [20] presented recently a very interesting work related to the nearest planes algorithm. They show that nearest planes can be viewed as an instance of enumeration (more commonly studied with regard to solving the exact shortest vector problem) and apply known improved variants of enumeration to nearest planes to obtain theoretical and practical improvements over [19]. In particular, those improvements are randomization and pruning. The idea of randomization is to apply the attack many times with parameters that provide only a small success probability with random bases. Applying this approach with a parallel implementation of nearest plane is easily possible. The idea of pruning is to cut off parts of the search trees that contribute significantly to the running time but only slightly to the success probability. This leads to unbalanced search trees and makes parallelization more difficult, but not impossible as the parallel implementation of the pruned enumeration by Kuo et al. [18] shows (see also [10,16]).

While Liu and Nguyen show that their approach outperforms the nearest planes as proposed in [19], we observe the following. In a nutshell, the goal of [20] is to minimize the number of "false positives", i.e. the number of vectors returned by nearest planes that are not close to the target. Our goal, however, is to maximize the number of vectors we can find by calculating many nodes in parallel. Hence, the approaches are complementary and a combination of both approaches (for parallelization) would be very promising for future work.

2 Preliminaries

2.1 Lattice Background

For an integer n, we define $[n] = \{1, 2, \ldots, n\}$. We denote vectors by bold lower-case letters and matrices by bold upper-case letters.

A lattice Λ is a discrete subgroup of the space $\mathbb{R}^m$. Lattices are represented by linearly independent vectors $\mathbf{b}_1, \ldots, \mathbf{b}_n \in \mathbb{R}^m$, where n is called the dimension of the lattice. If $n = m$, the respective lattice has full rank. We call a set of vectors $\mathbf{B} = \{\mathbf{b}_1, \ldots, \mathbf{b}_n\}$ a basis of a lattice $\Lambda(\mathbf{B})$ if the vectors are linearly independent and n is equal to the rank of the lattice. The lattice $\Lambda(\mathbf{B})$ is defined by all integer combinations of elements of $\mathbf{B}$, i.e.,

$$\Lambda(\mathbf{B}) = \left\{ \mathbf{x} \in \mathbb{R}^m \mid \exists \alpha_1, \ldots, \alpha_n \in \mathbb{Z} : \mathbf{x} = \sum_{i=1}^{n} \alpha_i \mathbf{b}_i \right\}.$$

We are particularly interested in modular integer lattices. These are also the lattices one considers when solving LWE instances. A modular (or q-ary) lattice, for a given $q \in \mathbb{N}$, is a full-ranked lattice Λ such that $q\mathbb{Z}^m \subseteq \Lambda \subseteq \mathbb{Z}^m$. The determinant of a full-ranked lattice $\Lambda(\mathbf{A})$ is defined as $\det(\Lambda(\mathbf{A})) = \det(\mathbf{A})$. It is well known that the determinant of a lattice is well-defined (i.e. does not depend on the particular basis) and the definition can be generalized for lattices that are not full-ranked.

For a set of vectors $\mathbf{B}$, we write $\pi_{\text{span}(\mathbf{B})}(\mathbf{t})$ for the projection of the vector $\mathbf{t}$ onto the span of the vectors of $\mathbf{B}$, i.e., $\pi_{\text{span}(\mathbf{B})}(\mathbf{t}) = \mathbf{B}(\mathbf{B}^T\mathbf{B})^{-1}\mathbf{B}^T \cdot \mathbf{t}$.

The Gram-Schmidt orthogonalization $\widetilde{\mathbf{B}} = \{\widetilde{\mathbf{b}}_1, \ldots, \widetilde{\mathbf{b}}_n\}$ of a basis $\mathbf{B}$ is defined through $\widetilde{\mathbf{b}}_i = \mathbf{b}_i - \pi_{\text{span}(\mathbf{b}_1, \ldots, \mathbf{b}_{i-1})}(\mathbf{b}_i)$ for $i \in [n]$. Note that the Gram-Schmidt basis is typically not a basis of the lattice. The fundamental parallelepiped of a basis B is given by

$$\mathcal{P}(\mathbf{B}) = \left\{ \mathbf{v} = \sum_{i=1}^{m} \alpha_i \mathbf{b}_i \mid \forall i \in [m] : 0 \leq \alpha_i < 1 \right\},$$

and the shifted fundamental parallelepiped by

$$\mathcal{P}_{1/2}(\mathbf{B}) = \left\{ \mathbf{v} = \sum_{i=1}^{m} \alpha_i \mathbf{b}_i \mid \forall i \in [m] : -\frac{1}{2} \leq \alpha_i < \frac{1}{2} \right\}.$$

Analogously, we can consider the fundamental parallelepiped (and shifted parallelepiped) determined by the Gram-Schmidt vectors of a given basis by replacing $\mathbf{b}_i$ in the above definitions with $\widetilde{\mathbf{b}}_i$ – we denote these cases by $\mathcal{P}(\widetilde{\mathbf{B}})$ and $\mathcal{P}_{1/2}(\widetilde{\mathbf{B}})$, respectively. Note that, in these cases, the orthogonality of the basis vectors implies that $\mathcal{P}(\widetilde{\mathbf{B}})$ and $\mathcal{P}_{1/2}(\widetilde{\mathbf{B}})$ are n-dimensional rectangles.

The quality of a basis is typically measured with the Hermite delta δ. A basis $\mathbf{B} = \{\mathbf{b}_1, \ldots, \mathbf{b}_n\}$ of an n-dimensional lattice Λ has Hermite delta δ if $\|\mathbf{b}_1\| = \delta^m \det(\Lambda)^{1/n}$. Below we recall the learning with errors problem formally whose hardness we investigate in this work.

Definition 1. ((Search) LWE Problem). *Let n, q be positive integers, χ be a probability distribution on $\mathbb{Z}_q$ and $\mathbf{s}$ be a secret vector following the uniform distribution on $\mathbb{Z}_q^n$. We denote by $L_{\mathbf{s},\chi}^{(n)}$ the probability distribution on $\mathbb{Z}_q^n \times \mathbb{Z}_q$ obtained by choosing $\mathbf{a}$ from the uniform distribution on $\mathbb{Z}_q^n$, choosing e according to χ and returning $(\mathbf{a}, c) = (\mathbf{a}, \langle \mathbf{a}, \mathbf{s} \rangle + e) \in \mathbb{Z}_q^n \times \mathbb{Z}_q$. Search-LWE is the problem of finding $\mathbf{s} \in \mathbb{Z}_q^n$ given pairs $(\mathbf{a}_i, c_i) \in \mathbb{Z}_q^n \times \mathbb{Z}_q$ sampled according to $L_{\mathbf{s},\chi}^{(n)}$.*

Naturally, we can extend this definition to 'Matrix-LWE' in which LWE samples (with a common secret vector) are concatenated to obtain a vector $\mathbf{t} = \mathbf{As} + \mathbf{e}$ and we are again asked to recover $\mathbf{s}$. By adopting this view, we can now view the matrix $\mathbf{A}$ as determining a q-ary lattice with $\mathbf{As}$ being a lattice point and $\mathbf{t}$ being the 'noisy' lattice point, the recovery of which is required to solve the LWE instance.

2.2   Definitions on Parallel Computing

We now recap some concepts pertaining to parallel computing. *Threads* (of computation) are sequences of instructions that can be executed independently from one another. Variables that are accessed by all threads are said to be *shared* variables, while variables of which each thread has a private copy of are said to be *private* variables. A *task* is computational work that is assigned to a thread. For the sake of simplicity, we deal with tasks that are never preempted from one thread to be assigned to another. *Barriers* are synchronization points for threads. Threads are only released from a specific barrier when every thread in the system reaches it. A *parallel zone* denotes a region of the code that is executed by all the threads in the system. Threads are created at the beginning of the parallel zone and die at the end of the region. Finally, a *single zone* denotes a region of the code that is executed by a single, unspecified, thread.

3   The Decoding Attack

3.1   The Idea

Since LWE is essentially a closest vector problem instance (given a modular lattice L and a target vector $\mathbf{t}$, find the lattice vector that is closest to $\mathbf{t}$), one natural approach is to apply the well-known nearest plane algorithm (due to Babai [4]) to recover a lattice point relatively close to the 'noisy' target point. In short, the idea of nearest plane is to solve the problem by dealing with one dimension after the other. For every basis vector $\mathbf{b}_i$, it subtracts the integer multiple c_i of $\mathbf{b}_i$ that minimizes the distance to the hyperplane spanned by the basis vectors $\mathbf{b}_1, \ldots, \mathbf{b}_{i-1}$ from the target vector and continues with the smaller basis $\mathbf{b}_1, \ldots, \mathbf{b}_{i-1}$ and the new target vector. At the end, it returns the sum of all vectors $c_i\mathbf{b}_i$, which is obviously a lattice vector.

Understanding why the result is (to some extent) close to the target vector requires more effort, but fortunately there is an easy geometric interpretation of the output: When called on an LWE instance $\mathbf{t} = \mathbf{As} + \mathbf{e}$, the (polynomial-time) algorithm nearest plane returns the unique lattice point $\mathbf{v}$ such that $\mathbf{t} - \mathbf{v} = \mathbf{e}$ lies in the shifted Gram-Schmidt fundamental parallelepiped $\mathcal{P}_{1/2}(\widetilde{\mathbf{B}})$.

One phenomenon which arises when examining lattices bases is that the logarithms of the norms of the Gram-Schmidt vectors appear to decline linearly, this phenomenon being known as the 'Gram-Schmidt Log Assumption'. As noted in [19], this phenomenon also manifests in the case of the modular lattices arising from LWE. If the last vectors in the Gram-Schmidt basis are too short, the 'search rectangle' $\mathcal{P}_{1/2}(\widetilde{\mathbf{B}})$ will be long and narrow and the returned point will in general be far from the actual closest lattice point.

One natural way to improve the success probability is to apply a basis reduction (typically BKZ) before running nearest plane. This will lead to "more orthogonal" basis vectors, which leads to a smaller gradient being for the log of norms of the Gram-Schmidt vectors and therefore to a search rectangle that is less narrow in the last dimension.

Another natural improvement and forming the crux of the Lindner-Peikert algorithm is to recurse on more than one plane at each step, i.e., instead of subtracting one multiple of the last basis vector, we subtract several, each leading to a vector close to the span of the other basis vectors. Each such vector value then leads to a further set of recursive calls as opposed to just one. Clearly, however, if we even deviate from the nearest plane algorithm by recursing on not just the closest plane but the closest and second-closest plane at each level, we obtain exponential complexity. In the nearest planes algorithm, the number of such branches at each level is specified by a vector $\mathbf{d}$, leading a generalization with the original nearest plane algorithm corresponding to $\mathbf{d} = (1, 1, \ldots, 1)$. Similarly to $\mathcal{P}_{1/2}(\widetilde{\mathbf{B}})$, the search rectangle of nearest plane, we define

$$\mathcal{P}^{\mathbf{d}}_{1/2}(\widetilde{\mathbf{B}}) = \left\{ \mathbf{v} = \sum_{i=1}^{m} \alpha_i \tilde{\mathbf{b}}_i \mid \forall i \in [m] : -\frac{d_i}{2} \leq \alpha_i < \frac{d_i}{2} \right\}$$

as the search rectangle of nearest planes.

To find the optimal choice of the vector $\mathbf{d}$, assuming the Gram-Schmidt Log assumption holds, we can observe that, to minimize the probability of the exact closest vector not being found through our projections, we should recurse on more planes when $\|\tilde{\mathbf{b}}_i\|$ is small and on fewer planes when $\|\tilde{\mathbf{b}}_i\|$ is large. In general, as observed in [19], the entries of $\mathbf{d}$ should be chosen to maximize $\min_i(d_i \cdot \|\tilde{\mathbf{b}}_i\|)$. Such issues are dealt with in the work of Lindner and Peikert, with natural optimal conditions being arrived at. However, since this work is concerned only with the nearest planes algorithm and not with obtaining the optimal distribution of time between the pre-processing and the main algorithm, we do not discuss such issues further.

3.2 Variants of Nearest Planes

Nearest planes traverses the tree as follows: for a given target vector $\mathbf{t}$, it calculates a new target vector $\mathbf{t}'$ and calls nearest planes with the new target vector (i.e. goes down the tree by one level). In every node, a part of the result is calculated. To get the final results, the algorithm goes up the tree again, combining the partial results of every level. In contrast to this, we have implemented a variant which has a slightly different workflow. Instead of going up and down on the tree in a depth-first manner, we go down and right in a breadth-first manner. This implies that we do not accumulate the target vector when we go up in the tree, but we pass the parts of the target vector to the lower nodes and accumulate while we go down on the tree. In the next section we describe in more detail our chosen variant for implementation.

4 Parallel Implementation

In this section we explain the mapping of the algorithm's workflow on a weighted tree and the parallelization of the traversal and computation of the tree.

4.1 Mapping of the Workflow on a Weighted Tree

The workflow of the algorithm can be viewed as a traversal of a tree, with $\prod_{i=n-k}^{n} \mathbf{d}_i$ is the number of nodes in level k. The values in $\mathbf{d}$ dictate the number of branches per level on a reversed order: position $\mathbf{d}_n$ indicates the number of branches on the first level, $\mathbf{d}_{n-1}$ indicates the number of branches on the second level, and so on.

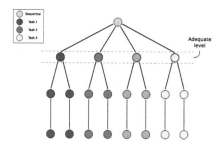

Fig. 1. Map of the algorithm's workflow on a tree, partitioned into tasks, for $\mathbf{d} = \{1, 2, 4\}$, for a number of threads ≥ 4 (Color figure online).

Figure 1 shows a tree with an array $\mathbf{d} = \{1, 2, 4\}$. A new target vector is calculated for each node, on a certain level k, and used in the level $k + 1$ by its child nodes. The processing of vectors in a given level $k + 1$, after the execution of nodes in the level k, is a process referred to as *going down* in the tree.

As opposed to direct implementation of nearest planes [19], which does not need to carry vectors from one level of the tree to the other, our implementation hands error vectors from a given level k to its subsequent level $k + 1$. This is equivalent to process the tree in a depth-first manner, versus to process the tree in a breadth-first manner, in our implementation. This has a direct impact in data collection, further discussed in Sect. 4.3.

4.2   Approach

Our parallel implementation is based on creating a task for each branch of the tree, starting at some level, as seen in Fig. 1 (tasks are in different colors). Tasks are very well suited for the parallelization of this algorithm because, unlike other abstractions, such as threads, it is easy to specify parallel workload (branches of the tree). Our parallelization scheme is based on sequentially executing (and *going down*) a certain number of levels on the tree, until an *adequate level* is reached. Conceptually, an *adequate level* k is a level which satisfies:

1. The number of nodes and child nodes on the level provide enough computation to utilize the capacity of all running threads
2. The computation associated to the levels between 1 and k is not a significant part of the overall computation of the tree.

This means that the *adequate level* depends on the number of running threads and on the amount of computation required by the nodes on the levels that precede it. Then, once the *adequate level* has been reached, the implementation defines as many tasks as the number of nodes on the level. Each task entails the computation of each node on the *adequate level* and its child nodes. Tasks can then be executed in parallel, by unspecified computation units, without any need for synchronization. There are a couple of data structures and variables that need to be initialized accordingly. For example, each task receives its own target vector and has his own variable for *len*.

Each task traverses itself a tree, rooted by the node that is on its starting level. All tasks receive the value of the *adequate level*, so that they can calculate the number of child nodes that they have, by accessing the vector **d** accordingly.

4.3   Implementation

In our implementation, we calculate the *adequate level* as the first level on the tree that has at least as many nodes as the number of running threads. Since the *adequate level*, as it is defined by us, is straightforward to compute, we split the original loop into two different loops, as shown by steps 6 and 16 in Algorithm 1. From here on, we refer to these loops as loops lp1 and lp2, respectively. Note that it is also trivial to compute the number of nodes #nodes in the *adequate level*.

In addition to this, our parallel implementation differs from the Lindner and Peikert implementation in two other ways. The first difference is that, instead of going through the tree in a recursive depth-first manner, we traverse it iteratively in a breadth-first manner. The second difference is that we do not add up multiples of the basis vectors to find a lattice vector. Instead, we update the target vector by subtracting a multiple of a basis vector. This leads to an error vector (i.e., a vector **e** such that the original target vector subtracted by **e** is a lattice vector), which can easily be used to calculate the desired close lattice vector.

Algorithm 1. Nearest Planes

Input: $\mathbf{B} = \{\mathbf{b}_1, \ldots, \mathbf{b}_m\} \subset \mathbb{R}^m$, $\mathbf{d} \in (\mathbb{Z}^+)^m$, $\mathbf{t} \in \mathbb{R}^m$, $al \in \mathbb{N}$, $\#nodes \in \mathbb{N}$
Output: All error vectors $\mathbf{e} \in \mathcal{P}_{1/2}^{\mathbf{d}}(\{\tilde{\mathbf{b}}_1, \ldots, \tilde{\mathbf{b}}_m\})$ such that $\mathbf{t} - \mathbf{e} \in \Lambda(\{\mathbf{b}_1, \ldots, \mathbf{b}_m\})$

```
 1  begin
 2  │   calculate Gram-Schmidt basis B̃ = {b̃₁, …, b̃ₘ};
 3  │   OpenMP_parallel_region
 4  │   │   OpenMP_single_region
 5  │   │   │   len = 1;
 6  │   │   │   for k = n; k ≥ n − al; k = k − 1 do
 7  │   │   │   │   for i = 0; i < len; i = i + 1 do
 8  │   │   │   │   │   Let {c₁, …, c_{d_k}} ∈ ℤ^{d_k} be the distinct integers closest to  ⟨b̃_k,t⟩/⟨b̃_k,b̃_k⟩;
 9  │   │   │   │   │   for j = 1; j ≤ d_k; j = j + 1 do
10  │   │   │   │   │   │   t*_{i·d_k+j} = t_i − c_j · b_k;
11  │   │   │   │   │   end
12  │   │   │   │   end
13  │   │   │   │   t = t*;
14  │   │   │   │   len = len · d_k;
15  │   │   │   end
16  │   │   │   for node = 0; node ≤ #nodes; node = node + 1 do
17  │   │   │   │   create_task
18  │   │   │   │   │   len = 1;
19  │   │   │   │   │   for k = n − al − 1; k ≥ 1; k = k − 1 do
20  │   │   │   │   │   │   for i = 0; i < len; i = i + 1 do
21  │   │   │   │   │   │   │   Let {c₁, …, c_{d_k}} ∈ ℤ^{d_k} be the distinct integers closest to
        │   │   │   │   │   │   │   ⟨b̃_k,t⟩/⟨b̃_k,b̃_k⟩;
22  │   │   │   │   │   │   │   for j = 1; j ≤ d_k; j = j + 1 do
23  │   │   │   │   │   │   │   │   t*^{node}_{i·d_k+j} = t_i − c_j · b_k;
24  │   │   │   │   │   │   │   end
25  │   │   │   │   │   │   end
26  │   │   │   │   │   │   t = t*;
27  │   │   │   │   │   │   len = len · d_k;
28  │   │   │   │   │   end
29  │   │   │   │   end
30  │   │   │   end
31  │   │   end
32  │   end
33  │   return t;
34  end
```

This parallel execution is implemented with OpenMP. Our implementation has a parallel region, that creates as many threads as defined by the user. Inside the parallel region, a single region (region executed by one, unspecified, thread) embodies both loops lp1 and lp2. These regions are represented in Algorithm 1, steps 3 and 4. While both loops are executed sequentially, by a given thread t, t creates #nodes tasks in lp2, each of which entailing the body of the lp2 loop. As soon as tasks are created, they are assigned to one thread, which means that the issue of tasks is, very likely, overlapped with the execution of other tasks, by a different thread. The OpenMP runtime manages the task scheduling among the running tasks.

Workload Balance. The *adequate level* is defined to be the first level on the tree that contains a number of nodes that is at least as big as the number of threads. This is because all the tasks are, computationally speaking, very well balanced (in terms of FLOPS they are, in fact, equal). This means that, as long as (1) the number of nodes in the *adequate level* is a multiple of the computing units, (2) the computing units compute the same number of tasks and (3) computing units are equally capable, the workload distribution is balanced.

Data Collection. A vector of #nodes pointers is allocated outside of the parallel region, and defined as shared in the parallel region, which means that every thread has access to it. As tasks have an id (from 1 to #nodes), it is easy for threads to write in a different location, that will be available outside of the parallel region. Once the parallel region is finished, which means that every task is also finished (there is an implicit barrier at the end of the parallel region), the structure is accessed and the shortest (error) vector among all the stored vectors is chosen.

5   Results

We evaluated the running time of nearest planes on LWE instances proposed by Lindner and Peikert [19] for their encryption scheme. For a given secret size n, we selected the optimal lattice dimension m for a basis that is reduced with Hermite delta $\delta = 1.006$, i.e., $m = \sqrt{n \log(q)/\log(1.006)}$.

Table 1. Runtime in seconds (R) and speed-up (S) for our implementation for LWE instances proposed in [19]

	$m = 404$						$m = 517$					
	number of enumerations											
	2^{12}		2^{15}		2^{18}		2^{12}		2^{15}		2^{18}	
Threads	R	S	R	S	R	S	R	S	R	S	R	S
1	7.04	1.00	56.03	1.00	446.93	1.00	11.65	1.00	92.63	1.00	736.19	1.00
2	3.61	1.95	28.54	1.96	227.43	1.97	5.93	1.96	47.14	1.96	373.78	1.97
4	1.87	3.77	14.88	3.77	117.18	3.81	3.06	3.81	24.19	3.83	192.71	3.82
8	1.01	6.99	8.04	6.97	63.81	7.00	1.65	7.07	13.16	7.04	104.20	7.06
16	0.66	10.71	5.36	10.45	42.01	10.64	1.08	10.75	8.64	10.72	67.93	10.84

	$m = 597$						$m = 667$					
	number of enumerations											
	2^{12}		2^{15}		2^{18}		2^{12}		2^{15}		2^{18}	
Threads	R	S	R	S	R	S	R	S	R	S	R	S
1	15.54	1.00	124.31	1.00	979.78	1.00	19.36	1.00	156.34	1.00	1229.38	1.00
2	7.88	1.97	63.03	1.97	499.26	1.96	9.91	1.95	78.20	2.00	624.76	1.97
4	4.07	3.82	32.37	3.84	257.64	3.80	5.07	3.82	40.36	3.87	321.76	3.82
8	2.21	7.05	17.45	7.12	140.85	6.96	2.75	7.04	21.83	7.16	173.44	7.09
16	1.43	10.86	11.46	10.85	92.28	10.62	1.79	10.80	14.22	10.99	112.54	10.92

Given the runtime of our nearest planes implementation, we can estimate the time we require to solve LWE instances of practical dimensions with high probability. To this end, we select the encryption scheme by Lindner and Peikert [19] and revisit the proposed security with respect to our practical algorithm. We consider the sequential attack and attackers that are in possession of 128 and 2^{21} cores.

There are two main reasons to consider 128 cores. Firstly, it is not common that shared memory CPU system have higher core counts. Secondly, our experiments show that the sequential runtime of nearest planes is about 2^{-9} seconds, which means that 128 cores can output $128 \cdot 2^9 = 2^{16}$ close vectors per second, which is exactly the bound proposed by Lindner and Peikert [19].

Those values can therefore be used to predict the security of the instances with their runtime assumption against the decoding attack with randomization and a perfect balance between the basis reduction and the decoding step. For an adversary with many resources, we consider a parallel attack on 2^{21} cores, which is about the number of cores of the leading supercomputer in the last top500 list[1], a rank for high-performance computers.

Our experiments confirmed that the runtime of nearest planes is nearly linear to the number of returned vectors (#enum in the following), see Table 1 and Fig. 2. Considering the fact that our implementation is not optimal, it is reasonable to assume that an attacker has an implementation that scales (almost) perfectly linear. It is not surprising that the time for nearest planes depends on the dimension of the lattice. Nevertheless, we choose the runtime of nearest planes for our smallest parameter set as a lower bound, which renders our estimates very conservative. Together with the prediction of nearest planes given in [19], it is possible to find the Hermite delta and number of enumerations that distribute the computational amount equally between nearest planes and BKZ and minimize the expected computational effort.

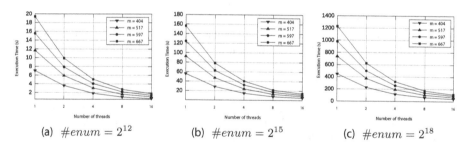

(a) $\#enum = 2^{12}$ (b) $\#enum = 2^{15}$ (c) $\#enum = 2^{18}$

Fig. 2. Performance of our implementation executing the nearest planes algorithm on random lattices, for dimensions 404, 517, 597 and 667, with $\#enum = 2^{12}$ in (a), $\#enum = 2^{15}$ in (b) and $\#enum = 2^{15}$ in (c). Runtime in seconds (less is better).

Acknowledgments. Özgür Dagdelen is supported by the German Federal Ministry of Education and Research (BMBF) within EC-SPRIDE. This work has been co-funded by the DFG as part of project P1 within the CRC 1119 CROSSING.

---

[1] http://www.top500.org/.

References

1. Albrecht, M.R., Fitzpatrick, R., Göpfert, F.: On the efficacy of solving LWE by reduction to unique-SVP. In: Lee, H.-S., Han, D.-G. (eds.) ICISC 2013. LNCS, vol. 8565, pp. 293–310. Springer, Heidelberg (2014)
2. Albrecht, M.R., Cid, C., Faugère, J.C., Fitzpatrick, R., Perret, L.: On the complexity of the BKW algorithm on LWE. Des. Codes Crypt. **74**(2), 325–354 (2013)
3. Albrecht, M.R., Faugère, J.-C., Fitzpatrick, R., Perret, L.: Lazy modulus switching for the BKW algorithm on LWE. In: Krawczyk, H. (ed.) PKC 2014. LNCS, vol. 8383, pp. 429–445. Springer, Heidelberg (2014)
4. Babai, L.: On Lovász' lattice reduction and the nearest lattice point problem. Combinatorica **6**(1), 1–13 (1986)
5. Bai, S., Galbraith, S.D.: Lattice decoding attacks on binary LWE. Cryptology ePrint Archive, Report 2013/839 (2013). http://eprint.iacr.org/
6. Bai, S., Galbraith, S.D.: An improved compression technique for signatures based on learning with errors. In: Benaloh, J. (ed.) CT-RSA 2014. LNCS, vol. 8366, pp. 28–47. Springer, Heidelberg (2014)
7. Blum, A., Kalai, A., Wasserman, H.: Noise-tolerant learning, the parity problem, and the statistical query model. J. ACM **50**(4), 506–519 (2003)
8. Brakerski, Z., Gentry, C., Vaikuntanathan, V.: (leveled) fully homomorphic encryption without bootstrapping. In: ITCS, pp. 309–325 (2012)
9. Brakerski, Z., Vaikuntanathan, V.: Fully homomorphic encryption from Ring-LWE and security for key dependent messages. In: Rogaway, P. (ed.) CRYPTO 2011. LNCS, vol. 6841, pp. 505–524. Springer, Heidelberg (2011)
10. Dagdelen, Ö., Schneider, M.: Parallel enumeration of shortest lattice vectors. In: D'Ambra, P., Guarracino, M., Talia, D. (eds.) Euro-Par 2010, Part II. LNCS, vol. 6272, pp. 211–222. Springer, Heidelberg (2010)
11. Ducas, L., Durmus, A., Lepoint, T., Lyubashevsky, V.: Lattice signatures and bimodal gaussians. In: Canetti, R., Garay, J.A. (eds.) CRYPTO 2013, Part I. LNCS, vol. 8042, pp. 40–56. Springer, Heidelberg (2013)
12. Gentry, C.: A fully homomorphic encryption scheme. Ph.D. thesis, Stanford, CA, USA (2009)
13. Goldreich, O., Goldwasser, S., Halevi, S.: Public-key cryptosystems from lattice reduction problems. In: Kaliski Jr, B.S. (ed.) CRYPTO 1997. LNCS, vol. 1294, pp. 112–131. Springer, Heidelberg (1997)
14. Güneysu, T., Lyubashevsky, V., Pöppelmann, T.: Practical lattice-based cryptography: a signature scheme for embedded systems. In: Prouff, E., Schaumont, P. (eds.) CHES 2012. LNCS, vol. 7428, pp. 530–547. Springer, Heidelberg (2012)
15. Han, D., Kim, M.-H., Yeom, Y.: Cryptanalysis of the Paeng-Jung-Ha Cryptosystem from PKC 2003. In: Okamoto, T., Wang, X. (eds.) PKC 2007. LNCS, vol. 4450, pp. 107–117. Springer, Heidelberg (2007)
16. Hermans, J., Schneider, M., Buchmann, J., Vercauteren, F., Preneel, B.: Parallel shortest lattice vector enumeration on graphics cards. In: Bernstein, D.J., Lange, T. (eds.) AFRICACRYPT 2010. LNCS, vol. 6055, pp. 52–68. Springer, Heidelberg (2010)
17. Kannan, R.: Minkowski's convex body theorem and integer programming. Math. Oper. Res. **12**(3), 415–440 (1987)
18. Kuo, P.-C., Schneider, M., Dagdelen, Ö., Reichelt, J., Buchmann, J., Cheng, C.-M., Yang, B.-Y.: Extreme Enumeration on GPU and in Clouds. In: Preneel, B., Takagi, T. (eds.) CHES 2011. LNCS, vol. 6917, pp. 176–191. Springer, Heidelberg (2011)

19. Lindner, R., Peikert, C.: Better key sizes (and attacks) for LWE-based encryption. In: Kiayias, A. (ed.) CT-RSA 2011. LNCS, vol. 6558, pp. 319–339. Springer, Heidelberg (2011)
20. Hojsík, M., Půlpánová, V.: A fully homomorphic cryptosystem with approximate perfect secrecy. In: Dawson, E. (ed.) CT-RSA 2013. LNCS, vol. 7779, pp. 375–388. Springer, Heidelberg (2013)
21. Lyubashevsky, V.: Lattice signatures without trapdoors. In: Pointcheval, D., Johansson, T. (eds.) EUROCRYPT 2012. LNCS, vol. 7237, pp. 738–755. Springer, Heidelberg (2012)
22. Micciancio, D., Peikert, C.: Trapdoors for lattices: simpler, tighter, faster, smaller. In: Pointcheval, D., Johansson, T. (eds.) EUROCRYPT 2012. LNCS, vol. 7237, pp. 700–718. Springer, Heidelberg (2012)
23. Nguyên, P.Q.: Cryptanalysis of the Goldreich-Goldwasser-Halevi Cryptosystem from Crypto 1997. In: Wiener, M. (ed.) CRYPTO 1999. LNCS, vol. 1666, p. 288. Springer, Heidelberg (1999)
24. Plantard, T., Susilo, W.: Broadcast attacks against lattice-based cryptosystems. In: Abdalla, M., Pointcheval, D., Fouque, P.-A., Vergnaud, D. (eds.) ACNS 2009. LNCS, vol. 5536, pp. 456–472. Springer, Heidelberg (2009)
25. Pöppelmann, T., Güneysu, T.: Towards practical lattice-based public-key encryption on reconfigurable hardware. In: Selected Areas in Cryptography, pp. 68–85 (2013)
26. Regev, O.: On lattices, learning with errors, random linear codes, and cryptography. In: STOC, pp. 84–93 (2005)

Cryptographic Protocols II

Timed-Release Secret Sharing Schemes with Information Theoretic Security

Yohei Watanabe$^{(\boxtimes)}$ and Junji Shikata

Graduate School of Environment and Information Sciences,
Yokohama National University, Yokohama, Japan
watanabe-yohei-xs@ynu.jp, shikata@ynu.ac.jp

Abstract. In modern cryptography, the secret sharing scheme is an important cryptographic primitive and it is used in various situations. In this paper, timed-release secret sharing (TR-SS) schemes with information-theoretic security is first studied. TR-SS is a secret sharing scheme with the property that participants more than a threshold number can reconstruct a secret by using their shares only when the time specified by a dealer has come. Specifically, in this paper we first introduce models and formalization of security for two kinds of TR-SS based on the traditional secret sharing scheme and information-theoretic timed-release security. We also derive tight lower bounds on the sizes of shares, time-signals, and entities' secret-keys required for each TR-SS scheme. In addition, we propose direct constructions for the TR-SS schemes. Each direct construction is optimal in the sense that the construction meets equality in each of our bounds, respectively. As a result, it is shown that the timed-release security can be realized without any additional redundancy on the share size.

1 Introduction

Secret sharing schemes were proposed independently by Shamir [14] and Blakley [1]. In a (k, n)-threshold secret sharing $((k, n)$-SS for short) scheme (e.g. see [14]), a dealer shares a secret among all participants, and then, k participants can reconstruct the secret while any $k - 1$ participants obtain no information on the secret. Since Shamir and Blakley proposed secret sharing schemes, various research on them have been reported.

On the other hand, "time" is intimately related to our lives. We get up, eat something, do a job, and get asleep at a time of our (or someone's) choice. For the above reason, it appears that cryptographic protocols associated with "time" are useful and meaningful. Actually, as those protocols, *timed-release cryptographic protocols* introduced in [11] are well-known.

From the above discussion, it is worth considering a secret sharing scheme with timed-release security. Therefore, we study such a scheme, which we call a *timed-release secret sharing* (TR-SS) scheme, in this paper.

Timed-Release Security. Informally, the goal of timed-release cryptography is *to securely send a certain information into the future*. For instance, in timed-release

B. Ors and B. Preneel (Eds.): BalkanCryptSec 2014, LNCS 9024, pp. 219–236, 2015.
DOI: 10.1007/978-3-319-21356-9_15

encryption, a sender transmits a ciphertext so that a receiver can decrypt it when the time which the sender specified has come, and the receiver cannot decrypt it before the time. The timed-release cryptography was first proposed by May [11] in 1993, and after that, Rivest et al. [13] developed it in a systematic and formal way. Since Rivest et al. gave a formal definition of timed-release encryption (TRE) in [13], various research on timed-release cryptography including timed-release signatures (e.g., [7,8]) and timed-release encryption have been done based on computational security. In particular, TRE in the public-key setting has been recently researched on intensively (e.g., [3–5]), and very recently Watanabe and Shikata [16] proposed computational secret sharing schemes with timed-release functionality. On the other hand, information-theoretically (or unconditionally) secure timed-release cryptography was proposed by Watanabe et al. [15]. In addition, they investigated not only encryption but also key-agreement and authentication codes with information-theoretic timed-release security. To the best of our knowledge, however, there is no paper which reports on the study of secret sharing schemes with information-theoretic timed-release security.

Our Contribution. In adding timed-release functionality to secret sharing schemes, we conceive the following two types of schemes.

One is a secret sharing scheme such that information associated with time (called *time-signals*) is required whenever a secret is reconstructed, which means a secret sharing scheme with a simple combination of traditional secret sharing functionality and timed-release functionality. For realizing it, we propose (k, n)-TR-SS in this paper. In (k, n)-TR-SS, a dealer can specify positive integers k, n with $k \leq n$, where n is the number of participants and k is a threshold value, and future time when a secret can be recovered; and the secret can be reconstructed from at least k shares and a time-signal at the specified time. On the other hand, participants cannot reconstruct the secret without the time-signal even if they can obtain all shares. Specifically, we define a model and security notions of (k, n)-TR-SS, and we derive lower bounds on the sizes of shares, time-signals, and entities' secret keys required for (k, n)-TR-SS. Moreover, we provide a direct construction of (k, n)-TR-SS, which is constructed by using polynomials over finite fields and provably secure in our security definition. In addition, we show that the direct construction meets the lower bounds on the sizes of shares, time-signals, and entities' secret keys with equalities. Therefore, it turns out that our lower bounds are tight, and that the direct construction is optimal.

Another one is a *hybrid* TR-SS, which means a secret sharing scheme in which traditional secret sharing functionality and timed-release functionality are simultaneously realized. In our hybrid TR-SS, a secret can be reconstructed, if one of the following condition is satisfied: a secret can be reconstructed from k_1 shares and a time-signal at a specified time as in the (k_1, n)-TR-SS; or a secret can be reconstructed from k_2 shares as in the traditional (k_2, n)-SS. Hence, we consider two threshold values k_1, k_2 to define a model of the hybrid TR-SS, and we propose (k_1, k_2, n)-TR-SS as such a model, where $k_1 \leq k_2 \leq n$. Specifically, in (k_1, k_2, n)-TR-SS, a dealer can specify future time, and arbitrarily chooses k_1, k_2 and n. At least k_1 (and less than k_2) participants can reconstruct a secret with a time-signal at the specified time, and at least k_2 participants can reconstruct a secret *without* any time-signal (i.e. they can reconstruct from *only* their shares). Specifically, we define a model and security notions of (k_1, k_2, n)-TR-SS, and we derive *tight* lower bounds on the sizes of shares, time-signals, and entities' secret keys required for (k_1, k_2, n)-TR-SS. Moreover, we provide a direct constructions of (k_1, k_2, n)-TR-SS, which is an *optimal* construction, which meets the above lower bounds with equalities.

In particular, a theoretically-interesting point in our results includes that the timed-release security can be realized without any additional redundancy on the share size in both schemes.

Applications of TR-SS. Our TR-SS is a secret sharing scheme with timed-release property, hence we can add timed-release functionality to applications of secret sharing schemes. Here, we consider information-theoretically secure key escrow with limited time span (see [2] for computationally secure one) as one of applications of TR-SS. In a key escrow scheme, a user sends shares of his secret key using encryption (or other cryptographic protocols) to trusted escrow agents in advance. Even if the user is less able to access an encrypted data (e.g. by accidental loss of the secret key), he can get the secret key reconstructed from agents' shares. However, considering the corruption of agents in practice, it is desirable to restrict the agents' power since they can access all encrypted data corresponding to the secret key. To achieve this, a key escrow scheme with limited time span (a.k.a. a time-controlled key escrow scheme) was proposed [2]. In the time-controlled key escrow scheme, a user and escrow agents can update a secret key and its shares at each time-period without any interaction. Therefore, at each time-period t, agents only have the power to access data encrypted at t (i.e. if some agents are corrupted, they cannot access data encrypted before t). By using TR-SS to generate shares of a secret key, we can realize information-theoretically secure time-controlled key escrow schemes.

Furthermore, TR-SS can also provide other cryptographic protocols with timed-release functionality. For example, we can construct information-theoretically secure TRE in the two-user setting from $(1, 1)$-TR-SS and the one-time pad as follows. For a plaintext M and a shared key K, a sender chooses a random number r whose length is equal to the plaintext-length, and computes a ciphertext $C := M \oplus r \oplus K$. Then, the sender specifies future time, and he generates one share from the secret r by $(1, 1)$-TR-SS. A receiver can compute $C \oplus K = M \oplus r$ by using the shared key K in advance, however, he cannot obtain M until the specified time comes since he can get r only after the specified time. In a similar way, it is expected that TR-SS is useful for building other timed-release cryptographic protocols such as timed-release authentication code [15] in the two-user setting, and that TR-SS might be able to provide some new timed-release cryptographic protocols, e.g., timed-release threshold encryption.

Organization of This Paper. The rest of this paper is organized as follows. In Sects. 2 and 3, we describe (k, n)-TR-SS and (k_1, k_2, n)-TR-SS, respectively, which are based on the ideas according to [10, 14, 15]. Specifically, in each section, we define a model and security of each scheme, and derive lower bounds on the sizes of shares, time-signals and secret keys required for each scheme, respectively. Furthermore, we propose a direct construction of each scheme, and show it is provably secure and optimal.

Notation. Throughout this paper, we use the following notation. Generally speaking, X indicates a random variable which takes values in $\mathcal{X}$ (e.g., A, B, and C are random variables which take values in $\mathcal{A}, \mathcal{B}$, and $\mathcal{C}$, respectively). For any finite set $\mathcal{Z}$ and arbitrary non-negative integers z_1, z_2, let $\mathcal{PS}(\mathcal{Z}, z_1, z_2) := \{Z \subset \mathcal{Z} | z_1 \leq |Z| \leq z_2\}$ be the family of all subsets of $\mathcal{Z}$ whose cardinality is at least z_1 but no more than z_2.

2 (k, n)-Timed-Release Secret Sharing Scheme

In this section, we propose a model and a security definition of (k, n)-TR-SS. In (k, n)-TR-SS, a time-signal at the specified time is always required when a secret is reconstructed. In other words, a secret cannot be reconstructed without a time-signal at the specified time even if there are all shares.

2.1   The Model and Security Definition

First, we introduce the model of (k, n)-TR-SS. Unlike traditional secret sharing schemes [1,14], we assume that there is a trusted authority (also called a trusted initializer) TA whose role is to generate and to distribute secret keys of entities. We call this model the *trusted initializer model* as in [12]. In (k, n)-TR-SS, there are $n+3$ entities, a dealer D, n participants $P_1, P_2, \ldots, P_n$, a time-server TS for broadcasting time-signals at most τ times and a trusted initializer TA, where k, n and τ are positive integers. In this paper, we assume that the identity of each user P_i is also denoted by P_i.

Informally, (k, n)-TR-SS is executed as follows. First, TA generates secret keys on behalf of D and TS. After distributing these keys via secure channels, TA deletes it in his memory. Next, D specifies future time, as D wants, when a secret is reconstructed by participants, and he generates n shares from the secret by using his secret key. And, D sends each share to each participant respectively via secure channels. The time-server TS periodically broadcasts a time-signal which is generated by using his secret key. Note that there is no interaction between TS and D, hence TS may not know when the specified time is. When the specified time has come, at least k participants can compute the secret by using their shares and the time-signal of the specified time.

Formally, we give the definition of (k, n)-TR-SS as follows. In this model, let $\mathcal{P} := \{P_1, P_2, \ldots, P_n\}$ be a set of all participants. And also, $\mathcal{S}$ is a set of possible secrets with a probability distribution P_S, and $\mathcal{SK}$ is a set of possible secret keys. $\mathcal{T} := \{1, 2, \ldots, \tau\}$ is a set of time. Let $\mathcal{U}_i^{(t)}$ be the set of possible P_i's shares at the time $t \in \mathcal{T}$. Also, $\mathcal{U}_i := \bigcup_{t=1}^{\tau} \mathcal{U}_i^{(t)}$ is a set of possible P_i's shares for every $i \in \{1, 2, \ldots, n\}$, and let $\mathcal{U} := \bigcup_{i=1}^{n} \mathcal{U}_i$. In addition, $\mathcal{TI}^{(t)}$ is a set of time-signals at time t, and let $\mathcal{TI} := \bigcup_{t=1}^{\tau} \mathcal{TI}^{(t)}$. Furthermore, for any subset of participants $\mathcal{J} = \{P_{i_1}, \ldots, P_{i_j}\} \subset \mathcal{P}$, $\mathcal{U}_{\mathcal{J}}^{(t)} := \mathcal{U}_{i_1}^{(t)} \times \cdots \times \mathcal{U}_{i_j}^{(t)}$ denotes the set of possible shares held by $\mathcal{J}$.

Definition 1 $((k,n)$-**TR-SS**$)$. *A (k,n)-timed-release secret sharing $((k,n)$-TR-SS) scheme Π involves $n + 3$ entities, $TA, D, P_1, \ldots, P_n$, and TS, and consists of four phases, Initialize, Extract, Share and Reconstruct, and five finite spaces, $\mathcal{S}, \mathcal{SK}, \mathcal{U}, \mathcal{T}$, and $\mathcal{TI}$. Π is executed based on the above phases as follows.*

(a) *Initialize. TA generates a secret key $sk \in \mathcal{SK}$ for TS and D. These keys are distributed to corresponding entities via secure channels. After distributing these keys, TA deletes them from his memory. And, D and TS keep their keys secret, respectively.*[1]

(b) *Share. A dealer D randomly selects a secret $s \in \mathcal{S}$ according to P_S, and chooses k and n. If D wants the secret s to be reconstructed by participants at future time $t \in \mathcal{T}$, on input the secret $s \in \mathcal{S}$, specified time $t \in \mathcal{T}$ and a secret key sk, D computes a share $u_i^{(t)} \in \mathcal{U}_i^{(t)}$ for every P_i $(i = 1, 2, \ldots, n)$. And then, D sends a pair of the share and specified time, $(u_i^{(t)}, t)$, to P_i $(i = 1, 2, \ldots, n)$ via a secure channel.*[2]

(c) *Extract. For broadcasting a time-signal at each time t, TS generates a time-signal $ts^{(t)} \in \mathcal{TI}^{(t)}$ by using his secret key sk and time $t \in \mathcal{T}$, where for simplicity we assume that $ts^{(t)}$ is deterministically computed by t and sk.*

(d) *Reconstruct. At the specified time t, any set of at least k participants $\mathcal{A} = \{P_{i_1}, \ldots, P_{i_j}\} \in \mathcal{PS}(\mathcal{P}, k, n)$ can reconstruct the secret s by using their shares $u_{i_1}^{(t)}, \ldots, u_{i_j}^{(t)}$ $(k \leq j \leq n)$ and a time-signal $ts^{(t)}$ at the specified time.*

In the above model, we assume that Π meets the following *correctness* property: If D correctly completes the phase *Share* and TS correctly completes the phase *Extract*, then, for all possible $i \in \{1, 2, \ldots, n\}$, $t \in \mathcal{T}$, $s \in \mathcal{S}$, $u_i^{(t)} \in \mathcal{U}_i$, and $ts^{(t)} \in \mathcal{TI}^{(t)}$, it hold that any $\mathcal{A} \in \mathcal{PS}(\mathcal{P}, k, n)$ will correctly reconstruct the secret s at the end of phase *Reconstruct*, namely, $H(S \mid U_{\mathcal{A}}^{(t)}, TI^{(t)}) = 0$.

Next, we formalize a security definition of (k, n)-TR-SS based on the idea of the information-theoretic timed-release security [15] and secret sharing schemes (e.g. see [10]). In (k, n)-TR-SS, we consider the following two kinds of security. The first security which we consider is basically the same as that of the traditional (k, n)-SS: less than k participants cannot obtain any information on a secret. In addition to this, as the second security we want to require that even at least k participants cannot obtain any information on a secret before the specified time comes (i.e., before a time-signal at the specified time is received), since

---

[1] If we consider a situation in which TS is trusted and has functionality of generating keys and distributing them to participants by secure private channels, we can identify TA with TS in the situation. However, there may be a situation in which the roles of TA and TS are quite different (e.g., TA is a provider of secure data storage service and TS is a time-signal broadcasting server). Therefore, we assume two entities TA and TS in our model to capture various situations.

[2] More precisely, there is no need to keep the specified time confidential (D only has to send shares via secure channels).

we consider timed-release security in this paper. Therefore, we formally define secure (k, n)-TR-SS by Shannon entropy as follows (if readers are not familar to Shannon entropy, see [6] for the excellent instruction).

Definition 2 (Security of (k, n)-TR-SS). *Let Π be (k, n)-TR-SS. Π is said to be secure if the following conditions are satisfied:*

(i) *For any $\mathcal{F} \in \mathcal{PS}(\mathcal{P}, 1, k - 1)$ and any $t \in \mathcal{T}$, it holds that $H(S \mid U_{\mathcal{F}}^{(t)}, TI^{(1)}, \ldots, TI^{(\tau)}) = H(S)$.*

(ii) *For any $\mathcal{A} \in \mathcal{PS}(\mathcal{P}, k, n)$ and any $t \in \mathcal{T}$, it holds that $H(S \mid U_{\mathcal{A}}^{(t)}, TI^{(1)}, \ldots, TI^{(t-1)}, TI^{(t+1)}, \ldots, TI^{(\tau)}) = H(S)$.*

Intuitively, the meaning of two conditions (i) and (ii) in Definition 2 is explained as follows. (i) No information on a secret is obtained by any set of less than k participants, even if they obtain time-signals at all the time; (ii) No information on a secret is obtained by any set of more than $k - 1$ participants, even if they obtain time-signals at all the time except the specified time.[3]

Remark 1. We can also consider the following security definition (the condition (iii)) instead of (i): No information on a secret is obtained by collusion of TS and any set of less than k participants, namely, this is defined as follows.

(iii) *For any $\mathcal{F} \in \mathcal{PS}(\mathcal{P}, 1, k - 1)$ and for any $t \in \mathcal{T}$, it holds that $H(S \mid U_{\mathcal{F}}^{(t)}, SK) = H(S)$.*

Note that the condition (iii) is stronger than (i). However, we do not consider (iii) in this paper because of the following two reasons: first, the condition (i) is more natural than (iii), since it does not seem natural to consider the situation that any set of less than k participants colludes with TS in the real world; and secondly, our lower bounds in Theorem 1 are still valid even under the conditions (ii) and (iii), in other words, even if we consider the conditions (ii) and (iii), we can derive the same lower bounds in Theorem 1 since Definition 2 is weaker. Interestingly, our direct construction in Sect. 2.3 also satisfies (iii), and *tightness* of our lower bounds and *optimality* of our direct construction will be valid not depending on the choice of the condition (i) or (iii). Furthermore, we do not have to consider an attack by dishonest TS only, since TS's master-key is generated independently of a secret.

2.2   Lower Bounds

In this section, we show lower bounds on sizes of shares, time-signals, and secret keys required for secure (k, n)-TR-SS as follows. Due to space limitation, the proof is given in Appendix A.

---

[3] In this sense, we have formalized the security notion stronger than the security that any set of more than $k - 1$ participants cannot obtain any information on a secret *before* the specified time, as is the same approach considered in [15]. Actually, if we remove $TI^{(t+1)}, \ldots, TI^{(\tau)}$ from (ii) in Definition 2, we obtain the same lower bounds on sizes of shares, time-signals and secret keys as those in Theorem 1.

Theorem 1. *Let Π be any secure (k, n)-TR-SS. Then, for any $i \in \{1, 2, \ldots, n\}$ and for any $t \in \mathcal{T}$, we have*

$$(i)\ H(U_i^{(t)}) \geq H(S), \qquad (ii)\ H(TI^{(t)}) \geq H(S), \qquad (iii)\ H(SK) \geq \tau H(S).$$

As we will see in Sect. 2.3, the above lower bounds are tight since our construction will meet all the above lower bounds with equalities. Therefore, we define optimality of constructions of (k, n)-TR-SS as follows.

Definition 3. *A construction of secure (k, n)-TR-SS is said to be optimal if it meets equality in every bound of (i)–(iii) in Theorem 1.*

Remark 2. The secret sharing scheme such that the size of each participant's share is equal to that of the secret is often called an *ideal* secret sharing scheme. The construction of (k, n)-TR-SS in Sect. 2.3 is optimal, hence, in this sense we achieve *ideal* (k, n)-TR-SS. In terms of the share size, an interesting point is that the timed-release property can be realized without any additional redundancy on the share size. Therefore in the sense of the bound on the share size, our results are also regarded as the extension of traditional secret sharing schemes.

2.3   Direct Construction

We propose a direct construction of (k, n)-TR-SS. In addition, it is shown that our construction is optimal. The detail of our construction of (k, n)-TR-SS Π is given as follows.

(a) *Initialize.* Let q be a prime power, where $q > \max(n, \tau)$, and $\mathbb{F}_q$ be the finite field with q elements. We assume that the identity of each participant P_i is encoded as $P_i \in \mathbb{F}_q \backslash \{0\}$. Also, we assume $\mathcal{T} = \{1, 2, \ldots, \tau\} \subset \mathbb{F}_q \backslash \{0\}$ by using appropriate encoding. First, TA chooses uniformly at random τ numbers $r^{(j)}(j = 1, \ldots, \tau)$ from $\mathbb{F}_q$. TA sends a secret key $sk := (r^{(1)}, \ldots, r^{(\tau)})$ to TS and D via secure channels, respectively.

(b) *Share.* First, D chooses a secret $s \in \mathbb{F}_q$. Also, D specifies the time t at which participants can reconstruct the secret. Next, D randomly chooses a polynomial $f(x) := c^{(t)} + \sum_{i=1}^{k-1} a_i x^i$ over $\mathbb{F}_q$, where $c^{(t)}$ is computed by $c^{(t)} := s + r^{(t)}$ and each coefficient a_i is randomly and uniformly chosen from $\mathbb{F}_q$. Finally, D computes $u_i^{(t)} := f(P_i)(i = 1, 2, \ldots, n)$ and sends $(u_i^{(t)}, t)$ to $P_i (i = 1, 2, \ldots, n)$ via a secure channel.

(c) *Extract.* For sk and time $t \in \mathcal{T}$, TS broadcasts t-th key $r^{(t)}$ as a time-signal at time t to all participants via a (authenticated) broadcast channel.

(d) *Reconstruct.* First, a set of at least k participants $\mathcal{A} = \{P_{i_1}, P_{i_2}, \ldots, P_{i_k}\} \in \mathcal{PS}(\mathcal{P}, k, k)$ computes $c^{(t)}$ by Lagrange interpolation from their k shares: $c^{(t)} = \sum_{j=1}^{k} (\prod_{l \neq j} \frac{P_{i_j}}{P_{i_j} - P_{i_l}}) f(P_{i_j})$. After receiving $ts^{(t)} = r^{(t)}$, they can compute and get $s = c^{(t)} - r^{(t)}$.

The security and optimality of the above construction is stated as follows.

Theorem 2. *The resulting (k, n)-TR-SS Π by the above construction is secure and optimal.*

Proof. First, we show the proof of (i) in Definition 2. Assume that any $k - 1$ participants $\mathcal{F} = \{P_{i_1}, \ldots, P_{i_{k-1}}\} \in \mathcal{PS}(\mathcal{P}, k-1, k-1)$ try to guess $c^{(t)}$ by using their shares. Note that they know $r^{(t)} = c^{(t)} - s$ and

$$f(P_{i_j}) = (1, P_{i_j}, \ldots, P_{i_j}^{k-1}) \begin{pmatrix} c^{(t)} \\ a_1 \\ \vdots \\ a_{k-1} \end{pmatrix},$$

for $j = 1, \ldots, k - 1$. Thus, they can know the following matrix:

$$\begin{pmatrix} 1 & P_{i_1} & \cdots & P_{i_1}^{k-1} \\ 1 & P_{i_2} & \cdots & P_{i_2}^{k-1} \\ \vdots & \vdots & \ddots & \vdots \\ 1 & P_{i_{k-1}} & \cdots & P_{i_{k-1}}^{k-1} \end{pmatrix} \begin{pmatrix} c^{(t)} \\ a_1 \\ \vdots \\ a_{k-1} \end{pmatrix}. \tag{1}$$

However, from (1), they cannot guess at least one element of $(c^{(t)}, a_1, \ldots, a_{k-1})$ with probability larger than $1/q$. Therefore, $H(S \mid U_{\mathcal{F}}^{(t)}, TI^{(1)}, \ldots, TI^{(\tau)}) = H(S)$ for any $\mathcal{F} \in \mathcal{PS}(\mathcal{P}, 1, k - 1)$ and any $t \in \mathcal{T}$.

Next, we show the proof of (ii) in Definition 2. Without loss of generality, we suppose that τ is a specified time, and that all participants try to guess $r^{(\tau)}$ by using $c^{(\tau)}$ and time-signals at all the time except the time τ, since they obtain $c^{(\tau)} = s + r^{(\tau)}$ from their shares. They get $\tau - 1$ time-signals $r^{(1)}, \ldots, r^{(\tau-1)}$. However, since each time-signal is chosen uniformly at random from $\mathbb{F}_q$, they can guess $r^{(\tau)}$ only with probability $1/q$. By the security of one-time pad, we have $H(S \mid U_1^{(\tau)}, \ldots, U_n^{(\tau)}, TI^{(1)}, \ldots, TI^{(\tau-1)}) = H(S)$. Hence, for any $\mathcal{A} \in \mathcal{PS}(\mathcal{P}, k, n)$ and for any $t \in \mathcal{T}$, we have $H(S \mid U_{\mathcal{A}}^{(t)}, TI^{(1)}, \ldots, TI^{(t-1)}, TI^{(t+1)}, \ldots, TI^{(\tau)}) = H(S)$.

Finally, it is straightforward to see that the construction satisfies all the equalities of lower bounds in Theorem 1. Therefore, the above construction is optimal. $\qquad\square$

3 (k_1, k_2, n)-Timed-Release Secret Sharing Scheme

In this section, we consider the following problem, "Can we realize traditional secret sharing functionality and timed-release secret sharing functionality simultaneously?". Therefore, we propose (k_1, k_2, n)-TR-SS, where k_1 and k_2 are threshold values with $1 \le k_1 \le k_2 \le n$. (k_1, k_2, n)-TR-SS can realize timed-release functionality —a secret can be reconstructed from at least k_1 shares and a time-signal at the specified time— and traditional secret sharing functionality —a secret can be also reconstructed from only at least k_2 shares— simultaneously. In the case that $k = k_1 = k_2$, (k, k, n)-TR-SS can be considered as traditional (k, n)-SS (for details, see Remark 3).

3.1   Model and Security Definition

In this section, we propose a model and a security definition of (k_1, k_2, n)-TR-SS. First, we introduce a model of (k_1, k_2, n)-TR-SS. In (k_1, k_2, n)-TR-SS, there are same entities and sets as those of (k, n)-TR-SS. The main difference from (k, n)-TR-SS is that a dealer D can specify two kinds of threshold values, k_1 and k_2 with $k_1 \leq k_2 \leq n$: k_1 indicates the number of participants who can reconstruct a secret s with the time-signal at the time specified by the dealer; and k_2 indicates the number of participants who can reconstruct s without any time-signals. We give the definition of (k_1, k_2, n)-TR-SS as follows.

Definition 4 ((k_1, k_2, n)-TR-SS). *A (k_1, k_2, n)-timed-release secret sharing ((k_1, k_2, n)-TR-SS) scheme Θ involves $n + 3$ entities, $TA, D, P_1, \ldots, P_n$, and TS, and consists of five phases, Initialize, Extract, Share, Reconstruct with time-signals and Reconstruct without time-signals, and five finite spaces, $\mathcal{S}, \mathcal{SK}, \mathcal{U}, \mathcal{T}$, and $\mathcal{TI}$. Θ is executed based on the following phases as follows.*

(a) *Initialize. This phase follows the same procedure as that of (k, n)-TR-SS (see Definition 1).*

(b) *Share. A dealer D randomly selects a secret $s \in \mathcal{S}$ according to P_S. Then, D chooses k_1, k_2 and n, and specifies future time $t \in \mathcal{T}$ when at least k_1 participants can reconstruct s. Then, on input the secret s, the specified time t and a secret key $sk \in \mathcal{SK}$, D computes a share $u_i^{(t)} \in \mathcal{U}_i^{(t)}$ for every P_i $(i = 1, 2, \ldots, n)$. And then, D sends a pair of the share and specified time, $(u_i^{(t)}, t)$, to P_i $(i = 1, 2, \ldots, n)$ via a secure channel, respectively.*

(c) *Extract. This phase follows the same procedure as that of (k, n)-TR-SS (see Definition 1).*

(d) *Reconstruct with time-signals. At the specified time t, any set of participants $\mathcal{A} = \{P_{i_1}, \ldots, P_{i_j}\} \in \mathcal{PS}(\mathcal{P}, k_1, k_2 - 1)$ can reconstruct the secret s by using their shares $(u_{i_1}^{(t)}, \ldots, u_{i_j}^{(t)})$ $(k_1 \leq j < k_2)$ and a time-signal of the specified time $ts^{(t)}$.*

(e) *Reconstruct without time-signals. At anytime (even before the specified time), any set of participants $\hat{\mathcal{A}} = \{P_{i_1}, \ldots, P_{i_j}\} \in \mathcal{PS}(\mathcal{P}, k_2, n)$ can reconstruct the secret s by using only their shares $(u_{i_1}^{(t)}, \ldots, u_{i_j}^{(t)})$ $(k_2 \leq j \leq n)$.*

In the above model, we assume that Θ meets the following *correctness* properties:

1. If D correctly completes the phase *Share* and TS correctly completes the phase *Extract*, then, for all possible $i \in \{1, 2, \ldots, n\}$, $t \in \mathcal{T}$, $s \in \mathcal{S}$, $u_i^{(t)} \in \mathcal{U}_i^{(t)}$, and $ts^{(t)} \in \mathcal{TI}^{(t)}$, it holds that any $\mathcal{A} \in \mathcal{PS}(\mathcal{P}, k_1, k_2 - 1)$ will correctly reconstruct the secret s at the end of phase *Reconstruct with time-signals*, namely, $H(S \mid U_{\mathcal{A}}^{(t)}, TI^{(t)}) = 0$.

2. If D correctly completes the phase *Share*, then, for all possible $i \in \{1, 2, \ldots, n\}$, $t \in \mathcal{T}$, $s \in \mathcal{S}$, and $u_i^{(t)} \in \mathcal{U}_i^{(t)}$, it holds that any $\hat{\mathcal{A}} \in \mathcal{PS}(\mathcal{P}, k_2, n)$ will correctly reconstruct the secret s at the end of phase *Reconstruct without time-signals*, namely, $H(S \mid U_{\hat{\mathcal{A}}}^{(t)}) = 0$.

Next, we formalize a security definition of (k_1, k_2, n)-TR-SS in a similar way to that of (k, n)-TR-SS as follows.

Definition 5 (Security of (k_1, k_2, n)-TR-SS). *Let Θ be (k_1, k_2, n)-TR-SS. Θ is said to be secure if the following conditions are satisfied:*

(i) *For any $\mathcal{F} \in \mathcal{PS}(\mathcal{P}, 1, k_1 - 1)$ and any $t \in \mathcal{T}$, it holds that $H(S \mid U_{\mathcal{F}}^{(t)}, TI^{(1)}, \ldots, TI^{(\tau)}) = H(S)$.*

(ii) *For any $\hat{\mathcal{F}} \in \mathcal{PS}(\mathcal{P}, k_1, k_2 - 1)$ and any $t \in \mathcal{T}$, it holds that $H(S \mid U_{\hat{\mathcal{F}}}^{(t)}, TI^{(1)}, \ldots, TI^{(t-1)}, TI^{(t+1)}, \ldots, TI^{(\tau)}) = H(S)$.*

In Definition 5, intuitively, the meaning of (i) is the same as that of (k, n)-TR-SS (Definition 2), and the meaning of the condition (ii) is explained that no information on a secret is obtained by any set of at least k_1 but *no more than k_2* participants, even if they obtain time-signals at all the time except the specified time. We also consider a more strong security notion in a similar to (k, n)-TR-SS, however, we do not consider such a strong notion for the same reason as in the case of (k, n)-TR-SS.

Remark 3. In the case that $k = k_1 = k_2$, the model and security definition of secure (k, k, n)-TR-SS (Definitions 1 and 2) are the same as those of traditional (k, n)-SS. Therefore, the model and security definition of (k_1, k_2, n)-TR-SS can be regarded as the natural extension of those of traditional secret sharing schemes.

3.2 Lower Bounds

In this section, we show lower bounds on sizes of shares, time-signals, and secret keys required for secure (k_1, k_2, n)-TR-SS as follows. Due to space limitation, the proof is given in Appendix A. The proof is similar to that of Theorem 1, however, in the proof there are several technical points which are complicated than that of Theorem 1 (See Appendix B for details).

Theorem 3. *Let Θ be any secure (k_1, k_2, n)-TR-SS. Then, for any $i \in \{1, 2, \ldots, n\}$ and for any $t \in \mathcal{T}$, we have*

$$(i) \ H(U_i^{(t)}) \geq H(S).$$

Moreover, if the above lower bound holds with equality (i.e. $H(U_i^{(t)}) = H(S)$ for any i and t), we have

$$(ii) \ H(TI^{(t)}) \geq (k_2 - k_1)H(S), \qquad (iii) \ H(SK) \geq \tau(k_2 - k_1)H(S).$$

As we will see in Sect. 3.3, the lower bounds in Theorem 3 are tight since our construction will meet all the above lower bounds with equalities. Therefore, we define optimality of constructions of (k_1, k_2, n)-TR-SS as follows.

Definition 6. *A construction of secure (k_1, k_2, n)-TR-SS is said to be optimal if it meets equality in every bound of (i)–(iii) in Theorem 3.*

3.3   Optimal (but Restricted[4]) Construction

We can consider a naive construction based on (k_1, n)-TR-SS and (k_2, n)-SS, however, this naive construction is not optimal since the share size is twice as large as the underlying secret size (see Appendix C for details). To achieve an optimal construction, we use the technique as in [9]: In the phase *Share*, the dealer computes public parameters, and the public parameters are broadcasted to participants or else stored on a publicly accessible authenticated bulletin board. The detail of our construction is given as follows.

(a) *Initialize.* Let q be a prime power, where $q > \max(n, \tau)$, and $\mathbb{F}_q$ be the finite field with q elements. We assume that the identity of each participant P_i is encoded as $P_i \in \mathbb{F}_q \backslash \{0\}$. Also, we assume $\mathcal{T} = \{1, 2, \ldots, \tau\} \subset \mathbb{F}_q \backslash \{0\}$ by using appropriate encoding. First, TA chooses ℓ, which is the maximum difference between k_2 and k_1. Note that k_1 and k_2 will be determined by a dealer D in the phase *Share*. Then, TA chooses $\tau\ell$ numbers $r_i^{(t)}$ $(1 \leq i \leq \ell)$ and $(1 \leq t \leq \tau)$ from $\mathbb{F}_q$ uniformly at random. TA sends a secret key $sk := \{(r_1^{(t)}, r_2^{(t)}, \ldots, r_\ell^{(t)})\}_{1 \leq t \leq \tau}$ to TS and D via secure channels, respectively.

(b) *Share.* First, D randomly selects a secret $s \in \mathbb{F}_q$, and chooses k_1, k_2 and n such that $k_2 - k_1 \leq \ell$. Also, D specifies the time t when at least k_1 participants can reconstruct the secret. Next, D randomly chooses a polynomial $f(x) := s + \sum_{i=1}^{k_2-1} a_i x^i$ over $\mathbb{F}_q$, where each coefficient a_i is randomly and uniformly chosen from $\mathbb{F}_q$. Then, D computes a share $u_i^{(t)} := f(P_i)$ and a public parameter $p_i^{(t)} := a_{k_1-1+i} + r_i^{(t)}$ $(i = 1, 2, \ldots, k_2 - k_1)$. Finally, D sends $(u_i^{(t)}, t)$ to $P_i(i = 1, 2, \ldots, n)$ via a secure channel and discloses $(p_1^{(t)}, \ldots, p_{k_2-k_1}^{(t)})$.

(c) *Extract.* For sk and time $t \in \mathcal{T}$, TS broadcasts a time-signal at time t, $ts^{(t)} := (r_1^{(t)}, r_2^{(t)}, \ldots, r_\ell^{(t)})$ to all participants via a (authenticated) broadcast channel.

(d) *Reconstruct with time-signals.* Suppose that all participants receive $ts^{(t)} = (r_1^{(t)}, r_2^{(t)}, \ldots, r_\ell^{(t)})$. Let $\mathcal{A} = \{P_{i_1}, P_{i_2}, \ldots, P_{i_{k_1}}\} \in \mathcal{PS}(\mathcal{P}, k_1, k_1)$ be a set of any k_1 participants. First, each $P_{i_j} \in \mathcal{A}$ computes $a_{k_1-1+i} = p_i^{(t)} - r_i^{(t)}$ $(i = 1, 2, \ldots, k_2-k_1)$ and constructs $g(x) := \sum_{k_1}^{k_2-1} a_i x^i$. Then, each P_{i_j} computes $h(P_{i_j}) := f(P_{i_j}) - g(P_{i_j})$ $(j = 1, \ldots, k_1)$ such that $h(x) := s + \sum_{i=1}^{k_1-1} a_i x^i$. Then, they compute $s = \sum_{j=1}^{k_1} (\prod_{l \neq j} \frac{P_{i_j}}{P_{i_j} - P_{i_l}}) h(P_{i_j})$ by Lagrange interpolation from $(h(P_{i_1}), \ldots, h(P_{i_{k_1}}))$.

(e) *Reconstruct without time-signals.* any $\hat{\mathcal{A}} = \{P_{i_1}, P_{i_2}, \ldots, P_{i_{k_2}}\} \in \mathcal{PS}(\mathcal{P}, k_2, k_2)$ computes $s = \sum_{j=1}^{k_2} (\prod_{l \neq j} \frac{P_{i_j}}{P_{i_j} - P_{i_l}}) f(P_{i_j})$ by Lagrange interpolation from their k_2 shares.

---

[4] In this optimal construction, a dealer is only allowed to choose k_1 and k_2 such that $k_2 - k_1 \leq \ell$, where ℓ is determined by TA in the phase *Initialize*. In this sense, this construction is restricted.

The security and optimality of the above construction is stated as follows.

Theorem 4. *The resulting (k_1, k_2, n)-TR-SS Θ by the above construction is secure. Moreover, it is optimal if $k_2 - k_1 = \ell$.*

Proof. First, we show the proof of (i) in Definition 5. Assume that $k_1 - 1$ participants $\mathcal{F} = \{P_{i_1}, \dots, P_{i_{k_1-1}}\} \in \mathcal{PS}(\mathcal{P}, k_1 - 1, k_1 - 1)$ try to guess s by using their shares, public parameters, and all time-signals. $\mathcal{F}$ can compute $g(x)$ from public parameters and the time-signal at the specified time, hence they can get $h(P_{i_l}) = f(P_{i_l}) - g(P_{i_l})$ $(l = 1, \dots, k_1 - 1)$. Thus, they can know the following matrix:

$$\begin{pmatrix} 1 & P_{i_1} & \cdots & P_{i_1}^{k_1-1} \\ 1 & P_{i_2} & \cdots & P_{i_2}^{k_1-1} \\ \vdots & \vdots & \ddots & \vdots \\ 1 & P_{i_{k_1-1}} & \cdots & P_{i_{k_1-1}}^{k_1-1} \end{pmatrix} \begin{pmatrix} s \\ a_1 \\ \vdots \\ a_{k_1-1} \end{pmatrix}. \tag{2}$$

However, from (2), they cannot guess at least one element of $(s, a_1, \dots, a_{k_1-1})$ with probability larger than $1/q$. Therefore, for any $\mathcal{F} \in \mathcal{PS}(\mathcal{P}, 1, k_1 - 1)$ and any $t \in \mathcal{T}$, we have $H(S \mid U_{\mathcal{F}}^{(t)}, TI^{(1)}, \dots, TI^{(\tau)}) = H(S)$.

Next, we show the proof of (ii) in Definition 5. Without loss of generality, we suppose that τ is a specified time, that $k_2 - k_1 = \ell$, and that $k_2 - 1$ participants try to guess s by using their shares, public parameters, and time-signals at all the time except the time τ. First, they cannot guess at least one coefficient of $f(x)$ with probability larger than $1/q$ since the degree of $f(x)$ is at most $k_2 - 1$. Therefore, they attempt to guess one of $a_{k_1}, \dots, a_{k_2-1}$ by using their $k_2 - 1$ shares, public parameters and $\tau - 1$ time-signals, since if they obtain any one of these coefficient, they can get $f^*(P_{i_l})$ $(l = 1, \dots, k_2 - 1)$ such that the degree of $f^*(x)$ is $k_2 - 2$ and reconstruct s by Lagrange interpolation. They know $\tau - 1$ time-signals, however, these time-signals $\{(r_1^{(j)}, \dots, r_\ell^{(j)})\}_{1 \le j \le \tau-1}$ are independent of the time-signal $(r_1^{(\tau)}, \dots, r_\ell^{(\tau)})$ at τ. Hence, by the security of one-time pad, they cannot guess each a_{k_1-1+i} $(= p_i^{(\tau)} - r_i^{(\tau)})$ $(1 \le i \le k_2 - k_1)$ with probability larger than $1/q$ since each $r_i^{(\tau)}$ is chosen from $\mathbb{F}_q$ uniformly at random. Therefore, we have $H(S \mid U_{l_1}^{(\tau)}, \dots, U_{l_{k_2-1}}^{(\tau)}, TI^{(1)}, \dots, TI^{(\tau-1)}) = H(S)$. Hence, for any $\mathcal{A} \in \mathcal{PS}(\mathcal{P}, k_1, k_2 - 1)$ and any $t \in \mathcal{T}$, we have $H(S \mid U_{\mathcal{A}}^{(t)}, TI^{(1)}, \dots, TI^{(t-1)}, TI^{(t+1)}, \dots, TI^{(\tau)}) = H(S)$.

Finally, if $k_2 - k_1 = \ell$, it is straightforward to see that the construction satisfies all the equalities of lower bounds in Theorem 3. Therefore, the above construction is optimal if $k_2 - k_1 = \ell$. □

Acknowledgments. We would like to thank anonymous referees of BalkanCryptSec 2014 for their helpful comments. The first author is supported by JSPS Research Fellowships for Young Scientists. This work was supported by Grant-in-Aid for JSPS Fellows Grant Number 25·3998.

A   Proof of Theorem 1

The proof of Theorem 1 follows from the following lemmas.

Lemma 1. $H(U_i^{(t)}) \geq H(S)$ for any $i \in \{1, 2, \ldots, n\}$ and any $t \in \mathcal{T}$.

Proof. The proof of this lemma can be proved in a way similar to the proof of Lemma 4. For arbitrary $i \in \{1, 2, \ldots, n\}$, we take a subset $\mathcal{B}_i \in \mathcal{PS}(\mathcal{P} \setminus \{P_i\}, k-1, k-1)$ of participants. Then, for any $t \in \mathcal{T}$, we have

$$
\begin{aligned}
H(U_i^{(t)}) &\geq H(U_i^{(t)} \mid U_{\mathcal{B}_i}^{(t)}, TI^{(t)}) \\
&\geq I(S; U_i^{(t)} \mid U_{\mathcal{B}_i}^{(t)}, TI^{(t)}) \\
&= H(S \mid U_{\mathcal{B}_i}^{(t)}, TI^{(t)}) \\
&= H(S),
\end{aligned}
\tag{3}
$$
$$
\tag{4}
$$

where (3) follows from the correctness of (k, n)-TR-SS and (4) follows from the condition (i) in Definition 2. □

Lemma 2. $H(TI^{(t)} \mid TI^{(1)}, \ldots, TI^{(t-1)}) \geq H(S)$ for any $t \in \mathcal{T}$. In particular, $H(TI^{(t)}) \geq H(S)$ for any $t \in \mathcal{T}$.

Proof. For any $\mathcal{A} \in \mathcal{PS}(\mathcal{P}, k, n)$ and any $t \in \mathcal{T}$, we have

$$
\begin{aligned}
H(TI^{(t)}) &\geq H(TI^{(t)} \mid TI^{(1)}, \ldots, TI^{(t-1)}) \\
&\geq H(TI^{(t)} \mid U_{\mathcal{A}}^{(t)}, TI^{(1)}, \ldots, TI^{(t-1)}) \\
&\geq I(S; TI^{(t)} \mid U_{\mathcal{A}}^{(t)}, TI^{(1)}, \ldots, TI^{(t-1)}) \\
&= H(S \mid U_{\mathcal{A}}^{(t)}, TI^{(1)}, \ldots, TI^{(t-1)}) \\
&= H(S),
\end{aligned}
\tag{5}
$$
$$
\tag{6}
$$

where (5) follows from the correctness of (k, n)-TR-SS and (6) follows from the condition (ii) in Definition 2. □

Lemma 3. $H(SK) \geq \tau H(S)$.

Proof. We can prove in a similar way to the proof of Lemma 6. We have

$$
\begin{aligned}
H(SK) &\geq I(TI^{(1)}, \ldots, TI^{(\tau)}; SK) \\
&= H(TI^{(1)}, \ldots, TI^{(\tau)}) - H(TI^{(1)}, \ldots, TI^{(\tau)} \mid SK) \\
&= H(TI^{(1)}, \ldots, TI^{(\tau)}) \\
&= \sum_{t=1}^{\tau} H(TI^{(t)} \mid TI^{(1)}, \ldots, TI^{(t-1)}) \\
&\geq \tau H(S),
\end{aligned}
$$

where the last inequality follows from Lemma 2. □

Proof of Theorem 1: From Lemmas 1–3, the proof of Theorem 1 is completed. □

B   Proof of Theorem 3

The proof of Theorem 3 follows from the following lemmas.

Lemma 4. $H(U_i^{(t)}) \geq H(S)$ for any $i \in \{1, 2, \ldots, n\}$ and any $t \in \mathcal{T}$.

Proof. The proof can be proved in a way similar to the proof in [10, Theorem 1]. For arbitrary $i \in \{1, 2, \ldots, n\}$, we take a subset $\mathcal{B}_i \in \mathcal{PS}(\mathcal{P} \setminus \{P_i\}, k_2 - 1, k_2 - 1)$ of participants. Then, for any $t \in \mathcal{T}$, we have

$$H(U_i^{(t)}) \geq H(U_i^{(t)} \mid U_{\mathcal{B}_i}^{(t)}, TI^{(1)}, \ldots, TI^{(t-1)}) \tag{7}$$

$$\geq I(S; U_i^{(t)} \mid U_{\mathcal{B}_i}^{(t)}, TI^{(1)}, \ldots, TI^{(t-1)})$$

$$= H(S \mid U_{\mathcal{B}_i}^{(t)}, TI^{(1)}, \ldots, TI^{(t-1)}) \tag{8}$$

$$= H(S), \tag{9}$$

where (8) follows from the correctness of (k_1, k_2, n)-TR-SS and (9) follows from the condition (ii) in Definition 5.   □

Lemma 5. If $H(U_i^{(t)}) = H(S)$ for any $i \in \{1, 2, \ldots, n\}$ and $t \in \mathcal{T}$, $H(TI^{(t)}) \geq H(TI^{(t)} \mid TI^{(1)}, \ldots, TI^{(t-1)}) \geq (k_2 - k_1)H(S)$ for any $t \in \mathcal{T}$.

Proof. The statement is true in the case that $k_1 = k_2$, since Shannon entropy is non-negative. Therefore, in the following, we assume $k_1 < k_2$. For arbitrary $i \in \{1, 2, \ldots, n\}$, we take a subset $\mathcal{B}_i \in \mathcal{PS}(\mathcal{P} \setminus \{P_i\}, k_2 - 1, k_2 - 1)$ of participants. For any $t \in \mathcal{T}$, we have

$$
\begin{aligned}
H(TI^{(t)}) \geq & H(TI^{(t)} \mid TI^{(1)}, \ldots, TI^{(t-1)}) \\
\geq & I(TI^{(t)}; U_1^{(t)}, U_2^{(t)}, \ldots, U_n^{(t)} \mid TI^{(1)}, \ldots, TI^{(t-1)}) \\
= & H(U_1^{(t)}, U_2^{(t)}, \ldots, U_n^{(t)} \mid TI^{(1)}, \ldots, TI^{(t-1)}) \\
& - H(U_1^{(t)}, U_2^{(t)}, \ldots, U_n^{(t)} \mid TI^{(1)}, \ldots, TI^{(t)}) \\
= & H(U_1^{(t)}, \ldots, U_{k_1}^{(t)} \mid TI^{(1)}, \ldots, TI^{(t-1)}) \\
& + H(U_{k_1+1}^{(t)}, \ldots, U_{k_2}^{(t)} \mid TI^{(1)}, \ldots, TI^{(t-1)}, U_1^{(t)}, \ldots, U_{k_1}^{(t)}) \\
& + H(U_{k_2+1}^{(t)}, \ldots, U_n^{(t)} \mid TI^{(1)}, \ldots, TI^{(t-1)}, U_1^{(t)}, \ldots, U_{k_2}^{(t)}) \\
& - H(U_1^{(t)}, \ldots, U_{k_1}^{(t)} \mid TI^{(1)}, \ldots, TI^{(t)}) \\
& - H(U_{k_1+1}^{(t)}, \ldots, U_{k_2}^{(t)} \mid TI^{(1)}, \ldots, TI^{(t)}, U_1^{(t)}, \ldots, U_{k_1}^{(t)}) \\
& - H(U_{k_2+1}^{(t)}, \ldots, U_n^{(t)} \mid TI^{(1)}, \ldots, TI^{(t)}, U_1^{(t)}, \ldots, U_{k_2}^{(t)}) \\
\geq & H(U_1^{(t)}, \ldots, U_{k_1}^{(t)} \mid TI^{(1)}, \ldots, TI^{(t)}) \\
& + H(U_{k_1+1}^{(t)}, \ldots, U_{k_2}^{(t)} \mid TI^{(1)}, \ldots, TI^{(t-1)}, U_1^{(t)}, \ldots, U_{k_1}^{(t)}) \\
& + H(U_{k_2+1}^{(t)}, \ldots, U_n^{(t)} \mid TI^{(1)}, \ldots, TI^{(t)}, U_1^{(t)}, \ldots, U_{k_2}^{(t)})
\end{aligned}
$$

$$- H(U_1^{(t)}, \ldots, U_{k_1}^{(t)} \mid TI^{(1)}, \ldots, TI^{(t)})$$
$$- H(U_{k_1+1}^{(t)}, \ldots, U_{k_2}^{(t)} \mid TI^{(1)}, \ldots, TI^{(t)}, U_1^{(t)}, \ldots, U_{k_1}^{(t)})$$
$$- H(U_{k_2+1}^{(t)}, \ldots, U_n^{(t)} \mid TI^{(1)}, \ldots, TI^{(t)}, U_1^{(t)}, \ldots, U_{k_2}^{(t)})$$
$$= H(U_{k_1+1}^{(t)}, \ldots, U_{k_2}^{(t)} \mid TI^{(1)}, \ldots, TI^{(t-1)}, U_1^{(t)}, \ldots, U_{k_1}^{(t)})$$
$$- H(U_{k_1+1}^{(t)}, \ldots, U_{k_2}^{(t)} \mid TI^{(1)}, \ldots, TI^{(t)}, U_1^{(t)}, \ldots, U_{k_1}^{(t)})$$
$$\geq \sum_{i=k_1+1}^{k_2} H(U_i^{(t)} \mid TI^{(1)}, \ldots, TI^{(t-1)}, U_{\mathcal{B}_i}^{(t)})$$
$$- \sum_{i=k_1+1}^{k_2} H(U_i^{(t)} \mid TI^{(1)}, \ldots, TI^{(t)}, U_1^{(t)}, \ldots, U_{i-1}^{(t)})$$
$$= (k_2 - k_1) H(S), \tag{10}$$

where (10) follows from (7) in the proof of Lemma 4, the assumption of $H(U_i^{(t)}) = H(S)$, and the following claim.

Claim. If $k_1 < k_2$ and $H(U_i^{(t)}) = H(S)$ for any $i \in \{1, 2, \ldots, n\}$ and $t \in \mathcal{T}$, $H(U_i^{(t)} \mid U_{\mathcal{A}_i}, TI^{(t)}) = 0$ for any $i \in \{1, 2, \ldots, n\}$, any $\mathcal{A}_i \in \mathcal{PS}(\mathcal{P} \setminus \{P_i\}, k_1, k_2 - 1)$, and any $t \in \mathcal{T}$.

Proof. First, for arbitrary $i \in \{1, 2, \ldots, n\}$, we take subsets $\mathcal{B}_i := \mathcal{PS}(\mathcal{P} \setminus \{P_i\}, k_1 - 1, k_1 - 1)$ and $\mathcal{A}_i := \mathcal{PS}(\mathcal{P} \setminus \{P_i\}, k_1, k_2 - 1)$ of participants such that $\mathcal{B}_i \subset \mathcal{A}_i$. Then, for any $t \in \mathcal{T}$, we have

$$H(U_i^{(t)}) \geq H(U_i^{(t)} \mid U_{\mathcal{B}_i}^{(t)}, TI^{(t)})$$
$$\geq H(U_i^{(t)} \mid U_{\mathcal{B}_i}^{(t)}, TI^{(t)}) - H(U_i^{(t)} \mid U_{\mathcal{B}_i}^{(t)}, TI^{(t)}, S) \tag{11}$$
$$= I(U_i^{(t)}; S \mid U_{\mathcal{B}_i}^{(t)}, TI^{(t)})$$
$$= H(S \mid U_{\mathcal{B}_i}^{(t)}, TI^{(t)}) - H(S \mid U_{\mathcal{B}_i}^{(t)}, U_i^{(t)}, TI^{(t)})$$
$$= H(S \mid U_{\mathcal{B}_i}^{(t)}, TI^{(t)}) \tag{12}$$
$$= H(S), \tag{13}$$

where (12) follows form the correctness of (k_1, k_2, n)-TR-SS and (13) follows from the condition (i) in Definition 5.

From (11) and the assumption of $H(U_i^{(t)}) = H(S)$, we have

$$H(U_i^{(t)} \mid U_{\mathcal{B}_i}^{(t)}, TI^{(t)}) = H(U_i^{(t)} \mid U_{\mathcal{B}_i}^{(t)}, TI^{(t)}) - H(U_i^{(t)} \mid U_{\mathcal{B}_i}^{(t)}, TI^{(t)}, S).$$

Therefore, we have

$$H(U_i^{(t)} \mid U_{\mathcal{B}_i}^{(t)}, TI^{(t)}, S) = 0.$$

Hence, we have

$$H(U_i^{(t)} \mid U_{\mathcal{A}_i}^{(t)}, TI^{(t)}) = H(U_i^{(t)} \mid U_{\mathcal{A}_i}^{(t)}, TI^{(t)}, S) \leq H(U_i^{(t)} \mid U_{\mathcal{B}_i}^{(t)}, TI^{(t)}, S) = 0.$$

Since $H(U_i^{(t)} \mid U_{\mathcal{A}_i}^{(t)}, TI^{(t)}) \geq 0$, we have $H(U_i^{(t)} \mid U_{\mathcal{A}_i}^{(t)}, TI^{(t)}) = 0$. □

Proof of Lemma 5: From the above claim, the proof of Lemma 5 is completed. □

Lemma 6. *If* $H(U_i^{(t)}) = H(S)$ *for any* $i \in \{1, 2, \ldots, n\}$ *and* $t \in \mathcal{T}$, $H(SK) \geq \tau(k_2 - k_1)H(S)$.

Proof. We have

$$\begin{aligned}
H(SK) &\geq I(TI^{(1)}, \ldots, TI^{(\tau)}; SK) \\
&= H(TI^{(1)}, \ldots, TI^{(\tau)}) - H(TI^{(1)}, \ldots, TI^{(\tau)} \mid SK) \\
&= H(TI^{(1)}, \ldots, TI^{(\tau)}) \\
&= \sum_{t=1}^{\tau} H(TI^{(t)} \mid TI^{(1)}, \ldots, TI^{(t-1)}) \\
&\geq \tau(k_2 - k_1)H(S),
\end{aligned}$$

where the last inequality follows from Lemma 5. □

Proof of Theorem 3: From Lemmas 4–6, the proof of Theorem 3 is completed. □

C Naive Construction of (k_1, k_2, n)-TR-SS

Our idea of a naive construction is a combination of (k_1, n)-TR-SS (Sect. 2.3) and Shamir's (k_2, n)-SS [14].

(a) *Initialize.* Let q be a prime power, where $q > \max(n, \tau)$, and $\mathbb{F}_q$ be the finite field with q elements. We assume that the identity of each participant P_i is encoded as $P_i \in \mathbb{F}_q \backslash \{0\}$. Also, we assume $\mathcal{T} = \{1, 2, \ldots, \tau\} \subset \mathbb{F}_q \backslash \{0\}$ by using appropriate encoding. First, TA chooses uniformly at random τ numbers $r^{(j)}(1 \leq j \leq \tau)$ from $\mathbb{F}_q$. TA sends a secret key $sk := (r^{(1)}, \ldots, r^{(\tau)})$ to TS and D via secure channels, respectively.

(b) *Share.* First, D chooses a secret $s \in \mathbb{F}_q$. Also, D specifies the time t when at least k_1 participants can reconstruct the secret and chooses t-th key $r^{(t)}$. Next, D randomly chooses two polynomials $f_1(x) := s + r^{(t)} + \sum_{i=1}^{k_1-1} a_{1i}x^i$ and $f_2(x) := s + \sum_{i=1}^{k_2-1} a_{2i}x^i$ over $\mathbb{F}_q$, where each coefficient is randomly and uniformly chosen from $\mathbb{F}_q$. Then, D computes $u_i^{(t)} := (f_1(P_i), f_2(P_i))$. Finally, D sends $(u_i^{(t)}, t)$ to $P_i(i = 1, 2, \ldots, n)$ via a secure channel.

(c) *Extract.* For sk and time $t \in \mathcal{T}$, TS broadcasts t-th key $r^{(t)}$ as a time-signal at time t to all participants via a (authenticated) broadcast channel.

(d) *Reconstruct with time-signals.* First, $\mathcal{A} = \{P_{i_1}, P_{i_2}, \ldots, P_{i_{k_1}}\} \in \mathcal{PS}(\mathcal{P}, k_1, k_1)$ computes $s + r^{(t)}$ by Lagrange interpolation:

$$s + r^{(t)} = \sum_{j=1}^{k_1} (\prod_{l \neq j} \frac{P_{i_j}}{P_{i_j} - P_{i_l}}) f_1(P_{i_j}),$$

from $(f_1(P_{i_1}), \ldots, f_1(P_{i_{k_1}}))$. After receiving $ts^{(t)} = r^{(t)}$, they can compute and get $s = s + r^{(t)} - ts^{(t)}$.

(e) *Reconstruct without time-signals.* Any $\hat{\mathcal{A}} = \{P_{i_1}, P_{i_2}, \ldots, P_{i_{k_2}}\} \in \mathcal{PS}(\mathcal{P}, k_2, k_2)$ computes

$$s = \sum_{j=1}^{k_2} (\prod_{l \neq j} \frac{P_{i_j}}{P_{i_j} - P_{i_l}}) f_2(P_{i_j}),$$

by Lagrange interpolation from $(f_2(P_{i_1}), \ldots, f_2(P_{i_{k_2}}))$.

It is easy to see that the above construction is secure, since this construction is a simple combination of (k_1, n)-TR-SS and Shamir's (k_2, n)-SS. Also, the above construction is simple, however not optimal since the resulting share size is twice as large as that of secrets.

References

1. Blakley, G.: Safeguarding cryptographic keys. In: Proceedings of the 1979 AFIPS National Computer Conference, pp. 313–317. AFIPS Press, Monval (1979)
2. Burmester, M., Desmedt, Y.G., Seberry, J.: Equitable key escrow with limited time span. In: Ohta, K., Pei, D. (eds.) ASIACRYPT 1998. LNCS, vol. 1514, pp. 380–391. Springer, Heidelberg (1998)
3. Cathalo, J., Libert, B., Quisquater, J.-J.: Efficient and non-interactive timed-release encryption. In: Qing, S., Mao, W., López, J., Wang, G. (eds.) ICICS 2005. LNCS, vol. 3783, pp. 291–303. Springer, Heidelberg (2005)
4. Chalkias, K., Hristu-Varsakelis, D., Stephanides, G.: Improved anonymous timed-release encryption. In: Biskup, J., López, J. (eds.) ESORICS 2007. LNCS, vol. 4734, pp. 311–326. Springer, Heidelberg (2007)
5. Chan, A.F., Blake, I.: Scalable, server-passive, user-anonymous timed release cryptography. In: 2005 Proceedings of the 25th IEEE International Conference on Distributed Computing Systems, ICDCS 2005, pp. 504–513 (2005)
6. Cover, T.M., Thomas, J.A.: Elements of Information Theory, 2nd edn. Wiley-Interscience, New York (2006)
7. Garay, J., Jakobsson, M.: Timed release of standard digital signatures. In: Blaze, M. (ed.) FC 2002. LNCS, vol. 2357, pp. 168–182. Springer, Heidelberg (2003)
8. Garay, J.A., Pomerance, C.: Timed fair exchange of standard signatures. In: Wright, R.N. (ed.) FC 2003. LNCS, vol. 2742, pp. 190–207. Springer, Heidelberg (2003)
9. Jhanwar, M.P., Safavi-Naini, R.: Unconditionally-secure robust secret sharing with minimum share size. In: Sadeghi, A.-R. (ed.) FC 2013. LNCS, vol. 7859, pp. 96–110. Springer, Heidelberg (2013)

10. Karnin, E., Greene, J., Hellman, M.: On secret sharing systems. IEEE Trans. Inf. Theor. **29**(1), 35–41 (1983)
11. May, T.: Timed-release crypto (1993)
12. Rivest, R.L.: Unconditionally secure commitment and oblivious transfer schemes using private channels and a trusted initializer (1999)
13. Rivest, R.L., Shamir, A., Wagner, D.A.: Time-lock puzzles and timed-release crypto. Technical report, Technical memo MIT/LCS/TR-684, MIT Laboratory for Computer Science (1996). (Revision 3/10/96)
14. Shamir, A.: How to share a secret. Commun. ACM **22**(11), 612–613 (1979)
15. Watanabe, Y., Seito, T., Shikata, J.: Information-theoretic timed-release security: key-agreement, encryption, and authentication codes. In: Smith, A. (ed.) ICITS 2012. LNCS, vol. 7412, pp. 167–186. Springer, Heidelberg (2012)
16. Watanabe, Y., Shikata, J.: Timed-release computational secret sharing scheme and its applications. In: Chow, S.S.M., Liu, J.K., Hui, L.C.K., Yiu, S.M. (eds.) ProvSec 2014. LNCS, vol. 8782, pp. 326–333. Springer, Heidelberg (2014)

A Signature Scheme for a Dynamic Coalition Defence Environment Without Trusted Third Parties

Jan C.A. van der Lubbe $^{(\boxtimes)}$, Merel J. de Boer, and Zeki Erkin

Cyber Security Group, Department of Intelligent Systems, Faculty of EEMCS,
Delft University of Technology, Mekelweg 4, 2628 CD Delft, The Netherlands
{j.c.a.vanderLubbe,z.erkin}@tudelft.nl

Abstract. Secure communication among multiple parties is very important, especially in joint military operations and during peacekeeping missions. Unfortunately, in practice the communicating partners cannot fully trust each other and having a trusted party is almost impossible. Nevertheless, the partners need to communicate and occasionally add new parties to the communication. It is essential to add new partners without too much effort and a trusted third party. In this paper, we consider the expansion of a distributed (n,n)-signature scheme to a distributed $(n+1, n+1)$-signature scheme. The presented solution is a modification of the distributed El Gamal signature scheme of Park and Kurosawa. By introducing additional secret numbers and two oblivious third parties that use homomorphic encryption and the EED-model, the El Gamal scheme is modified to a distributed $(n+1, n+1)$-signature scheme, enabling us to add new partners for secure communication efficiently.

1 Introduction

Combined joint task forces, where 'combined' indicates the cooperation between different nations and 'joint' indicates the cooperation between the different services of a nation's armed forces, are becoming increasingly important in military operations. Combined joint task forces are for instance deployed in peacekeeping missions all over the world. Each coalition partner will participate in the combined joint operation for a certain period of time. After that period of time it will be relieved by another nation. This results in a very dynamic task force, where coalition partners regularly join and leave the task force, as it happens in e.g. NATO-ISAF mission in Afghanistan.

The cooperation between the different nations in the combined joint task force should be enhanced when there is a combined joint network available. It is expected that the coalition partners share their operational information as long

This research was supported by the Royal Naval College (KIM) of the Ministry of Defence in Den Helder and the Dutch COMMIT programme. M. J. de Boer is with the Maritime Warfare Centre of the Royal Netherlands Navy and conducted her MSc research in this paper during her study at Delft University of Technology.

B. Ors and B. Preneel (Eds.): BalkanCryptSec 2014, LNCS 9024, pp. 237–249, 2015.
DOI: 10.1007/978-3-319-21356-9_16

as they participate in the combined joint task force. On the contrary, when a partner leaves the task force, that partner should no longer be able to receive the shared information. And when a new partner joins the task force, it should have access to the shared information. In other words, access control is essential in a combined joint network.

To provide access control, it must be possible to authenticate users that log on to the combined joint network. To authenticate a user it is essential that users have their own private key and that the public keys are certified by a Certification Authority (CA). The certificate guarantees that the public key concerned belongs to the user. The CA creates this certificate by signing the pair (user ID, public key) with its own private key. The CA is a very important factor in the combined joint network and all coalition partners in general take part in it. To create the public key certificates the coalition partners need a signature scheme that allows them to place a signature jointly. A limiting condition is that the coalition partners do not have a commonly trusted party that can be used to provide the coalition partners with their secret signing keys.

When the coalition partners want to be able to place a signature jointly without addressing a Trusted Third Party(TTP) there are several distributed key generation [1,4,9,13] and signature protocols [8,12,14,16,18,21] available. Most schemes implement a threshold, all n group members have a part of the secret signing key but only a threshold of t parts are necessary to construct the signature; the so-called (t, n) scheme. The jointly generated signature can be verified using one public key. If the signature may only be placed when all group members agree, there will be a need for a n-out-of-n signature scheme. All shares of the secret signing key are needed to construct the signature. One can use a specific (n, n) scheme or create one out of a (t, n)-signature scheme by choosing threshold t equal to n.

Another approach is the use of multi-signatures [17,19]. Here, every member of the group has his own secret signing key and a corresponding public key. Every group member sequentially signs the document, calculates the verification key to verify the current sequel and passes it to the next member in line. The last member publishes the signature and the corresponding verification key.

Assume that a coalition consisting of n members has initialised an arbitrary (n, n)-signature scheme without using a TTP since there is no commonly trusted party. All members have a valid share of the secret signing key and the members can jointly create a signature on any document without revealing the secret shares to each other. At a certain moment in time the group may need to expand with one additional member. The joining member wants to have its own share of the secret signing key, the group wants the old signatures to stay valid and the public key must be kept unchanged. The consequence is that the secret key remains the same and must be redistributed between the $n + 1$ group members.

Note that joining and leaving a (t, n)-signature scheme is a generally known research topic. Several proposals for joining or leaving the group when a (t, n)-signature scheme is used already exist [2,3,7,22,24], but these schemes update the shared secret when the group changes. Joining a (t, n)-signature scheme without changing the secret is possible using the secret redistribution protocol of [10], but this protocol does not work when $t = n$.

The aim of this paper is to address the problems that occurs when a (n, n)-signature scheme should be expanded to a $(n + 1, n + 1)$ scheme and the secret key remains unchanged.

This paper is organised as follows. Section 2 puts the considered problem into a more specific context and gives a set of requirements to state the limiting conditions. Section 3 proposes a signature scheme that can cope with the expansion using two Oblivious Third Parties and homomorphic encryption. Section 4 evaluates the proposed solution based on the set of requirements in Sect. 2. Finally, Sect. 5 draws conclusions and points out some recommendations.

2   Problem Definition

The combined joint coalitions become more important in international relations every day, and it is also very important to bring about thorough information security in such coalitions. The following scenario gives a framework for information security. Note that even though we focus on combined joint forces for military operations, the scenario we sketch here is of general importance and can occur in many different situations, not only military.

2.1   Scenario

The combined joint task force consists of several nations and several services of armed forces. There is a staff, consisting of staff members of each nation represented in the coalition, to manage the combined joint task force. The staff needs to be accommodated, for example in a naval setting this is on a staff ship that provides a combined joint information network. The staff and all units participating the combined joint operation can exchange information by using this network.

In this combined joint network, there is a need for a mission network that contains all relevant information for the mission and has a sufficient security level. In addition, there is a need for private national networks for the different delegations. The separation between the network compartments is hard and Boundary Protection Devices (BPD) will guard the information flow between the compartments. The router will only exchange information between the compartments if it is permitted by the BPD.

Since there are many users in this network with different authorisations and access rights, there is a need for a thorough Public Key Infrastructure (PKI) and access control. To achieve this, every nation needs to have its own national TTP, this can be a government institution. This does not imply that there is a commonly trusted TTP for all coalition members. The TTPs have their own private key and a corresponding public key, the public key must be available within the coalition task force. The authentication of users is based on the use of cryptographic credentials that are stored on a smart card. The infrastructure for these smart cards will be available at the staff ship. The following framework is based on [25] and is presented here to give an idea of the network structure.

Almost all aspects of this framework are interesting to specify further but here only the core problem of expanding the distributed Certification Authority (CA) using a $(n + 1, n + 1)$-signature scheme is considered.

Initialisation of the Combined Joint Network

1. Each nation's TTP generates a private key and a public key for each user of his nationality and for each application, server or database that uses access control in the private national network. Requirements for these keys are:
   - The keys need to satisfy the agreed key length.
   - The keys must be forward secure and suitable for both authentication and encryption. This may be achieved with one or two sets of keys.
   - Each user needs to identify himself to acquire his unique set of keys.
   - The national TTP supervises that the credentials of a user are stored on the person's smart card according to procedure.
   - The national TTP provides the applications, servers and databases with their credentials.
2. Together the national TTPs of the participating nations are the Certification Authority. The 'distributed CA' will sign the public key certificates. There is no higher level CA available so the distributed CA will be the root CA. The TTPs generate a signing key in a distributed fashion using a (n, n)-signature scheme, so each nation has a part of the signing key and all key parts are necessary to place the signature. The public verification key is placed on a shared server. To prove that the verification key is trustworthy it can be signed separately by each national TTP.
3. Each national TTP provides the other TTPs with a list of all occurring ID's within his responsibility.
4. Each national TTP offers a public key and the appropriate ID to the distributed CA to be certified.
5. The distributed CA checks if the public key and ID offered satisfy the certifying policy that has been agreed on. Each national TTP checks that the concerning ID hasn't been granted a certificate before and participates in the distributed signing scheme. After signing the ID and public key, in other words the certificate, the distributed CA places the certificate on a shared server that is accessible to every user in the combined joint network. All information on the shared server is public and will only be protected by read/write rights.
6. The national TTPs determine, in mutual consultation, for all occurring functions what that user needs to know to do his job, in other words what the access rights are.
7. Each national TTP places his list of ID's including the corresponding function, need-to-know and access rights on the shared server.

Conditions to Work with the Combined Joint Network

1. Confidentiality, integrity, non-repudiation and forward security are required through the communication and information sharing between the nations and

within the nations. To provide forward security and non-repudiation one can use the proposal of [26],

2. Each terminal has a smart card reader. Each user logs on to his nations operating system or the mission operating system.

   - He authenticates himself to the system by using the private key on his smart card. The server gets the public key certificate from the shared server and checks if the public key certificate is valid by verifying the CA signature on the certificate with the verification key. Now the server knows the public key certificate is valid and it can authenticate the user by checking his signature with the public key from the certificate, this final check also contains a hash chain to guarantee that the public key has not been revoked. There is no additional Certificate Revocation List needed. The server also authenticates itself to the user.

   - The server looks up the access rights of the user in the Access Control List on the shared server. If the user has the right to access the system he will be granted access, if not he will be excluded from the system.

3. A user logs on to a specific application or places a request for information on a server or database in the same fashion as stated above at step 2. When the user is allowed to receive the requested information, the data will be transferred. Besides the access control, the Boundary Protection Device will guard all communication between the sender and receiver. This device relies on security labels and must intervene when the communication does not meet the security policy.

4. It must be possible to search in released national information and shared mission information. Released national information will be made available in physically separated databases to protect the national-eyes-only information when a coalition partner is searching the database for information.

The base of the entire framework is step 2 in the initialisation phase, the distributed CA. The national TTPs have initialised an arbitrary (n, n)-signature scheme without using a higher level TTP. This will work as long as there are n national TTPs in the coalition. But an essential aspect of coalition task forces is that they are very dynamic. Over time a coalition often changes in composition: coalition partners join and leave. This means that the distributed CA must cope with these changes. In this paper only the first aspect of joining the coalition will be considered.

When the joining nation trusts the distributed CA of the coalition, it may decide to join the coalition without demanding its own share of the secret signing key to join the distributed CA. Then, the already existing public key certificates remain valid and the certificates of the joining nation are signed by the distributed CA that still consists of n members. On the other hand, the joining nation can demand its own share of the secret signing key. One possibility is to initialise a new $(n + 1, n + 1)$-signature scheme, so all $n + 1$ members have their own secret share. The consequence is that all certificates need to be signed again, this time by the distributed CA consisting of $n + 1$ members. Another approach is to redistribute the secret signing key of the (n, n)-signature scheme among the $n + 1$ members. In this case the signature remains the same and the existing certificates will remain valid. This last approach is of great interest since this will guarantee a flexible distributed CA.

2.2 Set of Requirements

In this subsection the requirements concerning the flexible distributed CA are stated.

1. At initialization the distributed CA consists of n members, which jointly generate a distributed secret key and one public key using a suitable protocol. Generation of the keys only takes place at initialization. The secret signing key and the corresponding public key remain the same until the distributed CA is dissolved or the secret key is compromised.
2. The n members are able to create a signature together using a suitable (n, n)-signature scheme. This scheme makes it possible to create the signature without revealing the secret shares. The scheme they use must be expandable to a $(n + 1, n + 1)$-signature scheme.
3. When the distributed CA is expanded, the shares of the secret key, shared by n members, should be determined again and distributed among $n + 1$ members. After redistributing the secret, the n old members may not be able to create a valid signature without cooperation of the $n + 1^{th}$ member. One can assume that the old secret shares will not be erased by the n old members. And no member will give his secret share to another member since this can be used against him. Note that the members of the distributed CA all want to have a veto, in this light they do not trust each other.
4. It must be impossible for any member to find the entire secret key throughout the entire lifetime of the distributed CA.

3 Modified Distributed Signature Scheme

In general, existing basic secret sharing schemes enable the old members to construct the $n + 1^{th}$ share, which is not desired in our scenario. Therefore, in this section we propose a new solution. Since the old members can find the $n + 1^{th}$ secret share, it is essential to have an additional component, like a random number, that verifies the participation of the $n + 1^{th}$ member. Instead of preventing the old members from finding the $n + 1^{th}$ secret share, a method to detect the participation of all members is used. To achieve this, the use of an Oblivious Third Party is unavoidable. To keep the OTP really ignorant, the work done by the OTP must be divided over two OTPs. The OTPs will perform some operations on their encrypted input, so homomorphic encryption is necessary. And the members of the distributed CA may not learn about each others secret shares or random numbers. To provide this, the EED-model of [6] is used. The building blocks used to modify the distributed signature scheme are the Oblivious Third Parties, homomorphic encryption and the EED-model.

Oblivious Third Party. The OTPs are a compromise between complete independent calculation and the use of a TTP. Assume that the OTPs are entities outside the coalition that are completely independent from each other and are not influenced by any of the coalition members. The OTPs can only perform the required calculations on the input and will always calculate the correct output. The OTPs are not trusted with secret information so everything that is sent to the OTPs will be encrypted. Assume that the OTPs have their own set of keys. By using a homomorphic cryptosystem the OTPs can perform operations on the encrypted data as if it were plain text.

Homomorphic Encryption. A homomorphic cryptosystem has the property $E(x) \oplus E(y) = E(x \oplus y)$ for some operation $\oplus$. Using this property one can calculate $E(x \oplus y)$ without first decrypting x and y. This way the OTPs will not learn anything about x and y. Some homomorphic cryptosystems are RSA [23], Paillier [20] and ElGamal [11]. Since existing distributed secret sharing schemes and signature schemes use an addition of secret shares, the OTPs must work with a cryptosystem that is homomorphic in addition.

EED-model. To use the homomorphic property of a cryptosystem, all shares that are added must be encrypted using the same key. Therefore all members of the distributed CA need to agree on a set of keys and all members need to know the secret key. By encrypting a share with the corresponding public key, the information will be protected against the OTPs, but all members can decrypt it since they all have the secret key. To solve this, the members need to encrypt their share twice using the EED-model of [6].

The EED-model is a smart sequence of encryption and decryption, in which the secret share is first encrypted with the public key of OTP_B. After that the result will be encrypted again, this time with the members' joint homomorphic public key. The double encrypted secret share will be sent to OTP_B. The OTPs will use his own secret key to decrypt it. After that the share still is encrypted and can only be decrypted by the members.

In addition to this model, OTP_A is introduced to keep OTP_B truly ignorant. The members will send their double encrypted share to OTP_A, which encrypts it with his own public key before sending it to OTP_B. So OTP_A provides an extra encryption shell around the EED-model.

In the following two subsections a proposal for a modified distributed El Gamal signature scheme based on [21] is presented. In the first subsection the distributed CA will be initialised with n members following the scheme given in [21]. This scheme is a (t, n)-signature scheme, where $t = n$. In the second subsection, we describe our proposed scheme that expands the (n, n)-signature scheme to a $(n + 1, n + 1)$-signature scheme when a $n + 1^{th}$ member joins. The secret signing key of the distributed CA will not be redistributed. Instead all members will generate an additional random number and the OTPs will create a public reference out of the $n+1$ random numbers; this is a measure designed to prevent the old members from finding the $n+1^{th}$ secret share after redistribution. The modified scheme presented in this section does not redistribute the secret and detects whether all members have joined the signing process by means of the additional random numbers.

3.1   Distributed El Gamal (n,n)-signature Scheme

The public keys where the n members need to agree on are p, q and g. Here p and q are large primes such that q divides $p-1$ and generator g generates the subgroup G_q of $\mathbb{Z}_p$ of order q. The scheme of [21] is divided in a key generation protocol and a signature issuing protocol. First a sub-protocol to generate random numbers is given.

Protocol to Generate Random Numbers (PGRN)

1. Each member P_i chooses $x_i \in \mathbb{Z}_q$, at random and broadcasts $y_i = g^{x_i} \mod p$.
2. Every P_i computes $y \triangleq \prod_{i=1}^n y_i$. Note that $x \triangleq \sum_{i=1}^n x_i$ and thus $y = g^x$.

Key Generation Protocol

1. $P_1, \dots, P_n$ execute the PGRN protocol. Let the public output be y and the secret key of P_i be x_i.
2. The public verification key of the group is (p, q, g, y).

Signature Issuing Protocol. Let m be a message and h be a one way hash function.

1. $P_1, \dots, P_n$ execute the PGRN protocol. Let the public output be $v(= g^\beta \mod p)$ and the secret output of P_i be β_i. Let $w = v \mod q$.
2. Each P_i reveals $\gamma_i \triangleq wx_i + h(m)\beta_i \mod q$.
3. Each P_i verifies that for $\forall l$, $g^{\gamma_i} = (y_l)^w (v_l)^{h(m)}$.
4. Each P_i computes $t = \sum_{i=1}^n \gamma_i$ satisfying $t = wx + h(m)\beta \mod q$. The validity of the signature (t, w) is verified by $w \equiv (g^{t/h(m)} y^{-w/h(m)} \mod p) \mod q$. Note that $w = (g^\beta \mod p) \mod q$.

3.2   Expansion to $(n+1, n+1)$-signature Scheme

When a member joins the distributed CA, the public keys (p, q, g, y) remain valid as well as the secret key $x = \sum_{i=1}^n x_i$. To initialise the expanded signature scheme, the members delegate some operations to two OTPs, namely OTP$_A$ and OTP$_B$. Because the new member does not have his own share of the secret signing key, all members need to generate a random number and register it using the OTPs to make it verifiable that all members joined in the signing process.

The proposed modified scheme differs at two points from the distributed El Gamal (n,n)-signature scheme stated in the previous subsection. The first contribution is the initialisation protocol that registers the random numbers r_i. The second contribution is the added r_i in the signature issuing protocol to verify that all members joined the process.

Initialisation Protocol

1. Each P_i generates a random number r_i and keeps it secret.

2. All P_i jointly agree on a set of keys for an additively homomorphic cryptosystem, e.g., Paillier [20]. The public key will be $(p, g, w_{CA}(= g^{a_{CA}} \mod p))$ where p is a large prime, generator $g \in \mathbb{Z}^+$ and a_{CA} is a random number, $1 \le a_{CA} \le p-2$. The secret key a_{CA} is known by all P_i. Then, all P_i jointly choose a random number k_{CA} to encrypt their secret r_i with. They compute $\gamma_{CA} = g^{k_{CA}} \mod p$ and $\delta_{CA,i} = (r_i)(w_{CA}^{k_{CA}}) \mod p$.

3. Each P_i encrypts his $\gamma_{CA,i}$ with the public key of OTP_B. This public key will be $(p, g, w_B(= g^{a_B} \mod p))$ where p is a large prime, generator $g \in \mathbb{Z}^+$ and a_B is a random number, $1 \le a_B \le p-2$. The secret key of OTP_B is a_B. Each P_i chooses a random number k_i to encrypt their homomorphic secret numbers $\delta_{CA,i}$ with. They compute $\gamma_i = g^{k_i} \mod p$ and $\delta_{B,i} = (\delta_{CA,i})(w_B)^{k_i} \mod p$.

4. Each P_i sends $(\gamma_i, \delta_{B,i})$ to OTP_A.

5. OTP_A encrypt $\delta_{B,i}$'s with his own public key $(p, g, w_A(= g^{a_A} \mod p))$ and a randomly chosen secret k_A and sends $(\gamma_i, \delta_{A,i})$ to OTP_B. Thus, OTP_A computes

$$\gamma_A = g^{k_A} \mod p \text{ and } \delta_{A,i} = (\delta_{B,i})(w_A)^{k_A} \mod p . \tag{1}$$

6. OTP_B decrypts $\delta_{B,i}$, using his own secret key and the γ_i's he received from OTP_A. He computes for each $\delta_{A,i}$,

$$D_{a_b}(\delta_{A,i}) = \frac{\delta_{A,i}}{\gamma_i^{a_B}} \mod p = \frac{r_i(w_{CA})^{k_{CA}}(w_B)^{k_i}(w_A)^{k_A}}{g^{k_i a_B}}$$

$$= r_i(w_{CA})^{k_{CA}}(w_A)^{k_A} \mod p = (\delta_{CA,i})(w_A)^{k_A} = \delta_{OTP_A,i} . \tag{2}$$

7. The result $\delta_{OTP_A,i} = (\delta_{CA,i})(w_A)^{k_A}$ is again homomorphic since k_A is the same for each i. Now, OTP_B calculates $\delta_{OTP_A} = \sum_{i=1}^{n} \delta_{OTP_A,i}$ and sends it back to all P_i. This results in:

$$\delta_{OTP_A} = \sum_{i=1}^{n} \delta_{OTP_A,i} = \sum_{i=1}^{n} (\delta_{CA,i})(w_A)^{k_A}$$

$$= \sum_{i=1}^{n} r_i(w_{CA})^{k_{CA}}(w_A)^{k_A} = (r)(w_{CA})^{k_{CA}}(w_A)^{k_A} \mod p . \tag{3}$$

8. Each P_i decrypts δ_{CA} of δ_{OTP_A} with their joint secret key a_{CA} and γ_{CA} and sends the result δ_r to OTP_A. They compute

$$D_{a_{CA}}(\delta_{OTP_A}) = \frac{\delta_{OTP_A}}{(\gamma CA)^{a_{CA}}} \mod p = \frac{(r)(w_{CA})^{k_{CA}}(w_A)^{k_A}}{g^{k_{CA} a_{CA}}}$$

$$= (r)(w_A)^{k_A} \mod p = \delta_r . \tag{4}$$

9. OTP_A compares δ_r's of all participants. In case they are all same, OTP_A then decrypts δ_r with his own secret key a_A and γ_A, resulting r:

$$D_{a_A}(\delta_r) = \frac{\delta_r}{(\gamma_A)^{a_A}} \mod p = \frac{(r)(w_A)^{k_A}}{g^{k_A a_A}} \mod p = r . \tag{5}$$

10. OTP_A keeps r secret, calculates $R = h(g^{-r})$ and publishes R in a table with the number of members, corresponding $h(\cdot)$ and time it was generated.

The only secret information that OTP_A will receive is r and this number must be kept secret. But if OTP_A reveals r to one of the members, this member cannot forge the signature. To do so, he will need both r and the secret key x, which he will not find unless all members with a share of the secret key are influenced by him.

If the two OTPs work together, they will know more secret information. This situation is comparable to using only one OTP. In this case steps 1 to 4 remain the same, after that the one OTP will decrypt the $\delta_{B,i}$ which results in the $\delta_{CA,i}$'s. The OTP will add the $\delta_{CA,i}$ together and encrypts the result δ_{CA} again with his own key. Then he sends it to each P_i, they decrypt the δ_{CA} and sends δ_r back to the OTP. Now the OTP only needs to decrypt δ_r using his secret key (step 9) to find the secret number r. After this the OTP will perform step 10. This scheme is much simpler than the one presented above, but it also includes a great risk. At one moment in this scheme the OTP has the $\delta_{CA,i}$'s available. The OTP is not able to decrypt this information, but every member of the distributed CA can. If the old members can get hold of these $\delta_{CA,i}$'s, especially the $\delta_{CA,i}$ of the newly joint member, they can forge the signature since the new members have no share of the secret key. Therefore the two OTPs must be prevented from working together.

Modified Signature Issuing Protocol

1. Each member broadcasts $c_i = g^{\beta_i + r_i} \mod p$, $y_i = g^{x_i}$, $b_i = g^{-r_i}$ to all other members. Note that $x_{n+1} = 0$ and $\beta_{n+1} = 0$.
2. Each P_i reveals $a_i = g^{\gamma_i}$, where $\gamma_i \triangleq wx_i + h(m)(\beta_i + r_i) \mod q$. Here w remains equal to $v \mod q$ with $v = g^\beta \mod p$.
3. Each P_i verifies that $\forall \ell$, $a_\ell = (y_\ell)^w (c_\ell)^{h(m)}$.
4. Each P_i computes $a = \sum_{i=1}^{n+1} a_i = g^t$, where $t = \sum_{i=1}^{n+1} \gamma_i$ satisfying $t = wx + h(m)(\beta + r') \mod q$, and each P_i computes

$$b = \prod_{i=1}^{n+1} b_i = \prod_{i=1}^{n+1} g^{-r_i} = g^{-\sum_{i=1}^{n+1} r_i} = g^{-r'}. \tag{6}$$

The validity of the signature (a, y, w, b) is verified by

$$w \equiv (a^{1/h(m)} y^{-w/h(m)} b \mod p) \mod q. \tag{7}$$

Besides this, one must verify that $R_{\#n} \equiv h(b)$.

To guarantee that this scheme works and the n old members cannot conspire against the $n + 1^{th}$ member, time-stamping is necessary. Otherwise the n old members can use their old random numbers and backdate the signature. Since there is no TTP that can provide the time-stamping service, it is not possible to use absolute time-stamping [15]. Relative time-stamping by the distributed

CA itself can be a solution. At initialisation of the expanded distributed CA, the $n + 1$ members must create a 'root'-time-stamp to start the $n + 1$ period. When each new time-stamp is related to the previous time-stamp and the 'root'-time-stamp with $n + 1$ members, it will be feasible to use relative time-stamping. A possible relative time-stamping scheme is the binary linking scheme in [5] since the suggestions of [15] are considered in this solution.

4   Evaluation

In this section the set of requirements of Sect. 2 will be evaluated.

At initialisation the distributed CA consists of n members, who jointly generate a distributed secret key and one public key using a suitable protocol. Generation of the keys only takes place at initialisation. The secret signing key and the corresponding public key remain the same until the distributed CA is dissolved or the secret key is compromised. This requirement is achieved, the secret and public key remain the same but there is an additional verification key that changes when the distributed CA expands.

The n members are able to create a signature together using a suitable (n, n)-signature scheme. This scheme makes it possible to create the signature without revealing the secret shares. The scheme they use must be expandable to a $(n + 1, n + 1)$-signature scheme. The modified El Gamal signature scheme is expandable with one member at a time.

When the distributed CA is expanded, the shares of the secret key by n members should be determined again and redistributed among $n + 1$ members. After redistributing the secret, the n old members may not be able to create a valid signature without cooperation of the $n + 1^{th}$ member. One can assume that the old secret shares will not be erased by the n old members. And no member will give his secret share to another member since this can be used against him. Note that the members of the distributed CA all want to have a veto, they do not trust each other. This requirement can not be achieved with the methods examined in this paper. All $n + 1$ members keep their veto because of the added random number in the modified signature scheme, but the secret key is not redistributed.

It must be impossible for any member to find the entire secret key throughout the entire lifetime of the distribute CA. Since the secret key is not redistributed the members will not learn anything more about the secret key than their own share.

5   Conclusion

This paper proposes a new scheme to expand a (n, n)-signature scheme to a $(n + 1, n + 1)$-signature scheme. The solution presented in this paper does not implement the initial idea of redistributing the secret key. Although redistributing the secret key does not seem possible with the currently available protocols, it should be examined further. An advantage of the presented solution is that there is no limit to the amount of joining members. Also the Oblivious Third Parties are kept completely ignorant, which reduces the amount of trust the coalition members need to have in the OTPs. The members only rely on the OTPs for correct calculations. Unfortunately the presence of OTPs is essential in this solution.

References

1. Algesheimer, J., Camenisch, J.L., Shoup, V.: Efficient computation modulo a shared secret with application to the generation of shared safe-prime products. In: Yung, M. (ed.) CRYPTO 2002. LNCS, vol. 2442, pp. 417–432. Springer, Heidelberg (2002)
2. Blakley, B., Blakley, G.R., Chan, A.H., Massey, J.L.: Threshold schemes with disenrollment. In: Brickell, E.F. (ed.) CRYPTO 1992. LNCS, vol. 740, pp. 540–548. Springer, Heidelberg (1993)
3. Blundo, C., Cresti, A., De Santis, A., Vaccaro, U.: Fully dynamic secret sharing schemes. In: Stinson, D.R. (ed.) CRYPTO 1993. LNCS, vol. 773, pp. 110–125. Springer, Heidelberg (1994)
4. Boneh, D., Franklin, M.: Efficient generation of shared RSA keys. J. ACM **48**(4), 702–722 (2001)
5. Buldas, A., Laud, P., Lipmaa, H., Villemson, J.: Time-stamping with binary linking schemes. In: Krawczyk, H. (ed.) CRYPTO 1998. LNCS, vol. 1462, pp. 486–501. Springer, Heidelberg (1998)
6. Cartrysse, K., van der Lubbe, J.: Providing privacy to agents in an untrustworthy environment. In: van Blarkom, G., Borking, J., Olk, J. (eds.) Handbook of privacy and privacy-enhancing technologies, pp. 79–96 (2003)
7. Chai, S.Z., Zhang, Q.: A general threshold signature scheme based on elliptic curves. Adv. Mater. Res. **756–759**, 1339–1343 (2013)
8. Damgård, I.B., Koprowski, M.: Practical threshold RSA signatures without a trusted dealer. In: Pfitzmann, B. (ed.) EUROCRYPT 2001. LNCS, vol. 2045, pp. 152–165. Springer, Heidelberg (2001)
9. Damgård, I., Mikkelsen, G.L.: Efficient, robust and constant-round distributed RSA key generation. In: Micciancio, D. (ed.) TCC 2010. LNCS, vol. 5978, pp. 183–200. Springer, Heidelberg (2010)
10. Desmedt, Y., Jajodia, S.: Redistributing secret shares to new access structures and its applications (1997)
11. ElGamal, T.: A public key cryptosystem and a signature scheme based on discrete logarithms. IEEE Trans. Inf. Theory **31**(4), 469–472 (1986)
12. Fouque, P.-A., Stern, J.: Fully distributed threshold RSA under standard assumptions. In: Boyd, C. (ed.) ASIACRYPT 2001. LNCS, vol. 2248, pp. 310–330. Springer, Heidelberg (2001)
13. Gennaro, R., Jarecki, S., Krawczyk, H., Rabin, T.: Secure distributed key generation for discrete-log based cryptosystems. J. Cryptol. **20**(1), 51–83 (2007)
14. Gennaro, R., Jarecki, S., Krawczyk, H., Rabin, T.: Robust threshold DSS signatures. In: Maurer, U.M. (ed.) EUROCRYPT 1996. LNCS, vol. 1070, pp. 354–371. Springer, Heidelberg (1996)
15. Just, M.: Some timestamping protocol failures. In: Internet Society Symposium on Network and Distributed Network Security, San Diego, CA, USA, pp. 89–96, 11–13 March 1998

16. Katz, J., Yung, M.: Threshold cryptosystems based on factoring. In: Zheng, Y. (ed.) ASIACRYPT 2002. LNCS, vol. 2501, pp. 192–205. Springer, Heidelberg (2002)
17. Kawauchi, K., Minato, H., Miyaji, A., Tada, M.: A multi-signature scheme with signers' intentions secure against active attacks. In: Kim, K. (ed.) ICISC 2001. LNCS, vol. 2288, p. 328. Springer, Heidelberg (2002)
18. Kim, S., Kim, J., Cheon, J.H., Ju, S.H.: Threshold signature schemes for ElGamal variants. Comput. Stand. Interfaces 33(4), 432–437 (2011)
19. Mitomi, S., Miyaji, A.: A multisignature scheme with message flexibility, order flexibility and order verifiability. In: Dawson, E., Clark, A., Boyd, C. (eds.) Information Security and Privacy. Lecture Notes in Computer Science, vol. 1841, pp. 298–312. Springer, Berlin Heidelberg (2000)
20. Paillier, P.: Public-key cryptosystems based on composite degree residuosity classes. In: Stern, J. (ed.) EUROCRYPT 1999. LNCS, vol. 1592, p. 223. Springer, Heidelberg (1999)
21. Park, C., Kurosawa, K.: New ElGamal type threshold digital signature scheme. IEICE Trans. Fundam. Electron. Commun. Comput. Sci. E79–A(1), 86–93 (1996)
22. Perez, G., Gomez Skarmeta, A., Zeber, S., Spagnolo, J., Symchych, T.: Dynamic policy-based network management for a secure coalition environment. IEEE Commun. Mag. 44(11), 58–64 (2006)
23. Rivest, R.L., Shamir, A., Adleman, L.M.: A method for obtaining digital signature and public-key cryptosystems. Commun. ACM 21(2), 120–126 (1978)
24. Sun, H.M., Shieh, S.P.: Construction of dynamic threshold schemes. Electron. Lett. 30(24), 2023–2025 (1994)
25. Zeber, S.: Managing Identity and Access in the Defence Environment. Defence Research and Development Canada, Ottawa (2002)
26. Zhou, J., Bao, F., Deng, R.: Validating digital signatures without TTP's time-stamping and certificate revocation. In: Boyd, C., Mao, W. (eds.) ISC 2003. LNCS, vol. 2851, pp. 96–110. Springer, Heidelberg (2003)

Author Index

Printed in the United States
By Bookmasters